Advance Praise for

REVOLUTION

"KT McFarland has been at the center of Republican foreign policy-making for decades, starting in the 1970s when she first worked on the National Security Council, continuing through the Reagan Administration, Fox News, and then as President Trump's first Deputy National Security Advisor. Well written and perceptively argued, *Revolution* provides interesting insights into the beginning stages of Trump's foreign policy and the reasoning behind it."

—HENRY A. KISSINGER, Former Secretary of State

"KT McFarland's foreign policy experience spans decades. She was a junior aide to Kissinger, a foot-soldier in the Reagan Revolution, and a national security and foreign policy leader of the Trump Revolution. Her insights into American national security—past, present and future—are indispensable."

—JOSEPH LIEBERMAN, Former Senator

"KT McFarland has personal insider knowledge of how big the fight for freedom is and how dangerous the opponents of freedom both inside the United States and outside are to all of us. An important testimony to the great struggle of our times."

—NEWT GINGRICH, Former Speaker of the House

"Over the years KT McFarland has had the courage to challenge conventional wisdom on foreign policy, and has almost always been right. In this book she sounds the alarm about the strategic, technological and economic threats posed by an aggressive, rising China, and lays out what America can do about it."

—MATT SCHLAPP, Chairman of American Conservative Union

"KT McFarland is an exceptional student, writer, and professional warrior. She had the extraordinary experience of learning from the masters of foreign policy and defense in the Nixon and Reagan presidencies, Secretary of State Henry Kissinger, and Defense Secretary Cap Weinberger and the others that mattered. She's a pro's pro! She watched it up close; learned the lessons of diplomacy, both the successes and the failures, and was prepared to offer that experience to the new Trump White House. She now shares those lessons with you the reader. If 'in the room decision making' interests you, this is a must read!"

—ED ROLLINS, Former White House Assistant to President Reagan, National Campaign Director Reagan-Bush '84

"KT McFarland has been focused on the national security interests of the United States since her time as a young aide to Dr. Henry Kissinger. She has never stopped studying how to protect the U.S. since that time, through her time advising President Trump's 2016 campaign and setting up its national security shop and in her distinguished media career before and after. Now comes her account of the 'Revolution' we are all living through. 'The Washington elites were stunned by Trump's victory,' McFarland writes in the opening pages of this eyewitness account. If they want to get over their shock while also recognizing the growing perils to the country from abroad, this timely important book is the place for them—and all Americans—to start."

—HUGH HEWITT, Nationally Syndicated Radio Talk Show Host, President of the Richard Nixon Foundation

REVOLUTION

REVOLUTION

Trump, Washington,
and We the People

KT MCFARLAND

A POST HILL PRESS BOOK

Revolution:
Trump, Washington and "We the People"
© 2020 by KT McFarland
All Rights Reserved

ISBN: 978-1-64293-404-5
ISBN (eBook): 978-1-64293-405-2

Cover photo by Tom McCall
Cover design by Juan Pablo Manterola
Interior photos edited by Justin Hoch

In several cases, this book deviates from the more accepted capitalization and grammatical rules. This is deliberate, to give special emphasis to certain offices, organizations, and unofficial groupings.

Post Hill Press
New York • Nashville
posthillpress.com

Published in the United States of America

To my husband, Alan Roberts McFarland—
the love of my life,
the song to my soul,
and the north star to my purpose

CONTENTS

PART THREE: WE THE PEOPLE

PART ONE

TRUMP

CHAPTER 1

Why I Joined the Trump Revolution

I was as surprised as anyone by Donald Trump's victory. As a FOX News National Security Analyst, I had spent the day at our studios in midtown Manhattan, watching election commentary, and occasionally providing analysis myself. I was convinced Hillary Clinton would win and, as President, take us even further along the path of economic and global decline. She might have been a less combative President than Trump, but she would have done nothing to stop the erosion of American power and increased indebtedness. She would not have taken the steps necessary to restore America to robust economic growth. As a result, she would have presided over the slow decline of American power and influence and, in time, other countries would rise to take our place on the world stage. In the past, Clinton had picked the wrong foreign policy priorities. She had neglected the aggressive rise of China, yet pushed for interventionism abroad, especially in the Middle East and North Africa. I took no joy in being on cable news that day; I was just going through the motions, resigned to Hillary Clinton's blowout victory.

But as polls started closing across the country, and Trump unexpectedly won a few key counties and then some key states, the chatter in the green room at FOX changed. Was there a chance Trump might pull an upset victory? After I finished my last FOX Business News appearance, I headed to Trump's election night headquarters a few blocks away to watch the impossible first become possible and then inevitable. County after county and state after state posted unexpected wins for Trump. Someone said the Clinton campaign had just cancelled their victory party caterer and the Hudson River fireworks display. Trump's upset victory was actually going to happen.

I was a Trump supporter from the beginning. As a fellow New Yorker, I had followed him over the years and liked a lot of what he said, especially when it came to foreign policy. Trump had the guts to stake out contrarian positions at odds with both Republicans and Democrats. He may have expressed his views in an unconventional manner, but he had a better track record than most of the experts. I had given foreign policy advice to a number of presidential candidates over the last decade or so, but they were more or less interchangeable. None impressed me as having understood the urgent necessity of reorienting our attention away from the Middle East and toward Asia.

Trump was the outlier. Finally, here was a Republican candidate who wasn't afraid to face reality, to admit the mistakes we made in foreign and economic policy, and commit to a major course correction. If he could ever manage to get elected, Trump might actually get something done, no matter how many people he offended along the way.

I joined Trump's National Security Advisory Committee in the fall of 2016, after the Republican Convention, and was one of the few well-known and experienced foreign policy experts to do so. I participated in prep sessions for his final debates, and was impressed by his ability to cut through the details and zero in on the core of an issue, almost intuitively.

I'd already had several interviews with his personnel team, and thought I might be offered a senior position in his Administration if he actually did win. If so, I would be going back to my roots in government service, and fulfilling the dream of a lifetime. As I stood in the middle of the VIP section of Trump's election night headquarters, I should have been over the moon with excitement and possibility. I should have been jumping for joy.

But I wasn't. Instead, I felt an ominous sense that something life-altering—maybe for the better, maybe not—was about to happen to the country and to me. It was a deep feeling of foreboding that nothing would ever be quite the same again. My instincts were right, just not in the way I anticipated.

By the 2016 election, it was clear America was ready for change. By nominating Trump, the Republican Party had rejected the traditional Republican Establishment. By electing Trump, the country rejected the entire Washington Establishment, Republican and Democrat alike. The battle lines were now drawn. On one side were the elites of both parties who had governed America for decades and supported big government and a globalist, interventionist foreign policy. On the other side were the populists, the ordinary citizens who rarely got excited about politics, but were now mobilized in rebellion against a governing class they believed was arrogant, unresponsive, and unsuccessful. It was a revolt by the governed against the governing.

The Washington elites were stunned by Trump's victory. They had always taken for granted their inherent right to govern. They had assumed the country would elect one of their own in 2016, drawing yet again from one of America's political dynasties. The irony is many of Trump's supporters were just as stunned by his victory. They identified with his political-incorrectness and outsider status, but never actually thought he could beat Hillary and the Washington machine.

Since the 2016 election, that divide has grown wider, increasingly rancorous, and more personally destructive. We are now living in the Age of Trump, where the media is all Trump, all the time. Everything in Washington—every person, politician, journalist, analyst, issue, and policy—is now measured as being either pro-Trump or anti-Trump. Our political classes have locked the country into a full-scale, political civil war, which shows no sign of winding down. The outrage industry has cranked the discussion up to the point where we're always on edge. You can't even talk about the weather without being put into the pro-Trump or anti-Trump camp. There are no safe, neutral zones in Washington.

Pundits and politicians throw around words like "populist" and "nationalist," "elitist" and "globalist" with wild abandon. The terms have been hijacked to sanctify or demonize people, depending on which camp they're in. They're the new equivalent of four-letter words—shorthand for everything that is good about your camp and bad about the other camp. It's the pro-Trump national populists versus the anti-Trump global elitists. As loaded as these terms have become, there is no common agreement

5

about what they actually mean. They mean one thing to the people who identify with them, and the compete opposite to the people who do not.

Each side sees the other as the enemy and refuses to acknowledge they might possess any redeeming attributes, or even that they may have an opinion worth listening to. The only thing both sides have in common is that they see themselves as virtuous and true, and people on the other side of the great divide as wrong and sometimes even criminally evil.

It's worth unpacking what these words mean to the people who identify with them, and to the people who do not. Without definitions, we're just talking past each other—or more likely, just screaming at each other.

CHAPTER 2

Washington Elites Versus American Populists

To the elites, populism means mob rule, and represents the worst in American society—the uneducated, dim-witted masses who have neither the experience nor intelligence to govern themselves. They are the people who shop at Walmart and eat at McDonald's. The elites see nationalists as the bigoted, narrow-minded, white (mostly male) supremacists who resent the rise of women, minorities, and immigrants. Barack Obama saw them as the bitter people who "cling to guns or religion or antipathy toward people who aren't like them or anti-immigrant sentiment or anti-trade sentiment as a way to explain their frustrations." Hillary Clinton said they belong in a "basket of deplorables," characterized by "racist, sexist, homophobic, xenophobic, Islamophobic" views. They see nationalists and populists as the people who are, and deserve to be, life's losers.

In their version of America, populists are people driven by their hatreds and prejudices, and therefore morally inferior. Conservatives are either angry whites unwilling to make way for deserving minorities, or a rapacious business class trying to perpetuate their unfair privileges in order to keep their ill-gotten spoils. The governing elites see these populist/nationalists as, at best, misguided and simplistic, and at worst, dangerous and evil—the same kind of people who supported Hitler and Mussolini and their racist, nationalist agendas in the 1930s and 40s.

In contrast, the elites see themselves as society's leadership class who, by education, experience, and temperament, are best suited to make decisions for the rest of us. They see themselves as upholding the American values of equality, fairness, and inclusiveness. They focus on those in our society who have been treated unfairly in the past—those who didn't have equal access to education, opportunity, civil rights, or legal redress. They believe it is the job of government to compensate people for wrongs done to them, including to their ancestors in decades past and to make up the difference with quotas and preferential treatment today. There is a whiff of self-righteousness about them, since they are convinced the things they believe in are universal truths, shared by all civilized people, and therefore beyond debate. It goes without saying that they believe that their motives are pure, and that their virtuous beliefs make them morally superior. Therefore, they are, and deserve to be, the final arbiters of our society and government.

When elitists look abroad, they see an interconnected world, which is moving beyond the nation state to a global society and worldwide economy where people, information, goods, and money should move freely across borders. They are part of a post-nationalist movement that sees the world evolving toward a more peaceful and prosperous place, where we will all be governed by universal norms and international organizations. Elitists equate nationalism with xenophobia, and believe pride in one's country has been the root cause of most of the wars of the last century. Their hope is that the next century will be one without trade wars, cold wars, or hot wars. It will be a world where international commerce and communication are so intertwined that we will naturally move toward a sort of utopia, bound together by commonly held beliefs, and governed by a global elite which rises above selfish national interests to create a more just and cleaner world.

As for Trump, elites consider him so dangerous that he must be stopped dead in his tracks. For the first two years of his Presidency, they were convinced the Mueller investigation would charge Trump with criminal offenses, and they shared fantasies that he would be hauled out of the White House in handcuffs and end up behind bars. When the Mueller

Report exonerated him, Congressional Democrats and the anti-Trump media doubled down. Even if there was no evidence of colluding with the Russians to steal the election, Trump must be guilty of obstructing justice…somehow or other, for something or other. There might not be enough evidence to convict him in a court of law, but they could ruin him in the political courtroom of public opinion. The Democrat-led House of Representatives would vote articles of impeachment against him and force him to stand trial in the Senate. Failing that, they could have never-ending investigations of Trump, his family, and his associates, going back decades. They would take anything he ever said or did, give it their own spin, and scream, "Impeachment! Impeachment!" They figured even if the Senate couldn't muster the two-thirds vote necessary to remove him from office, Trump would be so wounded politically that the voters would refuse to reelect him in 2020.

They're convinced that Trump is just too corrupt, too belligerent, too incompetent, and too evil to be America's president. They believe they have the right and even the responsibility to do whatever it takes, including suspending the rules, stretching the truth, and breaking the bounds of tradition to hound him from office.

They've convinced themselves that once he's gone the country will come to its senses and purge itself of all things, people, and ideas that are pro-Trump. Then Washington can get back to the pre-Trump normal: the Never-Trump Republicans will once again be back in charge of the Republican Party; and the Democrats will return to power and reinstate Obama's tax-and-spend program at home and globalist worldview abroad.

The people who call themselves populists and nationalists may not always have a clear idea of what they are, but they do know what they are not—most are neither wealthy, nor powerful, nor in charge. They see themselves as having been cast aside and trampled by the governing coastal elites who dominate the Democrat and Republican parties, Wall Street, Hollywood, the media, academic institutions and, especially, Washington, D.C.

They see themselves as the salt of the earth—patriotic, hard-working citizens, and the backbone of our nation. They love America—our culture, our history, our traditions—and believe they're the only ones upholding the traditional American values of hard work, self-reliance, personal responsibility, cohesive families, small government, balanced budgets, a strong military, and peace through strength. They pay their taxes, worship God, keep their families together, and believe in liberty and freedom. They think America is an exceptional nation, even if they're not quite sure why.

They're opposed to what they see as an entitlement society, where one group is favored over another, and granted special privileges for some alleged injustice, often far in the past. They see multiculturalism as a threat to America's melting pot culture of inclusiveness and assimilation. They believe the liberal elites are snobs who look down on them as second-class citizens whose opinions don't matter and whose votes shouldn't count— and they deeply resent it. They think they've been exploited by the richest catering to the poorest in our society, to the point where the American Dream is increasingly out of reach for those in the middle. They see liberals, or the modern incarnation of progressives/socialists, as irresponsible big spenders who are bankrupting the country, who are anti-law enforcement, anti-God, anti-military, and downright anti-American. Populists believe that elites advocate for the nanny state and cradle-to-grave big government, so they can be in charge of picking the winners and losers. They think elitists want to confiscate their hard-earned money and dole it out to people who, unlike them, have done nothing to deserve it.

Populists see Trump as the only guy who has ever acknowledged them or stood up for their interests. In three years he's improved the economy to the point where they and their neighbors all have jobs—and good ones at that. For the first time in years, they can take a family vacation and buy a new car. They are optimistic about their own, and their children's, future. They don't mind Trump's bluntness, political incorrectness, tweetstorms, or rascally behavior. Some of them even approve of all this because Trump is saying what a lot of them think but have been too afraid to say out loud. They can't understand the Washington insiders who are trying to throttle Trump and kick him out of office. To populists, Trump has been an exceptionally good president.

It's as if both groups are living in separate but parallel universes, each seeing themselves and each other in complete reverse, like a film negative where black is white and white is black, up is down, and left to right becomes right to left. There is no middle ground, no room for compromise, no ability to see the others as the others see themselves, no willingness to see ourselves as the others see us. There is little tolerance for the belief system of the other camp, or even the recognition that the people who disagree with them can still be good people, fully entitled to their own opinions. The question used to be: "Are you a Republican or a Democrat?" But even those lines have now become jumbled. Today it is: "Are you a populist or an elitist?" "Are you a nationalist or a globalist?" "Are you with Trump or against him?"

In other words, we've evolved into a society that does everything possible to emphasize what divides us politically, yet very little to nurture what unites us or champions our common purpose. All of us, from each side of the divide, are painfully aware that we have a serious national problem, even if we blame the other side for having started it and for keeping it going. The only thing both sides agree on is that it's not their fault. As far as they're concerned, the other side landed the first punch, and they're just defending themselves.

CHAPTER 3

Washington's Failed Economic & Foreign Policies

How did we get to this place? How did the American people, who were so united in common purpose after the September 11th attacks, get to the point where we are increasingly at each other's throats? We now self-segregate according to political beliefs, with each group watching its own media outlets, going to its own sporting events, and following its own entertainers. There are probably many causes for our present divide: a political system that rewards the extremes in each party; the Great Recession of 2008 and a financial culture that ignored risk and subsidized speculators; a weaponized media that finds profitability in creating division; social media that provides a platform for people on the fringes to move to center stage and scream at each other anonymously; an emphasis on multiculturalism that breaks us into subgroups; and the abandonment of civic education which once provided the glue that held us together by reminding us of our history, governance, and culture. But most of all it's been because for nearly twenty years we have pursued economic and foreign policies that worked well for some of our people but failed miserably for others. It didn't matter whether the Republicans or the Democrats were in charge in Washington. The average, hardworking "commoners" turned to Trump because they felt either ignored or ill-treated by everybody else.

That's what I have observed from outside the Washington bubble. First, a little background about me: after a successful career in government and politics, I married and moved to New York in the mid-1980s to raise a large family of five children and stepchildren. In 2006, after a long hiatus from government and politics to go on the mommy track, I re-engaged in public life. I ran for the U.S. Senate from New York, lost, and went on to carve out a new career in media. I became a national security commentator on FOX News, wrote a regular column for their website, and created and hosted *DEFCON3*, Fox's innovative web-based foreign policy program. I also hit the speakers' circuit, traveling around the country, and meeting with a wide range of people—security professionals, veterans, women, businessmen, advocacy groups—everyone from corporate executives to college students.

By about 2010, I noticed a distinct sense of unease that rippled across all these people. I wasn't quite sure what caused that distress, so I decided to do some informal polling of my own, using my audiences as focus groups. Whenever I gave a speech, I began my remarks with a survey of the audience.

"Raise your hand," I said, "if you think our economy is a mess—that the economic opportunities and security you've enjoyed won't be there for your children's or grandchildren's generations." Usually about a quarter of the hands went up.

"Raise your hand if you think America has forfeited our leadership role in the world—if you think we're getting pushed around by Russia, China, Iran, and even pip-squeaks like North Korea." At this point, about half the people had a raised a hand.

"Raise your hand," I continued, "if you think we've lost our way as a nation. Do you sense that the values we were raised on—hard work, personal responsibility, integrity, and fair play—have been replaced by a society of entitlement and instant gratification, where people are rarely held accountable for their actions?" At this point, two-thirds of the audience would have a hand in the air, some nodding in agreement.

"Finally," I would ask, "how many of you think the mess we're in is Washington's fault? How many of you believe the insiders have rigged the system to take care of themselves but not the rest of us?" By now everyone's hand was up, including the guy running the sound system. The results surprised me because, for the most part, I was speaking to groups of people who were successful, well-educated, and gainfully employed. Clearly, something very powerful was happening in American society.

The people I saw when I traveled around the country weren't imagining things, even if they themselves were not directly affected. Many Americans had not really recovered from the Great Recession of 2008, when we went through the worst economic and financial crisis since the Great Depression. Even though the economy, as a technical matter, had grown modestly in the years after 2008, the working and middle classes had actually lost ground. Median household income in the United States had not just stagnated; data from the Census Bureau noted it had fallen by more than $1,000 in inflation-adjusted dollars from 2008 to 2015.

Our great middle class, which for decades had been living proof of the American Dream for millions of people, was shrinking as more and more people fell out of the bottom and fewer people were able to move up into it. The rich were getting richer, but the poor were being permanently left behind. The percentage of people in the workplace had dropped significantly since the beginning of the 21st century, and our national debt was spiraling out of control. High taxes and over-regulation were suffocating economic growth, and the number of jobs open to the working and middle classes was shrinking. The Obama Administration assured us that the "green shoots" of recovery were starting to sprout up, even though, sadly, it would largely be a "jobless" recovery.

Whatever gains there were in those years went mostly to the top ten percent, especially to the top one percent. In many cases, the very people and corporations who caused the economic crisis of 2008 were the ones who benefited most from the solutions the government imposed. Take, for example, the big banks that triggered the crisis. Rather than do what banks are supposed to do—provide capital to companies to invest in growth—they created risky financial products to drive up bank profits and their own paychecks. When that shaky banking structure collapsed, both the Bush and Obama Administrations deemed certain banks "too big to fail" and bailed them out. Most of the bankers running them were allowed to keep their jobs and, after a brief adjustment period, went right back to doing the things that had gotten them into trouble in the first place: taking big bets with other people's money and receiving immense compensation for the gambles. If they lost their bets, no problem—they weren't made to pay for their mistakes. They walked away with big compensation packages and their retirement plans intact. It was a "heads-I-win, tails-I-don't-lose" arrangement. And, surprise, surprise! Many of those people were also major donors to the Democrat and Republican politicians who wrote the rules and bailed them out.

Even if the people I met with around the country were doing well themselves, they knew plenty of people in their communities who were not. They had friends, family members, or acquaintances who were gradually finding the American Dream, which used to be their birthright, slipping just out of reach. People began to worry that their children might see it disappear entirely.

The Washington Establishment was unaware of the growing anger of the working and middle classes. Or, if they did recognize something was happening around the country, they were unable or unwilling to do anything about it. Instead, establishment politicians promised more and more of the same: Democrats promised more government assistance programs and pledged to tax the rich to pay for them. They refused to acknowledge America already had some of the highest taxes in the world, and that the super-rich always seemed to find ways around them.

The rich don't pay taxes; they pay lobbyists and Members of Congress, so they *don't* have to pay taxes! They're granted tax loopholes, subsidies, and rebates by senators and congressmen grateful for their generous campaign contributions. Ultimately, promises to "tax the rich" don't result in higher taxes for the rich; they really mean more taxes for the middle class.

Republicans promised more of the same too: they would cut spending in order to cut taxes. But they never got around to eliminating expensive, lobbyist-protected government programs. Despite all the noise, our politicians, whether Republican or Democrat, never succeeded in doing more than nibbling around the edges of our problems. The Republicans never managed to cut spending enough to be noticed. The Democrats never managed to increase taxes enough to make any difference. Around and around they went—locked in a fantasy, always promising something new and different, but never delivering on any of it.

All the while, the economy was stagnating, the rich were getting richer and the poor were locked into permanent poverty. The working and middle classes were shrinking in size and prosperity, and our common problems of education, immigration, healthcare, and decaying infrastructure were never addressed. The only thing politicians did succeed in accomplishing was growing the size, scope, and cost of the Administrative State. Congress and the Executive Branch all hired more staff, at higher wages and with better health care than most of the taxpayers who were stuck paying for them. It was a car jack that could only be ratcheted in one direction—up and up and up. To my mind, the leaders of both political parties were recycling the same stale old policies that didn't work, and supporting the same people who had gotten us into this mess in the first place.

By 2016, Washington had become a boomtown. President George W. Bush had expanded the national security bureaucracy after the September 11th attacks. President Obama had expanded the welfare state after the Great Recession. Both of these efforts were popular in the immediate aftermath of their respective crises, so the government responded by raising budgets and adding new programs. But they soon took on a life of their own. The programs were never scaled down after the crises passed; they became the new baseline, often with newly-thought-of justifications for their perpetuation.

For those inside the Washington bubble, the 21st century was business as usual: politicians gave expensive new government programs to blocs of special interest groups in order to buy their loyalty come election time. They also voted special privileges, tax exemptions, subsidies, and waivers to industries and companies that contributed to their campaign coffers. Put simply, they were spending money we didn't have, to pay for programs we didn't need, in order to guarantee job security for politicians who didn't deserve it.

Together, Bush and Obama added a total of 500,000 new workers to the federal bureaucracy, costing an additional $50 billion a year. That's just the number of new employees to administer the new programs; it doesn't include the hundreds of billions of dollars already in the system. It's no wonder that four of the ten richest counties in the country are in suburbs surrounding Washington, D.C.

Meanwhile, the perception gap between the Washington Establishment and the rest of the country was growing, gathering both in size and momentum. One of the first people to comprehend what was happening outside the Washington-New York-California bubble was FOX News powerhouse journalist Lou Dobbs. In the early years of the 21st century, Dobbs began to focus his attention on examining and explaining how the elites on Wall Street and in Washington had abandoned the people on Main Street.

In 2004, when Dobbs was still at CNN, he wrote *Exporting America: Why Corporate Greed is Shipping American Jobs Overseas.* He examined the devastating impact on working class Americans when corporations and government eagerly pushed to relocate manufacturing overseas for cheap labor. Two years later, he followed with *War on the Middle Class: How the Government, Big Business, and Special Interest Groups are Waging War on the American Dream and How to Fight Back.* Dobbs joined FOX News in 2010, and his 2014 book, *Upheaval*, focused on how the governing class had betrayed the "middle class and those who aspire to it." For two decades Dobbs has been one of the leading voices of the anti-Washington and anti-Wall Street populist movement that has been sweeping the country.

The ever-perceptive author and columnist Peggy Noonan noticed it too. In early 2016 she noted that there was a "historic decoupling between the top and the bottom" of American society. The people at the top, whom she calls the "protected class," are the people in government, business, media, and the arts who set the rules, yet are themselves immune to the harm and suffering they're inflicting on the rest of their countrymen. "The protected make public policy," Noonan wrote, but "the unprotected live in it."[1]

Pulitzer-prize winning columnist Michael Goodwin, a life-long Democrat, shocked liberals by announcing his support for Trump. In his March 2016 *New York Post* opinion piece, *Why It's Time for a Trump Revolution*, Goodwin said he would vote for Trump because he was the only candidate willing to stand up for the middle and working classes.

It was slowly dawning on the rest of the country that it didn't matter to the protected class if the country voted Republican or Democrat, because they were all safely ensconced in their middle- and upper-class bubbles. They didn't sense the growing alienation of more and more Americans, nor see the shattering of their dreams.

---

[1] Peggy Noonan. "Trump and the Rise of the Unprotected." *Wall Street Journal.* February 25, 2016. https://www.wsj.com/articles/trump-and-the-rise-of-the-unprotected-1456448550

People inside the Washington universe were oblivious to what was happening around the country. Even if they were vaguely aware of it on paper, they didn't experience it firsthand. To them, it wasn't real life—it was just a set of statistics in a government study. The people in Washington never experienced the pain the rest of the country was suffering. Their houses were worth more than they had paid for them; their streets were quiet and safe. They lived in gentrified neighborhoods, with late-model cars parked out front. Their children got a good education, often in private schools, and proceeded to glide seamlessly into top colleges and then high paying jobs. They didn't have to worry about a drug epidemic in their schools or crime spreading to their neighborhoods. They were living pretty much the same as they had a decade before and, in many cases, even better.

The thing to remember about Washingtonians is that they never experience a recession because, unlike the rest of the country, government workers have job security for life, coupled with generous health care and retirement benefits. They usually get automatic pay raises, regardless of what's happening with the economy or the size of the budget deficit. Private sector businesses tighten their belts when times are tough; the government adds a few more notches.

If I hadn't traveled around the country in those ten years between 2006 and 2016, I doubt if I would have seen the growing frustration felt by so many Americans. By every yardstick I'm part of the elite, and live inside a comfortable bubble, albeit mine is in New York instead of Washington. I graduated from George Washington University with a degree in Chinese Studies, got a graduate degree in Politics, Philosophy and Economics from Oxford University, and studied nuclear weapons and national security in MIT's PhD program. In between, I worked in the Nixon, Ford, and Reagan Administrations, at the center of power. I worked my way up from secretary to research assistant on Henry Kissinger's NSC staff in the 1970s. I was one of the first women on the Senate Armed Services Committee Staff, and Secretary of Defense Caspar Weinberger's speechwriter and assistant in the Reagan years. After a long hiatus as a stay-at-home mom, I lost a bid for the U.S. Senate and then spent a decade in cable news. I have been happily married for over thirty-five years, with five terrific grown children, and live in an affluent, upper middle-class community.

I've had a first-rate education, several successful careers, and a fulfilling family life. For decades I have been blessed beyond measure.

But that's not where my life started out. I was born in the early years of the Baby Boom generation into a working-class Italian-American family in the Midwest. My parents never went to college. My father carried a labor union card and worked the night shift. My mother was a housewife. We lived paycheck to paycheck, and sometimes fell short a day or two before it arrived. But our neighborhood was safe, my parents owned their own home, our family had health care, and our public schools were just fine.

Even though I faced many of the same obstacles as the rest of my trail-blazing generation of women, I was able to go to college and then to graduate school. My family couldn't afford to pay for my education, but I managed to scrape together enough for tuition and room and board through a combination of part-time jobs, student loans, and scholarships. I had student debt when I graduated, but it was manageable. Within a few years of working full time, I had paid it all off and even saved enough for a down payment on a home of my own. A few years after that I married, raised a family, and over the decades have enjoyed personal and professional success. I have lived the American Dream. And I wasn't alone. Many of our friends and neighbors had started out life as I did, and they, too, had been able to move into the middle and even upper classes. The American Dream was alive and well when we were coming of age, and we were fortunate enough to turn that dream into reality.

But what about someone born into a working-class family in the Midwest in 2001, instead of 1951? I'm not at all sure they will have the same opportunities that I had fifty years before. It's no longer a given that they will have access to good public schools, live in safe neighborhoods, or be part of secure families. Yes, granted there are now many more educational and professional opportunities for women, often with less of the sexual harassment and discrimination that were par for the course for my generation. But college? Graduate school? Home ownership? Yes, they may be available now, too, but are they still affordable for someone trying to move into or stay in the middle class?

Many of the young men and women graduating from college today are saddled with tens, if not hundreds of thousands of dollars of student debt, which they will have to pay back during the same years when they hope to marry, start a family, and buy a home. Will the American Dream be as accessible to them as it was to the men and women of my generation? And if it is not there for the generation coming of age today, how likely is it that it will be available to their children's generation?

To my mind, it wasn't just that the Washington Establishment had failed the country's working and middle classes; they also had failed to pursue an effective national security policy for much of the last twenty years. They were so focused on a Middle East mindset that they lost track of the real strategic threats posed by a revanchist Russia and an expansionist China—both bent on advancing their agendas at our expense. Because of the shortsightedness of the foreign policy Establishment, the country has squandered many of the Reagan Revolution's hard-won gains.

When I left Washington in the 1980s, the near miraculous Reagan economic recovery was well along and America was on course to winning the Cold War—it was only a matter of time. It turned out to be sooner than anyone predicted. Just a few short years after Reagan left office the Iron Curtain came down and the Soviet Union collapsed. America was left standing as the world's sole superpower—militarily, economically, and politically. We were admired, emulated, and envied throughout the world.

The years that followed the end of the Cold War were heady times for America. We assured ourselves that, with the collapse of Communism, the world had changed. Liberal democracy had established itself as the final evolution of governance, the pinnacle of civilization. We had reached "The End of History," according to my former Rand Corporation colleague and now Stanford University Professor Francis Fukuyama.[2] Our political parties walked back from their extremes, and both Presidents George H.W. Bush and Bill Clinton governed from the political center, with bipartisan support. It was a time of unity, prosperity, and peace—if you will, an American golden age.

But then came 9/11. The United States was caught flat-footed as nineteen religious fanatics from a subnational, transnational death cult murdered thousands of Americans in surprise terrorist attacks in two of our country's most iconic cities. It was this generation's Pearl Harbor.

They say generals are always ready to fight the last war, but unprepared for the next one and September 11th proved the point. Prior to the attacks, our military and intelligence communities were geared toward

---

[2] Fukuyama, Francis. *End of History and the Last Man.* New York: Free Press, 1992.

large-scale conflict against major powers. But Osama bin Laden and al-Qaeda were different. They were an insignificant band of half-crazed zealots who had found a safe haven in Taliban-governed Afghanistan, one of the most primitive and inhospitable countries in the world. They didn't present a military threat to us, at least not a traditional one. Before September 11th, we hardly gave them a second glance.

After the attacks, we immediately went to war. Our military adapted in real time to deal with this new threat. They sent a small group of Special Forces to Afghanistan to destroy al-Qaeda. The American military's initial attack on al-Qaeda's strongholds in Afghanistan was brilliant, decisive, and effective. Our CIA and special operations units teamed up with Afghanistan's Northern Alliance tribesman to oust al-Qaeda from Afghanistan, and the Taliban government from Kabul. Within three months of 9/11, al-Qaeda was decimated and Osama bin Laden on the run and headed for the Tora Bora Mountains, the narrow mountain passes separating Afghanistan and Pakistan. His followers were reduced to a thousand or so fighters holed up in mountain caves. Osama bin Laden was so convinced they had lost that he wrote his last will and testament.

But that's when everything began to go wrong. There is still a lot of finger pointing for who was to blame, and no one admits to knowing exactly what happened next or why. But instead of sealing the caves and wiping out the last of the terrorists, somehow the remnants of al-Qaeda managed to slip through our grasp and escape into the remote, tribal region of northwest Pakistan.

We then made a second mistake. Instead of pursuing al-Qaeda into Pakistan, to finish them off ourselves, we stopped at the border and out-sourced what we thought would be the war's final stages to Pakistan, paying that country $2 billion a year to help find bin Laden and destroy what was left of al-Qaeda. Pakistan wanted our money, of course, but didn't necessarily share our interest in destroying al-Qaeda. They knew that if Osama bin Laden died, or was captured or killed, they might lose that $2 billion annuity. Furthermore, parts of the Pakistan government and intelligence services were in sympathy with and had close ties of long standing to the terrorists. So, Pakistan took us on a decade-long ride. They pocketed our money while elements of their government kept bin Laden in a safe house, under their watchful eye. Meanwhile, al-Qaeda had time to regroup, rebuild, adapt, and expand throughout the Middle East and North Africa.

Once al-Qaeda was beyond our reach in Pakistan, we came up with a new plan: we would remain in Afghanistan and make it al-Qaeda-proof. We moved into the former Soviet base at Bagram, built up a gigantic civilian and military infrastructure, and set about nation building. Our aim was to turn one of the most backward countries in the world, which had been riven by tribal blood feuds for millennia, and located in one of the most remote and inhospitable parts of the world into a modern, self-sustaining democracy. The United States and our allies poured hundreds of billions of dollars into this new effort. But as long as the Afghan government remained untrustworthy and incompetent, and the Taliban and al-Qaeda had a safe haven in Pakistan, our new mission proved to be mission impossible.

Soon enough the Taliban crept back into Afghanistan to fight a guerilla war against U.S. forces and the ineffective and corrupt Afghan government we had propped up. Our civilian and military leaders had forgotten the bitter lessons of Vietnam and the complications of asymmetrical conflict. One senior Afghan official summed up the problem when he said to me, "Don't blame us for trying to get as much from you as we can now. We are a poor country. We know you Americans will eventually pack up and go home. We have nowhere else to go. We are here forever." His analysis was prophetic. Most of our forces have left Afghanistan, but some still remain, fighting in a forever-war, with no prospect of ultimate victory.

I saw the futility of our efforts on another trip to Afghanistan in 2011, when I visited Bamiyan Valley, high up in the Hindu Kush mountains. The valley isn't very large—maybe five miles wide—with sandstone cliffs all around. My escort officer was Navy Lieutenant Commander Morgan Murphy, who had arranged for us to take a helicopter from Kabul with some Navy SEALs. Once we arrived at the Bamiyan heliport—which was nothing more than a small, rocky parking lot on the top of a cliff—the SEALs went their way, and we left to tour the valley in a military jeep. The entire area was covered in rocks and sandstone dust.

High up on one side of the valley was a small New Zealand Army base, part of the U.S.-led coalition effort. The base commander told me he was very proud to be there, because one of his forbearers had fought there in the 1830s, with the British Expeditionary Forces. On another sandstone cliff were two looming empty niches that had once housed the famous Bamiyan Buddhas and a third smaller one that still remained. The Buddhas had been carved in the fifth century by Hindus, but destroyed in the first year of the 21st century by the Taliban who declared them to be idolatrous offenses to Islam. We drove to the other side of the valley to the ruins of the ancient City of Screams, Shahr-e Gholghola, which had been carved out of the side of the cliff nearly a thousand years ago when the Silk Road connected Asia to Europe. Genghis Khan and the Mongol hordes invaded the valley three hundred years after it was built. When the people living in the cliffside city refused to surrender, he gave the order that every man, woman, and child be killed. Genghis Khan then left their cliffside dwellings intact as a testament to his wrath.

At the bottom of the valley, five beat-up, rusted, weed-infested Soviet tanks were parked at odd angles, their hatches open and looking as if they had been abandoned in a hurry years before. Alongside the tanks was the meandering trickle of the Bamiyan River. It was laundry day; women in hijabs or full burkas walked to the river balancing baskets of clothing on their heads. After washing their clothes, they spread them out on the rocks to dry. Next to the river was a pasture, with an old, wizened, and turbaned farmer, wearing the traditional Afghan garb of long tunic and loose trousers, bent over and slowly walking beside his two oxen, which were pulling a wooden plow through the rocky and arid ground.

To my mind, the Bamiyan Valley is the perfect example of the mistake we make time and again in foreign policy. We presume that everyone sees things the way we do, thinks the way we do, and wants what we want. But it's not true. Over the 2,500 years of the history of Bamiyan Valley, the only things that remain after all the conquests, invasions, and religious conversions are the Afghan farmer, his oxen and a wooden plow, and the women carrying their clothes to the river to wash. Over our decades of nation-building, that Afghan farmer had no doubt been offered an upgrade from his wooden plow—perhaps a steel plow or even a tractor. Those women had probably been offered washing machines and gas generators. But the farmer still plowed his field and those women still did their washing the same way their ancestors had two thousand years before.

When we left the valley to go back to the Bamiyan heliport and return to Kabul, we drove along the Laura Bush Highway, named for the former First Lady when she visited the area in 2008. It was pristine, well-built...

and empty. The only others on the highway were two boys, prodding a donkey along with a stick. They were walking on the edge of the highway because the donkey shied away from the paved road.

A week later I was back in New York City, in a taxi driving along Manhattan's FDR Drive. As usual, we were stuck in traffic. When we finally got moving, the taxi bounced along over the potholes and unevenly patched roadbeds. The United States had built a modern highway in the remotest part of the Third World but couldn't manage to properly repair the main roadway of one of America's largest and most important cities.

In Afghanistan, the Bush Administration made the mistake of thinking they could force democracy on a people who didn't want it—and then they made the same mistake again in Iraq. In 2003, intelligence reports surfaced that Saddam Hussein possessed weapons of mass destruction. So, in March 2003 America went to war again, diverting some of our forces and resources from Afghanistan before we had finished the job there in order to invade Iraq. The goal was to destroy Saddam Hussein's weapons before he could use them. As with Afghanistan, the U.S. armed forces were brilliantly effective in defeating Saddam Hussein's army in just a few weeks. Less than two months later, on May 1st, President Bush declared it "Mission Accomplished." We never did find those the weapons of mass destruction; either Saddam Hussein destroyed them, had secretly shipped them to Syria, or they had never existed in the first place. But no matter, we had defeated the Iraqi Army…or so we thought.

Yet, rather than declare victory and leave, we found a new rationale for remaining in Iraq, just as we had in Afghanistan. We would help them create a modern democracy, this time in the heart of the Muslim Middle East. We poured hundreds of billions of dollars into this new nation building effort, and hundreds of billions more to station American troops there. But it was no more successful than our efforts in Afghanistan.

We and our Iraqi allies were soon confronted with an indigenous guerrilla war by the people we supposedly had just defeated. Iraq was torn apart by sectarian civil war with the United States military in the middle, again propping up a corrupt, fledging government. So, Bush doubled down and by the time he left office in 2009 our military had regained lost ground and had nearly defeated the Sunni insurgency. When President Obama took office there was a glimmer of hope for Iraq. But when he withdrew all U.S. forces a few years later, it created a regional power vacuum which Islamic extremists rushed to fill, creating a short-lived Islamic State. The tragedy of Iraq is Bush shouldn't have gone in the way he did, and Obama shouldn't have gotten out the way he did.

During this same period, dictatorships across North Africa and the Middle East were shaken by spontaneous pro-democracy uprisings. With the exception of Iran's Green Movement, President Obama embraced them all, encouraging the demonstrators to topple their dictators and to create democratic governments in their wake. He even authorized a U.S. military intervention to depose Libya's longtime, brutal dictator Muammar Qaddafi.

President Obama was supported in this initiative by the entire foreign policy community, just as President Bush had been in the Afghan and Iraq wars a decade before. The Bush and Obama Administrations made many of the same mistakes in their Middle East wars, although they would no doubt both cringe at the comparison. Both assumed that the major obstacle to creating a democratic society was a brutal dictator standing in the way. Once the dictator was overthrown—whether by outside armed forces or internal uprisings—they believed democracy would flourish.

Bush tried to build democratic governments for them; Obama assumed they would build democracies on their own. Both strategies failed, with terrorists, militants, criminals, extremists, and opportunists rushing in to these countries to fill the voids.

Both presidents had the best of intentions, and each spent hundreds of billions of dollars on nation building, in the hopes of instantly creating the modern institutions that are essential for democratic government. They committed our armed forces to fight military wars that couldn't really be won. The region remains just too locked into its own ethnic, tribal, and religious divisions—not to mention its historic hatreds—to suddenly be transformed into a place of modern societies with Western-style freedoms, governance, and economies. In 2016, after fifteen years of war, much of the Arab Muslim world was wracked by instability, chaos, and violence.

The lesson is that the Washington foreign policy Establishment—of both parties during this era—made similar mistakes in the Vietnam, Afghanistan, Iraq, and Libyan wars. Democracy doesn't happen overnight. It takes years to build the institutions needed to underpin it—including a free press, an independent judiciary, transparency, equality under the law, and corruption-free armed forces and government. It's not something that can be imposed by outside forces, nor a small segment of the population. Many of the Eastern European democratic governments formed after the collapse of the Soviet Union succeeded because they had already developed some of those institutions prior to Communism. For political revolutions to succeed they must be organic and indigenous—and desired by a people who are willing to work years to build the institutions necessary for self-government. Put simply, it won't work if we want it for them more than they want it for themselves.

I am always struck by the nation builders in the foreign policy world who think that as long as we help a country write a constitution and hold elections, it will result in a pluralist society with equal rights for all. Have they forgotten about our own political history? We've had democracy for over 200 years and many of our people still vote along ethnic, geographic, gender, religious, or racial lines. How many times have you heard that a candidate has locked up the "black vote" or the "Hispanic vote," or has a gender gap with women voters? We have even coined a term for it: "identity politics." Why, then, are we surprised when Afghans or Iraqis or Syrians go to the polls and vote only for candidates from their own tribes?

As a result of all these miscalculations, nation building experiments, and ever-shifting goals, the United States has paid a real price in blood and treasure. We have wasted trillions of taxpayer dollars that could have been spent to fix our schools, rebuild our infrastructure, or fund advanced research and development projects. We have subjected the dedicated men and women in our armed forces to fifteen years of constant war in the Middle East, wars we had little chance of winning with the resources we allocated to them. We gave our military just enough to avoid losing, but never enough to win. These forever-wars have taken their toll on our military, in readiness, reenlistment, and morale. Our men and women in uniform were forced to endure back-to-back deployments, which put enormous strain on them as well as their families. Post-traumatic stress syndrome and suicide rates were skyrocketing. Our armed forces were stretched to the point of breaking, because they were forced to do more and more with less and less. After cutting back on research and development in order to pay for these fifteen years of war, our real adversaries were able to spring ahead and develop into peer competitors, especially in cyberwarfare.

Our leaders have a sacred duty to the men and women who serve America in uniform. We have created the most powerful armed forces in the history of the world, yet they have never flexed their own muscles at home. Civilian control of the military is written into our Constitution and it is one of America's great strengths. Members of our armed forces take an oath to defend that Constitution, which means obeying their civilian masters, even when they vote for other candidates and other political parties, even when they disagree with them, even when they know their civilian masters are making grave mistakes. In return, our civilian leaders owe them a debt of honor—to respect their advice, to provide adequate care for them and their families, and to never, ever, send them into combat casually, without a clear understanding of their purpose and prospects for success.

We were stuck in a Middle East mindset, and so distracted by the region's eternal tribal psychodramas and the evolving terrorist threat that we took our eye off the ball. Washington's foreign policy Establishment either ignored, or failed to appreciate, the real strategic threats to our future: the return of big power geopolitics, and the rise of an expansionist, mercantilist China seeking to replace us as the largest economy and most powerful country in the world by the mid-21st century. Were China to succeed, it would be in a position to rewrite the international rules of order to their benefit and at our expense. It wouldn't just be a setback to America; it would be the end of the American era.

My disagreement with the elites' mismanagement of the economy and of our foreign policy was one of the reasons I came to reject the Washington Establishment. It's not just my anger at their failure to provide opportunities for our working and middle classes while promoting their own self-interests. It's not just my personal nostalgia for the American Dream, and wanting this generation of young people to have the same opportunities that I had decades ago. It's the very practical realization that if the American Dream is no longer accessible to all of our people—the working class, the legal immigrants, the people in the industrial heartland and rural areas—the American experiment will not long endure. The American Dream is the foundation of American society: it is the social contract we have with each other and with our government. It is the glue that binds us. It holds out the promise that it's not what you were born with; it's what you make of yourself that counts. America is where dreams can become reality.

If we lose that hope, that promise, that dream, then we lose what really counts—the thing that makes America an exceptional nation. If we lose social mobility, a classless society, and our sense of common purpose, then there is little left to hold together our polyglot, diverse peoples. If America is to remain an exceptional nation, we need to restore the American Dream. The only way to do that is by guaranteeing that we remain the land of opportunity by renewing and reinvigorating American industries and businesses so they can once again create private sector jobs and economic growth for all our people.

CHAPTER 4

I Joined the Trump Revolution for the Same Reasons I Joined the Reagan Revolution

Somewhere in the middle of Barack Obama's presidency I concluded that the leaders of both political parties had lost their way. I rejected their elitist attitude and globalist direction, especially in foreign policy and national security. By the time the 2016 presidential campaign season began, I was already a committed populist and nationalist, or at least my versions of them.

Populism is a system of government of, by, and for the people. A populist is someone who believes in the rights, wisdom, and virtues of the common man. It follows that we are capable of governing ourselves, and that power should be vested in the hands of those ordinary folk. We are the best people to determine what kind of government we want, choose the leaders to represent us, and give them general direction on the policies we expect them to follow. Our equal rights and responsibilities are exercised in elections. We don't need a group of our "betters" to decide things for us.

Yet, while we believe in equal rights, we do not insist on equal outcomes. It is our own individual strengths and weaknesses, talents and shortcomings, circumstances and histories, preferences and opinions that are responsible for the choices we make and the different lives we live.

A populist democracy is not always the most efficient way of choosing leaders and doesn't necessarily lead to the most effective governments, at least in the short term. Sometimes voters make mistakes and come to regret the leaders they've chosen and the decisions they've made. But governments elected by the people are the only ones that are, by their very nature, self-correcting. In the end, power rests in the hands of the common man. Even the people we choose to represent us in the halls of government are there temporarily and conditionally. If the majority of citizens are dissatisfied, we can vote leaders out of office the next time around. If we don't like certain laws, we can elect people who will change them. If we don't like certain things in the Constitution, we can amend it.

To me, a self-avowed populist, populism is the purest form of democracy…where every person's vote is equal.…where no one person, or group of people, has the right to rule over the rest of us.…where no citizen is any better than any other and no group more entitled to power and privilege than any other.

Throughout history, most societies have been governed by small elite groups: hereditary monarchs, landed aristocracies, police and military forces, religious leaders, dictators, a professional civil service, or a large, self-perpetuating Administrative State. Sometimes their power has been out in the open for all to see; sometimes it's been hidden behind the curtains.

Inevitably, once a certain group of people are in charge, they want to stay in charge. They want to keep the privileges that being in power gives to them, their friends and their families. There is nothing sinister in this; it is just human nature. They want to keep things the way they are, with themselves in charge. Elitist governments eventually become so entrenched that transformative change has tended to come only with great difficulty and disruption—through political movements, revolutions, civil war, or coups—where a new group wrestles power from the old group.

One of the reasons for American exceptionalism is that we have been different from the very beginning. In the Declaration of Independence, we broke with thousands of years of human history to claim that our rights come to us directly from the Almighty, not through a king or a general or a prophet. Neither are our rights bestowed on us by any elite group of superiors who could choose to grant them or deny them to us as they saw fit. They are ours by Divine Right, they are unalienable, and no one can take them away from us.

Nearly two hundred and fifty years ago, Americans of all classes and regions joined together to fight a revolution against the rich, powerful, and entrenched hereditary monarchy of Great Britain for the right to govern ourselves. The Constitution our Founding Fathers wrote made it official—in America, power would be vested in the hands of the ordinary man, in "We the People." We are still a work in progress, and America remains an experiment in self-government that some think unrealistic or ill-guided. Granted, it has taken us some time to get there, but today every citizen—regardless of color, creed, gender, ethnicity, or national origin—has equal protection under the law with the same rights, including the right to vote. Our citizens are the ultimate check on whether government is fulfilling its promises, by exercising their right to vote through free and fair elections. If the majority of Americans come to feel the current batch of leaders are no longer serving the people's interests, we have the right and responsibility to replace them with leaders who will. Populism begets populists.

I'm not just a populist, I'm also a nationalist, a devoted believer in America, its systems and values—and one who believes that for too long the United States has put the interests of other countries ahead of our own. To me, nationalism is not nativist, racist, xenophobic, or any of the other negative connotations some have attached to it. My nationalism does not exclude Americans who are not like me; it opens wide its arms to include them.

The greatness of America is that we have come together to form something unique—an American society and culture that we have all contributed to, united by common values of equality, freedom, liberty, and purpose. It has been created by all of us, together and over time, with each new group of immigrants and cultures adding something special to the mix. American society is not an assortment of diverse subgroups, each emphasizing what sets them apart. Instead, it is a melting pot where different ideas, cultures, and traditions blend together to create a constantly evolving society. The new culture we have created together is greater, more inclusive, and more powerful than any of the different cultures our people might have been born into. The whole is greater than the sum of its parts. For me, nationalism is the conviction that America is an exceptional nation, and therefore it is worth celebrating, defending, and protecting.

During 2016, over two dozen Republicans were competing for the privilege of running against Hillary Clinton, the Democrat's inevitable presidential candidate. To my mind, most of them offered up the same-old, same-old standard platform that had failed so miserably in the past. The front runner was Jeb Bush, whose father and brother had both already been President. He was the poster boy for the Republican establishment, dynastic politics, and the very things I thought were holding us back. I may have converted to populism and nationalism, but it seemed to be a lonely stance. None of the presidential candidates had done so.

But when Trump entered the race, I got interested. Here was someone who thought the way I did on many key issues. He was just unorthodox enough, independent enough, and tough enough to break through the Republican lineup. If he secured the nomination, he might be the one to give Hillary Clinton a run for her money. And maybe, just maybe, if the impossible happened and Trump won, he could turn the country around.

Trump had talked about running for president for years, well before the populist movement had emerged as a political force. When he called a press conference on June 16, 2015, supposedly to reveal his decision, a lot of people treated it with a yawn. I watched it from the FOX green room and marveled at how unscripted he was. He seemed to say whatever came into his head at that particular moment. Every other politician in the country, especially everyone running for president, would have each word vetted in advance by his political and policy teams. The frontrunners would have poll tested every proposal, to make sure they connected to their base, but avoided insulting any special interest group. They would have mouthed pure pablum—beautifully phrased but signifying nothing. Not Trump. Tossing political correctness to the wind, he seemed to insult just about everybody from George W. Bush, Barack Obama, and John McCain to illegal immigrants.

At about the twenty-minute mark of the press conference, Trump still hadn't gotten to the point. Someone else in the FOX green room said, "Yeah, he's got our attention but he's not really going to run. He's just toying with us." But to the surprise of most of the "experts," even those at

FOX, Trump ended his long rambling remarks by throwing his hat into the ring. He walked off the stage, and descended down the golden escalator to the cavernous, floor-to-ceiling marble and gold lobby of Trump Tower—and past a huge crowd of roaring fans.

There has been endless speculation about why Trump decided to make the run in 2016—that the ratings for his hit television reality show, *The Apprentice*, were sagging and he wanted the free publicity to pump them up; that he couldn't resist the spotlight and running for President was the biggest show on earth; that he was insulted by Barack Obama's snarky, condescending attacks on him at the recent White House Correspondents' Dinner while Trump sat at a table just a few feet away from the podium; that he was sick and tired of all the pious politicians who spent almost all of their time raising money, but never delivered on their campaign promises.

I suspect it was a combination of all those things, but most of all I think he originally approached it as would a businessman. He looked at America's balance sheet the same way he would read a company's profit and loss statement. From that perspective, America was already in trouble financially, and it would only get worse over time. There was a gap between spending and revenues, which was widening every year and seemingly unstoppable. We had to borrow to make ends meet, and the amount of interest we would have to pay to keep going was potentially crippling.

Trump was a businessman and had been through bankruptcy himself. He knew that you couldn't keep borrowing forever; eventually banks will stop lending you money. Your choice is to either somehow start paying it back or to declare bankruptcy. In 2016 America was already nearly twenty trillion dollars in debt, and adding to it by borrowing nearly a trillion dollars each year. Congress was incapable of cutting expenditures, as were our recent Presidents. Countries may not be able to declare bankruptcy, but Trump thought we were headed toward a financial day of reckoning and that something had to be done.

Trump thought that the world was playing America like a sucker, taking advantage of us. It was partly our fault, because for the prior two decades our leaders had either refused to acknowledge it or let them get away with it. Trump saw himself as a hard-headed businessman who knew how to fix our problems, the same way a new CEO could turn around a poorly run company that still had great potential. He would grow the economy through tax cuts, regulatory reform, and a pro-energy policy, which in turn would create million of new jobs. He would re-examine the country's assets and liabilities, renegotiate our trade deals, refocus American foreign policy away from the Middle East to Asia (especially China), and make changes that, over time, would make ends meet.

I've heard him say that he'd met dozens of politicians over the years, including most of the presidential candidates. They all made the pilgrimage to Trump Tower to kiss his ring in hopes of getting his endorsement and campaign donations. In typical Trumpian fashion he insulted them behind their backs and made jokes about them at their expense. Maybe Trump had concluded it wasn't such a tough field. Why not give it a whirl?

What first attracted me to his campaign were his foreign policy positions. Over the years, he had occasionally dabbled in the rarefied world of diplomacy, war and peace, and international economics by tossing out a few soundbites that inevitably put him at odds with conventional wisdom. The foreign policy community was unimpressed. To the extent they noticed him at all, they were dismissive of his commonsense approach. "Trump doesn't know what he's talking about…he's had no foreign policy experience…he shouldn't be taken seriously." Pundits laughed at his pronouncements on trade, treaties, security, and diplomacy. As far as they were concerned, he had no business wading into their nuanced areas of experience and expertise.

But it turns out that Trump—the rank amateur—had a surprisingly accurate grasp on the big issues. Even though they would never admit it, the foreign policy community as well as many Bush and Obama Administration officials, in lockstep groupthink fashion, had gotten many of these very same issues totally wrong.

Here is the record: Trump was against the Iraq and Libya wars. He said they were futile, expensive, and would destabilize the Middle East. He thought that nation building, especially in places like Afghanistan, was a waste of our time and resources. He was against the Iran nuclear deal because it threw a life preserver to Iran's collapsing economy while we got very little in return. He said we had given away our leverage up front in the negotiations, in exchange for a temporary pause in Iran's nuclear program and got no halt at all to their missile program or their support of terrorist movements. Trump wasn't shy about giving our prosperous security allies in Europe and Asia a tongue-lashing for failing to contribute more to our common defense. Most important in my mind was that Trump went where most Republicans and even more Democrats were afraid to go—he publicly called out China for its trade abuses, intellectual property theft, and currency manipulation.

As Trump was heading into the final stretch of the campaign, I agreed to join his National Security Advisory Board and to help prepare him for the second debate. Trump hadn't done all that well in his first debate with Secretary Clinton and this second one was to focus on foreign policy, her strong suit. She was expected to wipe the floor with Trump and finish him off once and for all. Even though former Secretary of State Clinton was already the acknowledged master of foreign policy minutiae, she disappeared several days before the debate to prepare.

Trump, on the other hand, kept up his heavy schedule of campaign rallies around the country. To prepare for this all-important debate he wanted a one-hour briefing session with the twenty or so members of his National Security Advisory Committee, period. As far as I could tell, that would be his only foreign policy prep. No Q&A briefing books, no lengthy lectures from policy experts, and no hunkering down to read lengthy position papers. Senator Jeff Sessions organized the group, consisting mostly of retired generals and admirals, and we met with Mr. Trump at his Trump Tower conference room. We were given an agenda beforehand: Sessions would lead the meeting, and each of us in turn would give a brief summary of our assigned topics. This wasn't supposed to be anything like a debate prep in the traditional sense—a mock debate where the candidate would field the sorts of questions he could expect in the debate. It was certainly nothing like the debate practice sessions Secretary Clinton was reportedly conducting—with accomplished debaters serving as stand-ins for Trump and the news anchors. Trump's debate preparation was a one-hour session with a group of experts each offering a three-minute presentation on a different topic.

Or at least that was the plan. We were assembled in a large glassed-in conference room at Trump Tower, fiddling with our briefing papers, when candidate Trump blew into the room, top campaign advisors in tow. I had met Trump before, in passing, at a social event or two in New York, but this was the first time I was able to spend any time with him, or to exchange anything more than pleasantries. First, Trump is impressively tall, towering over the rest of us—especially the diminutive Senator

Sessions and Republican National Committee Chairman Reince Priebus, who had joined Trump's entourage. But even more than being tall Trump is large—broad shoulders, long arms, large head, the famous pompadour hair and very long legs. Trump dominates any room he enters, because he literally and physically takes it over.

We all sat down around a large mahogany conference table, with Trump in the middle on one side. I was directly across from him, sitting next to Senator Sessions. Trump called in the photographers to memorialize the event for the media, and after they left, we introduced ourselves one after another. Trump spoke briefly, saying most people spent too much time preparing, and ended up being stale in the actual debate. He wanted to be fresh. In other words, don't bore him to death with minutiae. This is your one shot at briefing him and it better be short, concise, and to the point.

Sessions had his checklist in front of him and started calling on people, checking off the topics accordingly. I got about three sentences into my analysis of Chinese leaders and their goals when Trump interrupted and started peppering me with questions. He zeroed in on trade. "What is China's trade surplus? Their growth rate? How good is their military?" This is how Trump responded to everyone—he would jump in and ask questions about the topics he cared about, not necessarily what you had prepared for. He often added his own opinion: "I don't think so," or "that's what I think, too." If Trump thought your answer was too long, or too in the weeds, he'd cut you off with, "yeah, I got that" and ask another question: "Could we stop them from stealing intellectual property? What about currency manipulation?" Then Trump would skip to another topic: "Could NATO beat Russia? Why didn't Germany contribute more to NATO? How big a problem was Arab immigration in Europe?"

The briefing was scheduled for an hour, but Sessions quickly lost control of the agenda. Trump was in charge. He was not the typical candidate, passively receiving a briefing by experts and memorizing statistics. He had opinions, questions, and switched back and forth from one topic to another in his rapid staccato. Trump's questions veered off in different directions, then a few minutes later he would circle back. By the end of the hour Trump was growing bored, got fidgety, and gave a clear signal that the briefing was over. He got up and breezed out of the room, with the campaign aides in tow.

I sat there dumbfounded. It was unlike any briefing I've ever been part of over my nearly fifty-year national security career, either ones I'd given or ones I'd received. I glanced down at Sessions's checklist. To my surprise, by the end of the hour we had gotten through more or less the entire agenda, but certainly not in a linear fashion. Trump was nothing like I expected, but I liked what I saw: thoroughly in charge, unconventional, self-confident, and totally unafraid of taking on conventional wisdom or established leaders.

Trump was the only candidate in a crowded field who didn't need the job—for status, for wealth, or for acclaim. If Trump were to somehow win the presidency, it would likely be a step down in lifestyle—the planes, housing, and other perks that came with being President of the United States weren't as good as what he already had. He was already world-famous. If he could win the presidency, he would be the first person in a long time, if ever, who would enter the Oval Office without owing anything to anybody.

Trump's independent wealth allowed him to embrace populism because he didn't need donors to pay for a campaign. He ran his own campaign, his way. He would pay for it himself; he didn't need contributions, with the strings that were inevitably attached, from friends, lobbyists, or special interest groups. Trump also didn't need the Republican Establishment to help him get votes. He didn't care what the Washington Establishment power brokers thought of him. His whole reason for running was to disrupt their system.

Trump was self-reliant not only politically but also in terms of public relations. He didn't need the media to get name recognition or to put him on the national radar—so he didn't have to curry favors from the media. One evening, after his top-rated FOX Business News show, anchor Lou Dobbs came back into the green room to talk politics with a few of his regular guests. It was right after Trump announced he was running, and most people were treating it like a joke. Not Dobbs. He predicted Trump would get the Republican nomination, and go on to win the presidential election. Why? Because Trump was already bigger than the media. He was already one of the most famous people in the country, and a genius at personal branding. Dobbs said Trump didn't need the media; the media needed him. Dobbs's prediction proved right. Trump was great for ratings, and higher ratings meant more advertising revenues.

Having Trump call in to a cable news program or radio show was an instant spike in ratings; having Trump participate in a debate meant millions more people would tune in. Having the name "Trump" in the headlines meant people would read the story. His very outlandishness meant he was guaranteed "click-bait." The more outrageous he was, the more ostentatious, the more flamboyant, the more the media covered him. Most politicians don't take risks. Trump thrives on taking risks. Most politicians make decisions behind closed doors and have a spin machine announce their bland stands so as not to alienate voters or donors. Trump made his decisions in the open—at press conferences or on Twitter—and he relished being politically incorrect, giving his competitors insulting nicknames, and skewering journalists.

The media are rarely willing to admit it, but Trump has been good for the entire range of media businesses. Without Trump in the primaries or the general election, the media would never have been able to ramp up their staffs or budgets. If 2016 had been another Clinton-Bush election, nobody outside of Washington would have gotten excited enough to bother following the campaign. With a President Hillary Clinton or President Jeb Bush in the White House, lots of normal Americans would have turned off the boring news channels and tuned into sports, cooking, and home improvement shows.

Trump recognized this from the beginning and skillfully exploited it. Even though their coverage was almost entirely negative, the media made Trump even more famous. They were eager to cover his every tweet, gaffe, and rally which put him front and center in voter's minds. There was Trump...and then there was everybody else. The *New York Times* estimated that Trump got nearly $2 billion in free advertising in the primaries—and got even more in the general election.[1] Some estimates are that he got over $5 billion through the entirety of his campaign.[2] This was summed up by a highway billboard in the Midwest after he won. It read something like this: "The media think Trump is stupid–But he was smart enough to get them to pay for his campaign!"

---

[1] Confessore, Nicholas and Karen Yourish. "$2 Billion Worth of Free Media for Donald Trump." *The New York Times*. March 15, 2018. https://www.nytimes.com/2016/03/16/upshot/measuring-donald-trumps-mammoth-advantage-in-free-media.html.

[2] Stewart, Emily. "Donald Trump Rode 5 Billion in Free Media to the White House." *The Street*. November 20, 2016. https://www.thestreet.com/story/13896916/1/donald-trump-rode-5-billion-in-free-media-to-the-white-house.html.

As surprising as Trump's victory was, just as stunning was the fact that the professional punditry, pollsters, and political class didn't even see it coming. It simply never occurred to them that the majority of their fellow Americans no longer felt confident about the country's future, or secure about their own. They were blind to it because they, and their inside-the-corridors-of-power group, didn't know anybody who felt that way, nor could they imagine why anyone would. On the rare occasions when Washington insiders did encounter people who didn't see things the way they did, they dismissed them as racists, sexists, homophobes, and xenophobes. They shamed Trump's supporters by claiming they were angry, "low information" voters, "deplorables" who just wanted to make America white again.

What they—and especially the critics in the liberal mainstream media—didn't understand was that most populists and Trump support-ers didn't care much about issues of race, gender, or sexuality, one way or the other. What they did care about was reclaiming the land of opportu-nity that used to be their birthright but was increasingly slipping just out of their grasp. They worried that their children would never even have a shot at it. They wanted to Make America Great Again, and they were tired of being told they should be ashamed for thinking that way.

Therein lies the indictment—the proof of just how disconnected the Washington Establishment and the media cartel that supports it had become from the people they were supposed to represent, speak for, and lead. The Trump voters were there all along, but the elites failed to see them. They let their own prejudices get in the way of their supposed anal-ysis. They forgot that in America, political movements aren't top down, they are always bottom up, which is why they are so powerful. In 2016 average Americans all across the country did what the Constitution had given them the right to do—launch a peaceful political revolution at the ballot box. They decided they'd finally had enough of the Washington elites and their failed and misguided policies. It was time to "throw the bums out."

The people Peggy Noonan called the "unprotected" were the people at the Trump rallies, the ones fueling Bernie Sanders's campaign, the ones who turned out in November to shake the Republican and Democratic political establishments to their very core. As Trump gathered momen-tum throughout the primary season, Washington's Republican elites went through the five stages of grief: denial, anger, bargaining, depression, and—for those who chose to remain in the GOP—finally, grudging acceptance. As for the liberal mainstream media and the Washington press corps? They just continued to laugh at him. Shortly after Trump announced his bid for President, I was with a small group of the most respected media mandarins of the Washington press corps, some conservative and some liberal. To a person, they all regarded Trump as a buffoon. One journalist asked sneeringly, "Who does he think he is?" In other words, how dare he run for president? They dismissed him—he wasn't among their accepted list of candidates.

That's when I knew for certain that the gap between the groupthink of the Washington Establishment would prevent it from comprehending what was going on in the rest of the country. Even after Trump defeated his seventeen Republican competitors, one after another, the experts wrote it off as a fluke—and claimed that the Republican party was committing political suicide. When Trump pulled even with Hillary in some of the polls, they still refused to believe it. Then, when Donald Trump was elected President, just twenty-four hours after the *New York Times* had given him a mere 15 percent chance of victory, the entire political establishment went apoplectic. The self-absorbed Hollywood glitterati insisted they would move to Canada rather than live in President Trump's America. Colleges across the country set up grief counseling sessions. Press commentators and pundits were stunned; some even crying on air. But the stock market soared.

Over the last several years literally hundreds of people had called me out for supporting Donald Trump—friends, acquaintances, even complete strangers who accosted me in the checkout line of the grocery store. "Didn't I realize he was rude, crude, a narcissist, and a liar?" "How could I be all right with his sexist, race-baiting, vulgarity?" "How could I work for a man who risked getting us into World War III, or who incites domestic violence?" One longtime colleague even insisted my name be removed from the cover of a book we co-authored, lest he be contaminated by having his name appear next to mine.

First, these people aren't telling me anything I didn't already know. Maybe I disagreed with some of their characterizations and conclusions, but I'm not blind or deaf to Donald Trump's shortcomings. I think he has contributed to making the country a more divisive and angry place.

But he's not done so in a vacuum. I also think he's gotten as good as he's given—by the Washington Establishment that despises him, by the ratings-hungry, weaponized media that push the anti-Trump message 97 percent of the time, and by the Never-Trump Republicans, Democrats, socialists, progressives, left wing intellectuals, the entertainment community, punditry, and politicians. Who started the fights? Everybody. Who's merely defending themselves against attack by others? Everybody. No one is without blame in this toxic environment—no one's hands are clean.

Second, I'm not "all right" with a lot of his behavior. I don't like his tweetstorms. Nobody does, including his wife. They can be nasty, petty, and unpresidential, even if they can sometimes also be very effective.

But there is something I find far worse than Trump's incivility and divisiveness. It is that for the last twenty years most of our leaders were too busy scoring political points over each other to take any steps to protect the interests of our middle and working-class citizens. Or that for decades our leaders stood politely by playing by the Marquis of Queensbury rules—while our adversaries and competitors played by no rules at all. They failed to stand up to and call out those who were taking advantage of our generosity for fear of somehow offending them or of rocking the boat. Too many of our senior statesmen who stood silently by while our competitors used sharp-elbowed tactics and ruthless policies, deliberately lied to our officials, and stole from our companies. The leaders of both political parties assured us for years, "Don't worry, our competitors all want to live in harmony with us as responsible members of the U.S.-led, liberal world order. Once we help them develop their economies and modernize their industries, they will open up their societies and be our trading partners and political allies."

Many of these leaders committed foreign policy malpractice, even if unintentionally. Now that some of our adversaries and competitors are poised to share our place on the world stage, it's become clear that they have no interest in playing by our rules. They want to rewrite the international rules to reflect their own preferences, and to serve their own purposes. Far from opening up their own societies, countries like China have tightened their grip on power and become even more authoritarian. Far from the peaceful rise they promised, China has moved aggressively to claim the South China Sea, one of the world's most important trade routes, as an internal Chinese lake. Even the liberal *New York Times* columnist Roger Cohen now admits that Chinese President "Xi's message is clear: We'll take your engagement, eat it, double down on repression and one day run the world."[3]

Leaving America vulnerable to exploitation by foreign powers? Ignoring the needs and interests of tens of millions of Americans? I find those far worse than Trump's angry tweets and belligerent counterpunches. Trump may be offensive to some, but at least he recognizes we're like the people on the Titanic, headed for a collision course with an iceberg unless we change direction. He's also willing to do whatever it takes to avoid such a disaster. Meanwhile, the Washington Establishment is more concerned with squabbling over rearranging deck chairs on the Titanic instead of turning the ship around.

While Trump's critics are offended by his behavior, I am disgusted by theirs. They are willing to put their own selfish interests ahead of the nation's. Their obsession with campaign contributions, media ratings, and electoral victory has driven them to condemn the country to another year of constitutional crises over impeachment. The consequence—our adversaries, especially China, have determined they need not yield to Trump's pressure to revise our trade and security relationships. They can sit on the sidelines, watch the anti-Trump forces destroy him, and wait for a more China-friendly compliant U.S. president to replace him.

One thing I'm convinced of is if the Republicans had nominated a typical establishment candidate in 2016—a Jeb Bush or Mitt Romney—he would have given a respectable showing but would have lost, nonetheless. If Hillary Clinton were now President, she would have neither the inclination nor the willpower to redirect American economic or foreign policy. She would be taking us further down the road to decline until a decade or so later, when it would be too late to alter course.

I know Trump can be an insufferable, noisy brawler, a Queens street-fighter. I know he isn't like other leaders. I know he's a black swan; an exceptionally rare and disrupting influence. That's exactly why I supported him then and continue to support him now. It is precisely the fact that he *is* an outsider, and one who isn't the least bit afraid of ruffling some feathers, that has allowed him to get things done that more

---

[3] Cohen, Roger. "Trump Has China Policy About Right." *The New York Times.* August 30, 2019. https://www.nytimes.com/2019/08/30/opinion/trump-china-trade-war.html.

polite and refined politicians couldn't. Trump is tough, blunt, politically incorrect, and unfettered by tradition. But he is also doggedly relentless and unwilling to give up something he believes in no matter how loud the chorus of critics, or the number of Democrats, cable news networks, journalists, academics, or Hollywood glitterati that clamor for his head. Donald Trump, warts and all, offers our best, and perhaps last, chance to Make America Great Again.

Once again, it was Peggy Noonan who put it best: "Trump supporters...chose him and back him because he *isn't* normal. They'd tried normal! It didn't work! Of course he's a brute, but his brutishness was the only thing that could surprise Washington, scare it, make it reform. Both parties are corrupt and look out only for themselves; he's the one who wouldn't be in hock to them and their donors. Is he weird? Yes. But it's a weird country now. He's the only one big enough to push back against what's pushing us."[4]

So far, I'm winning my bet. Granted, Trump is more combative than I had anticipated, but then again so are the countless number of his critics. Today's political divisiveness is a steep price to pay for restoring the country to economic growth and recalibrating our defense and foreign policies. The anger and resentment that has been stoked by all sides is something we cannot ignore. We will have to face up to it and work together to repair the damage this incivility has caused in the years ahead if we are ever to regain our national sense of purpose and faith in each other. But at least we will now have that option. Without Trump's policy reversals, and the economic growth and prosperity they have brought about, our ability to guarantee the security, peace, and prosperity for our people in the decades ahead would inevitably have declined, perhaps permanently.

Trump has also been far more successful in restoring economic growth, creating jobs, and tackling some of the accumulated abuses of the administrative and regulatory state. Today, the American economy is not only the strongest it has been in decades, across all groups in our society, it is easily among the strongest economies in the developed world. Trump has also begun to reorient our international relationships, and is in the process of ending the unnecessary, expensive, and unfair subsidies

---

[4] Noonan, Peggy. "I Love a Parade, but Not This One." *Wall Street Journal*. February 8, 2018. https://www.wsj.com/articles/i-love-a-parade-but-not-this-one-1518135401.

embedded in our security and trade agreements. His use of American economic power, through tariffs, and the threat of tariffs, has been far more effective in getting our adversaries and competitors to come around to our way of thinking than any use of our military power.

Trump still hasn't reduced our burgeoning debt, or actually lowered our trade deficits, but unlike traditional Washington politicians, he at least understands the urgency and necessity of doing so. Tax-and-spend Democrats, progressives, and socialists blame our deficits on tax cuts, and urge across the board tax increases, especially on high income earners. What they often fail to admit is that America's taxes are already some of the highest in the world. We don't have a revenue problem; we have a spending problem. Ultimately, Trump must find a way to break our unsustainable addiction to spending and the use politicians make of ramping up government programs to buy votes if he is to have lasting success.

Only by fixing the economy and by making us once again the land of opportunity for all our people, can we restore the American Dream to all our people. If we fail, we will become like all the other great nations in history, slowly fading into the background while others rise up to take our place. We will no longer be the exceptional nation nor the "Shining City on a Hill." Only if Trump (and the leaders who will come after him) can stay his course, can we Make America Great Again.

At one of our two debate prep sessions, I congratulated Trump for tipping his hat to Reagan by using his campaign theme, "Make America Great Again." Trump looked puzzled and I realized he either didn't remember it was originally Reagan's 1980 rallying cry or didn't care. He would make it his own, whether it was his idea first or not. No matter. The important thing for me was that Trump's goals were the same as those that worked so successfully for Reagan a generation before: grow the economy and create jobs by cutting taxes, eliminating burdensome over- regulation, and reducing the size and scope of government, rebuild our military, and avoid getting sucked into hopeless foreign wars. And most important, stand up to the real adversaries who pose a true strategic threat to the future of our country. Just as Reagan understood that it was the Soviet Union during the Cold War, Trump realizes that in the 21st century it is China.

So, despite his reluctance to acknowledge it, Trump probably comes the closest to being President Reagan's true heir. Not in temperament, of course, or character, humility, or personal popularity, but in foreign and economic policies and a dogged perseverance to see them through. The irony is every Republican presidential candidate for decades has declared himself to be a "Reagan Republican." Yet the only one who hasn't claimed Reagan's mantle is probably the one who comes closest to having the right to wear it.

The combination of Reaganomics (tax cuts, regulatory reform, and spending reductions) and Peace through Strength (defense buildup, deterrence, and the Star Wars missile defense program) stood at the core of the Reagan Revolution. Both positions were dramatic breaks with the conventional wisdom of the day, and rejections of the status quo. By 1980, the country was ready for massive change, even if the Washington Establishment was not.

The 1970s had been an exceptionally disappointing decade. The Vietnam War had escalated, with casualties climbing into the tens of thousands, with no end or victory in sight. Student-led anti-war demonstrations had broken out across the country. Finally, after years of fighting in the jungles of Southeast Asia against a guerilla Vietnamese army, Congress cut off the funding, so we packed up and left in humiliation and defeat. At the same time, President Richard Nixon was overwhelmed by the Watergate scandal. In 1974 he had resigned rather than face certain impeachment by the House of Representatives. In the years that followed, President Gerald Ford lost to Jimmy Carter, who presided over the decline of the American armed forces and an economy that was both stagnant and inflationary at the same time. Interest rates climbed so high that in some states they were considered usurious.

While we were struggling, the communist Soviet Union was thriving. Their top-down economic model was touted by some as superior to our free market capitalism. They were flush with revenues from high oil prices; they rebuilt their military, expanded their influence abroad, and seemed to be winning the Cold War. Even President Carter himself admitted that America was adrift, and suffering from a crisis of confidence and national malaise. He offered no answers. Instead, Carter recommended doing the same things that had gotten us into the mess in the first place. The Republican Party's establishment candidate, George H.W. Bush, offered more of the same.

By 1980 the majority of Americans had had enough. Rank and file Republican voters turned away from the candidate their party leaders clearly preferred and chose Reagan as their standard bearer. He went on to defeat a sitting President by winning over millions of Democrats to his cause. Reagan proposed economic and foreign policies that were radically different from those the Washington Establishment endorsed, but Reagan's were the ones voters embraced. He launched a pro-growth agenda to dramatically reduce personal and corporate taxes, streamline government, and cut through the tangle of bureaucratic red tape—all despite warnings from Washington insiders that he would fail spectacularly. But within three years Reaganomics had turned America around. His pro-growth policies unleashed free enterprise and economic freedom that created a near-miraculous economic revival. Under Reagan the economy grew by a third, creating 19 million new jobs, and improving Americans' standard of living by 20 percent. He is responsible for launching one of the longest and most significant periods of economic growth and job creation in our history.

Reagan had even more success in the foreign policy field. He refused to get drawn into overseas quagmires with unwinnable wars of intervention. He rejected the notion that the best we could hope for was an interminable uneasy peace between the United States and Soviet Union that depended on the threat of mutual nuclear annihilation. Reagan rebuilt our military, improved relations with our allies, gave hope to the people behind the Iron Curtain, and challenged Soviet President Gorbachev to "tear down this wall." The policies he laid down in the early 1980s led to Communism's collapse. Within a decade, the Berlin Wall came down, the Soviet Empire dissolved, and we won the Cold War without firing a shot. We were the world's sole remaining superpower.

Because of Reagan's sunny personality, humor, charisma, and considerable political skills, people outside of Washington tended not to appreciate just how much of a revolutionary he was. Reagan didn't merely overturn the policies of his predecessors; he replaced them with something entirely new. He didn't just tear down—he also built up.

Why do people still admire Reagan, even decades after his Presidency ended? It isn't due to the extraordinary success of Reaganomics and Peace Through Strength alone. It is because Reagan was the kind of exceptional leader who comes along but once in a generation, maybe only once in a century. Reagan shattered the conventional wisdom on taxes and economic growth, peaceful coexistence with communism, and Mutually

Assured Destruction. He stood up to the Washington Establishment and disrupted the status quo. But it is more than that—Reagan replaced the crisis of confidence Americans had about the country and our purpose in the world with a renewed sense of pride and patriotism.

The achievement of which Reagan was most proud was helping to reawaken the American spirit. He believed in his bones that we were the Shining City on a Hill, a beacon of hope for the entire world. His confidence in America's goodness and purpose was contagious. He got us to believe in ourselves again and, in so doing, restored the world's confidence in American leadership. He became the spark that lit the fire; the leader who inspired us to rise above the petty partisanship endemic to the politics of every age and realize the exceptional nation we have inherited and have a duty to preserve.

While fiercely criticized at the time, Reagan eventually took on Olympian stature among conservatives and Republicans. Even his critics ultimately gave him grudging respect. Clark Clifford, one of the senior statesmen of the Democratic Party, once called Reagan "an amiable dunce." Years later, though, ABC White House correspondent Sam Donaldson, who had been one of Reagan's fiercest media opponents, said,

> *Having a front-row seat to the Reagan Presidency certainly changed how I viewed this nation's Great Communicator, and I came to believe Clifford was only half right. Amiable, yes; dunce, most certainly not.... I came to respect Reagan's skills as a leader.... Will there be another like Ronald Wilson Reagan? Not in our lifetime. And that's too bad.*

Reagan was unfailingly polite, upbeat, and optimistic. Even when he was lambasting a policy he opposed, he did it with a smile on his face. He criticized policies, ideologies, and perspectives, but he didn't criticize the people who advocated for them. He had a unique ability to keep it professional—and never let it get personal.

Reagan's sunny optimism and ability to reach across party lines to get legislation passed worked well in the 1980s. He didn't go to war against the Democrats in Congress or rail at the media; he persuaded them, charmed them, and disarmed them. One of his most effective weapons against opponents was his sense of humor—that, and his demeanor that rarely let anyone get under his skin. He constantly expanded his base of support and was even more popular with the American people when he left the White

House than when he had entered it. The country seemed united and the body politic much healthier. Much of it was because Reagan himself set the tone. Although he was every bit as tough as Trump, Reagan worked hard at not presenting an easy target. He was liked even by his enemies.

Trump, on the other hand, is disliked, sometimes even by his allies. He actually seems to revel in it. He's a classic New Yorker, ready to take anyone on. He brags about being a counter-puncher. When attacked, he hits back, only harder. He is proud to be politically incorrect and relishes criticizing and offending those he thinks deserve it. It is probably the only way he can survive the constant hammering he takes from all sides. Unfortunately, this cycle of verbal combat lends itself to increasingly harsh criticism, which is taking its toll on the nation. It shows no sign of abating; indeed, it is getting more and more vicious by the day, as we move into the impeachment process and the intensity of the upcoming 2020 presidential election campaign.

Reagan inspired the United States and the world. I can't imagine Trump, at least as he is today, inspiring any of his opponents, except to further outrage. He is capable of bringing the country back together, if he so chooses. But right now, he's focused on defending himself and fulfilling his campaign promises—and not on outreach to his Democrat opponents. I still hope the rest might come later, either because Trump himself (after re-election) is able to change his approach, or because his successors do.

I joined the Trump Revolution for many of the same reasons I joined the Reagan Revolution in 1980. I wasn't blind to Trump's flaws. I supported him despite his roughness, unpredictability, and pugnacious street-fighter persona. In many ways, I supported him precisely *because* of those characteristics. I wanted someone who would challenge the status quo, break up the Washington power cartels, and reverse the economic and foreign policies that favored the elites at the expense of the working and middle classes. Trump was the only person running for President in 2016 who was willing to go up against Washington's governing class and to have the resilience to keep fighting until he broke through. Today, Trump remains strong, even if alone, in fighting the swamp of the Washington Establishment and the Administrative State, the special interests which support them, and the liberal media and their fake news which benefit from them.

CHAPTER 5

@ The Real Donald Trump

For each of our presidents, character and personality have played a major role in what they've been able to achieve. But the Presidents who stood at the major inflection points in our history, those who led genuine political revolutions, were always larger-than-life characters who came to dominate the politics and media not just of their time in office, but of their entire era. George Washington, Andrew Jackson, Abraham Lincoln, Teddy Roosevelt, Franklin Delano Roosevelt, Ronald Reagan. You could fill a bookcase with analyses and psychoanalyses on any one of them.

But Trump is likely to have an entire library all to himself. Since everything else in Washington divides into two camps these days, it's no surprise that there are two radically different versions of Donald Trump's character and personality. His supporters see him as a larger-than-life counterpuncher. He will swing back at anyone, almost regardless of their prominence, who swings at him first, only harder. But the punches he takes and throws are all for his supporters. He is their fearless champion.

They don't pay a lot of attention to what Trump says, because over the years career politicians have demonstrated that words by themselves are cheap. They care more about what Trump does. They believe that, unlike other politicians, Trump is actually keeping his campaign promises, or at least trying to keep them, even in the face of unprecedented attacks and sabotage by the Washington Establishment and its fervently Trump-hating media supporters.

Trump's critics—who dominate 95 percent of the press, airwaves, internet, Twitterverse, and most of Washington, D.C.—see him as a textbook narcissist. To them, Trump has a dangerously excessive need for attention and admiration—he can't feel empathy, respect, or love for anyone but himself. To them he's a liar, bully, and brute.

Both of these assessments have a whiff of truth to them. But neither get to the core of why Trump is the way he is. I followed Trump for years before his run for President, observed him personally in the months I worked with him, and continue to follow him closely after leaving Washington. Putting hyper-praise or hyper-criticism aside, this is what I have seen.

My former FOX News colleague, the talented primetime anchor Martha MacCallum, may have unintentionally hit upon what really drives Trump. She made a guest appearance on *FOX and Friends* in July 2018, to preview her coverage of Trump's official State Visit to Great Britain. He had just left the NATO Summit meeting in Brussels and was heading to London, where he was scheduled to meet Prime Minister Theresa May and have a formal dinner with the Queen at Blenheim Palace. The big news of the day in much of Britain was that England had just lost in the World Cup semi-finals, 2-1 in overtime.

MacCallum relayed Trump's rather unusual reaction to London's morning press, which heaped praise on the all-England team. Trump was stunned by their reaction to the match, and their unanimous praise of the team. The headlines read, "They exceeded all expectations," "They tried their best," "They're our heroes!" According to MacCallum, Trump said, "Can you believe it? They *lost*! They didn't *win*! Why are they saying nice things about losers?"

Remember when Trump said on the campaign trail, "America doesn't win anymore? I'm going to make America win again. We're going to win so much you're going to get tired of winning."

For Trump, the only thing that counts is winning. It doesn't matter how you do it, how many rules you have to break, how many people you offend, how much you humiliate your competitors, or even yourself, in order to achieve victory. Everything is fair game. The only thing that matters for Trump is the bottom line, whether you've won or lost.

In Trump's New York world of real estate, banking, business, and even entertainment, everything has a constant, real-time bottom line. There is nothing ambiguous or subjective about it. You either made money that day or you didn't. You either closed the year profitably—in the black—or you lost money and were in the red. Your quarterly ratings either went up or they went down.

Washington operates differently, with lots of blue smoke and mirrors, behind-the-scenes power brokers and special interest groups. There are so many interpretations, nuances, and subtleties involved, particularly from political commentators, that it's all but impossible to keep a running score. Just about anything can be spun as a victory by your side, or a failure by your adversaries. The only metric to judge whether you've won or lost happens every two or four years at election time. In between, victory is too subjective and hard to quantify.

It's as if Trump has internalized the legendary 1950s football coach Vince Lombardi's dictum: "Winning isn't everything; it's the only thing." That attitude has fallen into disrepute in modern times. It has been replaced by a kinder, gentler, more egalitarian way of thinking. "It's not whether you win or lose, it's how you play the game that counts." Today, every child gets the same participation trophy, everyone gets to play, and no one keeps score. Whenever the game ends, there are no winners or losers. But Trump's combative personality was formed when he was a young man in the 1950s—and in many ways he's still there.

I think that's why he feels no shame when he's called out for fudging facts a bit, or changing positions, or holding two seemingly contradictory positions at once. Trump doesn't worry about whether his tweets insult journalists, senators, or foreign leaders. Occasionally, he can even denigrate loyal, long-standing aides in private or in public; if they're not helping him win, they're expendable. He doesn't see it as necessarily provocative when he tosses out threats about going to war, or picks fights with our allies, or risks rupturing other long-standing international relationships. He doesn't intend for the positions that he takes along the way to become permanent; they're just negotiating tactics. Trump's tariff and trade wars aren't meant to last; they're leverage he can use to drive a better deal. They are all part of the back and forth, the push and pull, the means necessary to achieve Trump's end goal of winning. Trump's world is black and white—you're either winning (or on the course to winning) or you're losing. It's not always pretty, admirable, or commendable. But it *is* effective—and it is a key to Trump's personality.

Since Trump makes all the big decisions himself and thus takes all the risks, he expects to get all the credit if he succeeds. I think that this braggadocio lies at the heart of his ongoing war with the media. They go at him 24/7. It's all Trump, all the time, and it's almost all pointedly and viciously negative. They won't give him credit for any of his successes. "He didn't really win the election; the Russians did it… He may have brought North Korean President Kim Jong-Un to the negotiating table, but nothing will come of it… He's not responsible for creating millions of new jobs; that began under Obama… The new U.S.-Mexico-Canada trade agreement isn't anything new; it's just recycled NAFTA… We may have high economic growth rates now, but it's just a sugar high and cannot possibly last." Yada, yada, yada.

In my experience, people brag incessantly for one of two completely different reasons: Either they have too little self-confidence—or too much. Insecure people constantly drop names of famous people, inflate their resumes, and tell you how powerful or rich they are. They're trying to convince themselves as much as you. Their deep sense of insecurity or inferiority pushes them to validate their self-worth by stretching the truth. If they can convince you into thinking they're important, then they'll believe it too, like a reflection in the mirror.

On the other hand, some braggarts are supremely confident in themselves and their flawless judgment. They constantly talk about their own achievements because experience has taught them that it is the only way they can get proper credit for their successes. For these people, the problem isn't with them, it's with you. They've done really great things— they're successful, brilliant, rich—but it doesn't seem to have registered with others. Their braggadocio isn't meant to convince themselves, it's to remind everybody else.

For the most part, Trump falls into the second category. Unless and until the liberal media give him credit for something, he's going to keep coming back at them with accusations of tainted analysis and "fake news." But the media is never going to give him credit for his successes. Why? In part because they just can't stand him. They despise everything about him. Furthermore, he's not from the Washington insiders club where they're longtime members. But rarely mentioned is that it is in their self-interest to never acknowledge any of Trump's successes, and to continue their anti-Trump obsession. After all, their ratings are up, media profits are soaring, and the Trump Presidency is the biggest reality TV show of all time. It's just too good a thing to walk away from. So, the war between the president and the press is likely to continue, almost indefinitely.

Most of my time with Trump after the Inauguration was spent in the Oval Office in his morning intelligence briefings or throughout the day, as I helped him prepare for meetings and calls with foreign leaders. I soon learned that if you begin a conversation with Trump by giving him credit for one of his success—not in a fawning, faux-credit way, but by offering legitimate praise for one of his genuine achievements—he drops the self-aggrandizing and starts paying attention to what you have to say. He needs to win, and he needs you to acknowledge his victory and give him full credit for it. Once that's out of the way, he can get down to business. If not, he never gets past the winning/losing dynamic, and insists on repeating stories of his previous successes, leaving little time for the topic you have come to discuss. When Trump is in private, with people he knows already respect and admire him, he doesn't do the bragging routine. He doesn't need to remind you of his wins because you already know.

One of the constant themes from anti-Trumpers is that he is stupid and crazy. If so, then how do they explain his successes, not just in one field, but in most of the things he's tried? Trump has the Midas Touch: He built a real estate empire in the most competitive place in the world: Manhattan. He's built hotels and golf resorts, both at home and abroad. He's a businessman who made millions, nearly went bankrupt, then came roaring back to make billions. When other men his age were having their mid-life crises, Trump created a whole new genre of television, Reality TV, and cast himself in the starring role of a top-rated series. And in his seventies, when most of his contemporaries were retiring to Florida to work on their golf game and play with the grandkids, Trump decided to run for president...and win...by championing the working class. Three years later, the people he thumped still can't wrap their minds around his victory. Like comedian Rodney Dangerfield, Trump still "can't get no respect."

What Trump's critics fail to appreciate is how practical he is, and that he possesses that most uncommon of virtues, especially in Washington: common sense. Let me give you an example. Early in the Administration, the Oval Office seemed infested with flies—the big, black kind that buzz all around, land on something for a second, and fly away when you try to swat them. I certainly found them annoying when I was in the Oval Office for a thirty-minute meeting, but Trump had to suffer them all day and they were driving him nuts. At the intelligence briefing one morning, a big black hairy fly landed on Trump's desk, right next to his ubiquitous glass of Diet Coke. He said, "We've had exterminators come in, but nobody can get rid of these damned flies." I tried to make a joke out of it and said maybe it wasn't a fly at all, but a miniature intelligence drone from one of the anti-Trump networks. He didn't think that was very funny. He ignored me and continued, "Whatever happened to fly paper? You know, the long yellow strips that hung from the ceiling? Nobody uses fly paper anymore, but it worked just fine."

Later that day, my office got a call from CIA saying that Deputy Director Gina Haspel was sending over an envelope marked for KT McFarland, *Eyes Only*, and asked that it be delivered directly into my hands. I had no idea what this was all about, but it was very irregular, and seemingly clandestine. When the package arrived, I opened it up only to find several strips of sticky yellow fly paper, with a note: "You will know what to do with this." That evening, as I walked past the Oval Office on my way home, I stuck my head in and saw two White House handymen up on ladders putting the fly paper on an invisible ledge of the crown molding that circled the ceiling.

A few days later, we were back in the Oval Office for the morning intelligence briefing. President Trump looked at Gina Haspel, smiled, and pointed to the ceiling. He said, "See, no more flies." Gina Haspel not only has a sense of humor, she is also one of the most talented intelligence officers in the business. She went on to break the glass ceiling at the CIA as the first female director in history.

President Trump doesn't like long, boring meetings. He gets especially frustrated with people who go on and on, making the same point again and again. He's a man of action; no one can accuse him of paralysis by analysis. Briefing Trump is unlike briefing anyone else. He's in charge of setting the agenda, not the briefer. He assumes control of every briefing at the very beginning, and treats it like it's a conversation, even a debate. He likes to throw out alternative interpretations, and canvas others in the room for their opinions, even if they're not experts. He likes to bounce around from topic to topic, sometimes pulling an idea out of thin air and batting it around.

I asked one of his longtime assistants at Trump Tower why he did it, and whether he was always like that. The explanation I got might have been more apocryphal than true. I've never found anyone who could confirm it firsthand. According to the story, when Trump was in the process of buying Mar-a-Lago, he and the seller agreed on a price which was considered a bargain by any measure. As Trump was going to the closing, he bragged to the valet who parked his car that he was about to buy the best piece of real estate in all of Palm Beach. The valet congratulated him then suggested Trump might want to walk out on the lawn of Mar-a-Lago in the middle of the day and look up at the sky. Trump did—and realized Mar-a-Lago was directly under the flight path in and out of Palm Beach airport. Trump went back to the seller's agent and insisted that they knock a million or so off the sale price because of all the noise. They agreed, and renegotiated a deal with even more favorable terms for Trump. Once the sale was final, he got the Palm Beach authorities to change the flight path. Whether the story is true or not, the point is that Trump often asks the most unlikely of people for their opinions, and sometimes it pays off.

Another criticism from anti-Trumpers is that he's constantly "winging it." Again, that's not what I observed. His "spontaneity" is deliberate. He wants you to think he came up with something off the top of his head, because it reinforces his aura of unpredictability. I've never seen him announce a major policy or personnel decision out of the blue. He has already chewed it over in private, querying his staff and friends, tossing out ideas in Oval Office briefings, floating trial balloons. He has usually made the decision on a firing, hiring, or policy change well before he first tweets it out. But he keeps it to himself, like a card up his sleeve, often not sharing it even with his closest aides. He's saving the announcement for an opportune moment when it will do him the most good—when he wants to change the national conversation, divert the press's attention away from something else, or deflect some criticism. Only then does he tweet it out or drop it in what appears to be an offhand way at a public event.

In most Administrations, presidential summit meetings are carefully choreographed. For months leading up to the historic event, each side has dozens of internal meetings and departmental debates. They prepare position papers outlining options and make recommendations for their bosses, who in turn do the same thing for the next level above them, on up to the Cabinet Secretary and maybe even to the President. That's followed by lots of back and forth between the two countries' staffs, each offering ideas and responding to the other side's demands. The final positions have been worked out well in advance by the experts of both sides. Any contentious issues have already been resolved, all joint agreements already printed out and ready for signature—even the concluding press statements are written ahead of time. By the time the two leaders finally do meet, there is often nothing left to do but sit for a formal private meeting where each leader reads his talking points with the cameras flashing away. There are no surprises, no last-minute changes, nothing left to chance, no risk of something going haywire.

"Choreographed" is not how Trump did things in business, and it's not how he does things as president. In New York, the big real estate companies are family-owned and operated. The founder is the patriarch and CEO of the empire. His siblings, children, and grandchildren are responsible for different parts of the business, but he is still the only boss that counts. Non-family staff, no matter how talented, loyal, or well-compensated, are still just employees. The CEO of a privately held real estate empire is more all-powerful than the CEO of a public company who has to answer to a board of directors or shareholders. Trump, like the chieftains of other great New York real estate families, answered to no one. He was used to giving orders to people who obeyed. When they didn't, he would fire them. When two major New York real estate developers do business with each other, it's like two titans doing battle—each sizing the other up, looking for his weaknesses, understanding his strengths, figuring out his bottom line and yours. It's a very personal business where the boss makes the big decisions, and leaves it to the staff to sort out the details.

Trump now sees himself as America's CEO. He expects to do business and negotiate directly with the other country's CEO, the same way he has always done, face to face. He wants to get a sense of the man, read his body language, see how tough he is or isn't before deciding how to proceed. He believes only the top man can take bold steps, break logjams, and make tough calls. Yes, he is used to getting input from his staff in advance, but he is the one who ultimately decides the negotiating strategy and tactics.

As president, Trump intends to be the one doing the negotiating, not one of his Cabinet officers, and certainly not some deputy assistant secretary of something or other who Trump has never even met. Their job is to implement his decisions, not the other way around.

In business when Trump wanted to buy something, he would usually get the process started by throwing out a low-ball bid, expecting that with the back and forth of negotiating, he would end up settling for something higher. He would use any and every tactic to get the deal he wanted—threats, flattery, intimidation. He might not have intended to carry out the threats, but the other side didn't know that. After all, Trump has done some pretty crazy things in the past. He is constantly looking for leverage, any angle he could use to further his cause. But most of all, Trump is unpredictable. He changes positions, switches his approach, walks away from a deal, runs towards it. Trump uses his unpredictability as another tool in his negotiating toolbox.

Trump's approach can be especially effective against leaders who are unaccustomed to, and uncomfortable with, his unconventional way of doing business. For example, the Chinese approach to business and diplomatic negotiations is the polar opposite of Trump's. They work in a methodical, deliberative fashion, patiently studying the other side's issues and personalities, sometimes for years. They carefully follow the other country's domestic politics. They know the various pressures facing the other leader, and how they might exploit them during negotiations. It is only after prolonged and intense analysis and internal debate that they formulate their own positions. Yet, while they are very good at conducting scripted diplomacy, they are at a disadvantage when dealing with someone like Trump, who delights in doing the unpredictable and thrives on spontaneity.

Most presidents have approached U.S.-China summit meetings with similar extensive preparation, although perhaps not as much as the Chinese. In previous Administrations, the Americans, as well as the Chinese, start preparations at the bottom of the hierarchy and work their way up to the top for final decisions. For Trump, the process starts at the top—with him—and works its way down the chain.

I had several meetings with Chinese officials right after Trump took office, to lay the groundwork for a presidential summit to be held at

Mar-a-Lago in the early spring of Trump's first year in office. A delegation came from Beijing for meetings with various officials across the Executive Branch, culminating with a meeting in the W   House with me and other senior NSC officials. When I arrived at the conference room, the Chinese already had their large briefing books laid out on the table in front of them, with several pages of prepared remarks sitting on top—that had no doubt been carefully crafted back in Beijing. They had a script of items they wanted agreed to in advance of the summit between Presidents Xi and Trump, and needed them nailed down before taking things to the next step. The head of the Chinese delegation read through his talking points, with his aides taking extensive notes on everything that was said. When he finished, I was expected to respond by reading from the American talking points. It was maddening to them that we did not have a similarly well-crafted position.

I explained that President Trump had an unconventional approach, very different from what they were used to with previous presidents. Trump wanted to meet with the Chinese president first, get to know him, and share some general thoughts before setting out his positions at subsequent meetings. This was clearly not what the leader of the Chinese delegation expected, and that initial meeting wrapped up quickly. He was no doubt frustrated when he headed back to Beijing to report to his bosses, who were probably even more unhappy with the results.

At a follow-up meeting with Chinese Ambassador Cui Tankai, I tried to give some context to the Trump approach. I said when I worked for Dr. Kissinger on the National Security Council in the early 1970s, one of my jobs was to type up the notes of the meetings he had with foreign leaders. Most of them followed a fairly standard routine: first pleasantries, followed by discussion of the specific outstanding issues between our two countries, ending with plans to meet again.

I said Kissinger's meetings with Chinese leaders, beginning with his secret trip to China in July 1971, were completely different, and probably unique, at least in the annals of American diplomatic history. When Kissinger first met with Chinese Premier Zhou Enlai in Beijing, it was the only contact between American and Chinese officials in a generation, because we broke relations with each other when the Communists assumed power. There was no set agenda, and the two men talked for hours. They discussed the broad sweep of history, world trends, how they saw other nations, and their goals for their own. As Kissinger writes in his memoirs, it was like two college professors in the faculty lounge.[1]

I went on to explain to the Chinese Ambassador that those initial meetings weren't to haggle out the specifics of issues we had with each other. Rather, they were a way for both leaders to get a sense of what was possible in any relationship between the U.S. and China going forward. Those conversations, more philosophy than foreign policy, set the groundwork for a relationship that has endured for decades, even as both of our countries went through leadership changes, and pursued different policies.

I explained that President Trump felt the same way. Trump also wanted a long and enduring relationship, but the first step was for each President to get a measure of the other. Trump was not a politician. He wasn't familiar with all the code words of diplomacy, nor had he followed the minute details of the U.S.-Chinese relationship over the years. His upset victory was the result of the American people's decision to have a new group of leaders who would take the country in a different direction than it had followed for the last two decades. An important aspect of it would be the U.S.-Chinese relationship.

I pointed out that President Xi, although different in background and experience from President Trump, was also taking his country in a new direction, and would become a leader of great consequence in Chinese history.

The Chinese Ambassador realized we were not going to get through his list of talking points, so he closed his folder. He leaned back in his chair and begin speaking in a different tone. He said that while I was in the White House Situation Room typing up those notes of the Kissinger-Zhou meeting in the 1971, he was driving a tractor on a state farm in rural China, where his family had been sent during the Cultural Revolution.[2]

While he was talking, I recalled a conversation I had with Kissinger a few years before I joined the Trump Administration. He observed that the current generation of Chinese leaders had either been "prisoners or jailers" during the Cultural Revolution. They had either been Red Guard

---

[1] Kissinger, Henry. *On China*. London: Penguin Press, a division of Penguin Random House, 2011. 240.

[2] "A Conversation With Cui Tiankai." Council on Foreign Relations. July 1, 2013. https://www.foreignaffairs.com/print/1113333.

student radicals who attacked senior Chinese leaders, or the children of those leaders who were sent to forced labor camps with their parents.

The urbane and sophisticated Chinese Ambassador sitting across the table from me, like a number of China's senior leaders, was now in his sixties, and had come up through the ranks together with these senior leaders. Many of them, including Chinese President Xi Jinping, were China's "princelings," born in the 1950s into some of the most prominent political families in China.

On the eve of Xi's first state visit to the United States, in September 2015, the *New York Times* profiled the new Chinese president. The article described how his father, one of the country's senior-most officials, was purged by Mao and at the beginning of the Cultural Revolution in the 1960s. Even though Xi's father was one of the founders of Communist China, he was attacked by Mao's shock troops, the student Red Guard, who spread across the country arresting, beating, and even killing Communist party leaders, university professors, and government administrators. The Red Guard denounced them for being insufficiently Communist, and they and their families were banished to rural villages to work on state farms or in factories. Practically overnight, they had gone from lives of privilege and power in Beijing to living and working in grinding poverty, while being forcibly "re-educated." Most of them were eventually rehabilitated after the Cultural Revolution ended a decade later. Many of their sons, privilege restored, went on to university and government service.

When the Cultural Revolution ended, some of the Red Guard students entered the security services and also rose to prominence.

Whether prisoners or jailers in the 1960s, the violence and chaos of those years had left scars on their entire generation. They carry with them an abhorrence of dissent, uncertainty, and social unrest. They experienced firsthand what can happen in China when the forces of revolution, zealotry, and violence are unleashed. It underlies their insistence on strict adherence to order and hierarchy, both in the way they order their societies and conduct their diplomacy.[3, 4]

---

[3] Ramzy. Austin. "In Xi Jinping's Tears, a Message for China's People." *The New York Times.* March 3, 2016. https://www.nytimes.com/2016/03/04/world/asia/china-xi-jinping-tears.html?module=Promotron&region=Body&action=click&pgtype=article.

[4] Buckley, Chris. "2019 Is a Sensitive Year for China. Xi Is Nervous." *The New York Times.* February 25, 2019. https://www.nytimes.com/2019/02/25/world/asia/china-xi-warnings.html.

Ambassador Cui said that because of his upbringing, he too felt an obligation to work for peace. I'm not sure he was particularly pleased with the Trump approach, but he seemed resigned to it. Cui said all the right things, whether he meant them or not. But it was clear to me that the Chinese leaders thought they were now being forced to operate in unfamiliar territory. What I realized then was that Trump's unusual way of doing things allows him to drive the agenda. The other side may start out with all sorts of issues and demands, but unless Trump decides to engage, it doesn't go anywhere.

Trump's approach is risky, of course, because either side could fail to read the other accurately. In business, if a deal blows up, it's usually neither fatal nor the last word. You can always recover. In international relationships, that's not the case. If the other side miscalculates, you could both unintentionally move in a dangerous direction, making it harder to walk back. This is particularly true for Trump, who is new to the complicated dance of diplomacy. Trump might give up something important without realizing it, or do something offensive without meaning to. The Trump approach is most effective if you have the best cards to play and the most leverage. If the situation were to reverse at some point in the future, say, for example, if the Chinese came to believe they were so powerful that they no longer needed to take the U.S. position into serious account, Trump's approach could well end in disaster.

Donald Trump may be the most famous tweeter of all time. Twitter and Facebook had been around years before Trump ran for President, but he was one of the first political candidates to realize the power of social media, figure out how to harness it, and use it to his advantage.

We live in an impersonal era of mass communications and mass marketing. As more and more people are glued to their devices, they have fewer human interactions; most of their relationships are online. The issue today isn't getting your message out. People are already bombarded to death with social media messaging. The key is getting your message to penetrate the wall of media clutter.

Trump's tweets break through. When you read one of his tweets, you know it was Trump's own fingers that tapped out those 140 characters and hit "send." Trump's Twitter feed has become a reality show about being President, with the biggest audience in the world watching.

He may send a tweet out to hundreds of millions of people, but when you read it on your own handheld device, you and Trump have a type of immediate and intimate connection. Sometimes he's complaining that he's not getting the credit he deserves, sometimes he's ranting about the people he's mad at. Sometimes he's making fun of politicians or commenting on sporting events. But it always feels personal—like he's talking straight to you the way people talk to their families and friends.

Some of Trump's tweets are trial balloons, some deliberate signals to allies or adversaries, some launch new policies, some are unnecessarily cruel ways to announce firing and hiring decisions, and some sound more like the complaints of a petulant child rather than comments worthy of a president. Nevertheless, Trump's tweets are endlessly attention grabbing and immediate. If Trump is in his bathrobe at 6:00 a.m. and catches a morning talk show host trashing him, five minutes later he sends out a tweet trash-talking him back. Trump takes to Twitter to announce to the world he's firing his Secretary of State rather than telling him in advance and in person. He calls the North Korean dictator "Lil Rocket Man" and they proceed to engage in a heated tweet-a-thon over whose nuclear weapons are bigger. A few weeks later, he gushes that they're sending each other love letters.

Trump knows he can reach millions of people in seconds, and it's a powerful weapon for him to give up, even though many have urged him to do so. Once, in his office in Trump Tower during the Transition, several of us were sitting around his desk, trying to brief him on something or other. He was distracted, looking down at his cell phone and tapping away. He didn't hear a thing we were saying. He suddenly interrupted us, proudly held up his cell phone and said, "What do you think of this?" Without waiting for an answer, he hit "send." Trump chuckled and said, "I've just gotten to thirty million people, probably millions more because my followers retweet it." He repeated it, to emphasize the wonderous power of it. "I just pressed send and now hundreds of millions of people all around the world are reading it." We had to wait until we left his office and could check our own cell phones to see what he said—none of us could read his tweet from across his desk. Only after millions of people had already heard from Trump were we able to catch up.

Trump has figured out the key to breaking through the clutter is to make his tweets personal, humorous, biting, and politically incorrect.

Prior to Trump, and even today, most politicians use social media to push out bland, non-controversial, carefully scripted tweets scrubbed of anything which might give any offense to anyone. They're just a lot of white noise. Which Twitter feed do you think most people want to follow— Donald Trump's or one belonging to a politician whose tweets sound like they're written by robots?

But sometimes his tweeting can get him in trouble. When he goes off on tweetstorms, especially when they're more angry than funny, Trump can sound like a grouchy old man, flailing out at his enemies. But the tweetstorms are his one way of letting off steam. Remember, Trump doesn't drink, he doesn't smoke, he doesn't jog, he doesn't sleep much. He works non-stop, even on vacations. His only hobby is golf, and even that was always tied into his golf resort business empire. Now that he is president, his golfing partners are politicians and foreign leaders.

Under normal circumstances being president is one of the most difficult jobs in the world. But Trump's task has been made exponentially harder because he has had to put up with the most negative press coverage of any president in history. For example, the *Washington Post* has six opinion columns every day. On most days, all six of them are critical of something about Trump: his personality, his policies, his style and, yes, even his hair. Every day the *New York Times* has several anti-Trump columns on its editorial pages, and a considerable number of anti-Trump headlines scattered across its news pages. It's the same with CNN anchors and their guests. MSNBC has become the Trump conspiracy theory channel. He has to live a town where most of the people hate him—over 94 percent of Washingtonians voted against him. Trump has had to operate under the shadow of a two-year investigation into the legitimacy of his election victory. Even though the Mueller investigation is finished, with no crimes found, Trump now has to put up with a dozen Congressional committees obsessed with trying to find some evidence of wrongdoing in order to justify impeachment.

Trump was pummeled in the press every hour of every day for more than two years, with cable news pundits speculating on how the Mueller probe was going to find Trump guilty of some of the worst crimes in American history. Former Obama intelligence chiefs, implying they had inside information, suggested Trump was a Russian agent and would be charged with treason. Journalists, quoting "anonymous sources" insisted that Trump, his children, his aides, and his former business associates would soon be arrested for committing some crime or other. Now it turns out most of it was just made up wistful thinking on the part of the anti-Trump media.

Trump's frustration is entirely justified, and his tweetstorms are understandable. Even so, there are times when Trump can be his own worst enemy. If Trump could find another way to vent his aggravation, instead of sharing it with the world, his approval ratings would probably soar. Then others would be calling Trump one of our greatest presidents, relieving him of the need to say so himself.

Another key to understanding Trump is to look at what he does, not what he says. Trump's supporters dismiss what he says and focus on what he has done, especially for them. Trump's critics, especially inside the Washington bubble, ignore all that he has accomplished and focus solely on what he says. That's what Trump's supporters understand about him, and his critics never seem to comprehend.

What Trump says and what he does are often two very different things. For example, Trump complained about Special Counsel Robert Mueller, his investigation, and his staff incessantly. He tweeted regularly about the "13 angry Democrats" on Mueller's staff and listed how many of them contributed to Hillary's campaign. Yet, despite all his noise about the Office of Special Counsel, and the constant criticism he received as a result, Trump never once tried to limit their access, or put conditions on their actions, or interfere in any way with their investigation. He didn't shut them down. Just the opposite, he cooperated with them fully and instructed everyone on his staff to do so as well.

What rarely gets noticed is that despite all of Trump's clamor, he hasn't changed his positions or his behavior to appease his critics. He's well aware of what they're saying—remember he's a news junkie—and of course it gets to him. Even so, he is unwilling to give up on his policies to curry their favor or capitulate to them in hopes of getting better press treatment. In other words, he's tough enough to take the most vicious and constant media attacks in American history. It would have driven most people to despair. Yet Trump remains resilient in spite of it all. He calls himself a counter-puncher. But it's more than that. He simply never, never, never gives in.

It's one of the things that Trump's fans love about him. He keeps coming back again and again for more, like a plastic punching bag doll that keeps popping back up every time it's knocked down. It's also one of the things Trump's critics can never understand. They've convinced themselves time and again that Trump can never survive the latest knock-down punch. But they're always wrong.

Next time you see a video clip of Trump sitting at his desk, pay attention to how he crosses his arms. Most people cross their arms by tucking one or both hands into the opposite elbows, hugging their body about waist high. Sometimes it's a relaxing pose, but it can also be stern and imposing. When Trump crosses his arms it's downright belligerent. He balls each hand into a fist and tucks in under the opposite tricep, hugging his body right under his armpits. Try it on yourself. It makes you both look and feel pretty tough, not like somebody who's about to throw in the towel. Trump may not like the criticisms, but I think there is a part of him that actually relishes the fight.

CHAPTER 6

Trumpism–Before and After Trump

The national conversation may be focused on Trump, but Washington is completely obsessed with him. It's all Trump all the time, and there is no middle ground. You either love him or hate him. You're either for him or against him. You either want him out of office as soon as possible or want him re-elected to a second term. The Age of Trump tends to block out the larger picture of what is happening.

I believe the forces at play today are bigger than Trump versus the Washington Establishment. They are much more profound even than populism and nationalism versus elitism and globalism. I believe we are in the midst of a tug of war between average Americans and today's governing class over who gets to run the country. Who is in charge today, and who will be in charge tomorrow? Is it *We the People* or the permanent Washington Establishment? It is the ongoing battle that has been with us from the founding of our Republic and it breaks out into the open every generation or so. And, while I do not believe history repeats itself, I do believe it rhymes. The era we are living in today is not the first time Americans have fought over who should govern the country, nor will it be the last.

People may call today's political war the Trump Revolution, and refer to its principles as Trumpism, but the forces that set it in motion began stirring years ago. Trump didn't start this populist rebellion. I don't believe it was even his original reason in running for president. Trump's genius was in sensing this rebellion was happening, grasping its significance, connecting with it, and ultimately picking up the flag to lead it.

He became the champion to the millions of Americans who had been cast aside by the governing class, the people who had no voice in the corridors of power. I've heard it again and again from the people who were with Trump on the campaign, the people who traveled on the plane with him, and the ones who went with him to city after city. No matter how the Trump campaign got started, something happened as they went around the country campaigning. Thousands of average Americans started spontaneously showing up for Trump rallies. They didn't come as a result of any get-out-the-crowd efforts by Trump's campaign staff; he didn't even have a ground game. But once people got word Trump was coming to town, they were willing to stand in line for hours, even in the rain, in the hopes of getting into the arena where he was scheduled to speak. Trump and his campaign staff soon began to see the human faces behind the government's economic balance sheet. These were people who wanted to work but couldn't find jobs, or those who had to work two jobs to make ends meet. These were the forgotten Americans that all the other candidates had overlooked.

Unlikely as it seemed for a billionaire candidate, Trump was able to connect with these tens of millions of people who felt they had been left behind, whose values had been tossed aside, whose patriotism had been derided, and who had been mocked for their religious beliefs. I remember being at FOX one day and watching an interview with a poor, single mother in New Hampshire. She said that she was for Trump because he could identify with her problems. Here was a Fifth Avenue billionaire with his own personal fleet of planes, helicopters, and limousines who was able to connect with a woman who worried about how much it cost to fill her tank at the gas station! He was able to relate to working folks in a way Hillary Clinton, Jeb Bush, and the Washington Establishment couldn't even comprehend. He spoke their language in a way that was neither condescending nor complicated. Donald Trump, Jr. said it best when he called his father a "blue-collar billionaire."

One of the reasons people were drawn to Trump was because his campaign promises weren't the products of dozens of advisors coming up with detailed plans designed to appeal to certain special interest groups. He didn't really have a platform. He had some themes he thought up on his own and tried out at the rallies; if they resonated, these themes became part of his stump speech. Having been with Trump after the election and seen how his mind works, I'm convinced he senses these things intuitively; he understands the problems and decides how to deal with them instinctively. Trump himself has never been good at explaining why he thinks the way he does, the reasoning behind his policies, or going into detail about the concepts themselves. He doesn't get beyond a few lines in off-the-cuff remarks or the 140 characters in a tweet. His formal speeches sometimes do but they're written by others.

2020 will be a year of many things—Democrats pushing impeachment, presidential candidates battling it out within their parties, and a national election likely to be one of the most vitriolic in American history. What it is not likely to be is a year of national discussion and debate on the very real domestic and foreign problems facing us. Policy discussions will be crowded out by scandal and screaming.

Wherever we find ourselves at the end of 2020—whether Trump is resoundingly elected to a second term; whether he is removed from office by the impeachment process or the November election; whether the Democrats take a hard-left turn to embrace socialism—the forces underlying Trumpism will continue. The Trump Revolution began before Trump, and it will continue after he has left the stage. That is because the main tenets of Trumpism—Make America Great Again, America First, and Peace Through Strength—are driven by the American people themselves. Trump has been their standard-bearer, the person they chose to carry out their mandate. But if, for whatever reason, he is not able to carry the movement to its conclusion, other leaders will rise to complete the Trump Revolution.

I can't claim to speak for Trump; nobody can. Trumpism is his and his alone to define. But I do agree with the majority of his goals, if not always his methods of achieving them. So, let me make the arguments Trump won't, and the case for Trumpism that he doesn't. Unlike Trump, I didn't arrive at the same places Trump does intuitively or instinctively. I have gotten there only after years of analysis and reflection. I have had to take the long way 'round. Let me share with you how I got there, first in identifying problems and then finding the solutions.

Make America Great Again…America First…Peace through Strength…American Exceptionalism. They are more than slogans designed to fit on bumper stickers. They aren't merely campaign promises, casually given and quickly forgotten. There is a good case to be made for every one of them and why they will revive the country's economy, bring us prosperity, ensure peace, redefine America's leadership role in the world, and restore our faith in America and our future.

CHAPTER 7

Make American Great Again

Trump spent a lot of time on the campaign trail promising to Make America Great Again, echoing Reagan's campaign 1980 theme, "Let's Make America Great Again." What both men saw in their day was an America headed for decline, and both promised radical change to turn things around.

Trump and Reagan knew the first priority had to be the economy. America, more than many other nations, needs a growing economy for our system to work. Had we failed to turn the economy around in Reagan's day, and were we to fail now in our own time, we would be heading down the well-worn path European welfare states have already taken. Many of the once-great nations of Europe are today locked into stagnant economies, with no net new employment, weighed down by persistently and consistently high unemployment levels, and ever-increasing demands for government services. The European nations' experiments with the social welfare state and, more recently, unrestricted immigration, are now deemed less than successful, even by many of their own people.

That's why the economic recovery of the Trump Administration has been so astounding. When Trump was elected in November 2016, we were stuck in a rut of little to no growth. Now, nearly three years into Trump's Presidency we are in a sudden and significant cycle of growth and prosperity. Even the Trump-bashing *New York Times* was forced to admit that, "We have run out of words to describe how well the economy is doing." The economy has not only recovered robustly, but also rapidly. The Washington Establishment, the left-liberal media, Democrats and Never-Trump Republicans were taken completely by surprise.

By the end of the Obama Administration, the American economy was limping along, with liberal economists claiming that 1–2 percent growth and high unemployment were the new normal, the best we could expect in a modern technology-driven economy. As I write this, projections are that the American economy could grow 2–3 percent annually during Trump's Presidency. Trump's turnaround has occurred even more rapidly than Reagan's, whose reforms didn't result in economic growth until the third year of his Presidency, when the tax cuts were finally phased in.

Trump's plan included repeating what Reagan had done in the 1980s: cutting personal and corporate taxes, streamlining regulations, and reducing the size and scope of government. It's no surprise that Trump's economic plan was so similar to Reagan's—one of the people he turned to was Arthur Laffer, the same man who helped design Reaganomics. But Trump has one enormous and game-changing advantage Reagan lacked. In the last few years American engineers and entrepreneurs have invented fracking, horizontal drilling, and 3D mapping, which have completely revolutionized America's natural gas and oil industry, seemingly overnight. By taking the shackles off our domestic energy industry we have one thing that has bedeviled the American economy and foreign policy for decades: We now have an unending and reliable supply of inexpensive domestic oil and natural gas. This, coupled with tax cuts and regulatory reform, has taken an economy which was dead in the water when Trump took office and created rapid, sustained, and widespread growth as well as millions of new jobs.

Within just a few years, America has transformed from an energy importer into an energy exporter. As we look to the future, we should explore the idea of building an energy consortium with our neighbors to the north and south. The United States is now the world's number one energy exporter, surpassing Saudi Arabia, Russia, and Iran. If we were to partner with our energy rich neighbors, the western hemisphere could replace the oil rich nations of the Middle East as the world's major energy hub.

The reasons Reagan and Trump's economic plans are considered so radical is that they dismiss the conventional wisdom shared by liberal Democrats and establishment Republicans alike—that the only way government can increase revenues is by raising taxes, and that our modern economy needs government intervention to function. Reaganomics and Trumponomics turn that on its head. They insist that higher taxes and heavy-handed regulations stifle economic growth. Only by lowering taxes and cutting red tape can we free up the private sector to invest in growth and innovation, which, in turn, allows small businesses to expand and big businesses to grow more competitive in the global marketplace. When entrepreneurs and inventors find it easier to create new industries, the economy expands. As a result, more people have jobs and more money in their pockets because of higher wages and fewer taxes. They work harder, spend more, feel confident about the future, and the economy arcs upward. Reagan, like President Kennedy before him, believed, "The soundest way to raise revenues in the long run is to cut rates now." They remembered the thing that most of Washington seems to forget—that taxes are paid by the people who work. No jobs, no tax revenues. No jobs, no savings.

It's like taking one step back to take two steps forward. It may seem counterintuitive at first, but every single time we've had big tax cuts in the past, it has proved true, whether it was the Kennedy tax cuts in the 1960s, Reagan tax cut in 1980s, or Trump's tax cuts today. Many institutions predicted disaster would result from the Trump tax cuts. The Congressional Budget Office (CBO) predicted that federal revenues would fall by $163 billion in 2018, but in actuality they were up by $189 billion. Maybe the best explanation for why this works is simply human nature. If people can keep the fruits of their labor for themselves and their families, they will work harder than if they had to turn them over to the government to decide things for them.

Reagan and Trump's critics, even the establishment types in their own Republican party, pounced on their tax cut plans as unrealistic. They were both accused of being foolish, heartless, and irresponsible. Reagan's tax cut plan was called "voodoo economics," by none other than the Republican Party's establishment candidate of the day, George H.W. Bush! When Trump proposed a similar plan thirty-six years after Reagan, critics pounced, predicting he would bankrupt the country and trigger a financial crisis.

Trump, like Reagan before him, believes that higher taxes choke the nation's economic growth. After paying all those additional taxes, large corporations, and small businesses alike have less money to invest in new ventures, build new plants, and hire new workers. Higher corporate taxes also force businesses to focus their time and efforts on how to avoid paying those additional taxes. They devote their resources and energies to hiring lawyers and accountants to hunt for loopholes and tax shelters or arranging with Congress to get preferential legislation. Their time and money could have been better spent inventing and experimenting with new products, building new plants, and manufacturing more goods.

Trump's corporate tax cuts unleashed trillions of overseas profits to be reinvested in American industries and infrastructure. American companies produce 30 to 40 percent of all goods worldwide and sell much of it overseas. Before Trump, our corporate tax rates were the highest in the industrialized world. In our global economy, that meant many American and international corporations "parked" their overseas profits abroad, either in savings or as investments in foreign countries, rather than bringing those profits home and being forced to pay America's much higher taxes. They made more money by investing in countries with comparatively low tax rates.

It was not a lack of patriotism that made them avoid investing in America; it was a lack of profits. International companies can build anywhere in the world. They might have preferred to build factories in America and create more jobs for Americans. But high U.S. corporate taxes meant that doing business here came with an added cost over doing business in low tax countries—not very incentivizing for a competitive business. It became too expensive to make things in the United States. There is a reason Americans move out of high tax states like New York and retire to low tax states like Florida. They do it so they can keep more of their hard-earned wages and savings. Businesses do the same by moving to countries with lower taxes.

Not surprisingly, over the years many American corporations shifted their manufacturing abroad. As our high corporate taxes drove jobs away from our shores, millions of Americans missed out on the opportunities our companies created when they built new factories overseas. As a result, the U.S. government doesn't get any tax revenues at all, either from these corporations or the potential new workers.

Although it was a nail-biter, Trump's tax reform bill to cut personal and corporate taxes finally passed a year after he was elected. But it was without one Democrat legislator in either the House or Senate voting for it, and in the face of complete opposition by the liberal media and progressive economists. Other economists predict that some $2 trillion dollars "parked" overseas can now come home to be invested in rebuilding infrastructure, new plants, and new industries in America. Automobile companies are building new plants in Michigan. Apple is manufacturing in America instead of Asia.

Remember that old math question? Do you get more from a smaller slice of a bigger pie, or bigger slice of a smaller pie?

Democrats, progressives, and socialists say forget about eventually growing the pie, just give us a bigger slice now. And while you're at it, add a few more claimants who deserve a piece too. But since their pie never grows any bigger, everyone's piece keeps shrinking.

Reaganomics and Trumponomics say it's better to grow the pie, so even if government gets a smaller slice now the pie will grow bigger with more investment, more growth, and fewer claimants. In the end, government gets more revenues with a smaller slice of a bigger pie than it gets from a bigger slice of a smaller pie. And it's not just government that wins. Everybody wins because it's more pie for all!

The one way to see immediate growth is by regulatory reform. No matter who is president, tax cuts spark economic growth. But changes in our tax system require legislation, which first has to work its way through Congress. Once passed into law, it takes a year or more to show appreciable change in the economy. There was one thing, however, that Trump could do immediately, on his own authority without Congressional approval, to jump-start the economy. He could roll back and streamline the excessive and burdensome regulations imposed on businesses during the Bush and Obama years.

Trump began to zero in on regulatory reform during his campaign. In their book *Trumponomics*, Moore and Laffer describe a meeting Trump convened with some of the country's leading businessmen in May 2016. They told Trump the key to creating jobs wasn't just cutting taxes, but cutting back on growth-killing hyper-regulation. Moore and Laffer went on to recount how one executive told Trump, "We are being strangled by regulation and red tape. If you want to make America great again, please put a muzzle on the regulators."[1]

Freedomworks, a conservative watchdog group, noted that Obama added over 500 new regulations on his own initiative, without Congressional approval.[2] Layering on burdensome and often unnecessary regulations hits small businesses particularly hard. They usually operate with a small administrative staff, and narrow profit margins, especially when they are starting out. Yet they have to meet the same regulatory requirements as big mega-businesses which have a far larger administrative infrastructure already in place. For them, another dozen or so regulations can be written off as the cost of doing business. It eats into their profit margins, but doesn't put them out of business. For a small business owner, whose chief administrative officer might be a family member doing the books at the kitchen table, the new regulations sometimes mean putting another employee on the payroll, just to make sure they're in compliance. For a small business owner, it's the difference between solvency and bankruptcy.

Sam Batkins of the American Action Forum, another pro-growth think tank, claims the Obama Administration cost the economy over $800 billion.[3] The Competitive Enterprise Institute reports that the price of the federal regulations before Trump's reforms was approaching $2 trillion, nearly $15,000 per household each year.[4]

Trump's regulatory reforms had an immediate and positive effect, even greater than the most optimistic of its architects anticipated. Study after study showed that the Administrative State's hyper-regulations were literally strangling the American economy.

Perhaps the biggest factor in our sudden economic growth is America's energy revolution. For years we knew natural gas and oil were inside rock formations in the United States, but we didn't have the technological

---

[1] Moore, Stephen and Arthur B. Laffer. *Trumponomics: Inside the America First Plan to Revive Our Economy*. New York: St. Martin's Press, 2018, 189.

[2] Pye, Jason. "Regulator-In-Chief: Obama Administration Has Issued 600 Regulations with Costs of $100 Million or More." FreedomWorks. August 8, 2016. https://www.freedomworks.org/content/regulator-chief-obama-administration-has-issued-600-regulations-costs-100-million-or-more.

[3] Batkins, Sam. "$9.8 Billion in Regulatory Costs." American Action Forum. March 28, 2016. https://www.americanactionforum.org/week-in-regulation/9-8-billion-regulatory-costs/.

[4] Crews, Clyde Wayne. "Ten Thousand Commandments 2016." Competitive Enterprise Institute. May 3, 2016. https://cei.org/10KC2016.

sophistication to extract these resources at low enough prices to make it competitive. While President Obama was talking about peak oil in 2010, and oil prices were well north of $100, some hardscrabble American entrepreneurs were inventing fracking technologies, horizontal drilling, and 3D mapping. Many saw this period as the economic bonanza of a lifetime. The Obama Administration saw it as a new industry it could regulate and slow walk.

Immediately after taking office, Trump reversed course and encouraged oil and natural gas production. It was indeed a bonanza. Vast new oil and natural gas reserves were put into production. Energy prices came down quickly, exports went up…way up…and American manufacturing was once again very competitive.

Trump also added clean coal back into the energy mix. Cars, trains, trucks, and airplanes run on energy. Manufacturing runs on energy, both in raw materials and production costs. It's not just the creation of new jobs in the energy sector; it means new job creation across the board in every industry that uses energy to manufacture its products, which is just about every industry. By having a cheap domestic source of energy, America-made products will always be cheaper than those made in countries that have to pay the added costs of importing oil and natural gas. This means American-made products are once again competitive in a global economy.

It's difficult to overestimate just how significant the fracking revolution is. We have won the energy triple crown. First, we now have an entirely new and lucrative industry as the world's largest energy exporter. Second, we no longer have to rely on Middle East oil to fuel our economy. Not only is Middle East oil expensive and its supply unreliable, it has swept us into the violence and psychodrama of that part of the world for decades. Third, our abundance of natural gas allows us to reduce dependence on some of the dirtier fossil fuels by replacing them with cleaner natural gas.

Since the Industrial Revolution, one of the single greatest determinants of wealth for nearly 200 years has been energy—first coal then oil and natural gas. Countries with energy resources used them to become economic powerhouses. Britain, Germany, and the United States led the industrial revolution in the 1800s because of their abundance of coal. The Soviet Union's expansion a century later was built on oil and natural gas exports. The Arab oil states have become wealthy beyond imagination merely by exporting their oil. The importance of energy has only grown in the two hundred years since the Industrial Revolution. Guaranteed access to energy supplies has won wars and failure to access energy has toppled empires. Energy, especially oil, is not just about money. It's also about power. The electricity produced by these fossil fuels has been the greatest multiplier of the value of human labor in history.

Prior to Trump's election, and even afterward, liberal politicians, progressives, socialists, and left-wing economists issued dire warnings that Trump's policies would cause the growth rate to contract, the stock market to plummet, and the economy to dive into a tailspin. The opposite has happened. Immediately after Trump's upset victory, the stock market started climbing and has continued upward ever since. His pro-growth policies have created millions of new jobs, high paying and geared for the future. Unemployment and welfare claims are down, while blacks, Hispanics, and women have the lowest unemployment rates not just in decades, but in history.

Optimism about people's future financial opportunities is the highest it has been in seventy-five years. Why? Because Trump, like Reagan, cut taxes, eliminated job strangling bureaucratic overregulation, and took the shackles off our domestic energy industry. America has gone from an energy importer to the world's greatest energy exporter in just a few years. We are now the world's oil and natural gas superpower. Suddenly, manufacturing industries are building factories in America again, new technologies are being invented at home, and the people who were left behind for the last twenty years are once again finding America is the land of opportunity—for all.

As proof of just how successful Trump's economic program has been, it's amusing to go back to what Reagan said about his plan. "I knew our economic policies were a success when they stopped calling them Reaganomics." Trump's critics, like Reagan's, can't deny the stunning success of the program. So, instead of giving Trump the credit, they claim it was really Obama who did it and Trump swooped in to reap the rewards. Obama himself claimed credit for the turnaround when he said that, "when you hear how great the economy is doing right now….when you hear about this economic miracle" it's because he started it. Right after Trump was elected, those same people were predicting his programs would lead to financial ruin! Reagan was right. When other people start taking credit for your program, you know it's a success. It's no surprise that "Trumponomics" is a term now rarely mentioned by his critics in the press, politics, or the public square.

CHAPTER 8

America First

Before sending a new U.S. Ambassador off to his overseas posting, Reagan's Secretary of State George Shultz would summon him to the State Department's Mount Olympus, the Seventh Floor. The new Ambassador would walk out of the elevator banks and enter a world entirely different from the rest of the rather industrial looking State Department. He would be greeted by a receptionist and after some delay be invited to walk down the hall to the Secretary of State's official office. He would proceed along a plush carpeted corridor and through formal reception rooms filled with American antiques. Portraits of every Secretary of State beginning with Thomas Jefferson looked down upon him. It was guaranteed to fill the new diplomat with a sense of awe and purpose.

When the Ambassador finally arrived at the Secretary's door, Shultz would walk him over to a large standing globe and ask him to point out his country. Inevitably the new Ambassador would spin the globe around and proudly put his forefinger on the country where he was heading. Shultz would then spin the globe around again and put his large hand down on the United States. "That's your country," he would say. It was his way of making the point that the Ambassador's job was to represent America's interests to the country to which he was being sent, not the other way around.

In today's world, however, announcing you want to put American interests first has become a cause for alarm for many in the establishment. They see America First as an effort to reverse decades of American foreign policy, abdicate our world leadership role, reject our long-standing alliances, and abrogate our trade agreements and security treaties. They equate nationalism with a throwback to the world as it was in centuries past. They believe ultra-nationalism is behind racial intolerance, fanaticism, trade wars, and military conflict. It has gotten to the point where several of America's most powerful technology companies have taken the position that they should not work with the American government and military, for fear they would be complicit in promoting America's engines of war. Yet they are willing to work with Chinese civilian companies, ignoring the fact that they work hand in hand with their military and intelligence services.

According to one of the main champions of globalism, Pulitzer prize-winning *New York Times* columnist and bestselling author, Thomas Friedman, the defining characteristic of the 21st century is that advances in technology and communications have leveled the playing field. They've created a new "flat" world where ideas, goods, finance, and people move freely across national borders, even continents. The tech giants may be American-based and they may have invented most of their products here, but their biggest market is the rest of the world. They have no special loyalty to Washington. To them, national borders are something to be overcome and nation states something to be transcended. Technocrats may sell their products to citizens of different countries but their world is the internet, cyberspace, and the Cloud. The world has now entered a new era where supranational organizations and global businesses increasingly take the place of old-fashioned nation states with their own borders, citizens, and currencies.

Our economies are now intertwined and interdependent, not just within our own regions but across oceans and hemispheres. The Third World is no longer some remote and primitive place. It is being incorporated more and more into the economies of First World countries. It's no longer just nation dealing with nation, it's small businesses in one country dealing directly with their suppliers and distributors half way around the world. Globalists believe a global economy necessitates global rules of order. They believe the best way to keep world peace is through a well-ordered set of international organizations where member states are committed to following an agreed upon set of rules and regulations, based on their universally shared values and goals.

Globalists point out the most pressing problems we face in the 21st century—climate change, refugee movements, pandemics, terrorism, weapons of mass destruction—pay no heed to national borders. They can only be dealt with on a global scale, with all nations following the rules set down by international organizations made up of the most intelligent and capable people each country has to offer. Nationalism is deemed selfish and narrow minded because it puts one nation's interest ahead of others. If everyone were to put their own interests first, they argue, the world would descend into chaos and jungle law would prevail. They pound the final nail in the coffin by noting that nationalism was the xenophobic rallying cry of Nazi Germany and Fascist Japan that led to World War II.

This all sounds perfectly reasonable if you subscribe to the idea that other nations will set aside their own narrow self-interests, even if it causes them short-term hardship, and follow these international rules of order. I do not, or at least, I no longer do. There is increasing evidence that in the 21st century some countries no longer feel bound by those longstanding rules. Russia invaded its neighbors and seized territory in Georgia and Ukraine. It continues to brazenly interfere in democratic elections throughout the western world. It has hacked into our vital infrastructure systems. Iran is supporting terrorism throughout the Middle East while using surrogates' power to attack Israel and wage war against rival Sunni states.

Similarly, China continues to exploit the World Trade Organization to give itself an unfair advantage in exports and currency rates. The Chinese government demands international companies share valuable R&D as a precondition for doing business there. When they haven't been able to acquire it legally, they have stolen it from American businesses. They have penetrated the communications and storage systems of a vast array of American enterprises, and vacuumed up data from our government, health care industry, and defense industries.

A number of countries have already launched cyberattacks on American businesses. With the advent of the cyber age, we are entering a terrifying new world. As Pulitzer Prize-winning author and *New York Times* columnist David Sanger writes, cyberweapons "remain invisible, the attacks deniable, the results uncertain."[1] There is no international organization that can police cyberwar. If anything, the world is growing more aggressive and nationalist, not less.

The postwar world has been referred to as Pax Americana. It has given us a world at peace. Regional security treaties have prevented large scale conflict and another world war. Trade agreements have encouraged the development of poorer nations. The United Nations prohibits powerful countries from invading or expropriating weaker states. These international organizations and agreements were launched by the all-powerful United States in the 1940s and 50s, in the aftermath of a war that left the rest of the developed world devastated.

What happens when there is no longer a benevolent, all-powerful, first-among-equals country to enforce global rules? The United States has assumed that role throughout most of the postwar, and post-Cold War periods. But what if the world moves into a post-Pax Americana era? If the United States is no longer the power that cannot be ignored? If others step into that role? What if the world returns to an era of great power rivalries, where a handful of the world's economic and military powerhouses advance their own interests at the expense of others? Won't globalism be the first casualty? Is there any guarantee that these new masters of the universe, ambitious to establish their own regional hegemonies, won't expand their commercial and political reach and power? Will they continue to follow the rules of the current international system, especially if following the rules no longer suits their interests? If a rising nation breaks out of the pack and replaces the United States as the world's richest and most powerful nation, is there any guarantee it will be as generous and fair-minded as we have been?

In the global community, the gloves are now coming off. Russian expansionism into Ukraine and open interference in our elections as well as Chinese mercantilism and militarization of the South China Sea have demonstrated that these nations will play by the rules of the liberal world order only so long as it suits their interests.

While globalists assure us that everything will be fine after America's decline, evidence points in the other direction. According to former

---

[1] Sanger, David E. *The Perfect Weapon: War, Sabotage, and Fear in the Cyber Age.* New York: Crown Publishing Group, 2018.

Australian Prime Minister Kevin Rudd, a lifelong China watcher, Chinese President Xi Jinping has made it clear that rather than embracing an American led global world order, China aims to change it. Xi now claims that China should "show the way in reform of the global governance system."[2]

I'm a former defense planner. I look at capabilities, not just intentions. Capabilities take years to development. Intentions can change overnight, especially in authoritarian countries where an all-powerful leader makes all the decisions. What happens if that leader is no longer in charge, because he dies or is overthrown, and is replaced by a new leader with different designs? It's important to anticipate what intentions a country's leader has, but it is even more important to anticipate what capabilities and resources a leader has at his disposal should his intentions change.

Nationalism, to me, a self-proclaimed nationalist, isn't some hooded version of hate-spewing ultra-nationalism. It is not a group of people hiding out of sight until the "big reveal," when right wing, white supremacist zealots take out their guns and take over the country. It is nothing of the sort. The nationalism I subscribe to is a straightforward rejection of the globalist and internationalist mindsets that have dominated the national security community for the past several decades. These institutions and attitudes may have worked well in the past, but I worry that they will not necessary work in the future. Sadly, I believe globalists have been unconcerned and unresponsive to the changing international situation, and unrealistic in failing to acknowledge what looks like a gathering storm.

America First means putting, advancing, and protecting America's interests ahead of other countries, not necessarily at the expense of others' interests. But if we must choose between our own interests and the interests of other countries, our choice should be clear.

During the first week of the Trump Administration, National Security Advisor General Flynn and I called an all-hands meeting with the several hundred-person National Security Council staff. It's the largest

---

[2] The Hon. Kevin Rudd, "Xi Jinping, China and the Global Order: The Significance of China's 2018 Central Foreign Policy Work Conference." Address to the Lee Kuan Yew School of Public Policy of the National University of Singapore on June 26, 2018. https://asiasociety.org/sites/default/files/2019-01/Xi%20Jinping_China%20and%20the%20Global%20Order.pdf. See also: "Xi says China must lead way in reform of global governance." Reuters. June 23, 2018. https://in.reuters.com/article/china-diplomacy-idINKBN1JJ0GK.

staff on the White House grounds, and the only place we could assemble everyone together was in the auditorium of the Executive Office Building. Even so, every seat was taken, and a number of people were standing in the aisles and along the wall.

During the Q&A session, one of the senior NSC staff members raised his hand and asked me to define what President Trump meant by America First. It wasn't a hostile question…exactly…but his tone was less than friendly—a mixture of condescension and criticism.

I answered that Trump's America First policy was not, as the questioner implied, a throwback to the America First movement of the 1930s, which advocated American neutrality in the war between Germany and Europe, in part because some of its supporters identified with German Fascists.

I chuckled and said, "Look, if you think Donald Trump is secretly signaling that he identifies with American isolationists or is a covert neo-fascist, you're dead wrong. First of all, Trump isn't that subtle. Second, I doubt if Donald Trump even knows what the America First movement was. And even if someone told him about it, he couldn't care less what happened seventy-five years ago."

I went on to explain that Trump's America First is based on the conviction that the United States should reassert its sovereignty over international organizations and agreements. We should base our foreign policy on what is best for America—for our economy, our trade relationships, our security, and our budget. Other countries—China, Russia, Iran, and Germany—don't put aside their own self interests in dealing with the United States. They see to their own national interests first. In fact, I said it would be a dereliction of duty for any leader NOT to put his own country's needs first. I received no applause.

In addition to reasserting American sovereignty over international organizations, America First advocates a recalibration of our existing trade agreements and security treaties so the United States no longer subsidizes countries that no longer need it. It does not mean that we want to abandon them, or become a go-it-alone bully, or retreat into isolationism. America First does not mean America Alone.

Aided by America's generosity, many of the countries that were once poor and undeveloped, or devasted by the Second World War, have grown richer and more powerful, shifting the relative balance between us. Yet our bilateral arrangements have not shifted accordingly; they have remained much the same for fifty years, and in some cases for even longer. By not readjusting our relationships to reflect the changing times, our leaders have, in effect, *not* put the American people first. This change has happened slowly and incrementally, but the time has come to deal with it.

In the aftermath of World War II, the United States emerged as the most powerful country in the world—economically, militarily, politically, morally, and diplomatically. We had won the war, and our society and continental homeland remained intact. On the other hand, our former adversaries, and even some of our allies, were devasted. Their factories were destroyed and some of their cities were unrecognizable. British Prime Minister Winston Churchill described Europe as "a rubble-heap, a charnel house, a breeding ground of pestilence and hate." But it wasn't just the physical damage; their political institutions had been found wanting and their people were living in desperate conditions. After the war ended, we could have returned home to enjoy our hard-won peace. Instead we picked up the mantle of leadership.

But then we did something unique in the annals of world history. Rather than use our wealth and power to create an empire or subjugate the vanquished or exploit the weak, we did just the opposite. We helped the war-ravaged countries to rebuild, including even those countries responsible for starting the war.

We contributed over $13 billion in aid to European nations ($100 billion in today's dollars) with the Marshall Plan. We gave them monies and resources to rebuild their factories, their cities, their governments, and their societies. We did the same for Japan and Korea.

To help these countries reconstruct their industries and create jobs, we signed trade agreements which put our own industries at a disadvantage so their fledgling companies could prosper. We let their goods enter the United States practically tariff-free, while we let them impose significant tariffs on goods they imported from us. These tariffs not only gave these countries additional tax revenues when American goods were sold, they also ensured these countries' domestically manufactured goods were consistently priced lower than ours, in both their markets and in ours.

It was this same thinking that led us to create mutual security agreements with our allies and former enemies in Europe and Asia, and assume a far greater proportion of the shared defense burden. By subsidizing these alliances, the other members could devote resources to their economic recovery, rather than their armed forces.

After being wartime allies with the USSR, we soon found ourselves locked in a Cold War. We had already fought two World Wars in Europe and we did not want to fight a third, especially in the nuclear age. We formed the North American Treaty Organization (NATO) to provide for the common defense of the United States and most western European nations, including a defeated West Germany. It was a mutual defense treaty designed to deter and defend against encroachment and attack by the Soviet Union and Communist Warsaw Pact of Eastern European nations. Our NATO allies provided rent-free land for our bases and modest contributions of military personal and equipment. Even though NATO was designed to protect Europe, the United States contributed nearly 70 percent of the defense budget, which includes most of the high ticket-price items like weapons systems as well as communications and logistics equipment.[3]

The United States would remain in Europe after World War II as a check against an expansionist Soviet Union and the communist Eastern Bloc. According to British General Hastings Ismay, NATO's first Secretary General, the North Atlantic Treaty Association was created in the aftermath of World War II to "keep the Soviet Union out, the Americans in, and the Germans down."

We made similar multilateral agreements with several Asian nations, including the Southeast Asian Treaty Organization (SEATO), and the ANZUS treaty with Australia and New Zealand. We entered into bilateral defense treaties with Japan and South Korea. We did so to contain the Soviet Union as well as China and prevent the spread of communism. We also hoped that once the European and Asian economies grew, they would become our trading partners, to the benefit of all.

The international system the United States created after World War II, and our trade and security subsidies to allies and adversaries, were farsighted and succeeded brilliantly. They were largely responsible for guaranteeing one of the longest periods of great power peace since the fall of the Roman Empire. Our post-war policies were, in fact, so successful

---

[3] Block, Eliana. "Verify: Does the US fund 90 percent of NATO expenses?" WUSA9. July 11, 2018. https://www.wusa9.com/article/news/local/verify/verify-does-the-us-fund-90-percent-of-nato-expenses/65-572789169.

that many of those once devastated nations are now economic power-houses themselves. Many of them now have healthier economies than our own, with higher growth rates and lower unemployment; some are even running budget surpluses. They no longer need high tariffs on American goods. They can also afford to contribute more toward our common defense.

In 2016, Trump was one of the only presidential candidates to acknowledge that times have changed. Many of these postwar trade agreements, coupled with our high taxes and the tangle of burdensome and often contradictory regulations, meant many companies bore the burden of our foreign policy and tax system. They created factories abroad to take advantage of lower labor costs, and these manufacturing jobs are not coming back. Instead, Trump talked about creating jobs in new industries like oil and natural gas, and training American workers for new tech manufacturing jobs.

The globalists of the foreign policy community disparage President Trump and the America First nationalists as being unaware or unappreciative of the role our post-war trade and security agreements have made in keeping the peace for these last seven decades. On the contrary. These agreements have been so successful that these countries no longer need American subsidies. The agreements themselves are still important for our mutual peace and prosperity, but they should be recalibrated to reflect the change in circumstances.

Our trading partners are up in arms at the thought of changing our terms of trade. Of course they are! Why should they voluntarily give up the trade subsidies they have enjoyed for decades! It's given them marketplace advantage since their goods can be sold for less than ours, all other things being equal. But these subsidies were never intended to last forever. They were just supposed to provide a bridge from devastation to recovery. Now that these countries have crossed over from recovery to prosperity, those bridges are no longer necessary nor, from our perspective, affordable or desirable.

During one of my initial meetings with Trump in late December during the Transition, press reports indicated President Obama had just imposed sanctions on Russia for election interference. I briefed Trump and the senior staff who were with him at Mar-a-Lago about what the sanctions package consisted of, and the long history of the United States and Russia imposing economic sanctions on each other and expelling diplomatic personnel.

It wasn't clear Trump was giving me his full attention at that point. He looked off in the distance as if he was mulling something over in his head. Before I finished talking, Trump leaned back from the table and said, "You know what? Obama's actually done me a favor. He's given me leverage with Putin. He (Obama) put the sanctions on, but I can take them off for big concessions."

I was looking at the sanctions from a foreign policy perspective, concerned that we might be walking into a full-blown U.S.-Russia crisis when we took office three weeks later. Trump was already thinking about leverage and driving a harder bargain when he negotiated with Putin.

Trump's approach is unorthodox. His constantly shifting positions and deliberately calculated unpredictability make for more or less constant "breaking news headlines." They fuel our domestic outrage industry and drive the Washington Establishment nuts. "Trump's raised tariffs on Canadian automobiles! Doesn't he realize that will start a trade war?"

Trump is not trying to start trade wars. He's trying to end them and make sure America comes out on top. For example, China has been in a one-sided trade war with the United States for decades, stealing our intellectual property, denying us reciprocal access to their markets, and imposing unequal tariffs on our goods. In years past, when we had the leverage to demand changes our former presidents didn't use it for fear of offending China and losing the support of Wall Street globalists who got rich off the China trade. It was easier for our leaders to pretend the problem wasn't there.

More recently, some of our leaders have acknowledged the problem; they've asked the Chinese to respect our intellectual property and give us more equitable access to their markets. While the Chinese have rarely refused outright, they've accomplished the same thing with delays, denials, and deception. In the last decade or so, our economy hasn't been strong enough to give us the kind of leverage necessary to force the Chinese to change. Why should China give up the competitive advantages they have enjoyed for decades if they don't have to? Negotiating without leverage isn't negotiating; it's begging. It is just so many empty words.

Trump entered office determined to stand up to the Chinese and demand reciprocal treatment on trade matters. His pro-growth economic policy and the "Trump Bump" it created put us in a stronger position, and Trump imposed tariffs as negotiating leverage. He's not a protectionist nor does he want trade wars. Bringing our tariffs up to parity with tariffs the Chinese impose on us is just Trump's opening bid, not his final position. For example, before Trump took office, China imposed a stiff twenty-five percent tariff on cars made in America, while our tariff on Chinese-made cars exported to America was only two percent. Of course they didn't want to give up that advantage! So Trump raised our tariffs to rates commensurate to theirs with the intention of lowering them together. Trump has said a number of times that he doesn't want tariffs, he wants zero tariffs; he wants no trade barriers on either side. To Trump's critics, it's brinksmanship. To Trump, it's driving a hard bargain to make a deal.

Like so many of the words that divide us today—populist, globalist, nationalist, elitist—"free trade" is a term tossed around but with no universal agreement on what it means. To Trump's critics, "free trade" is what we have now. But it's not really. Most people think the phrase "free trade" means the same thing as fair trade. But before President Trump, America's trading relationships were lopsided—our trading partners imposed high tariffs on our goods; we imposed much lower tariffs on theirs. Trump spent some time at the beginning of the Administration trying to find the right way to describe what he wanted, since free trade and fair trade are such ambiguous terms. He decided on the word "reciprocal," which leaves no doubt that the tariffs should be the same on both sides. Best of all, according to Trump, would be for all countries to eliminate tariffs, trade barriers, and subsidies.[4]

Rudy Giuliani once told me the key to understanding Trump's negotiating style is to realize he treats international diplomacy the way he treats a New York real estate deal. When he bids on a project, he lowballs his opening bid. The seller counters with an unrealistically high price. Trump realizes he will have to raise the offer and, after a lot of back and forth, the seller will accept a bid somewhere in the middle. This unconventional approach has worked to his advantage in negotiations abroad, even as it has given fuel to his media critics and political adversaries at home.

---

[4] Bryan, Bob. "Trump makes stunning reversal, says there should be 'no tariffs, no barriers' at G7 summit weeks after imposing huge tariffs on US allies." *Business Insider*. June 9, 2018. https://www.businessinsider.com/trump-suggests-dropping-all-tariffs-trade-barriers-at-g7-summit-2018-6.

During the campaign Trump promised to renegotiate unequitable trade and security deals with just about everybody. In the first three years of his Presidency Trump has shamed our NATO allies into raising their defense budgets by $100 billion[5], gotten North Korean Dictator Kim Jong-un to the negotiating table, and brokered new and more favorable deals with our North American and Asian trading partners. To him, that is what presidents are supposed to do: negotiate good deals for America. He is the Commander in Chief, but he also sees himself as the country's Negotiator in Chief.

---

[5] Allen, Julie. "Nato members increase defence spending by $100 billion after Donald Trump called them 'delinquents.'" *The Telegraph*. January 27, 2019. https://www.telegraph.co.uk/news/2019/01/27/nato-members-increase-defence-spending-100-billion-donald-trump/.

CHAPTER 9

China First

Trump's critics point to his policy of America First as evidence of all that is wrong with Trump—he's anti-immigrant, racist, isolationist—you know the litany. But a foreign policy that puts America's interests first is what American leaders are *supposed* to do. Putting China First is certainly what China's leaders have done since they re-emerged from hibernation to rejoin the world in the 1970s.

The problem isn't that Trump wants to put American interests first or that China puts its own interests first. *It's that for decades American leaders have put China's interests first.* Central to the Trump foreign policy agenda is his plan to recalibrate our trading relationship with China. During the 2016 campaign, Trump's many media critics strung together clips of all the times he said "China," "China," "China." These montages were designed to show Trump as a hysterical, China-obsessed opportunist, pandering to the out-of-work people in the Rust Belt who needed someone to blame for the fact that their jobs had moved overseas. As is often the case with Trump's critics, they missed the point. Trump made it clear that, once elected, he would do what previous Presidents had shied away from. He would call China out for its aggressive, mercantilist trade policies, forced technology transfer, intellectual property theft, and currency manipulation. He pledged to stop the hemorrhaging of American jobs which had been sacrificed in order to help propel China's extraordinary economic growth and entry into the international trading system.

For decades, I had subscribed to the globalist's view that if the industrialized world helped China to modernize, their government would naturally move toward free market capitalism, open up their society, and adopt individual freedoms and human rights. After all, the same template had worked with great success before, both in Europe and Asia. For example, our efforts to help Japan and South Korea build modern economies resulted in democratic governments, stable societies, valued trading and security partners, as well as strong American allies.

By engaging China in the same way, the conventional wisdom was that as China developed, it too would become an important stakeholder in the U.S.-created liberal world order. The same reasoning held that China would never seek to present a military threat to us or our allies, nor was it likely to become expansionist in Asia or further afield. Even if China were to remain officially "communist" in the 21st century, it would, for all intents and purposes, be a benign, pro-Western variety of communist.

The problem is that things haven't turned out that way. As Vice President Pence has noted, "America had hoped that economic liberalization would bring China into a greater partnership with us and with the world. Instead, China has chosen economic aggression, which has, in turn, emboldened its growing military."[1]

Now, with President-for-Life Xi Jinping, China has become more assertive abroad and more authoritarian at home. According to the *People's Daily*, the Chinese government's official newspaper, "Western-style democracy used to be a recognized power in history to drive social development. But now it has reached its limits." China will not be content to be one of the major great powers in the 21st century. It hopes to once again become *the* great power. Turns out Trump was right all along.[2]

For millennia, China was the richest and most powerful country in Asia. It was also the world's largest economy from the beginning of

---

[1] "Remarks by Vice President Pence on the Administration's Policy Toward China." The Hudson Institute. October 4, 2018. https://www.whitehouse.gov/briefings-statements/remarks-vice-president -pence-administrations-policy-toward-china/.

[2] Curran, James. "How America's Foreign Policy Establishment Got China Wrong." *The National Interest*. December 17, 2018. https://nationalinterest.org/feature/how-america%E2%80%99s -foreign-policy-establishment-got-china-wrong-39012.

recorded time until the 1800s. But then the Industrial Revolution swept through Europe, the United States, and Japan. Their economies roared ahead. They invented machines that took the place of manual labor. Farming, building, transportation, communications, and manufacturing—just about every aspect of people's lives was affected. Standards of living leaped ahead in a generation and societies changed rapidly. As these industrialized countries became wealthy and powerful, they also created colonial empires and built advanced militaries.

China, for various reasons, did not embrace industrialization and their power waned as a result. The technologically and militarily superior European nations and Japan, and to a lesser extent the United States, exploited China's weaknesses, both within China and throughout Asia. Wars were fought and won by the countries with the most advanced militaries. China was left behind, with two-thirds of its population living in poverty and working on subsistence-level rural farms. It was governed by an educated, elite class of Mandarin bureaucrats. Presiding over it all was an imperial court and a dynastic emperor. China was governed as it had been for five thousand years; people were living and working in conditions that had not changed for centuries.

In the early years of the 20th century the last emperor of the final Chinese dynasty was overthrown and replaced by a democracy of sorts. Nationalist China, however, was weak and ineffective. After World War I, an expansionist Imperial Japan took advantage of China and invaded its coastal cities, leaving much of the most populous country in the world without a functioning government.

While the industrialized nations and nationalist China were preoccupied with fighting the Japanese during World War II, a small band of communist rebels, led by Mao Zedong, began to consolidate territory across China. After the Japanese surrendered to the Americans in 1945, the communists defeated what was left of nationalist China's army and, in 1949, created the Communist People's Republic of China. The defeated nationalist government fled to Taiwan, an island off China's east coast. The two Chinas both claimed to be the one China. The United States sided with the Taiwan-China and refused any contact with the People's Republic on the mainland. Communist China joined with the communist Soviet Union to create the Sino-Soviet Alliance and both swore enmity to the United States.

That's how things had stood for over two decades, when I joined Henry Kissinger's National Security Council staff in 1970. The United States had had no official contact with anyone from the People's Republic of China for a generation.

Then, in one of the most dramatic and consequential moments of modern diplomatic history, President Nixon and Secretary of State Kissinger reversed the course of American diplomacy and re-opened relations with China. They believed having a friendly relationship with communist China would drive a wedge in the already cracking Sino-Soviet alliance, and allow us to have better relations with each of them than they had with each other. It worked. For the next two decades we engaged in a sort of triangular diplomacy, tilting toward the junior member of the triad, China. It became our strategic counterweight to the more powerful, more aggressive, and expansionist Soviet Union.

Communist China entered a new phase in its development in the late 1970s when their larger-than-life founding patriarch, Mao Zedong, died. China's new leader, Deng Xiaoping, committed the country to rapid, intense technological and economic transformation. He pushed China to do in four decades what it had taken the rest of the world nearly four centuries to do. The West, led by the United States, approved. We enthusiastically stepped in to help with China's industrial and economic development, convinced that a modern China would also be a pro-America China.

American companies obliged and built factories in China to take advantage of its cheap, unskilled labor in order to manufacture goods for export to the West. "Made in China" became synonymous with cheaply made, low quality, and mass produced goods, which were exported to the West, especially America, at prices our own companies couldn't possibly compete with. As Chinese goods moved up the manufacturing food chain, what began as lower value goods became increasingly more sophisticated, value-added products like steel, aircraft, and automotive parts. Today, China is our peer competitor in some areas of high technology goods.

Throughout their rapid industrialization, Chinese leaders said China was "little brother to America's big brother" and assured us they sought only a "peaceful rise." They insisted they were for free trade, the rule of law, freedom of the seas, and an international system that advanced a global marketplace, stability, and peace. In 2000, with American support, we welcomed China into the World Trade Organization as a developing nation, which gave the nation enormous advantages. Their goods would enter the developed nations practically tariff-free while our goods remained subject to much higher tariffs. This protected Chinese industries from American and European competition, allowing their companies to develop much more rapidly. Our assumption was that once China became a developed nation, the lopsided tariffs would be removed and an equal playing field would emerge.

It turns out the conventional wisdom was wrong but we didn't notice it at first. After the September 11th attacks, we became preoccupied with the Middle East—with the Afghan and Iraq wars, the rise of terrorism and radical Islam, the fight against the Islamic State, and Iran's race to go nuclear. We took our eye off the ball in Asia. When we did have issues with China over trade and security matters, our leaders—both Republican and Democrat—chose to downplay our differences or ignore them entirely.

Had we been paying attention, we would have noticed that China was moving incrementally but steadily toward exploiting their trading relationships with the West through ruthless mercantilist policies. It is now clear, even to those who failed to see it before, that China's sharp-elbowed trade policies have violated both the spirit and the letter of World Trade Organization rules. They have forced international companies seeking to do business in China to turn over billions of dollars of intellectual property as a precondition. China's government-controlled sovereign wealth funds have bought American companies in order to obtain our R&D and trade secrets. When the Chinese couldn't legally acquire what they wanted, their military hacked into American companies' computer systems and stole their most valuable technologies, as the 2014 Justice Department indictment of five Chinese military hackers demonstrates.[3] Once the Chinese got the technology they needed, they used it to create their own government-subsidized companies. Then, by manipulating the currency and dumping exported goods at bargain prices, they were able to drive their American competitors out of business.

---

[3] Li, Zoe. "What we know about the Chinese army's alleged cyber spying unit." CNN. May 20, 2014. https://www.cnn.com/2014/05/20/world/asia/china-unit-61398/index.html.

At the same time, they continued to exploit the trade subsidies that the western nations had granted them in prior decades. Ironically, even though China is now one of the most developed nations in the world, boasting of the world's second largest economy, it has adamantly refused to give up its "developing nation" status with the World Trade Organization.

China has also been busy translating its new economic power into commensurate military might throughout the world. China's leaders are building a first world-style military, including a blue-water navy with global reach. They have begun aggressively throwing their weight around in East Asia, especially in the South and East China Seas. They've taken contested, uninhabited islands at the southern edge of the South China Sea and built them into ports. They reassured the world they were doing this in order to support Chinese fishing fleets and insisted they had no intention of ever militarizing the islands.

When neighboring nations objected and international tribunals ruled that these islands belonged to other countries, China simply ignored their decisions. Instead, they did what they specifically promised not to do: they converted these small, man-made islands into military airstrips, naval ports, and bases. China is now in a position to claim the sea lanes and airspace in between those islands and their coastline as Chinese territory. If allowed to stand, the South China Sea will, for all intents and purposes, become an internal Chinese Lake. They alone will be able to exploit its underwater resources and rich fishing areas. One of the world's most important maritime trade routes will be under total Chinese control, rather than what it used to be just a few years ago: a free sea lane through which navies and merchant vessels of all nations had unfettered access.

China's expansion into the South China Sea now appears to be part of a much larger plan to create a global maritime system of trade routes. China is building a string of ports from Southeast Asia through South Asia to Africa and the Middle East. They are ostensibly for commercial trade, but it would be an easy leap to repurpose those ports for Chinese military use, as they have already done in Djibouti on the east coast of Africa.

China also has begun an ambitious plan to build a new Silk Road trade route with its One Belt-One Road infrastructure program, aimed at creating a Eurasian trade route from China to Europe, with a presence in every country in between. It is working with some seventy nations along the route to build railroads, highways, and even new cities. They will be built by Chinese engineers and workers, to Chinese standards, and China will be the senior partner in trade and commercial relationships, inevitably giving them political as well as economic influence. China has extended generous loans to many of the countries along its maritime and land routes. When those countries fail to meet their payments, China takes over control of the asset.

Over two thousand years ago, Rome created an empire that stretched from Europe to the Middle East and beyond. Its effects are still felt today in language, culture, and governance. China has set out to create a modern-day version of the Roman Empire. Chinese leaders are building a Eurasian empire, not by conquering lands through invasion, but by dominating their economies with these new land and maritime trade routes that they will control. Ultimately, they will be in a position to push the United States out of Asia and out of the Western Pacific, or at least dictate the terms by which we remain.

In 2018, Chinese President Xi Jinping ended term limits and in effect became President for life. At the same time, he tightened control over all aspects of the Chinese government, military, and society. He curtailed access to the internet, crushed all opposition, including even minor disagreements with his policies. He relocated a million Chinese Muslims to "reeducation" camps. He is well along toward creating the world's first total surveillance state. In the not-too-distant future, China's 1.3 billion people will be monitored at all times with nationwide cameras, facial and voice recognition systems, and constant location tracking. Chinese citizens will be judged by a social points system, where regime loyalists are rewarded with better pay, jobs, and opportunities, while those who do not fall into line will have even normal activities curtailed. Anyone not in lockstep with Xi's groupthink will be unable to board planes or trains, rent apartments or get jobs. They will be banished from Chinese society while living in the midst of it. The planned system is already in place in several Chinese cities and is expected to go nationwide by 2021.

According to CFR China scholar Elizabeth Economy,

> *"What makes Xi's revolution distinctive is the strategy he has pursued; the dramatic centralization of authority under his personal leadership; the*

intensified penetration of society by the state; the creation of a virtual wall of regulations and restrictions that more tightly controls the flow of ideas, culture and capital into and out of the country; and the significant projection of Chinese power."[4]

Contrary to what many of our leaders have said for the last thirty years, China has not become a more open and liberal society. Instead, Xi has taken China in the opposite direction. Human rights, individual opinions and preferences, and democracy are seen as threats to Communist Party rule. China will soon be an even more tightly controlled, top down, authoritarian state, with no room for anything other than what the Communist Party chooses to allow.

We compounded the mistake of reassuring ourselves about China's benign intentions by taking our technological superiority for granted. China might have dizzying rates of economic growth and build a new city a week. It might even someday replace us as the world's largest economy and leading manufacturing country. But we assured ourselves that those things wouldn't be as important as America's insurmountable technological lead. After all, we led the Industrial Revolution; we invented the Information Age. We have always been and will always remain the world's innovation capital. We told ourselves we could make up for China's quantitative lead with our qualitative superiority. But just because that is how things have been in the past, there is is no guarantee that this is how things will remain in the future.

In 2015 Chinese leaders unveiled *Made in China 2025*, an ambitious plan to make China the world's most technologically advanced economy. Just as their infrastructure programs are designed to link the nations of Europe and Asia into one giant China-dominated trading block, *Made in China 2025* is their ambitious program to marshal all sectors of their economy, military, society, and government in order to leapfrog the United States in advanced technology. *Made in China 2025* is a plan to focus on taking the lead in ten next-generation industries—pharmaceuticals and medicine; the automotive, rail, shipping, and aerospace industries; green energy; semi-conductors; information technology; artificial intelligence; and robotics. While America has been preoccupied

---

[4] Economy, Elizabeth C. *The Third Revolution: Xi Jinping and the New Chinese State*. New York: Oxford, 2018.

with our own political infighting at home, and wasted trillions of dollars trying to turn Middle Eastern nations into modern democratic societies, the Chinese have spent billions to build the infrastructure of the digital future throughout the world.

If Huawei, China's flagship telecommunications company, is the first to roll out a 5G internet, China will leapfrog the United States in developing the next generation of mobile communications. 5G is much more than just a faster internet service; it will provide the world with the infrastructure on which all future data-driven advanced technologies will depend. Put simply, the Chinese government, working through Chinese companies, would have unfettered access to all communications everywhere. For all intents and purposes, it would own and control access to the future.

The *People's Daily*, the Chinese Communist Party's official newspaper, now talks openly of the failure of the current international order. It claims a new international order is taking shape, with China setting the rules. It's difficult to see how this new authoritarian big brother state, which crushes all opposition at home, will be any less ruthless in dealing with less powerful countries that don't follow Beijing's preferences.

I traveled to China several years ago as one of the leaders of a delegation of former Nixon Administration officials. One of the highlights of the trip was a dinner hosted by the Chinese government in the Great Hall of the People in Tiananmen Square. It is a vast structure, built in 1959 for the tenth anniversary of the founding of the People's Republic of China. It's more utilitarian than architecturally distinguished, with triple height ceilings, broad hallways, and gigantic rooms. It's China's main national building, with banquet halls, auditoriums, and government offices. It's also used for elaborate, multi-course, official dinners, for important speeches by government leaders, for cultural performances, and the National People's Congress. The State Banquet Hall, its largest, can hold 7,000 people for dinner. Compare that to a White House State Dinner in its historic East Room, which can accommodate less than 150. China's Great Hall of the People is meant to overwhelm visitors with its vastness, and it does.

Our banquet was in one of the smaller dining rooms, which still dwarfed the number of guests. There were fifty Americans and 150 Chinese, diplomats, government officials, and United States-Chinese

Friendship Society members. Before the dinner began, I joined several others on the stage to talk about the United States-China relationship that began with Nixon's historic trip some four decades before. I said that over the years we had not always agreed on everything, because we are different societies with our own unique cultures and histories. But, in spite of our differences, we had always found a way to work together. My remarks were friendly, noncommittal, and rather bland—and designedly so.

As I returned to my table, I turned to introduce myself to my dinner partner, a senior official from the Chinese foreign ministry. Rather than start out by exchanging niceties, which is normal for these situations, he immediately scowled at me. In a stern voice he lectured me that America should stop making such a fuss about a Chinese dissident who had recently defected to the United States and was then a hot topic in the western media.

He said, in very good English, "Why do you focus on this one person, who is a criminal and a deviant, and ignore what we have done for hundreds of millions of Chinese people? We have moved 300 million people out of poverty in one generation. This one criminal is not important." After he finished his rant, he abruptly got up and left the dinner.

His performance was extraordinary, and totally out of character for one of China's senior diplomats. It was the first time I had heard a Chinese official openly and unequivocally criticize America. He made no attempt at subtlety or innuendo. It was an in-your-face tirade and deliberately rude. Second, he made it unmistakably clear that he thought the rights of one person meant nothing in the greater scheme of things. But looking back, I now realize that his conduct and remarks were indicative of the new wind blowing through China—more aggressive, ultra-nationalistic, and unconcerned about giving offense, especially to Americans. So much for the "little brother-big brother" relationship.

Many foreign policy experts forget that in dealing with other countries it is not how we see them that matters, it is how they see themselves. It is not what we perceive to be facts in any given situation, it is what they believe them to be.

For millennia, the Chinese had seen themselves as being the very center of the universe, the oldest and greatest civilization in the history of the world. The Chinese word for their country is Zhongguo, which literally translates as "Middle Kingdom." The word is made up of two Chinese characters, or ideograms: the first, "zhong," for center; the second, "guo," for kingdom. China's people and leaders believe they have been the most important, most powerful, most populated, most homogenous, and the most advanced people in history. For them, China isn't just a country, it is and has always been *the* center of the universe, which ordered the world to its purpose, and to which all nations paid homage. There has never been a time when China didn't exist. They believe world history began with China and all Chinese should therefore share a sense of national pride and historic importance.

When the West—first Europe and then the United States—became powerful beginning in the 18th century, the Chinese believe that they did so only by exploiting China and other lesser nations. Although China was forced to endure several centuries of "humiliation" at Western hands as a result, they have now recovered and are ready to resume their pre-ordained position. Beginning with the Communist Revolution, they have slowly, steadily, and inexorably restored China to the point where it will soon become the world's sole superpower.

The narrative that the Chinese tell themselves is that they may have had a rocky period in the 19th and 20th centuries, but they're now poised to resume what they see as their rightful place on the world stage—as the kingdom at the center of the world. They believe that America is now a declining power, and it is China's destiny to once again control Asia, as they did centuries ago. They are convinced that the 21st century will be the Chinese century, in the same way that the 20th century was America's. They believe that nothing can stop their rise and that nothing can prevent our decline. Chinese President Xi Jinping has openly bragged that by 2025 China will dominate the world's high-tech industry and that by 2035 they will have pushed us out of the Pacific. By 2049, the hundred-year anniversary of the founding of the People's Republic of China, the Chinese believe they will run the world. They will replace the international system the United States created at the end of World War II with an international system more to their liking.

It should come as no surprise that this isn't how Trump sees things. One of his top foreign policy priorities has been to reset our relationship with China and to confront Chinese leaders over their aggressive, sharp-elbowed, mercantilist trade policies. Trump believes the United States has been taken advantage of for years by some of our trading and security partners, but especially by China. Throughout his campaign, Trump criticized former presidents for their naïveté in not recognizing this, and for their weakness in not standing up to China. He says they've played us for "chumps."

Generally speaking, when the Trump campaign became the Trump Tower Transition after the election, there was little focus on analyzing or proposing foreign policy positions the new Administration would pursue once it had assumed office. In the early days of the Transition, the National Security Council "staff" at Trump Tower consisted of myself, a few assistants, and periodic appearances by General Flynn, who was headquartered in Washington. Our time was spent interviewing people for jobs, and the traditional, introductory courtesy calls with foreign officials. The most useful meetings were those I arranged with former national security officials who shared their experiences and offered guidance to General Flynn and, in some cases, with President-elect Trump.

There was also a skeletal staff in the Washington Transition office, left over from Governor Christie's Transition planning team. They had been writing position papers for several months prior to the election, and meeting with outgoing Obama Administration staff after the election. But when Governor Christie was terminated as director of the Transition on the day after Trump's victory, there was little connection between the people in Washington and the people operating out of New York. Any decisions on foreign policymaking would have to wait until after Trump took office.

The one exception was how we would advise Trump on dealing with China, on both economic and national security policies. There was a behind the scenes tug of war right from the beginning, between the economic globalists, led by Gary Cohn and to a lesser extent by Treasury Secretary-designate Steven Mnuchin on the one hand, and the economic nationalists, led by Peter Navarro and Steve Bannon on the other. I joked that it was the "panda huggers" versus the "China hawks."

The globalists were from Wall Street and the international business community; they had gotten rich off the China trade. They were part of the global economy and their views were driven by what seemed best for international corporations and global businesses, not necessarily what was good for American workers. They might have been willing to pressure China for a few concessions here or there, but not at the risk of rocking the boat.

Trump's globalists also worried about America's indebtedness and instability in the global financial market. For years the United States has been forced to borrow money to make up the perennial gap between our expenditures and revenues. Our debt is over $20 trillion, and our largest foreign creditor is China, which holds over $1.1 trillion of U.S. Treasury notes, the United States government's official IOUs. Globalists were concerned that if our political relationship took a turn for the worse, China could inflict more pain on us that we could on them. China could cause a major United States financial crisis by liquidating all or a significant portion of their holdings of U.S. government debt, or refusing to extend their line of credit to the U.S. government. This would send interest rates soaring and cause American borrowing costs to ratchet up to dangerous levels. Since that kind of "nuclear option" could only come at significant costs to their own economy, it is unlikely the Chinese would pull the trigger. Still, the mere threat of doing so gave them enormous leverage over the U.S. government.[5]

The bottom line is that most globalists believe that it is only a matter of time before China surpasses the United States as the world's dominant economy, and it is inevitable that the Chinese will accrue all the political and economic clout that comes with it.

The "China hawks" took the opposite approach. Like the globalists, they agreed that if things remained as they were China was well along the way to becoming the world's most powerful economy. But, unlike the globalists, they did not believe it was inevitable. They believed the United States was still strong enough to stand up to China and insist on recalibrating the trade and investment relationship, but time was running out. Their push for Trump to take immediate steps to jump-start the American economy was not only for the sake of creating American jobs; it was also to regain political and economic leverage over China. They believed if we ever had a trade war with China, it was one the United States could ultimately win. The Chinese economy depends on exports and the United States is by an order of magnitude their largest market.

---

[5] Amadeo, Kimberly. "US Debt to China, How Much It Is, Reasons Why, and What If China Sells." The Balance. August 1, 2019. https://www.thebalance.com/u-s-debt-to-china-how-much-does-it-own-3306355.

Furthermore, Chinese exports to the United States are nearly five times the dollar amount of what we export to them. China's economic model depends on exports, especially to the U.S. market.

Trump had connected with Navarro several years before and found his ideas resonated with his own. Trump agreed with Navarro's claim that one of the reasons China had enjoyed such phenomenal growth over the last thirty years was because American trade policy allowed—and even encouraged—our Midwestern factory manufacturing, and the jobs that went with it, to move overseas to China. Their gain was our loss. Trump had campaigned as an unabashed economic nationalist, ready to take on anybody who was taking advantage of America—especially China. He has taken a strong stand against China's predatory trade practices and territorial expansion. I joined with the China hawks in believing Trump's policy shift had come just in the nick of time.

Today, many in the foreign policy community are catching up and acknowledging that the United States needs to challenge China's trade practices, even though they don't have the stomach for a sharp-elbowed engagement. One of our leading globalists, Pulitzer prize-winning *New York Times* columnist and bestselling author, Thomas Friedman, has come to realize "this is a fight worth having." He also agrees that it needs to happen now, before China is so big it can impose whatever terms it likes on its trading partners. Were our uneven trade and investment relationship to remain as it has been for the last twenty years, within the next decade or so China would become too strong to challenge.

I watched firsthand how Trump turned the American economy around and revealed the vulnerability that has now been exposed in the Chinese economy. China's growth rate has slowed, their stock market is at its lowest point in years, and their massive debt and real estate bubbles have sparked real fears in the country's business community. For the first time, China is in a vulnerable economic position.

The United States, on the other hand, is in the strongest economic position we have been in for decades. Because of the strong pro-growth policies Trump pushed from the beginning of his presidency, our economy is now growing again, rapidly, and at some of the highest rates in modern times. Our unemployment numbers are at historic lows. Millions of new jobs have been created with more on the horizon. Every socioeconomic group in the country is doing better.

Since much of our current export trade to China is agricultural, originating primarily from the Midwest, that is one of the few areas the Chinese can leverage in our trade negotiations—and they've been doing so aggressively. But it is not fair for one segment of our economy, or for one region of our country, to be held hostage to and to bear the entire burden of the trade war—and Trump is well aware of this. That is why he has guaranteed to make American farmers whole and compensate them for their losses during this prolonged negotiating period.

As I write this, in the fall of 2019, the United States and China are locked in a trade war, with on-again, off-again negotiations. Both Trump and Xi are tough negotiators and risk-takers. Neither side will make concessions unless absolutely necessary. President Trump believes we can "win" a trade war because China needs American trade more than we need theirs. Since China is an authoritarian state, President Xi may think he can force his people to endure hardships for a longer period than President Trump, who has to face the voters in 2020. Xi may also figure that Trump won't be president for long, either because he will be removed from office through impeachment or he won't be reelected, so China can just wait him out.

Trump has an opportunity to break the deadlock and turn the tables on China. He can capitalize on the successful bipartisan trade agreements he has already forged during his first three years in office, as well as those he is poised to complete soon. The new United States-Korea Free Trade Agreement (KORUS FTA) was Trump's first new trade agreement. He renegotiated the North American Free Trade Agreement (NAFTA), now called the United States-Mexican-Canadian Agreement (USMC). At the G7 Summit in August 2019, Japanese Prime Minister Abe and Trump announced they had negotiated a new trade agreement. Both Trump and British Prime Minister Boris Johnson have publicly committed themselves to a significant bilateral trade agreement that will take effect once Britain leaves the European Union in late 2019 or early 2020. Even German Chancellor Angela Merkel believes an independent Britain will become an economic competitor to the European Union.[6] A US-UK trade bloc would be formidable.

---

[6] Momtaz, Rym. "Merkel sees post-Brexit UK as 'potential competitor' to EU." Politico. October 13, 2019. https://www.politico.eu/article/angela-merkel-sees-post-brexit-uk-as-potential-competitor-to-eu-emmanuel-macron/.

At the beginning of the Administration, Trump pulled out of the Trans-Pacific Partnership, a 12-nation pact with our Pacific trade partners that excludes China. If President Trump can fi   way to rejoin it, on terms more favorable for the United States, he could be in a position to assemble a united front of Asian, British, and North American trading partners to stand with us in negotiating with China.

After all, China's European and Asian trading partners are also chafing under Chinese predatory trade policies, inequitable tariffs, and market access, some even more than we are. China's economic strategy so far has been to pick us off one at a time. If Trump can assemble the majority of the world's most powerful economies to join with the United States in confronting China over its unfair trade practices, the Chinese will have little choice but to renegotiate. Trump is the only leader who can present a united front to China and insist on new trade terms that are fair to all and maintained by all.

To a certain extent the Chinese official I met with in the Great Hall of the People was right. What they have achieved in four decades is an accomplishment unique in the history of the world. In a little more than a generation they have taken China from a nation of peasant farmers on the brink of starvation to a modern industrialized superpower. They have brought more than 300 million people out of poverty, the equivalent of the entire United States population. The Chinese people have worked and studied hard and the Chinese government has made smart investments in infrastructure and technology. We should give credit where credit is due.

But we should also acknowledge that much of it was made possible by the international trading system the United States created and has protected over the last seventy years. It gave China trade subsidies and preferential treatment even when it was to the detriment of our own economy. It is time to reconfigure our economic relationship to one of reciprocal free and fair trade. We recognize that China will continue to develop and grow, and we should not attempt to block or contain its progress. But we should no longer allow it to be at our expense. The days of the United States putting China First are over. It's time to put American interests first. As the Chinese are fond of saying, it could be a win-win policy, although perhaps not in the way they originally intended.

CHAPTER 10

Peace Through Strength

Trump's national security policy, like Reagan's, is *Peace Through Strength*. Nothing new there. It's also been the security policy of just about every Republican leader for forty years. On the surface, Peace Through Strength seems like a typical throwaway line or a convenient television sound bite. After all, who doesn't want peace? Who's against strength? It's sufficiently vague that it's allowed people to interpret it in different ways. Over the years, politicians, academics, experts, and diplomats have done just that. The neocons in the George W. Bush Administration used it to justify their pre-emptive invasion of Iraq in 2003. Senator Rand Paul interprets it in the opposite way—that Reagan's policy was to avoid getting drawn into the Lebanese civil war in the 1980s, and it remains a reason not to get drawn into unwinnable Middle East wars today.

I was in the Reagan Administration in the 1980s, when the Peace Through Strength policy was born. As the Defense Department's chief speechwriter, I was responsible for translating Reagan's defense policies and putting even the most complicated and technical of them into words an average person could understand.

"Peace Through Strength." Three harmless little words that could fit on a bumper sticker. But their meaning was profound, revolutionary even. Seen from today's prospective, they were also prescient, and just as relevant now as they were in the 1980s.

Reagan chose those three words carefully. Just as important as the three words he did use were the ones he did not. He never said our goal was simply peace—because there are a lot of ways to get to peace. Reagan wanted the peace that comes as a result of strength—not the peace that comes from conquest or capitulation. And Reagan didn't see America's strength as resting on our military might alone. He knew that our superior economic and political systems, innovative culture, and technological superiority could all be wielded in support of peace. Finally, he didn't want the peace that comes after military victory on the battlefield, especially between two nuclear powers. There are no winners in a nuclear war. It was not "Peace Through War."

Reagan wanted the peace that comes by avoiding and deterring conflict, when the enemy realizes the futility of waging war against America's superior military and economy. Potential adversaries are deterred from starting a war with us because they know they could never win. Reagan also believed America should never be the aggressor, even though our superior military might give us the capability to do so and emerge victorious. Reagan believed military aggression was contrary to everything America stands for. He wanted to build the strongest military in the world in order to deter our adversaries, not conquer them. America may finish wars, but we don't start them.

Reagan had a similar approach to the Cold War. He didn't want a hot war with the Soviet Union. But he didn't want a Cold War either. He wanted peace with the Soviet Union, but on our terms. It seems like common sense, but in the 1980s this strategy was not the conventional wisdom. The foreign policy establishment of the day, of both parties, believed we could never have peace with the Soviet Union. The best we could hope for was an endless Cold War, with both of us armed to the teeth with conventional and nuclear weapons. The experts thought we were condemned to a twilight zone between war and peace where we sought to avoid war, but didn't think we would ever have peace.

Reagan thought otherwise. When asked what his policy was toward the Cold War, he joked, "It's simple. We win, they lose." Experts dismissed him as uninformed and superficial, a second-rate actor past his prime, who just might be crazy enough to launch World War III. But he wasn't. Reagan did want to win the Cold War, but he didn't want to go to war to do it. He wanted to pit America's superior economic, political, and defense systems against the Soviet Union's deeply flawed equivalent systems. He believed the Soviet Union's greatest vulnerability was the inability of their top-down communist system to provide for their people. He believed the communist world would eventually collapse in on itself. But he wanted to hurry that day along. So, he marshalled all elements of our national power—economic, political, moral, diplomatic, military, and technological—to put great stress on their economy. Within a decade, the Soviet Union fell apart, and we won the Cold War without having to fire a shot. Reagan knew that American strength was rooted in its democratic connection to everyday people, and he was able to use that to ensure international peace.

One of the reasons I supported Trump is because, from what I could glean from his off-the-cuff statements and tweets, his version of Peace Through Strength was more in line with Reagan's than the other, more conventional Republican candidates. The Republican party had been dominated by neoconservative war hawks for over fifteen years. Bush's preemptive wars and nation building, despite the best of intentions, had failed in Afghanistan and Iraq. But rather than admit defeat, these conventional Republicans kept us on the battlefield fighting low intensity forever-wars—wars that we were unable to win, but also unwilling to end. All too often we were fighting to prop up leaders who didn't like us in countries that didn't matter.

At the same time, I believed Obama's policy of strategic patience was also fatally flawed. His long and tortured decision-making process resulted in paralysis by analysis. Obama was convinced that since our enemies would eventually fail and we would prevail, we didn't have to do anything other than wait for it to happen. I was convinced his doctrine of strategic patience was just another way of doing nothing for fear of failure. To passively sit back and wait for things to work out, convinced that the great arc of history will ultimately defeat our enemies, was fraught with problems. Even if Obama was right, and we would eventually come out on top, I worried it would take too long and carry too much risk while we waited…perhaps for decades.

To my mind, Trump and Reagan entered the White House facing similar situations with respect to the state of the U.S. military and they adopted similar defense postures. Trump, like Reagan, had inherited a war-weary and demoralized military. Trump, like Reagan, launched a defense buildup to make our military once again the most capable in the world. Reagan's goal in doing so in the 1980s was not in order to launch preemptive wars—as George W. Bush was later to do with Iraq. Trump's goal was more like Reagan's: have a strong military to deter war and, if deterrence failed, to fight and win wars.

Reagan explained the concept of Peace Through Strength in an Oval Office speech to the nation on March 23, 1983. He said our defense policy was "based on a simple premise: The United States does not start fights. We will never be the aggressor. We maintain our strength in order to deter and defend against aggression—to preserve freedom and peace." He believed that "We maintain the peace through our strength; weakness only invites aggression."[1] The speech, now referred to as the Star Wars speech, is famous because it was when Reagan first announced his plan to build a missile defense program to protect us against Soviet nuclear weapons. Reagan's original intention was for it to be a defense policy speech, to explain the reasoning behind the Reagan defense buildup and urge the American people to stay the course. I wrote the first draft of that speech, the part about defense policy, drawing from Reagan's own thinking. It is one of the things I am most proud of in my career, because it was the quintessential expression of a defense policy that remains relevant for all time.

On the campaign trail Trump described his defense policy in his own straightforward way: "I will make our Military so big, powerful & strong that no one will mess with us."[2] Like all things Trump, it was outspoken and blunt, and announced in a tweet. Trump may have lacked Reagan's eloquence, but he got the point across. Trump, like Reagan, launched a defense buildup that would ensure our military remained the strongest in the world. It was not with the intention of using our superior military strength to start wars, or impose our beliefs on others, or force nation building on backward states. Trump, like Reagan before him, wanted to

---

[1] "Address to the Nation on Defense and National Security." AtomicArchive. March 23, 1983. http://www.atomicarchive.com/Docs/Missile/Starwars.shtml.

[2] Trump, Donald J. (@realDonaldTrump). "I will make our Military so big, powerful & strong that no one will mess with us." January 24, 2016, 7:08 AM. "https://twitter.com/realDonaldTrump/status/691276412666261504.

rebuild our armed forces in order *not to have to use them.* The concept has been around since the Roman Empire: "*si vis pacem, para bellum.*" If you want peace, prepare for war.

But that leaves open the question of when *should* we go to war? Should it be only defensively, in response to attacks on our homeland? Or should we use our military offensively abroad to promote and advance other aspects of our foreign policy? Or something in between?

We have grappled with this question from the earliest days of our republic. Under what circumstances should we commit forces to battle? At one extreme, isolationists argue it should be only in order to defend ourselves. John Adams, one of our Founding Fathers and the second president, believed America "does not go abroad in search of monsters to destroy." John Quincy Adams, his son and our sixth president echoed the theme forty years later: "America is a friend of freedom everywhere, but a custodian only of our own."

At the other end of the spectrum are the interventionists who want to spread democracy abroad, even if it means going to war to do it. President Kennedy said in his Inaugural Address, "We shall pay any price, bear any burden, meet any hardship, support any friend, oppose any foe to assure the survival and the success of liberty." Kennedy sent American forces into Vietnam to stop the spread of communism in Southeast Asia. We left Vietnam three presidencies later, in failure.

Forty years later, President George W. Bush echoed some of Kennedy's themes in his second Inaugural Address. Bush justified the wars in Iraq and Afghanistan as necessary to protect our national security by ensuring these countries develop democratic governments. Judged against those goals, the Iraq and Afghanistan wars were failures as well.

Most presidents take a stab at defining when America should go to war. So do lots of legislators, academics, and thinktank intellectuals. Reagan himself didn't weigh in on the question while in office, but his closest friend and longtime colleague did, right after Reagan won reelection by a landslide victory. Reagan's defense secretary and my boss, Caspar Weinberger, gave a speech at the National Press Club in November 1984, titled "The Use of Military Force." I researched and wrote the speech, realizing it was an important statement of Reagan's Peace through Strength. The speech was over a year in the making, carefully vetted by the military, the White House, and by President Reagan himself. The speech laid out the conditions a leader should consider and the questions he should ask himself before committing American forces abroad.

The thinking behind the Weinberger Doctrine began shortly after a Hezbollah suicide bomber, operating under instructions from Iran, detonated himself and his truck bomb and killed 241 Americans while they slept in Marine barracks in Beirut.

The October 1983 attack, which killed more marines than any battle since Iwo Jima, ignited a heated discussion at the highest levels in the Reagan Administration. Some wanted to send in more American troops. Others, especially Weinberger and his military assistant, General Colin Powell, were against it.

Secretary Weinberger had been reluctant to put Marines in Beirut in the first place. They didn't have a military purpose, but were there as symbolic peacekeepers with the vague mission of helping diplomacy. Since there was no peace in Beirut, the American marines were attractive targets for several sides of the Lebanese civil war. As Weinberger had predicted, "they were sitting ducks" when a Hezbollah suicide bomber drove a truck full of explosives into the marine barracks.

Weinberger came back from a White House meeting in early 1984 and called me into his office. My speechwriters' office was just a few doors down the hall from the Secretary's suite of offices and I arrived quickly. Weinberger said he had talked to President Reagan about a speech he wanted to make that would put the Vietnam syndrome to rest.

In the Pentagon of the early 1980s, the Vietnam War was the elephant in the room in any discussion about when we should commit combat forces overseas, and Weinberger wanted to be on record with a clear and thoughtful discussion. He didn't want the United States drawn into another Vietnam-type war with vague and shifting objectives, creeping escalation, and limited chances of success. He was determined to lay down some guidelines to determine when America should go to war.

Weinberger was one of the few Cabinet officers who could go into Reagan's office alone, after larger meetings, and argue his case. Their friendship went way back to California, to the 1960s and Reagan's earliest days in politics. Weinberger was just a few years younger than Reagan but revered him. While they had different backgrounds growing up, they thought alike. Both believed in a strong military but both were reluctant to use it unless absolutely necessary. And both believed that if America went to war, America went to win.

To help prepare for his meeting with Reagan, Weinberger asked me to do research, sound out the military, and come back with some preliminary thoughts. He wanted to use the speechwriting process to kick-start his own thinking.

I spent hours talking to veterans and defense experts. I consulted the Service Chiefs, senior officers, and enlisted men. Secretary Weinberger's Military Assistant, General Colin Powell (later Secretary of State) shared much of Weinberger's thinking. So did my former Nixon Administration colleagues from the Kissinger days. The people who felt most passionately and spoke most thoughtfully were the colonels and one- and two-star flag officers. They had been the first and second lieutenant officers in Vietnam, and saw firsthand a war gone wrong. They also saw how the Vietnam War had practically broken the military because they were the ones who had to pick up the pieces after the civilian leaders moved on.

Many of them echoed the same thoughts I had years before as a young aide on Dr. Kissinger's West Wing NSC staff. I sat in the White House Situation Room, with the television on, watching American forces being evacuated by helicopter from the roof of the American Embassy in Saigon. I made a silent promise. "Never again should America fight a war without the support of the American people… never again should America go to war with vague goals and insufficient resources… never again should America go to war and lose."

After hours of conversations and interviews, and weeks poring over books, articles, and assessments of the good wars and the bad wars, I offered Weinberger a briefing paper outlining several points drawn from my research. The Vietnam War went wrong because its objectives were vaguely defined and kept changing; it dragged on for years, with ever mounting casualties; popular support waned, and anti-war demonstrations broke out across the country. Finally, Congress began putting conditions on continued funding and eventually cut it off. Yet, no president wanted to be the first one to lose a war. So, we fought on, stuck in a war we were unable to win, yet unwilling to end. Weinberger himself added the most crucial point—we should only go to war if we were prepared to do what it took to win.

The speech went through several drafts as it was circulated among the top brass at the Pentagon. When it was finished, we sent it to the National Security Council and White House for vetting. After some tweaking, the speech was ready by late spring 1984. Reagan was running for reelection that fall, and he asked Weinberger wait until after the vote, lest it risk becoming a political issue.

Weinberger laid down six principles to guide decisions in the gray areas that lay between self-defense and conquest. The gist of his speech was we should never hesitate to go to war if it meant defending our own lands or our vital national interests. But we should refrain from using force to "invade, conquer, or subjugate other nations."

The Weinberger doctrine:

1. The United States should not commit forces to combat unless the vital national interests of the United States or its allies are involved.

2. U.S. troops should only be committed wholeheartedly and with the clear intention of winning. Otherwise, troops should not be committed.

3. U.S. combat troops should be committed only with clearly defined political and military objectives and with the capacity to accomplish those objectives.

4. The relationship between the objectives and the size and composition of the forces committed should be continually reassessed and adjusted if necessary.

5. U.S. troops should not be committed to battle without a "reasonable assurance" of the support of U.S. public opinion and Congress.

6. The commitment of U.S. forces to combat should be considered only as a last resort.

At the time, the speech drew mixed reactions. *New York Times* columnist William Safire ridiculed Weinberger for insisting on "no more unpopular wars." Others, especially those in the military who had to carry on after the failures of the Vietnam War, were more sober-minded. Weinberger's principles were never meant to be items on a hard and fast checklist, but rather a series of things any president should consider before sending American forces abroad to fight. It was in that regard that Reagan recommended Weinberger's principles to future Presidents.[3]

After September 11th, attitudes changed. By that time, the lessons of the Vietnam War, fought more than a generation before, were a distant memory. President George W. Bush and his neocon advisors returned to a muscular military policy. American Special Forces attacked Afghanistan in order to destroy Al-Qaeda. Our forces were successful immediately, and within three months we had practically destroyed the people who had attacked us. But when Al-Qaeda quit Afghanistan and melted away into Pakistan, our mission changed. Instead of tracking down the remnants of Al-Qaeda and destroying them, we remained in Afghanistan to build a democracy. Our objective was to keep Al-Qaeda from returning to Afghanistan. We built a massive infrastructure, spent billions on extensive nation building efforts, and fought a guerilla war against the Taliban. Nearly twenty years and three presidents later, we are still fighting in Afghanistan. The war is stalemated, and our nation building, democracy promoting efforts have failed.

Of course, the Weinberger Doctrine needs to be adapted in the age of terrorism, asymmetrical conflict, and cyberweapons. But Trump understood instinctively what Presidents Bush and Obama did not learn from decades of postwar American history. Since it is far easier to start a war than it is to end one, only the defense of America's vital interests can justify the commitment of military forces to combat. And, to avoid encouraging any adversary from starting a conflict, the United States must have—and be perceived to have—the strongest military in the world.

When put into the context of events today, the Weinberger doctrine is similar to Trump's own unorthodox thinking when he talks about leaving the Middle East, Iraq, and Afghan wars for others to fight. Trump was an early and frequent critic of the Iraq and Afghanistan wars. He campaigned on the promise to end our involvement in these wars and to avoid getting stuck in similar Middle East quagmires in the future. He understood something fundamental about the Middle East that the neocons and liberal interventionists never did. They are convinced that all people everywhere see things the way we do, regardless

---

[3] Brands, H. W. *Reagan: The Life*. New York: Anchor Books, a division of Penguin Random House, 2015.

of their different cultures, histories, and traditions. But many do not. Americans think of peace as the default position of all societies, and war is what happens when peace fails. Once the war is over, people pick up the pieces and resume their normal lives. In the Middle East, war is often the default position, and peace is the brief pause while the factions regroup to fight again.

In his first address to the United Nations General Assembly in September 2017, Trump returned to a theme he uses frequently when talking about the goals of American foreign policy:

"In America, we do not seek to impose our way of life on anyone, but rather to let it shine as an example for everyone to watch."[4]

For the most part, President Trump has been true to his word. He inherited a war against the Islamic State. He pledged to win it and he did so by returning military decisions to those fighting on the battlefield rather than those observing from the White House Situation Room. The Islamic State has now collapsed, its leaders have been killed, and ISIS and radical Islamic terrorist groups are on the wane. Trump has avoided calls to add more American combat forces into the region. He has begun drawing down our forces in Afghanistan.

I was with Trump during his first military operation, bombing the chemical weapons facilities in Syria. The situation began just two months into the Trump Administration, when Syrian President Assad once again used chemical weapons on his own people. Several years before, President Obama had issued a warning to President Assad. He drew a "red line" and threatened Assad with serious consequences if he used chemical weapons. President Assad went ahead and used them anyway, calling Obama's bluff. At the time, Trump had been critical of Obama for drawing that red line in the first place and for compounding the problem by then backing down instead of enforcing it.

The morning after the chemical attack, I was with several others assembled for our regular morning intelligence briefing, waiting for President Trump to walk over from the Residence. We were standing in the small anteroom outside the Oval Office, where Trump's longtime

---

[4] "Remarks by President Trump to the 72nd Session of the United Nations General Assembly." United Nations. September 19, 2017. https://www.whitehouse.gov/briefings-statements/remarks -president-trump-72nd-session-united-nations-general-assembly/.

communications director, Hope Hicks, sat, as well as Trump's scheduling assistant, Madeline Westerhout.

Behind their desks are floor to ceiling windows looking out to the Rose Garden and the open-air columned walkway which connects the White House Residence to the West Wing offices. We could track Trump's regular morning commute from the Residence to the Oval Office. Rain or shine he walked outside, across the Colonnade, past the anteroom where we stood, and entered the Oval Office door directly from the outside. He walked briskly that day and wore a scowl. Once he sat down at the Resolute Desk, he immediately waved us all in. He was clearly agitated.

He had seen the morning news report about Syria's chemical attack, and saw pictures of the women and young children who had been gassed. He was outraged. We had hardly gotten into our seats when he said to no one in particular, "I want to take him out," meaning Syrian President Assad. In other words, he was suggesting we assassinate Assad. I was the senior NSC person at the meeting, and tried to catch the eye of the others in the room. No luck. Everyone was looking at their hands, heads down. Nobody said a thing.

I swallowed and said, "You can't do that, Mr. President. It would be an act of war. You would be starting an undeclared war with Syria. And there is also a law against assassinating foreign leaders."

Trump countered, "They're already at war with us." He stared me down.

None of my erstwhile colleagues came to my aid, so I continued. "It is also surprisingly hard to do it successfully. When we've tried this sort of thing in the past, it hasn't always worked. The intelligence is never without doubt. These guys are constantly moving around. You can never be sure exactly where they are at any given moment."

He folded his arms across his chest, in his belligerent pose, and barked at me, "I don't believe that."

"Reagan tried it when we bombed Qadaffi's compound in the 1980s in retaliation for a terrorist attack against our troops in Germany. Plenty of people died, supposedly including some of Qadaffi's own family, but Qadaffi himself wasn't there."

Trump continued to glare at me.

The only other woman in the room, the Vice President's National Security Advisor, retired Colonel Andrea Thompson, came to my aid.

"Mr. President," she said, "if we try to kill him and fail, a lot of Americans in Syria will die." The men in the room were still looking down at their shoes or fumbling with their papers.

I jumped back in, "But that doesn't mean we do nothing. For example, we could destroy the chemical weapons factories."

Trump said, "No. If we bomb the factories, chemical weapons could leak out." (He had a point. Many experts warned of the very same thing.)

"But we could bomb some other military sites," I continued. Trump nodded. "Okay, maybe." Warming to the idea, he turned to General Kellogg. "Call Mattis and see what he says." Kellogg left the Oval Office. He returned a few minutes later, saying, "I've talked to Mattis. He was already working on it. He'll have some options for you by this afternoon."

Mattis is a living legend. A much-decorated retired four-star Marine general, Mattis began his career as an 18-year-old enlistee. He commanded troops in the first Gulf War and in the Afghan and Iraq wars a decade later. He is a scholar, fierce warrior, geopolitical strategist, and worshipped by his beloved Marines, as well as everyone else in uniform, and thousands of others in the national security community, myself included.

Before Trump tapped him to be Secretary of Defense, he had been Obama's general in charge of Central Command, with responsibility over the entire Middle East. Mattis knew the area, knew what was militarily possible, had been in countless military operations in Afghanistan and Iraq, and had nerves of steel. Chairman of the Joint Chiefs of Staff General Dunford was the same. So was General John Kelly, then Secretary of Homeland Security (and later Chief of Staff). General H.R. McMaster, the new National Security Advisor brought in to replace Flynn, had seen plenty of military action in his army career, but had been at the White House for only five weeks. He was still feeling his way with Trump and the Cabinet and adjusting to his quasi-political role after decades of non-partisanship as a soldier.

But the rest of the national security team weren't battle crisis tested. Neither the president, vice president, Secretary of State nor anyone in their inner circles had ever been through a military operation. Furthermore, they were all preoccupied with the critically important first Summit between Trump and Chinese President Xi, scheduled for the coming weekend in Mar-a-Lago. I kept thinking about the worries I had during the Transition—that every president is faced with a foreign policy crisis in his first few months in office. How he handles it will affect the rest of his presidency.

By that afternoon, General Mattis and Joint Chiefs of Staff Chairman General Dunford presented Trump with a rough outline for a range of military options against Syria and Assad. For the next two days, the brand new NSC machinery went into overdrive, assembling a list of economic and diplomatic options against Assad. Whatever Trump decided, secrecy was essential. There had been serious leaks since the first days of the Trump Administration, not just political gossip and palace intrigue, but top-secret military and intelligence information. Since just about everything discussed at the NSC meetings appeared in the *New York Times* or *Washington Post*, or on CNN within hours, always negatively spun and slanted against Trump, this was no idle concern.

The President himself presided over several meetings in the Situation Room to go over a range of options. Despite press reports that he was reckless or trigger happy, I found him to be just the opposite. He might have been a rookie but he asked all the right questions. As was his custom, he peppered the staff with questions. "What could go wrong? Were Americans in danger? Would there be Syrian casualties?" And since we knew Russians were operating in the region, "What are the chances of Russian casualties? What is the likelihood this could escalate?" If anything, I thought Trump was a reluctant warrior, not afraid to use force, but wanting a frank assessment of the consequences, good and bad, before he made decisions. Once he decided to act, he left it to the experts to come up with options. He insisted on asking question after question in the briefings to fully understand things, and then made a measured sober decision. He knew the risks, he knew the stakes, and gave the order with his eyes wide open. Then he stepped back and let the military do their job. He didn't second guess their recommendations, hover over their shoulders, or dither about whether he had made the right decision.

Trump wanted to demonstrate to Assad and the world that chemical weapons use would not be tolerated. Trump also showed that he wasn't afraid to use force, as long as it was limited, properly resourced, and implemented with a well-defined objective in mind. But having made his point, Trump made it clear he would not get dragged back into a larger military commitment in the region.

If all went according to plan and the operation was a success, it would put down a marker to Assad or anyone else contemplating use of chemical weapons. Trump pointed out to us that this wasn't just about Assad. It would send a signal to the Chinese, North Koreans, Iranians, and others that he wasn't afraid of using force. Later, when Trump told North Korean President Kim that all options were on the table in dealing with their nuclear weapons program, including the military option, it wasn't an empty threat.

But it was a tough call, especially because of the timing. If something went wrong, if missiles went off course and landed on population centers, if they were shot down, if they set off a larger conflict, it would happen during Trump's first summit meeting with the Chinese leader, right in the middle of the official dinner. The entire world would be watching. If something—anything—didn't go off exactly as planned, Trump would own it for his entire time in office. A failed military operation at the beginning of his presidency would be a disaster for the effectiveness of his presidency, and put us at a disadvantage not just with China but with every other country we had issues with.

After the final Situation Room meeting, Trump stood up, thanked everyone, and said he would make his decision later that day. He decided on an option that would make the point to Assad but not be so aggressive that it mandated a response. Navy Tomahawk missiles would attack and destroy the airfield where the Syrians launched the chemical weapon attack.

Trump, General McMaster, the White House senior staff, and several Cabinet secretaries then left for Mar-a-Lago for the summit meeting with the Chinese President. Secretary of Defense Mattis and Chairman Dunford stayed at their command posts at the Pentagon. Vice President Pence, Homeland Secretary Kelly, Attorney General Sessions, and I remained at the White House to monitor events from the Situation Room.

There was no pre-existing protocol for who to inform and when—that had gone out the door with the Obama Administration. We deliberately hadn't prepared our own notification protocol in advance, for fear it would leak and endanger the mission. We had never done this before, so we weren't sure who we needed to call. I asked my advisor, Lieutenant Commander Sarah Flaherty, one of the few people on the NSC staff who had been involved with the operation from the start, to draft a list of people we should notify, with positions, names, and numbers. We didn't want to leave anyone out, so we called them all, personally and directly, once the missiles were in the air. Because we were so concerned news of the operation would leak out, we kept the group small.

No one had an entourage. It was just a handful of Cabinet secretaries and senior officials. Once the missiles launched, we fanned out to separate phones, each with a call list in hand, to inform our allies, the countries in the region, and key senators and congressmen. Most of us dialed the numbers ourselves. If our calls went to voicemail, we left messages. Can you imagine an Ambassador getting a call from the American Attorney General asking to call back immediately on an important issue of national security? It went well. A number of Congressional leaders appreciated the heads up. One senior Democrat and frequent Trump critic thanked me and rather sheepishly admitted he had never been called when the Obama Administration did military operations. Amazingly, nothing leaked to the press before the attack was over.

The one country we failed to reach was Israel. It was the Sabbath and we didn't have the private cell phone numbers of senior Israeli leaders. When I saw the Israeli Ambassador a few days later, I apologized for not being able to reach him. He chuckled and said don't worry. He understood the difficulty in reaching him and they figured out it was related to Syria.

After making our calls, Vice President Pence, the Attorney General, Homeland Security Secretary, White House Counsel Don McGahn, and key NSC staff members gathered in the Situation Room to wait. Other than Secretary Kelly and myself, none of the others had been through a military operation and we were all understandably anxious. Within the hour we got word from the Pentagon that the attack was 100 percent successful and there had been no leaks. The press was taken by complete surprise. They were focused on Mar-a-Lago and the Summit between Trump and the Chinese President. The press immediately switched gears, and Washington reporters scrambled for interviews with congressional leaders—who were able to say that they had been notified in advance. Even Democrats were pleased to report that the attack was a complete success and endorsed President Trump's first military operation with enthusiasm.

All the while the missiles were flying from destroyers in the Mediterranean to the air base in Syria, President Trump was in the middle of hosting a formal dinner with the Chinese President at Mar-a-Lago. It was Trump's first operation as Commander in Chief and he handled it like a pro. He wasn't afraid to take a measured risk and, once he made the call, left it up to the military to do their job.

The outside world had no inkling anything was going on. It looked like business as usual. Trump carried on with the meetings with the Chinese as if that were the only thing on his mind. So did his staff, those with him at Mar-a-Lago, and those of us back in the Situation Room.

For weeks afterward, he loved retelling the story of how he leaned over during the dessert course to tell Xi of the successful attack. Trump said the Chinese President looked stunned, sat completely still for a moment, and asked Trump, through his interpreter, to "please repeat" and then "repeat again." Trump went on to describe how he finished his "big, beautiful piece of delicious chocolate cake."

CHAPTER 11

Make Russia Great Again

I am a Cold Warrior, by education, training, experience, and commitment. I believe one of the greatest achievements in American diplomacy was our Cold War victory over the Soviet Union, which demonstrated to the world that democratic governments are superior to communist dictatorships and free market capitalism superior to a state-run command economy. Even sweeter is that we won this war not on a military battlefield, but in the battleground of ideas. Today, hundreds of millions of people are free because of our efforts. I was honored to have played a small part in helping bring it about, especially as a foot soldier in the "Reagan Revolution."

Today we view the Cold War as something that ended nearly thirty years ago. We believe we won it fair and square on the basis of our superior political and economic systems. Russian President Vladimir Putin thinks otherwise. He believes the West, especially the United States, tricked and cheated the Soviet Union and destroyed the Russian empire. He called the collapse of the Soviet Union the greatest geopolitical tragedy of the 20th century.

Vladimir Putin was born in 1952 in the war-torn city of Leningrad. As a young boy he watched his country struggle in the grim years after World War II, then slowly rebuild itself into a superpower, the greatest and most powerful communist country in the world. By the time he came of age in the 1970s, the Soviet Union was riding high—using windfall profits from selling oil and natural gas exports abroad to fund a military buildup, build a modern infrastructure, and expand its influence globally. At that point Putin could look forward to a long and successful career in the service of his nation as an ambitious young intelligence officer in the KGB, the Soviet spy agency. He was a true believer in Russia, the Soviet empire, and communism, in that order.

The beginning of the end of the Soviet Empire started in the early 1980s with the Solidarity movement in Poland. Anti-communist demonstrations encouraged by the West soon spread throughout Eastern Europe then the Berlin Wall came down in 1989, marking the end of the Communist Bloc. By late 1991, the Soviet Union itself fell apart. Suddenly, Russia went from a superpower and a military, ideological, and even an economic rival to the United States and the West, to a chaotic failure. The state-owned enterprises (which were the crown jewels of the nation) were de-nationalized and suddenly up for grabs. The institutions that had governed the Soviet Union and Warsaw Pact countries since the Russian Revolution disintegrated in a matter of months, leaving anarchy, corruption, and deprivation in their wake.

When the Soviet Union collapsed, seemingly overnight, Putin's dreams for the future—his own and his country's—collapsed with it. Ever since, Putin has made it his life's mission to rebuild Mother Russia's economy, government, and military in order to regain its superpower status. For the past three decades, he has pursued and consolidated his position as Russia's new Tsar. But Putin has been driven by more than just the quest for personal power. He sees himself as a great patriot who wants to Make Russia Great Again.

After the fall of the Soviet Union, Putin left the KGB and entered politics. He also went back to university and studied for a graduate degree at the St. Petersburg Mining Institute. In his 1997 dissertation, Putin laid out his blueprint for rehabilitating Russia. He recommended Russia do what had worked so successfully for it in the 1970s and 80s—export its abundant energy resources in order to accumulate great wealth for the state. Instead of investing in other parts of the economy, Putin argued that Russia should divert resources into rebuilding the energy sector. By creating state-owned enterprises, Moscow could bring the recently privatized oil and natural gas companies back under government control. He argued that Russia should build pipelines to Western Europe, and convince European countries and companies to substitute unreliable and expensive Arab oil with cheap and easily accessible Russian natural gas. Oil and gas prices might have been low in the 1990s when Putin devised his plan, but most experts at the time believed they would eventually rise again.

Energy prices are cyclical, depending on supply and demand. They rise, they fall, and they rise again. After reaching historic highs in the 1970s to early 1980s, oil prices fell in the late 1980s, which is one of the reasons the Soviet economy fell apart and the Soviet empire with it. Putin wanted to reposition the Russian energy industry so it was poised to reap the rewards when oil prices eventually rose again. Russia could use these new windfall profits to rebuild their society, their infrastructure, and armed forces. Russia would also gain the political leverage that came with being the main energy supplier to East, Central, and Western Europe. So, blueprint in hand, Putin quickly advanced to the top levels of the Russian government.

For years, Putin's plan succeeded. In the early years of the 21st century, oil prices began to rise, just as they had in the 1970s. Oil and gas profits soon poured into Russia, giving Putin the ability to centralize government, restore law and order, rebuild Russian society, rejuvenate their armed forces, and even create a large rainy-day reserve fund in case energy prices declined. Putin had Made Russia Great Again. But he also wanted to create a new Russian empire by bringing several former Soviet states back into the fold.

But just as victory was within his grasp, Putin's plan started unravelling. Young professionals in Moscow and St. Petersburg took to the streets between 2011 and 2013 to demonstrate against Putin's rule. The Ukrainian people rose up in early 2014 to topple their pro-Russian president and in February sent him packing to Moscow, in hopes of forging closer relations with the West. With lightning speed, the Russians sent special, unmarked forces into eastern Ukraine to stir up unrest along the Russian-Ukraine border. They also moved into and occupied Crimea. The Western powers, including the United States, were united in condemning Putin's actions and demanding that Russia leave Ukraine and Crimea. But their actions didn't match their words. The sanctions President Obama and the European governments imposed on Russia were mild. President

Obama refused to give Ukraine lethal weapons to fight the Russians. Even though the United States had potent economic weapons at our disposal, President Obama didn't use them against Russia.

I wrote an opinion piece for FOXnews.com at the time, fantasizing about an imaginary phone call between Obama and Putin. It was a tongue in cheek article, but I made the point that we should stand up to Putin, exploit our leverage over their markets, and give him a choice: He could stop interfering with the West, or we would crush Russia economically.[1]

Russia's great vulnerability then and now is that it is dependent on high oil prices to finance the government. Over half of Russia's exports come from oil and natural gas. They account for more than 30 percent of Russia's GDP, and 40 percent of government revenues. American break-throughs in fracking technology, combined with a decrease in worldwide demand, affected oil prices. They started falling and continued downward for two years, going from a peak of $115 per barrel in June 2014 to under $35 per barrel at the end of February 2016. The collapse of oil prices had a devastating effect on Russia. It forced a 50 percent devaluation in the ruble, and set off steep inflation. Government revenues fell sharply, forc-ing Russia to cut back on spending and to borrow abroad.

I attended a small luncheon in 2014 featuring remarks by the Rus-sian Ambassador to the United Nations. He railed on and on about the American interference in their affairs. He said the CIA was behind the Ukraine revolution. When several of us demurred, the Ambassador dis-missed our objections with the contemptuous wave of his hand. He said they even knew which Maidan Square hotel room the CIA used as their headquarters for stage-managing the anti-Russia demonstrations. He put the blame squarely on Secretary of State Clinton and several of her top aides who he claimed were in Kiev at the same, orchestrating efforts to tear Ukraine away from Russia.

Whether there was any truth to the Russian Ambassador's accusa-tions, I don't know. I was in Kiev later that spring with the Jamestown Foundation and met with several leaders of the Ukrainian revolution. They certainly didn't strike me as American intelligence operatives.

---

[1] McFarland, K.T. "How Obama could stop Putin's Ukraine power grab without firing a shot." FOX News. March 3, 2014. https://www.foxnews.com/opinion/how-obama-could-stop-putins-ukraine-power-grab-without-firing-a-shot.

But what matters in diplomacy is not what you believe about your country and theirs, or even what is true. It is what *they* believe.

Whatever Putin's intentions toward the United States might have been at the dawn of the 21st century, a decade or so later they took a decidedly anti-American turn. Putin blamed the United States for inciting the anti-Putin demonstrations. He blamed the United States for the anti-Russian revolution in Ukraine in 2014. Just as he had blamed the United States for the collapse of the Soviet Union a generation before, he now blamed us for interfering in their politics and thwarting Russia's rightful place in the world. Putin is now bent on revenge. He blames the United States for causing the collapse of the Soviet Union, and now wants to do the same back to us. By fanning the flames of our already adversarial politics, he hopes to drive us to the point of dysfunction.

Russia formally annexed Crimea at a signing ceremony at the Kremlin and Putin used the occasion to put on a show for his own people, and for the world. I've watched a video of the speech and, although I don't speak Russia, I have read the translated transcript. As hundreds of Russian officials sat quietly in their seats, looking straight ahead, the ornate gold doors at the back of the vast white hall opened and Vladimir Putin walked in. He strode past row after row of Russian officials and advanced to the podium bearing the double-headed eagle crest of the Russian empire. With Russian flags behind him, and crystal and gold chandeliers dating back to the days of the Tsars shining above him, Putin talked about the great Russian people, their shared history with Ukraine, and the valiant battles they fought together on the Black Sea and in Crimea. He then turned his remarks to modern times and raged against the West, especially the United States. He blamed the collapse of the Soviet Union on America, and claimed Russia had been robbed, tricked, and cheated ever since. He insisted that the West's goal was to contain the Russian motherland, and encircle it by expanding the anti-Russian NATO alliance to include countries which had once been part of the Soviet empire and sphere of influence.

The entire Russian leadership was in that room and as they cheered Putin on, a spontaneous rhythmic applause filled the room.

Putin seemed hungry for the world to accept the "New Russia," and recognize that he had Made Russia Great Again. But instead of basking in the glow of its restored superpower status, Russia was condemned by the world for Ukraine and Crimea, and forced to scramble to deal with budgetary shortfalls and a recession. Instead of the Sochi Winter Olympics being a dazzling showcase for the New Russia (*Novorossiya*), it was over budget at $50 billion and ridiculed for poorly constructed accommodations and facilities, and last-minute slapdash fixes. Instead of seeking an improvement in relations, as he did with Russian President Medvedev just a few years before, President Obama was now calling Russia a regional power and chiding Putin for being on the "wrong side of history."

Putin is a bully and, predictably, Obama's weak response on Ukraine and Crimea only emboldened him. We didn't realize it at the time, but Putin soon began mounting an assault on American democracy by meddling in our 2016 elections. Since then he has taken steps to sow even more discord in our already toxic political environment.[2]

As we look back over the last three years, it's difficult to draw any conclusion other than Putin's disinformation campaign in the United States is paying great dividends. Putin boasts that all the attention his country got during the 2016 presidential campaign and since is proof of "Russia's growing influence and significance." After the election, his efforts have borne even more fruit. The United States has spent nearly three years focused on Justice Department and Congressional investigations that grew out of Russia's election meddling. Putin's efforts to undermine American democracy may have done little to help Russia, but they have done enormous damage to the United States by casting doubt on our election process and stoking the fires of division.

One of the keys to understanding Trump is to watch what he does, not what he says. The irony of Trump's Russia policy is that despite his pro-Russia campaign rhetoric, and reluctance to criticize Putin, he has indeed imposed even more biting sanctions against Russia and some of its most powerful citizens than Obama did even in the closing days of his Administration. Trump's new sanctions have done significant damage to Russia's economy and banking system, and placed real impositions on some of Putin's closest cronies. According to an article in *Newsweek* in May 2018,

---

[2] Maza, Cristina. "U.S. May Give Ukraine More Lethal Weapons as Tensions Rise with Russia, Official Says." *Newsweek*. September 17, 2018. https://www.newsweek.com/us-may-give-ukraine-more-lethal-weapons-tensions-rise-russia-official-says-1125072.

Trump's decision to arm Ukraine with lethal weapons has caused problems for Russia's military.[3,4]

Putin's fierce anti-American rhetoric and actions are very popular with the Russian people, especially since his government controls the press. But the benefits of being anti-American in Moscow are nothing compared to the benefits of being anti-Trump and anti-Russian in Washington. The endless Congressional investigations are great for filling legislators' campaign coffers with cash. The media's anti-Trump hysteria is terrific for ratings. Reporters and columnists have become TV personalities by bashing Trump every day. They have fan clubs and get lucrative speaking gigs. Dozens of presidential hopefuls are running on an anti-Trump platform.

And being anti-Trump has become synonymous with being anti-Russian. The Washington ruling class still can't accept that Trump beat Hillary Clinton. Ever since the November 2016 election, they've floated dozens of theories of how the only reason Trump won was because the Russians intervened. Former Obama Administration officials, who give the impression that they have access to insider information, even claim that Trump is a Russian asset.

And then, when the Mueller investigation came up empty, everything went pouf! The endless rounds of Russia investigations have failed to show that Trump or his campaign colluded with the Russians. What they have found is how the Russians interfered with the 2016 election and continue to mount efforts, especially with social media, to subvert the American democratic process.

The Russia scare has so dominated our politics that today no American president or politician, Republican or Democrat, would dare seek an improvement of relations, even if Putin were to pivot, and cease and desist his efforts to wreak havoc on America's democratic process. If anything, the entire US-Russian relationship is likely to deteriorate even more in the years ahead, driving us further and further apart.

---

[3] Rogin, Josh. "Trump administration approves lethal arms sales to Ukraine." *The Washington Post.* December 20, 2017. https://www.washingtonpost.com/news/josh-rogin/wp/2017/12/20/trump-administration-approves-lethal-arms-sales-to-ukraine/?utm_term=.79a5b22c3e1a.

[4] Maza, Cristina. "Ukraine Tests Lethal Weapons Donald Trump Sent to Combat Russia." *Newsweek.* May 23, 2018. https://www.newsweek.com/ukraine-tests-lethal-weapons-donald-trump-sent-after-kiev-stopped-helping-941197.

The biggest tragedy is not just that we are now in a new Cold War with Russia, it is that we are pushing Russia into the arms of the Chinese, undoing fifty years of American national security policy. When the Communist revolutionaries seized control of China in 1949, the Soviet Union took the new government under its wing. They formed a close Sino-Soviet partnership, and the Soviet Union helped China become a nuclear weapons state. Individually both countries were hostile to the United States. When joined together, these two nuclear weapons nations posed an existential threat to us.

That's why the main goal of our national security policy for the last fifty years has been to separate the Chinese from the Russians, and to neutralize the threats to us by improving relations with each individually. In the 1970s Nixon and Kissinger were able to exploit the cracks developing between the two communist giants. Twenty years later, Reagan stressed the Soviet economy to the breaking point and the Soviet empire collapsed, thus neutralizing the one remaining nuclear superpower threat to the United States.

The American leaders who have come since, especially in the 21st century, have thrown all that away. They have failed to appreciate the threat posed by an increasingly aggressive, expansionist, mercantilist China, and the catastrophic effect a China-dominated world order will pose to the United States. These same leaders have seized on the specter of a menacing Russia to advance their own anti-Trump agenda. *But in so doing, they have unintentionally encouraged a new Sino-Russian entente, which will become increasingly anti-American in the years ahead.*

The anti-Trump establishment has done harm to our nation's security, although they are unlikely to acknowledge it. A new anti-American alliance between the two communist superpowers, with the economic domination of China and the military might of Russia, will present the United States with what could well be its greatest existential threat in the years ahead.

PART TWO

WASHINGTON

CHAPTER 12

The Trump Tower Transition

There has been considerable confusion and misunderstanding, and even some "fake news," about what happened during the Transition and early days of the Trump Administration. Trump's upset election was a shock to everyone, including the Trump campaign. The early days were chaotic, as campaign officials transformed into a government-in-waiting. It was filled with first-timers to government who inevitably made rookie mistakes.

But unlike most new presidents, Trump was cut no slack nor given a honeymoon period by the Washington Establishment. He was considered public enemy number one by many in the governing class and their allies in the liberal media who refused to accept that he had legitimately defeated their anointed candidate. Trump's personality added to the problem, especially over time. But from the very beginning, much of official and unofficial Washington was focused on removing him from office or at least preventing him from governing effectively.

I can't speak for everyone who was at Trump Tower in the early days. I was not among the five or six people in his inner circle who had been with him on the campaign. But I was one of the first people Trump appointed after the election and immediately became an integral part of what must surely be the most unique presidential Transition in modern American history.

I got to know Eric Trump during the campaign, so the day after the election I got in touch with him to pass along my congratulations. Like all the Trump children, Eric is in the real estate business. He works constantly and hard, is unfailingly polite and earnest, and is an integral part of a close-knit family. His role in the Trump Organization is to develop, build, and operate resorts and golf courses around the world, especially in Scotland, where my husband and I spend considerable time. I knew from our Scottish friends in real estate and construction that he is well regarded there, especially by the people who work for him. Scots don't hand out compliments or praise gratuitously. So, I was intrigued when I met Eric in a FOX News green room in early 2016, when we were both waiting to go on the air.

Each of us had some time between interviews (called "hits" in the TV business) so we talked about his father's foreign policy positions. I said I admired Trump for what he was saying on the campaign trail, especially his willingness to deviate from the Republican party line and criticize Bush as well as Obama. The thing that impressed me the most, though, was Trump's stance on China. Critics had dismissed Trump as having a China obsession. I told Eric that his father was the only candidate who seemed to understand that the main strategic, long-term threat we face isn't from terrorists, or the Middle East, or even Russia, but China. For decades we have helped China's rise, often at the expense of our own trade and industries. But if China someday replaces us as the world's dominant economy and most powerful nation, the Chinese will be in a position to rewrite the international rules of order to suit their own interests, regardless of and at the expense of our own. Were that to happen, America's days as the world's greatest power would be numbered, and our relative decline all but inevitable. It would also spell the decline of the U.S.-created liberal world order, and the rise of China's system of authoritarian government and state capitalism. Eric and I agreed to meet again and continue the conversation.

We had lunch a few weeks after we met. As we talked, I added depth and context to the positions that Trump seemed to arrive at instinctively. I explained how Trump's proposals were not in lockstep with the neoconservative war hawks who had come to dominate the Republican Party and predicted their criticisms would be harsh and relentless if his campaign got traction. But it was Trump's fearlessness in calling out NATO for their comparatively paltry contributions to our common defense and China for their intellectual property theft and unfair trade practices that would anger establishment Republicans even more. I did most of the talking, Eric most of the listening. Though national security issues were not something he had thought about in any detail before the campaign, Eric, like his father, has great instincts. Eric immediately grasped the larger points I made about the need to right the economy and rebuild the military. I said the time had come to address the inequitable trade and security relationships with our allies and competitors if we were going return the United States to economic growth and retain our world leadership position.

Eric and I stayed in touch off and on, and I continued to watch his father's campaign from afar. In the fall of 2016, I joined Trump's National Security Advisory Committee. Senator Jeff Sessions recruited me to help Trump prepare for two debates, and to look over one or two of his foreign policy speeches. I had also been interviewed by Trump's presidential personnel team over the summer, so knew that if lightning struck and Trump were to win, I was already in the mix for a top job, either at the United Nations or National Security Council.[1]

But I didn't give it much thought. I, like everybody else, assumed Hillary Clinton would be our next president. My only hope was that Trump might be able to make a clear break with the failed foreign policies of the last two decades. Then maybe next time around a Republican could win and finally return us to Reagan's Peace through Strength.

I got in touch with Eric right after the election and asked to be considered for a post in the Trump Administration. A week after Trump's victory, Eric invited me to come to their offices at Trump Tower. Sitting at the heart of Fifth Avenue, next to Tiffany's, across from the legendary Plaza Hotel, and diagonally across from Central Park, Trump Tower is one of the most famous buildings in Midtown Manhattan. Everything about it screams glitz and glamour—the restaurants in the basement, the high-end luxury shops on the first two floors, and the offices in the

---

[1] Balz, Dan. "'It went off the rails almost immediately': How Trump's messy transition led to a chaotic presidency." *The Washington Post.* April 4, 2017. https://www.washingtonpost.com/politics/it-went-off-the-rails-almost-immediately-how-trumps-messy-transition-led-to-a-chaotic-presidency/2017/04/03/170ec2e8-0a96-11e7-b77c-0047d15a24e0_story.html?utm_term=.7e516fd0dc13.

fifty-some floors above. Even the condominium apartments at the back of the building are exclusive and very expensive.

The lobby takes up the entire footprint of the building, and the ceiling extends at least three stories high. Everything is glossy marble—marble floors and marble walls—in shades of bronze, beige, and tan that blend together to make one continuous stretch of highly polished, gleaming surfaces. And what isn't marble is gold leaf. Along one wall sits a bank of elevators and a concierge desk—all with shining, golden-brass surfaces. In the middle of the vast lobby is a bank of open-sided escalators—also covered in golden-brass—taking people from one razzle-dazzle floor to another. Trump's penthouse apartment is even more ornate, with delicate gold-leaf painted on the extensive moldings, the antique French furniture, and sparking crystal chandeliers. The Trumps live and work in a building wrapped in over-the-top luxury.

After finishing for the day at FOX News, I walked the several blocks to Trump Tower. It was a dark and rainy night so walking into the sparkle of the Trump Tower lobby was a bit blinding at first. I went through the newly installed security checkpoints and was escorted straight up to the Trump Organization's suite on the 26th floor. Eric welcomed me into his small office and called in Reince Priebus to join us. Several people had already been named for key White House positions, including Priebus, Steve Bannon, and Jared Kushner, although their duties were still vague. General Mike Flynn, who had been Trump's main foreign policy aide during the campaign, was tapped as National Security Advisor. Priebus told me I was on the short list to be United Nations Ambassador or Deputy National Security Advisor.

As we began talking, I realized they knew very little about how the White House actually worked. I started giving them a primer on the Executive Office of the President and the White House staff. I was in the middle of explaining what the National Security Advisor did when we got the call that Trump was ready to see me.

The three of us walked down the short hallway and into Trump's corner office. The president-elect was on the phone but waved us over to sit in the chairs facing his desk. While he cradled the phone under his chin, I looked beyond him to the floor-to-ceiling glass walls, with their jaw dropping nighttime view of Central Park and Fifth Avenue. The other two walls were covered with photos, mementos, and over a dozen framed magazine covers, all featuring Trump. More pictures were leaning up against walls and lying on the floor. Compared to offices of other Manhattan powerbrokers, Trump's was surprisingly small and very cluttered.

Trump sat behind a large desk, his back to the windows, with papers, books, and a large multi-line business phone covering most of it. Eric and Reince pulled chairs from the small table at the other end of the office—which was also stacked high with books and papers—over to Trump's desk. This was the working office of a busy corporate executive, not a tidy ceremonial office of a government official.

Trump finished his phone call and turned to ask me a few questions about myself and my background, but he did most of the talking. He wanted a strong military. He wanted to renegotiate Obama's bad deals. He criticized President George W. Bush and the neocons. He complimented me for being one of his early supporters and quoted back to me from memory what I had said about him on FOX News—about his being right on key national security issues over the years—the futility of the Iraq and Afghan wars, the flawed Iran nuclear deal, and NATO members not paying their fair share. Trump said he had talked to Henry Kissinger, my old boss and mentor, who spoke highly of me and recommended Trump bring me into his Administration.

Trump finished up by saying he was considering me for several positions and asked if I had any preferences. I said I would be honored to serve in any capacity but thought I would be a good fit at the United Nations or National Security Council. After a few minutes, it was clear Trump was bored and tired, so I thanked him for considering me. Trump said he'd let me know soon.

Eric, Reince, and I walked back to Eric's office to go over the specifics of the jobs they were considering me for, and to talk generally about Trump's goals for the new Administration. It was clear that, while this handful of people had just pulled off one of the greatest upsets in American electoral history, they had very little idea of what was supposed to happen next, beyond interviewing and hiring people for top positions. They seemed unfamiliar with the different roles and responsibilities of people on the White House staff, especially the workings of the National Security Council.

I was flabbergasted. The entire Trump team was maybe three dozen people, including the interns. This was not only going to be a totally different presidential Transition, they were unlikely to get everything done they needed to before Inauguration day. Most presidents come into office with a large entourage of assistants and advisors, and an even larger pool of people who had been affiliated with the campaign as aides, donors, or political allies. Most presidential candidates have dozens of advisory committees on a range of issues, and hundreds of people who all expect jobs in the new Administration. They're almost all from Washington, and they're veterans at understanding how the system works.

Many have lifelong relationships with journalists, bureaucrats, and policy experts. They're part of a presidential package deal, with the president at the top and a legion of advisors primed to take positions in the White House or fan out to the Executive Branch for senior positions in the departments and agencies. They have an intimate understanding of the power structures at the White House and Cabinet departments. They know the difference in pecking order between an Assistant to the President, Deputy Assistant to the President, and Special Assistant to the President, and who is responsible for what and which perks and privileges come with the different jobs. They even know who rates reserved parking spaces, car service and White House Mess privileges. They've been working their way up the political appointees' food chain for decades and know everybody else who has been doing the same. Hillary Clinton had hundreds of people who had been on dozens of her advisory committees, who expected to fill the some four thousand jobs set aside for political appointees. Republicans have their people; Democrats have theirs. They consider themselves part of the governing class who move in and out of government, depending on which party holds the White House.

The incoming Trump Administration couldn't have been more different. This was the first political campaign for many, from the most senior advisors down to the most junior interns. This was also the first Transition any of them had been part of. Very few had ever worked in the White House or even in the departments and agencies that make up the Executive Branch. As far as I could tell, no one had ever worked in the West Wing before. In fact, most of them had never lived or worked in Washington at all. I hadn't stepped foot in the West Wing since the Reagan Administration, but I was as good as they were likely to get to give them the White House 101 briefing. I leaned across Priebus's desk, borrowed his yellow legal pad, and from memory sketched a floor plan of the West

Wing, marking what senior officials sat in which offices and what their responsibilities were.

I pointed out that the White House Mess and Situation Room were across from each other in the West Basement. I mapped out the first floor, with the Oval Office, and the Chief of Staff, National Security Advisor, and Press Secretary's suites in the four corners. The vice president's suite was between the Chief of Staff and the National Security Advisor; the Cabinet Room between the Oval Office and the Press Secretary. In the middle was the West Lobby which opened out to the West Lawn on one side and into the Roosevelt Room on the other. A narrow staircase connected the basement, first and second floors, where the White House Legal Counsel, and several economic, and domestic policy advisors had offices. I noted that it is actually rather a small space, although it always seems bigger in movies and television shows. As I continued to fill in the boxes, it suddenly dawned on me—not only had no one on the incoming team ever worked in the West Wing, it was unlikely any of them had even stepped foot in the White House.

Priebus seemed interested, so I kept going. I described the traditional functions of the different officials. I didn't think any of them, including Trump and perhaps even Flynn, knew what the National Security Advisor did beyond serving as the president's foreign policy staff aide—a personal assistant to prepare him for meetings, brief him on key issues as they arose, and help with speeches and press interviews. In other words, the same sort of things Flynn had been doing on the campaign trail.

I explained the National Security Advisor and the National Security Council (NSC) had two major roles: the most obvious one was to inform the President on the foreign policy, intelligence, and defense issues of the day; prepare him for meetings and phone calls with foreign leaders; join him for all relevant briefings; and take the lead in managing crises. But the NSC had a second role which was less obvious, but of greater consequence: as manager of the interagency foreign policymaking process.

Kissinger set up the NSC interagency management system in 1969, at the beginning of the Nixon Administration, in order to bring all the various foreign policy, defense, and intelligence communities in government together in one place and under direct White House control. Several times a week the National Security Advisor (NSA), or Deputy National Security Advisor (DNSA) convened meetings in the Situation Room, with Cabinet or sub-Cabinet officials of the State, Defense, Homeland Security, Justice, and Treasury departments, as well as the military and intelligence agencies and any other government entity that had a stake in the issue. The most senior national security officials of government sat around a conference table for several hours, presenting their agencies' positions and then thrashing out the pros and cons of each. The NSC was in the lead—it called the meetings, set the agendas and chaired the sessions. The National Security Advisor, with the help of the NSC staff, wrote the final report, which made recommendations to the President for his decision. Every Administration since Nixon's had followed Kissinger's organization chart. It put the responsibility for running the entire policy and decision-making process into the hands of the National Security Advisor and his Deputy.

I wasn't providing any particularly brilliant insights, but it was all new to Priebus and the one or two others who had since joined us, including Flynn. They may have just won the presidency, but they knew very little about actual governing. They had a lot of ground to cover in a short period of time in order to be ready to take over the reins of government in just two months' time. What worried me most was that none of them fully appreciated, or had even thought about, how difficult this was all going to be, and how many headwinds they would face, from all directions.

My first choice was not Deputy National Security Advisor. I didn't feel the allure of working in the White House that others might. I had worked in the West Wing for seven years in the Nixon and Ford Administrations, during an era of political upheaval as well as a golden age of American diplomacy. It was unlikely to get better than that. It would also require moving from New York to Washington, which meant dislocating my family. The NSC job would demand long hours and offer little recognition. It was a Washington insider's job, powerful inside the Beltway, but unknown anywhere else—the ultimate thankless task sort of job.

But as much as I wanted the prestige of an Ambassadorship, and the bright lights of the UN job, I realized that I would be far more useful to my country at the National Security Council, if that job were offered. If I really believed in the mission, more than my own ego and comfort, I could make a real difference in the White House, especially in the early days as the new people, including the new president, were getting their moorings. I knew Trump would have a hard time succeeding unless his people could quickly get control of the vast national security apparatus of government. If I was committed to the Trump Revolution, what was best for me should come in second place to what was best for the cause and the country.

In any event, it was a moot point. President-elect Trump offered the UN job to South Carolina Governor Nikki Haley and the Deputy National Security Advisor's job to me. Nikki Haley was a rising star in the Republican Party and they wanted to give her foreign policy experience to help in her bid someday for higher office. To her credit, Ambassador Haley did very well at the United Nations and was fearless in her defense of America's interests. Good for Donald Trump to recognize her potential.

I had known my soon-to-be-boss for about two years. He had been a guest on my FOXNews.com national security show, *DEFCON3*, several times in 2015 after he left the Defense Intelligence Agency, and again in 2016 when his book, *Field of Fight*, came out. Flynn was one of the first to recognize the value of both social media and on the ground information in intelligence gathering, and used them to great success in the Iraq and Afghan wars. It also made him controversial because he took on an entrenched intelligence bureaucracy to do it. What got him fired, though, was his outspoken criticism of the Obama Administration's claim that Al-Qaeda was on the ropes after Bin Laden was killed.

Flynn and I kept in touch off and on for the next two years, seeing each other at conferences and occasionally exchanging thoughts on national security issues. Flynn was one of the first people on Trump's campaign team and among his earliest appointments. As National Security Advisor, Flynn would be right down the hall from the Oval Office, and continue to serve as Trump's closest foreign policy, defense, and intelligence aide.

Flynn and I agreed we could work together well at the NSC, and our skill sets complemented each other's. Flynn was part of Trump's inner circle; I had met with Trump only twice. Flynn lacked White House experience; I knew how the national security government apparatus worked both from inside the West Wing and outside from a Cabinet department. Flynn was a Middle East expert, had been on the battlefield during war, and had also run a large government agency. My area of focus had been primarily Asia and nuclear weapons. I knew the media from my years at FOX News as a commentator, anchor, and columnist. Flynn's background was in military intelligence; mine was in geopolitics. Plus, he was amiable and, unlike a lot of generals, wasn't rank conscious. I thought we would make for good colleagues should I be offered the NSC Deputy's position.

I hadn't heard anything official from the Transition team by the time I joined my family in Long Island for Thanksgiving. So, I put it out of my head for a few days, switched my cell phone to voicemail and enjoyed the holiday. Our children and grandchildren had come from all around the country for a big family Thanksgiving dinner. Afterward, I snuggled with my five grandchildren in the living room, in front of a roaring fire, while we watched a rerun of the family movie classic, *Mrs. Doubtfire*.

Later that evening, I turned on my cell phone and saw there was a voice message from a number I didn't recognize in Palm Beach. It was Donald Trump offering me the Deputy National Security Advisor's position. So, I left my family to finish the vacation without me and the next day traveled to Washington to meet with Flynn and whatever staff there was at the Transition office.

Two days later I arrived at the nondescript entrance of a nondescript government office building a few blocks from the White House. I'm not sure what I expected, but it was nothing like what I found. The Transition headquarters was a gigantic, aging six-story Government Services Agency (GSA) office building that spanned an entire city block. It was boring gray stone on the outside, but the interior had been recently gutted and renovated. It now had a contemporary feel with a huge open floor space, and row after row of work stations, each with twenty or more desk cubicles. There were large and small glass-enclosed conference rooms and kitchens at both ends of each floor. Sections of floorspace were earmarked for each of the dozens of government departments and agencies which make up the Executive Branch of government. Some of the cubicles in each section had been reserved for the top officials and their aides. For example, the Secretary of State's desk was flanked by a dozen or so desks for the Deputy Secretary, Assistant Secretaries, Undersecretaries and so forth. It looked like the world's biggest call center, with room for thousands of people. And it was practically empty. Other than the security guards at the front door of the building, it was a virtual ghost town.

All I could think of was that this had been built to house the incoming Hillary Clinton Administration. Even the suite of offices set aside for the President's spouse had a decidedly masculine décor—the perfect setting for the incoming First Gentleman, Bill Clinton.

If she had won, these desks would have been filled the very next day, with the hundreds, perhaps even thousands, of people who had already been tapped for jobs in the Hillary Clinton Administration. The Transition from Obama to Clinton would have been seamless.

I wondered what had become of all those people who expected to be sitting at these desks, from Cabinet secretaries on down to interns. They were probably scattered all around Washington in their houses and apartments, still in shock. Many were no doubt bitter and resentful, feeling they had been "robbed" of the positions they had assumed to be rightfully theirs. No one, including the Trump people themselves, really expected that they would be the ones walking into the Washington Transition headquarters after the election.

I wandered around alone, past row upon row of empty desks, looking for the section that was reserved for the National Security Council. I found about a dozen or so people scurrying about in one corner of the third floor. I knew many of them, either personally or by reputation. They had come from the private sector, conservative-leaning thinktanks, or Congressional staffs, all volunteers hoping to join the new Administration. But they had no connection to Trump himself or the small cadre of people who had been at Trump Tower during the campaign and remained there after the election. Through no fault of their own they were operating in a vacuum, without much direction from anyone.

The real power center was in New York, housed in a small suite of offices on the 26th floor of Trump Tower. It's where Trump had presided over the Trump Organization for decades, and where he vowed to remain until the Inauguration. All the decisions, on issues both large and small, were made at Trump Tower, usually by Trump himself. It didn't matter that the government-provided official Transition headquarters was a few blocks from the White House. Trump was at Trump Tower, and that was all that counted. That's where the action was. If Trump was going to stay in Manhattan until the Inauguration, so would his top aides. He was the Sun King and all the courtiers wanted to be near him.

There was a daily parade of assorted people who made the trip to Trump Tower—job seekers, former candidates, people offering advice, old friends, well-wishers, and even former enemies—all to kiss the ring of the man who had unexpectedly just become the most powerful man in the world. He took all his calls at his office desk or in his penthouse apartment, whether it was with a foreign leader, a media mogul, or one of his golfing buddies. That's where he interviewed people, discussed their pros and cons with his friends and staff, and made the final job offers. The choices made during the Transition, especially selecting people for key national security positions, were being made in New York. As long as Flynn and I remained in Washington, it would be done without our input. While Flynn wanted to shift his focus from Trump Tower to Washington and begin setting up the NSC, it was clear one of us needed to be in New York. Since my family's apartment is a few blocks away from Trump Tower, we agreed I would stay in New York and Flynn would spend most of his time in Washington, which is where he lived.

I immediately turned around and left Washington for New York, arriving at the Trump Tower Transition office on the 14th floor, twelve floors below Trump's suite. It was not remotely like the official Transition headquarters in D.C. There were no guards at the door, nobody checking to see who was walking in, who had badges, or who had appointments (many visitors did not). The entire space of the New York office could have fit into one quarter of one floor of the D.C. office building. It consisted of one large and three small glass conference rooms, a dozen 10×10 offices, most of which had glass doors, and a large open bullpen with maybe three dozen metal desks and chairs. The only thing that looked remotely official was a wall of large flat screen TVs, each tuned to a different channel. Otherwise, the walls were bare. The whole place wasn't much larger than a medium sized medical clinic. Still, it was on the 14th floor of Trump Tower, one of the most luxurious of Manhattan's luxury office buildings, and had sweeping views of Fifth Avenue.

Small as it was, there were still a lot of empty offices and desks; with maybe twenty people of all ages milling around. It started filling up after Christmas and as we got closer to the January 20th Inauguration day. But even so, there were rarely more than forty people there at any one time, ranging from Chief of Staff Reince Priebus to the interns who sometimes answered the phones and otherwise drove the grown-ups around in a beat-up minivan. That was it.

I staked out one of the small glass conference rooms on the 14th floor and taped a large handwritten sign on the door that read "National Security Council." There was one long conference table with some faux leather chairs on wheels. I grabbed two otherwise underemployed interns who were hanging around the bullpen to help with anything that came up. They found some phones, plugged them in, put a dry erase board on the wall, and scrounged for some supplies. At least I now had someone to answer the constantly ringing phones.

My older daughter, Fiona McFarland, who was finishing up a month's vacation after leaving active duty as a Navy lieutenant and before joining McKinsey & Co, realized I was overwhelmed and said what I needed immediately was a military officer capable of organizing and standing up an operation. She offered to help out for a few days by putting together spreadsheets of duties, responsibilities, and schedules, and answered the backlog of several hundred congratulatory emails, letters, and calls from friends and strangers alike. In true Navy fashion, she had us up and running in a day. Before Fiona left for the business world a week later, she had arranged for her friend and colleague Lieutenant Commander Sarah Flaherty, a Navy helicopter pilot turned public affairs officer, to be temporarily assigned to me for the Transition. Flaherty is one of those people who can size up a situation, figure out what is needed, and then do it successfully, no matter what it is—everything from drafting crucial policy papers to mollifying snarky reporters, to briefing the president. She found some American and military standing flags for the elevator lobby and rounded up a few stray interns to man the doors and check IDs. She took over the spreadsheets, schedules, and was the point of contact with the D.C. Transition team.

We joked that it was like a tech start-up and we weren't far off the mark. I made sure one of us arrived at the office early, before anyone else, to guarantee the conference room remained ours. Others, including some of the senior staff, were still taking turns sitting on one of the two sofas in the lobby or looking for unclaimed desks when they weren't with Trump. Having a designated office space with people who were busy gave our NSC operation instant credibility. It was also a place to meet with people who dropped by on their way to and from Trump's office, everyone from former Secretary of Defense Robert Gates to football legend Jim Brown. Once we had secured NSC office space, I set about trying to get the lay of the land.

Trump's own office suite, on the 26th floor, was the nerve center not only of the Trump Organization but also the Trump Transition. A receptionist behind a small desk greeted people when they walked off the elevator and through the glass doors to the Trump Organization. There was no spacious lobby with plush leather sofas and chairs, just a narrow banquette that ran along the glass wall. Once that was filled, people stood, leaning against the walls of the narrow hallways. It was like the cramped waiting room of a doctor's office. Sometimes VIPs would wait on the banquette for thirty minutes, or even an hour, until Trump's long-time assistant, Keith Schiller, ushered them a few feet along the hallway into Trump's office. Others were whisked right in. There was no apparent schedule or agenda. Guests drifted in and out of the suite, and staff walked in and out of Trump's office. There were floor-to-ceiling glass windows along one wall, just as in Trump's office, with a spectacular panorama of iconic Manhattan landmarks. But everyone ignored the view, preferring to take stock of who was in the waiting room and speculating to themselves why.

Trump's door was rarely closed, and he would occasionally bellow out to his other longtime assistant, Rhona Graff, to get someone on the phone. His meetings were free flowing: one minute Trump would pepper his guests with questions, the next minute he ignored them and took a call, while they listened to every word. Occasionally, Trump would pull out his cell phone, type out a tweet, and press send—sharing what was on his mind at that moment with his millions of followers. Everything was in constant, energetic motion. To me it seemed chaotic, but to the people who had been around Trump for years, it was standard operating procedure. It was a security officer's nightmare.

The senior staff—just a handful of people including Reince Priebus, Steve Bannon, Jared Kushner, and General Flynn—if he was in New York—as well as a few others continued to operate the way they had during the campaign. They had the small offices on the 14th floor but were rarely there, preferring to stay on 26th floor with Trump throughout the day. They sat in on his meetings, were there for his phone calls, and managed the day-to-day scheduling, press queries, and personnel issues. They rarely left his side.

After a few days it was clear that I was a one-off at Trump Tower. I hadn't worked on the campaign as had everyone else. While I was respected for my background and experience, I didn't have the close personal relationships with Trump and the senior staff that had been forged on the campaign trail. So, we decided Flynn would travel back and forth between the two Transition offices. He would be in Washington to set up the NSC staff and come to New York and be with Trump for the important meetings. I would run the day-to-day activities in New York. We made sure one of us was always on hand with President-elect Trump.

By the time I arrived at Trump Tower, three weeks after the election, Trump had already received a number of congratulatory phone calls from foreign leaders. In a normal Transition, there is a strict protocol for which calls to take, and in what order. Allies first, followed by important countries, and so forth down the list. Each call is proceeded by staff briefings, outlining what the foreign leader is likely to say, and what the president-elect's response should be. The president-elect doesn't pick up the phone until the other leader is already on the line as a sign of respect. There are notetakers with him in the room or listening in from another room. Records are kept, transcripts written, and points for follow-up noted.

Not Trump. There was no protocol officer whispering in his ear, no talking points he was supposed to follow. He took the foreign leader congratulatory calls the same way he might have taken calls from business buddies congratulating him for closing a deal. He returned the calls in the order received. Occasionally he was put on hold while the foreign leader took his time picking up. Sometimes an aide was in the room with him and took notes, but not always. He was respectful of time zone differences, so he sometimes returned calls early in the morning or late at night from his apartment. Even in something as relatively insignificant as taking congratulatory calls from foreign leaders, it was clear that Trump would be his own man and make his own rules.

During one of my first meetings with Trump, he described what happened on election night. He and his family had stayed at the election night headquarters at the New York Hilton well past midnight waiting for the final results, and he didn't give his victory speech until about three o'clock Wednesday morning. By the time he arrived back at his Trump Tower apartment an hour or so later, it was midday in Tokyo. Japanese Prime Minister Abe was on the phone, the first leader to congratulate the new president-elect. The Prime Minister told Trump he very much looked forward to meeting him and his family and working with him. Trump said, "I'd like that too. If you're in New York, be sure to stop by Trump Tower." Trump chuckled when he related the story, saying Abe put his assistant on the next plane; the assistant then showed up at Trump Tower to organize the meeting between the two leaders.

A week after the election Prime Minister Abe himself was at Trump Tower, where he presented Trump with a very fancy, anti-slice golf club, since they are both avid golfers. Trump thanked him and said he would use the driver the next time he played at Mar-a-Lago. He then spontaneously invited Abe and his family to visit him there after the Inauguration. They could get to know each other and play some golf. Abe was thrilled, and the "Mar-a-Lago Summit" was scheduled for early February. Abe brought his clubs, and Trump arranged for some of the best pros in the world to make up their daily foursome.

It was vintage Trump. No briefing papers, no agenda, and no agreements. Just two leaders feeling each other out. The State Department was probably apoplectic. But it paid dividends. The friendship between the two men is genuine. They were able to forge a bond from the beginning, seeing eye to eye on a number of key issues, especially how to deal with China's increasing aggressiveness on trade and their militarization of the South China Sea.

After Trump told that story, I realized somebody needed to listen in to those calls with foreign leaders and take notes. I sat in his outer office, where several of his assistants had desks, and listened in on the mute key. The calls took a fairly standard course: the foreign leader would offer congratulations. Trump would say it was a historic, unprecedented victory that took everyone by surprise. After a few pleasantries, Trump usually asked about their economy and our trade relationship. Sensing an opening, a few of the leaders went through a list of what they wanted from the new Administration, hoping to get some sort of commitment from Trump. He made no promises, but inevitably ended each call with, "Stop by Trump Tower if you're in New York, or in Washington after the Inauguration. I'd love to show you around." The foreign leader was thrilled, thinking he had just received a personal invitation to visit the man the whole world wanted to meet, not realizing this was Trump's standard goodbye signoff, his equivalent of a New Yorker saying, "Let's do lunch sometime."

One of the things I had to do was field the inevitable follow-up call from the foreign leader's aide, who wanted to set a date as soon as possible for the visit Trump had just promised his boss.

During the Trump Tower Transition, I had a chance to talk to several of his longtime aides and assistants. Since I was recognized as one of the only people who knew how the White House worked, I was often asked for guidance by people who had been on the campaign or were now on the Transition but hadn't yet landed a position in the Trump Administration. One of the more memorable conversations I had was with Michael Cohen. I had seen him around Trump Tower but had no idea how he fit into the Trump operation, so I wasn't sure what to think when he asked me to come up to his office. He was on the 26th floor, in the Trump Organization's suite, just down the hall from Trump's office. Like everyone else's, Cohen's office was small, with just enough room for a desk and chair, and two guest chairs facing him.

He began by explaining that Trump told him he could have whatever job he wanted. But he wasn't sure what he should ask for, and hoped I could give him some ideas. I said that a president has lots of lawyers, but all with specific functions. There is the White House Legal Counsel, who works for the Office of the President; in other words his responsibility is to the institution of the presidency rather than the president personally. That office has over a hundred lawyers who work on everything from legislation to treaties to personnel issues.

I said the Attorney General is a lawyer too, but his job description is to be the chief law enforcement officer of government. He runs the Justice Department, which is responsible for the nation's legal affairs, the network of U.S. attorneys all across the country, and oversees the FBI.

Neither of those seemed like a good fit so I asked Cohen what he did now. He answered that he was Trump's lawyer. "I've been with him for years. I'm his personal lawyer." I asked him to elaborate. Did he work on Trump's taxes, or business contracts, or his real estate empire? "I'm involved in everything," Cohen answered. "I'm the guy who fixes his problems."

I tried to explain that most presidents do have personal lawyers, but they are not part of government. They are paid for by the president personally, out of his own pocket, and their one concern is looking after the interests of the president himself. I suggested that perhaps the best way for Cohen to continue working for Trump in the way he had was to stay out of Washington and remain at the Trump Organization. I don't think it was the answer he wanted to hear but Cohen said, "Yeah, you're probably right."

The most important thing I picked up from Trump's longtime aides was that he had his own unique, decidedly non-corporate management style. Apparently, the Trump Transition was operating much the same way the Trump Organization operated, where every morning Donald Trump would arrive at the office and call in his top assistants and family members for a staff meeting. There was no pre-set agenda. Trump would go around the room asking each one, "What's up today? What's going on?" They would discuss ongoing projects, ideas for future projects, and whatever problems had landed in that day's inbox. Trump would interject his own ideas, things he had been thinking about, things he had heard from the people he'd seen or spoken to, watched on cable news or read in the papers. As the day went on, Trump would have meetings, talk on the phone, and meet with a very wide circle of friends and acquaintances with whom he touched base regularly—billionaire buddies, business associates, family members, even the guys who operated the elevator or parked his car. His top aides and family had offices in the suite and all day long walked in and out of his office, getting his advice and constantly keeping him in the loop of what they were doing.

That's also how he operated when he first moved the entourage to Washington and into the White House. People walked into the Oval Office unannounced. If there was a schedule, Trump rarely stuck to it. Some meetings went on longer than expected, some were shorter. Trump made and received calls during meetings and throughout the day. Everything was fluid. Almost nobody kept a record of who was in what meeting, or what they talked about, or what papers were finding their way to Trump's desk. It was an archivist's nightmare.

The other thing I learned was that at one time or another, everyone did time in what I called Trump's "penalty box," when a person was singled out for punishment. It was like the penalty box in hockey—you're punished with a time-out, and when it's over you go back on the ice and resume play. Sometimes you were penalized because you screwed up, or didn't do what Trump wanted you to do, or got out in front of his decision. Sometimes it was because you got caught up in negative press stories which reflected badly on Trump or, worst of all, if you got positive press, but at Trump's expense.

The only warning you had that it was your turn in the penalty box was when Trump crossed his arms across his chest and glared at you. If you tried to say something, he looked right through you and ignored what you were saying. Then he'd turn to someone else in the room and ask him a question or say something flattering to him. When you were in the penalty box you were frozen off the ice, like you didn't exist. With few exceptions, nobody stayed in the penalty box for long. A day or two later Trump seemed to forget all about it, and it was someone else's turn to squirm. It was almost impossible to avoid the penalty box—everyone was there at one time or another, although some people were there more often. The key to surviving it was to keep your head down and stay quiet until he moved on. But the point was clear—he was the boss, and you were there only as long as he wanted you to be.

A large amount of the president-elect's time during the Transition was devoted to interviewing and choosing people for the key Cabinet positions. Trump wasn't like most presidential candidates who start the hiring process months before the election so they can be ready immediately if they win. When Trump was told the 2012 Romney campaign had binders full of candidates, who had all been interviewed and vetted well before the November election, Trump joked, "Yeah, but he forgot one thing—he had to win first."

Some said he refused to consider personnel issues because he was superstitious. Others claimed he didn't want to get ahead of himself. There was also a dose of practicality about it—Trump saw no need to devote and divert a lot of time and effort to choosing people for the Trump Administration until he knew there was going to be a Trump Administration. He would concentrate on winning, and then deal with it if he won. Until then, Governor Chris Christie would run Trump's Transition operation, presumably as a consolation prize for being passed over for vice president. Christie spent the summer months before the election vetting and assembling a list of candidates for the senior positions should Trump win. I never saw Christie's plan, but those who did said it was comprehensive, with a timeline of actions and decision points.

Complicating matters even more was the fact that by election time, Christie was on the outs with some of Trump's senior aides, especially the Trump family and Flynn. According to Flynn, "Christie took care of himself and his cronies, but that was about it." Flynn told me that when the Trump team met the day after the election to look over Christie's recommendations, they were so unhappy they tossed the plan in the trash. I never figured out why, but there had been bad blood between Flynn and Christie during the campaign, which broke out into the open after the election.

One of the great handicaps of the incoming Trump Administration was their having to start the hiring process all over again, once Christie's work was rejected. Any new Administration has thousands of positions to fill, not just the Cabinet secretaries and top jobs in the White House, but throughout the Executive Branch. It is important to fill them quickly with people supportive of the new president's agenda, who are already vetted and prepared to assume their responsibilities on day one. Because Trump's Transition was starting from zero, we were at a disadvantage from the very beginning.

Vice President-elect Pence was named chairman of the Transition, with Christie, Flynn, and several others as vice chairmen. The Transition was expanded within the next few days to include additional vice chairmen, myself included. Trump and his senior staff may not have had a sense of how government worked, but Trump knew how to hire and fire people, and create drama throughout the process. In the end, Trump got the hiring process he probably wanted all along; he was totally in charge.

Trump was his own one-man headhunting agency. He came up with his own suggestions, often getting recommendations from his friends, and conducted interviews for the top jobs himself. It was all done in a very public way by having the candidates come to Trump Tower and parade past a gaggle of cameramen and reporters who stood behind a velvet roped barricade right across from the elevators.

After going through the security checkpoint, anyone heading upstairs for an appointment approached the well-dressed concierge stationed in front of the elevators, who checked that they were on the approved list, and called upstairs for an escort to come down to the lobby. In the meantime, the cameras clicked away, and reporters shouted questions at the person standing awkwardly waiting to be met by someone from Trump's office. Twitter lit up with every senior person who walked through the lobby, reporters and pundits speculating on who was ahead or behind in the Cabinet officer sweepstakes. It was a constant parade of the most prominent, well known people in the country.

Trump chuckled that everyone who wanted to see him had to do either the "walk of shame" or the "walk of fame." His Republican primary opponents, outspoken critics, and even some Never-Trumpers had to endure the "walk of shame." They were forced to eat humble pie in front of the cameras as the price of admission to meet with Trump. Celebrities and Trump loyalists were treated to the "walk of fame." Reporters buzzed all day and night. Trump continued to dominate the news cycle, even during the traditionally slow period between the election and Inauguration.

Normally, a new Administration hires people who had been in the last Administration when their party was in power. When the White House changes hands, people in the Executive Branch leave for jobs in Washington thinktanks, law firms, and lobbying groups. Their places are taken by the people leaving Washington thinktanks, law firms, and lobbying groups. It's like a baseball game. The two teams alternate between being at bat or in the field. The team at bat strikes out and spreads out onto the field, while the other team leaves the field and heads to the dugout. One team is in the field trying to stop the runs, the other team is at bat trying to score some runs. In Washington there are always two teams, the political appointees currently in office and people in the shadow government ready to take their place after the next election. They move in and out of government as a full team. Occasionally, new people join the teams but not often since the rules and regulations favor people already playing. Instead, those already on the team move up the ranks with each inning.

The system is efficient, but not necessarily inclusive or effective. It sends a message to qualified outsiders wanting to serve in government: don't even bother applying. Washington is a closed union shop and these jobs belong to the insiders. The system discourages change and perpetuates the status quo. It also reinforces partisan groupthink, since creativity rarely comes from within an existing bureaucracy. People tend to double down on policies that failed in the past, instead of developing new ones. It also breeds contempt and condescension. It's as if Washington says to the rest of the country, "We know better than you do, so just be quiet, pay your taxes, and do as we say." Over time, the gulf between Washington's governing elite and the rest of the country grows wider as they become increasingly disconnected and disengaged with each other.

Trump wanted none of it. He was elected to change things, not slide into the way things were done in the past. Trump thought working in the

Bush Administration wasn't a badge of honor; it was a black mark. He didn't think much of the people who were responsible for what he saw as unfair trade agreements, which put the United States at a disadvantage in international and bilateral trade. He blamed Bush's interventionist neocons for the failed Afghanistan and Iraq wars. Trump wanted new blood, people from different backgrounds who had never been tainted or corrupted by working in Washington. That's what he meant when he promised on the campaign trail that he would drain the swamp.

The upside to his approach was he got new people who were not wedded to the failed policies of the past. He didn't have to put up with a lot of smug insiders who thought they were smarter than him or choose from a pool of people who would work at cross purposes to his own policies. The one thing guaranteed to rile up Trump was to tell him "this is the way we've always done things in the past." As with all things, Trump wanted to be the one making the decisions, negotiating the deals, and psyching out the opposition. Aides, including Cabinet secretaries, were there to carry out his decisions, not make them on his behalf.

And, to be fair, most of those traditional government workers wanted none of Trump. Some of the most experienced Republican national security experts had been Trump's loudest critics during the primary and even the general election campaign. They picked apart his policy positions, condemned his unscripted style, and loathed his personality. They signed Never-Trump petitions, belittled him on cable news, and wrote scathing op-ed columns in the *New York Times* and *Washington Post*. They vowed never to work in a Trump Administration, even in the unlikely chance that he got elected. Although many of them changed their tune after his upset victory, in Trump's eyes they had already made themselves ineligible.

The downside to Trump's approach was he had to start his Administration from scratch, hiring a large number of people who had never gone through the financial disclosure process, been vetted for a security clearance, or wetted by the press.

Thus, a lot of Washington Republicans were frozen out of jobs in the Trump Administration. Some made common cause with the disappointed Clintonistas, and a few even exceeded the Democrats in their Trump-hating fervor. To borrow from Shakespeare, "hell hath no fury like a Washington insider scorned." Together, both groups provided an endless supply of anti-Trump critics to feed the liberal media. They were quick to disparage the chaos of the early days of the Trump Administration. They were right—it was chaotic. But it was probably inevitable given Trump's pledge to shake things up. If a president wants to glide comfortably into the same old policies, he should hire the same old people. If a president wants to take the country in a different direction, he needs different people. But the new people will no doubt make rookie mistakes as they settle in. If the price Trump had to pay to get fresh talent was a shaky launch, it was a price worth paying.

While Trump didn't want to hire Bush veterans, he did want to pick their brains about the people he was considering for positions. Some of the best advice he got was from those Washington veterans, especially the ones who had previously served in top posts but were now retired. They knew the ins and outs of governing, and what qualities to look for when putting together a Cabinet. They could also weigh in on the merits of candidates on Trump's short list.

The one post that he didn't have a natural choice for was probably the most important one: Secretary of State. As a general rule, Trump interviewed several people for each Cabinet post. During the process some candidates fell out, others were added, and some put in different jobs than the ones they were first considered for.

He had met with dozens of people, and went back and forth between a handful, but hadn't settled on anyone. Flynn, concerned that Trump was being pushed into taking someone he wasn't comfortable with, wanted to buy him some time. He asked me to bring in another series of foreign policy wise men to see Trump. That would keep the press preoccupied speculating on who was falling ahead or behind in the Secretary of State horse race, allowing Trump to cast a wider net. For Trump, it wasn't just who had the best resume or who would give the wisest council. It was as much about Trump's gut reaction to the person, how he got along with him, the chemistry, that mattered most. He didn't spend a lot of time asking prospective nominees what they thought, as much as telling them what he thought and gauging their reactions. He assumed anyone who took the job would take orders from Trump, not overrule him, undercut him, or freelance. Trump was used to being the CEO of a company he owned personally, not a hired CEO with a board of directors above him or independent department heads below him. That's one of the reasons he cycled through so many top officials in the first two years. He was surprised when they thwarted some of his ideas, fired them, and then made them scapegoats when things didn't work out.

I realize Trump's critics will seize on this description of the relative anarchy of Trump's Transition as yet more evidence that he is unfit for office. But they are completely missing the point. Trump is effective because he doesn't do what his predecessors have done. That's how he won the Republican nomination and the 2016 election, and why he continues to receive widespread support from the people who elected him, despite the Democrats' impeachment efforts. They elected Trump to shake things up—a lot. A normal Administration just recycles the same people who had been in office the last time around, who perpetuate the same old policies and practices that got us into this mess in the first place.

As part of the series of meetings I arranged with former National Security Advisors and Flynn, I had asked former Secretary of Defense Robert Gates to join us at Trump Tower when he was in New York. I first knew Gates when we were on Kissinger's NSC staff in the 1970s. From there Gates went on to hold just about every senior foreign policy, defense and intelligence post in both Republican and Democratic Administrations— National Security Advisor, CIA Director, and Secretary of Defense—for both Bush and Obama. Gates was second to none in his insights into the national security process. I asked Gates to meet with Flynn and invited Jared Kushner to join us. True to form, Gates had some practical suggestions on the opportunities and pitfalls facing Trump. Kushner asked Gates if could come back and meet with Trump himself.

I met Gates in the lobby the next day and, predictably, the reporters at Trump Tower were abuzz with speculation. Photographers snapped pictures of Gates, and reporters shouted questions at him. "Is Trump going to offer you the State Department? Will you take it if he does? Aren't you against everything Trump supports?" Predictably, cable news led their prime-time coverage with pictures of Secretary Gates walking into Trump Tower, wearing his signature crumpled beige raincoat.

When Gates and I arrived on the 26th floor, we were asked to join the queue of people sitting on the banquette. I kept him company for nearly an hour, trying to make small talk, embarrassed that we had asked for the meeting and then kept Gates cooling his heels in the waiting room while others who arrived after him were ushered in to see Trump ahead of him. Finally, Gates was summoned in. Priebus, Bannon and several others were already in the room. Trump welcomed him, as if unaware of the insult of keeping him waiting for so long, and then grinned while he ribbed Gates for being critical of him during the campaign. He said, "You were one of the strongest against me. You said I couldn't win. I guess you were wrong!" Trump crossed his arms across his chest, leaned back in his chair and chuckled, remarking that Gates had to do the "walk of shame." Gates took the criticism in stride with a frozen smile but said nothing. Trump, having made his point, smiled back, and then motioned that Gates should begin.

Gates outlined the major national security issues he thought Trump would face and offered suggestions for early successes. Trump listened, didn't say much, but got to what was really on his mind. "Who do you think I should take for State? I've talked to a lot of people but haven't settled on anyone. What do you think? Who's the best?" Gates took his time in answering and said, "Well, if you want the person with the most experience, it would probably be me." Gates said it with a straight face—it wasn't clear whether he was being serious or not. Trump didn't say a thing, just looked at Gates. After a long and awkward pause when no one spoke or chuckled, Gates smiled. He continued, "If you really want to look outside the box, I've got a suggestion. You should look at Rex Tillerson, who is just stepping down as Chairman of Exxon Mobil." Gates said he had served with Tillerson on the Boy Scouts of America Board and found him very impressive.

Shortly thereafter, Trump met with Tillerson and tapped him for the job. Sadly, it was not a successful pairing for either of them.

CHAPTER 13

Figuring Out Foreign Policy

In early December, a few days after I started at Trump Tower, Bannon called me into his small office on the 14th floor, across the hall from our NSC office, and handed me a printout of an obscure news story about a new Chinese ship. He said, "What does your China guy think of this? Can you get me something?"

I thought to myself, "'China guy?' We don't have a 'China guy!'" The Trump Tower NSC office consisted of me, occasionally Flynn, Lieutenant Commander Flaherty, and two interns. But I said, "Sure, I'll get right on it."

I had no idea what the Transition team in Washington had in the way of China analysts, and anyway I needed a "China guy" right away and preferably one in New York to be on hand to meet with anyone who wanted a briefing. Flynn and I had already discussed the importance of getting the right Asia/China expert for the NSC, and I had proposed Matt Pottinger, whom I had known for years. Pottinger was a former *Wall Street Journal* reporter in their Asian bureau and spoke fluent Chinese. Then in his late thirties Pottinger did an about-face and joined the Marines to fight in Iraq and Afghanistan. He and Flynn had crossed paths there, and Flynn liked him. Pottinger had since left the Marines to be the Asia analyst at a Wall Street firm.

His wide-ranging background as a reporter in Asia, a Marine combat intelligence officer, and a Wall Street investment banker made for real world assessments and practical solutions. I thought he was one of the best China analysts in the country and, while he favored a tougher approach to China, he wasn't a hair-on-fire kind of guy. He was also fearless and I figured he would work well with Trump. I had no idea of Pottinger's political affiliation or whether he would even be interested in helping out. But I did have his cell phone number. Since I needed a "China guy" right away, I went ahead and called him.

I asked Pottinger if he could come right over to Trump Tower to write a short briefing paper on China. He said, "Sure. I've just been to the gym, so give me a few minutes to take a shower." I met Matt in the Trump Tower marble lobby within the hour, escorted him up to the 14th floor, sat him down at an empty desk, and he started writing. That day, Pottinger drafted a concise three-page policy paper on China, which became the foundation of the Trump Administration's China policy.

In the meantime, I asked another "China guy," Dr. Michael Pillsbury, to come up from Washington to prepare a paper on Chinese strategy. I'd known Pillsbury since I was a graduate student at MIT and he was finishing up his PhD at Columbia. He had spent decades studying Chinese military doctrine, translating their internal documents from the original Chinese, and traveling regularly back and forth to Beijing. Pillsbury had recently written a well-sourced, ground-breaking book, *The Hundred Year Marathon,* that traced how China's leaders had, since the 1970s, patiently followed a long-term plan to replace the United States as the dominant world power by the mid-21st century. It was a new interpretation of China's grand design. Many in the foreign policy community ignored it, especially the globalists, but it has been a wake-up call to others, myself included. Trump was familiar with the book, so I thought he would be receptive to Pillsbury's thesis. I asked Pillsbury to write a short paper outlining the themes of his book. Although Pillsbury didn't end up joining the Administration, he has played a significant behind the scenes role in advising Trump during the trade talks. Trump has referred to Pillsbury as America's "leading authority on China."

The next day, Pottinger came back to Trump Tower and wrote another short policy paper—this time on North Korea. I don't think we ever answered Bannon's query about the Chinese ship but Pottinger was certainly the right "China guy." A few days later, I called Matt's boss, Tom Kempner, co-founder of Davidson-Kempner Capital Management and longtime friend of my husband's, and asked if he would release Matt from his commitments to their firm, allowing Matt to stay at Trump Tower for the Transition and then into the Administration. "Look, Tom, what Matt can do for the country is so much more important than making you a little more money." It was one of the best hires of the Trump Administration. I was right about the president and Pottinger getting along. Today Pottinger sits at my old desk as Trump's Deputy National Security Advisor.

It is an understatement to say America's allies and adversaries were caught off guard by Trump's unexpected victory. They, like everyone else, assumed Hillary Clinton would win. Suddenly, they were forced to scramble to make connections to the new team. Not only was Trump a mystery, so were his top advisors. What did Trump mean by America First? Or Make America Great Again? What did his election mean for our allies and adversaries? But most of all they wanted to know, other than Trump himself, who was in charge?

In December the Chinese government sent their senior foreign policy official, Yang Jiechi, and a delegation to New York to meet with Trump's senior advisors. I had traveled to China several years before with a group of Nixon Administration alumni to retrace the steps of his historic 1972 trip, and had met Mr. Yang at a dinner in the Great Hall of the People in Beijing. During that trip I was presented with a red silk floral scarf and matching handbag in Hangchow, a city renowned for its silk products. Since the Chinese consider the color red a symbol of good fortune, I thought to honor our guests by wearing a red dress, the scarf, and carrying the handbag.

We met the Chinese delegation in a building a few blocks south of Trump Tower on Fifth Avenue, at the conference room of the Kushner family's real estate office. Jared Kushner didn't attend because it was a Saturday, when he and his family observe the Jewish Sabbath. The Trump team assembled before the meeting and went through our strategy of how we wanted this meeting to progress. We would briefly introduce ourselves, and Flynn would lead the discussion. He would talk about Trump's grassroots campaign, the historic nature of the election, and touch on Trump's themes. We wouldn't get into policy; we were in listening only mode.

As we waited for the Chinese delegation to enter the room, I noticed that Bannon hadn't taken off his battered oilskin jacket. While the rest of us were in business clothes, and I was primly attired in my respectful red dress and Chinese silks, Bannon looked like he was coming off a bender, had slept in his clothes, and just rolled out of bed—no shower, no shave. I politely asked if he wanted me to hang up his jacket—and he said, "Thanks, but no." When I asked a second time a few minutes later, Bannon barked, "I told you. *No.* I'm keeping this coat on. I know exactly what I'm doing here." The implication was he wasn't going to pay the Chinese the courtesy of cleaning up for the meeting. Like Trump and Bannon, I too advocated a much tougher stance on China, especially over trade and intellectual property issues, but I didn't see any value in humiliating them. There was no point in making this personal. There were more than enough substantive issues between us without any added insults.

Most of the people around Trump are fairly straightforward. One of the greatest mysteries to me is Steve Bannon. He is a working class Irish Catholic kid from Richmond who went to college on an ROTC scholarship and became a naval officer. When he got out of the Navy, Bannon went to high-powered graduate schools—first Georgetown and then Harvard Business School. He went on to have three successful careers—as a Wall Street investment banker (where he was apparently every inch the dapper, well-dressed businessman), a Hollywood producer, and head of a major conservative media company. His crowning achievement was helping elect a man who nobody thought could win the Presidency. Throughout his seemingly mainstream career, Bannon prided himself on being a renegade.

I saw at least three sides to Steve Bannon. Sometimes he was the bomb throwing rebel with a righteous cause; other times he was the thoughtful, even respectful intellectual; and occasionally, he lost his temper, even with me, and became a shouting, throw-things-around the room, in-your-face bully.

When many of the Transition staff at Trump Tower were focused on process and personnel and outreach, Bannon was the one thinking the big thoughts. But he didn't do it in a systematic way or extend it across the board to all national security issues. He was a gadfly and for a while China was his main focus.

I generally had good relations with Bannon. We both have daughters who graduated from Service Academies (his daughter, Maureen, from West Point; my daughter, Fiona, from the Naval Academy). I shared many of his convictions about how America needed a major course correction in foreign and domestic policy. I too believed that for too long America has put other countries' interests ahead of our own, and it was time to rebalance many of our foreign relationships, in both trade and security. I, too, believed the permanent Administrative State had become so entrenched that many bureaucrats and agencies have taken on a life and purpose of their own, independent from their political masters, and the American people.

I advocated taking the steps necessary to restore the American Dream, even if it means some temporary dislocation in our society as we move to replace the establishment elites with new people and new policies. The American Dream is the birthright of all Americans—regardless of color, race, ethnicity or gender. It is a promise that should be for all our people, for everyone in the vast melting pot that is America—from the newest immigrants to Mayflower descendants. What I didn't agree with Bannon on was his toleration and even encouragement of extremist groups and seeming sympathy with their prejudices.

From my earliest days at Trump Tower, I worried that few people on the Transition team, including the president-elect himself, fully appreciated, or had even thought about, how difficult it was going to be for them to govern, especially in the face of the unprecedented opposition they would face from every direction. President-elect Trump, for all his successes, wasn't used to working collaboratively, or acknowledging the contribution of others.

Meanwhile, America has a divided government which means nothing gets done without compromise and giving most of the credit to politicians with supersized egos. Presidents succeed only if they can find a way to work with ambitious legislators, many of whom have aspirations to occupy the Oval Office themselves someday. Presidents must also harness an independent bureaucracy whose attitude is, "Presidents may come and go, but we're here forever." Republicans have the added complication of an antagonistic press corps which leans heavily Democrat but refuses to acknowledge it. And in Trump's case, there would be a considerable number of Washingtonians who were committed to stopping his presidency dead in its tracks.

I worried that Trump and the people moving into the West Wing with him would make the mistake all too common among first timers—thinking that just because they won the election, they would be allowed to govern. Governing consists of a lot more than making speeches, negotiating deals, or proclaiming new policies. The president has to manage the entire Executive Branch, and compromise with Congress to get legislation passed and nominees confirmed. Trump and the people around him failed to recognize just how many obstacles their political opponents would throw in their path.

I was also concerned that they had no comprehension of the scope and magnitude of what it took to ensure the nation's security. Few had served in government before. I was one of the only people who had ever worked in the Executive Branch, or the White House, much less the West Wing and my experience was thirty years ago! I felt an enormous responsibility to do whatever I could to get the president-elect and his team ready in time.

What weighed most heavily on my mind was our need to be ready on day one to assume responsibility for the nation's security; and we would have to do it with only a skeleton team in place. The NSC would be the only functioning part of the Trump national security apparatus for weeks, if not months, while Trump formed the rest of his team. Incoming Cabinet secretaries, who had yet to be interviewed, vetted, or nominated, couldn't step foot in their departments until after they had been confirmed by the Senate. Deputies and other senior officials would take even longer to be in place, especially since many leading Democrat senators had made clear they would slow-walk all of Trump's nominees. We understood that Trump might not have a full complement of his own foreign policy and defense officials in place for as much as a year.

The United States is always most vulnerable at the changing of the guard—during the first few months of a new Administration when people are just figuring things out. An outgoing Administration is a well-oiled machine. By the time they leave office, the officials have worked together for years. Even if they have differences with each other, they've found a way to work through them. An outgoing Administration has also worked with their foreign counterparts for years, and whether friend or foe, they're known quantities to each other. They are the high school seniors who have had four years to figure things out.

A new Administration's team, on the other hand, are the high school freshman. It takes them months to get the hang of things. The Trump Administration would have an even more difficult time, since most were completely new to government. Most of the Cabinet had never worked together, didn't know each other, and were unfamiliar with the strange ways of Washington and the Administrative State. Since there had been little in the way of pre-election personnel selections, it would take weeks, even months before Trump officials would be running their departments.

Other countries know this about us and realize this is a period of great vulnerability for America. Our adversaries see this as their window of opportunity, when they can take advantage of a new Administration, exploiting the divisions between us, or even testing us with a crisis. Whether by coincidence or design, most new Administrations are tested within their first year. The Chinese forced down a U.S. spy plane in the early months of the George H.W. Bush Administration. The September 11th attacks were in President George W. Bush's first year. Three months into the Reagan Administration, the new president was nearly killed in an assassination attempt. Vice President George H.W. Bush was traveling the day Reagan was shot, and there was confusion at the White House over who was in charge in the interim and whether the United States should raise the worldwide military readiness level in case the Russians were somehow involved.

My most pressing concern was that we could have a full-blown North Korea crisis in the early days of the Trump Administration. President Obama had warned President-elect Trump that North Korea was his most immediate problem. Susan Rice and her team had given us similar warnings during their meetings with Flynn and me. Some experts thought North Korea was on the cusp of having long-range missiles and nuclear weapons capable of hitting the U.S. homeland. I worried the North Koreans could provoke a crisis by testing a new missile or a nuclear weapon in the first few days or even the first few hours after Trump took office. We could be faced with a defining national security crisis before most of my West Wing colleagues knew where their offices were, or how to turn on their computers.

I needed to stress this to my colleagues, without coming across as the office nanny. By mid-November, Priebus began convening daily senior staff meetings at 8:00 a.m. The people headed to top West Wing jobs were seated around the conference room table on the 14th floor of Trump Tower—Spicer, Bannon, Kushner, Deputy Chiefs of Staff Katie Walsh and Rick Dearborn, the vice president's top aides, and several others. Those not present listened in on speakerphone.

I sat in for Flynn and, when it was my turn to speak, reported that the NSC was moving quickly to hire at least a skeleton staff and process their security clearances with utmost urgency. Others in the room were impressed that we were moving out so promptly, and complimented me on being far and away the most organized of the incoming staff. "Not really," I said, "because we have to be up and running right from the start. We will be walking into an empty office—Obama's senior NSC officials will be gone. The safes will be empty, and the institutional knowledge of our relationships with friend and foe will go out the door with them. They will leave briefing books for us, but that's not the same as having a working knowledge of all the players and the issues. We will be responsible for the nation's security starting at 12:01 p.m. on Inauguration day. The Cabinet won't be confirmed until later. So, look around the room; it will be up to us. If a crisis comes on day one, it will be ours and ours alone to deal with."

There was a moment of silence as everyone in the room took that in. It was a sobering thought, and one I don't think any of them had contemplated before I said it. Later in the day, Deputy Chief of Staff Rick Dearborn pulled me aside, and said, "Tell me what you need—staff, office space, administrative support, anything—and it's yours." I gave him a list off the top of my head, starting with Megan Badasch, who had proved herself in the Trump campaign and early days of the Transition, but who was already earmarked for another position. She was not only calm in the face of the chaos all around us, but turned out to be the organizational wunderkind we needed. (Badasch became Special Assistant to the President and NSC Principal Deputy Executive Secretary.) By 7:30 a.m. the next morning, I had everything and everyone else I asked for.

I honestly think they believed they would walk into the West Wing on January 20th and find a staff in place, waiting to take orders, rather than vacant offices, empty desks, and no instruction manuals.

When I joined the Trump Administration, I had just finished heading up a several year project for the Nixon Foundation and Nixon Legacy Forums, which took an in-depth look at the Nixon/Kissinger foreign policy. I organized and led a series of panel discussions with about fifteen surviving members of the Kissinger-era National Security Council, who described the structure and content of foreign policymaking. The project culminated with six separate video interviews with Kissinger, which is to date his only oral history. I interviewed Kissinger for some eight hours total, with his longtime aide Ambassador Winston Lord. Kissinger discussed how he and Nixon created a structure which made the NSC the center of the interagency system. It has been the template for every Administration since. Kissinger also discussed their major foreign policy initiatives—the opening to China, détente and arms control agreements with the Soviet Union, the Vietnam War, and Middle East shuttle diplomacy. I was familiar with most of this, having worked as a junior aide in Kissinger's West Wing office when he was Nixon's and later Ford's National Security Advisor, and also from decades of association with Kissinger.

The Nixon Foundation project was, for me, a refresher course on the era, and a master class on national security. It was also a sobering reminder that even one of the most brilliant and successful diplomats of his era had to operate in a climate of unceasing criticism at home, and imperfect intelligence abroad. My time with Kissinger stood me in good stead when Donald Trump appointed me Deputy National Security Advisor a few months later. Sadly, when I finally got to the White House it wasn't as deputy to a universally respected Dr. Kissinger, but to General Mike Flynn, who was doomed, some would even say targeted, from the beginning.

CHAPTER 14

General Flynn

I had first meet Lieutenant General Mike Flynn in late 2014, after he had been fired by the Obama Administration. Like many in my field, I was familiar with his role in radically reforming the counter-intelligence programs in the Iraq and Afghanistan wars, and in bringing an entrenched military intelligence bureaucracy into the 21st century.

Flynn's thirty-three-year Army career had been spent in military intelligence, where he rose through the ranks to become head of the Defense Intelligence Agency (DIA), the premier intelligence agency serving all of the armed forces. Its primary focus is on gathering and analyzing intelligence on our enemies in order to assist the military, especially in fighting wars.

While at DIA, Flynn challenged the Obama Administration's claim that Al-Qaeda was on the ropes. He argued that while we may have killed Bin Laden, that didn't mean radical Islamic movements were finished. He predicted the rise of even more violent terrorist groups emerging from the ashes of Al-Qaeda, and the rise of ISIS. Flynn had been fired for speaking his mind, the same way General James Mattis had been pushed out for warning about the threats Iran still posed while the Obama Administration was eagerly negotiating a nuclear deal.

In my mind, both Flynn and Mattis were willing to speak inconvenient truths to senior officials in the Obama Administration—and had been punished for it. With time, both Flynn and Mattis were proven right in their assessments—Flynn on terrorist movements and Mattis on Iran. But even when you're right, or sometimes *because* you're right, you can make enemies. Mattis retired from the military, headed to the West Coast and a position at the Hoover Institute, and disappeared from public view until President Trump brought him back to Washington as Secretary of Defense.

After Flynn retired from the military, he remained in the Washington area and set up his own consulting firm. Flynn soon became a favorite on the talk show and speaker's circuits. His predictions about radical Islamic terrorist groups were coming true with the rise of ISIS and the establishment of the Islamic State. His book, *The Field of Flight: How We Can Win the Global War Against Radical Islam and Its Allies*, was published by Macmillan in July 2016 and became an instant bestseller.

Flynn first met Donald Trump in the summer of 2015 and by early 2016 had joined his campaign. He was at Trump's side through all the ups and downs of the primary season and weathered the hiring and firing of several campaign managers. As a nod to the military and his respect for the "generals," Trump even put Flynn on his short list for the Vice Presidency.

Trump and Flynn got along well and became travel buddies, but it was more than that. Flynn was the only person in Trump's innermost circle who had any foreign policy, intelligence, or military experience. When Trump declared his candidacy in June 2015, no serious national security expert would give him the time of day. Instead, they flocked to the campaigns of Jeb Bush, Marco Rubio, Ted Cruz, and the dozen other GOP candidates. Many proudly announced that they would never work in a Trump Administration. As a three-star Army general with a distinguished war record, Flynn's endorsement gave Trump some much needed credibility and expertise early on.

Flynn soon became the warm-up act at Trump rallies, criticizing Hillary Clinton for her role in the Benghazi attack, her misuse of classified information, and saying that if he had done what she had done, he'd be in jail. He stood at the podium at the Republican National Convention in Cleveland in August and reprised the role he had on the campaign trail. On prime-time television, with tens of millions of viewers in the United States and throughout the world, Flynn excoriated Hillary Clinton and led the audience in chants of "Lock her up. Lock her up."

When Trump unexpectedly defeated Hillary Clinton in November, it was only natural for him to reward Flynn for his loyalty on the campaign trail and offer him a senior position in the new Administration.

Flynn let it be known he was interested in being Secretary of Defense, and not Director of National Intelligence, which might have been a better fit given his background. Instead, Trump tapped him for National Security Advisor. I doubt if Trump—or Flynn for that matter—had anything more than a passing knowledge of what the National Security Advisor actually did. Neither of them had any appreciation for just how much someone like Flynn might struggle in the position.

Most former National Security Advisors had already spent a lifetime in the foreign policy community, as well as decades in the Executive Branch, by the time they were appointed to the coveted and powerful White House post. General Flynn had not. But he did have the one quality essential for any National Security Advisor—Flynn had the trust and confidence of his boss.

Flynn told me that Trump wanted Flynn at his side in the West Wing, to continue as one of his closest advisors, as he had been during the campaign. Flynn said Trump wanted his honest, unvarnished advice even if it was at odds with the bureaucracy. His straightforward, blunt style meshed well with Trump's own, and they saw foreign policy issues through the same lens. Even if they disagreed on some things, Flynn and Trump both knew who was boss, and whose opinion counted and whose didn't.

No matter who sits in the Oval Office, there are always a special set of challenges in working alongside any American president. Since Flynn had no prior White House experience, I thought he would benefit by spending time with some of the people who had held senior positions in previous Administrations. He could hear directly from them about the issues they had faced, about their successes and triumphs, and especially about their failures and regrets. They could also give him guidance on how to navigate as the president's personal representative in their dealings with all the national security-related departments and agencies of government, as well as the press.

Over the years, Flynn had been introduced to several former National Security Advisors, but didn't know any of them well. I wanted to give him the opportunity to talk one on one with a number of them, so Flynn could get their insider's perspectives on what he was about to face, especially with a president who had no prior government or Washington experience.

I also wanted these same former officials to have a chance to get to know Flynn. He wasn't in the mold of his predecessors, who had been in and out of the government, written scholarly articles for professional journals, and been active participants in the diplomatic and foreign policy associations. He was an unknown quantity to the opinion makers in that world. Inside intelligence community circles he was viewed as unconventional - some thought him brilliant, others thought him erratic. If Flynn was to be successful as National Security Advisor, he would need allies outside the Trump Administration, especially among these senior and well-respected statesmen. Their endorsement of Flynn also would go a long way in alleviating the skepticism many of them had of Donald Trump.

I reached out to a number of my friends and former colleagues to arrange meetings with General Flynn. Most were only too happy to share their experiences and gave generously of their time. During the course of three weeks in December, we had sessions with senior officials from the Reagan, George H.W. Bush, George W. Bush, and Obama Administrations: Secretary of the Navy John Lehman, Director of National Intelligence John Negroponte, Ambassador to Germany Robert Kimmitt, National Security Advisors Robert "Bud" McFarlane and Stephen Hadley, CIA Director and Secretary of Defense Robert Gates, and a handful of other former officials.

Their wise counsel was invaluable. Some offered policy suggestions, with their own lists of dos and don'ts. Some offered advice about the process—how to deal with Cabinet colleagues, the media, foreign diplomats, and legislators. They all stressed the importance of keeping the NSC in charge of the interagency process. They agreed that the most effective way for the National Security Council to serve the president was to act as the honest broker among all the different departments and agencies, giving each of them a fair hearing in the formulation of foreign policy and presenting their recommendations to the president for the final decision. All of them, including President Obama's National Security Advisor Susan Rice and her very able Deputy Avril Haynes, expressed concern that the NSC staff had grown too large over the years, and that reducing it should be a priority.

Far and away the most interesting meeting we had was with Henry Kissinger. Kissinger himself had had a long acquaintance with Donald Trump over the years, but it was more casual and social than professional. During the campaign, I helped arrange for him to brief Trump several times, as Kissinger has done for presidential candidate of both parties for decades. But Flynn himself had never met Kissinger, and we all thought it important that he do so.

Not only was Kissinger the architect of what some consider a golden age of American diplomacy, even today he continues to give insight and advice to the most important global figures of our time. Kissinger has known every major world leader since World War II, and remains a confidante to statesmen, entrepreneurs, and international businessmen. Even though Kissinger is now in his mid-nineties, he still travels around the globe several times a year and is often better informed on what's really on the minds of the world's most influential leaders than a lot of intelligence agencies. Indeed, I find Kissinger has become even more impressive in these later years, because he sees things in the great sweep of history, rather than the minutiae of the moment.

Flynn and I offered to meet Kissinger at his office in mid-town Manhattan so he wouldn't have to walk through the lobby of Trump Tower and run the gauntlet of reporters and photographers who had taken up permanent residence there. When we arrived at the Park Avenue office of Kissinger and Associates, he was already standing at the door, smiling, and leaning on his ever-present cane. He graciously welcomed us into his office suite, where tea and cookies had been laid out. His office has a spectacular view of the rooftops of Manhattan office buildings, but what immediately draws your eyes are what sit on the tables and hang on the walls. Both his office and his home are crosses between a living museum and a stroll through history. There is the statue of a Tang Dynasty horse that Chinese Prime Minister Zhou Enlai gave him during the early days of President Nixon's historic opening to China. There is the Nobel Peace Prize he was awarded for negotiating the Paris Peace Accords and an end to the Vietnam War. There are dozens of autographed pictures of Kissinger with every major premier, President, and king of the last seventy years.

I was anxious that this initial session between my first boss and my current boss go well. I had suggested to Flynn beforehand that he could best use the time to get Kissinger's assessment of the current United States-China relationship. Kissinger has long been revered in China as one of that country's greatest friends. He worked with Mao Zedong and Zhou Enlai, the legendary founding fathers of the People's Republic of China and has known every Chinese leader in the decades since. As a result, Kissinger's insights into Chinese foreign and domestic policy are second to none. My hope was that Kissinger could explain the Chinese leaders' mindset to the leaders in the Trump Administration, and Flynn could give him insights into Trump's attitudes toward China. Although the meeting was a bit awkward at first—Flynn was nervous to be meeting this living legend—it turned out to be time well spent for everyone. It was one of the most important meetings that Flynn had to help prepare him for what was sure to be one of the most unconventional presidencies in modern times.

Over the decades, the National Security Council had ballooned up to about 400 people. When I worked for Kissinger in the 1970s, the NSC staff consisted of about 100 people, including file clerks and secretaries like me. The myth is that the National Security Advisor can hire all of the 400 people on his staff—and they have become some of the most sought-after positions in government. In reality, he only gets to hire directly about twenty or so new people. Most of the people in administrative, technical, and support positions remain at the NSC from one Administration to the next. Added to these are the hundred or so "detailees"—civil servants from the foreign policy, military, and intelligence departments and agencies in the Executive Branch who are detailed for temporary assignment to the White House. These are considered plum jobs, and the agencies send their best people to give them invaluable experience at the nerve-center of government.

The detailees return to their home agencies some two or three years later with a sense of how things work at the top. In exchange, the White House gets first-rate talent and immediate access to foreign policy experts with years of experience. They all, no doubt, have their own political preferences, but the best of them don't let that get in the way of doing their jobs. Like the military, they are career professionals who are supposed to serve any president, regardless of party or whether they personally voted for him. I found almost all of them to be exceptional civil servants who were eager to help their new bosses succeed.

There were others, however, who were determined to sabotage the Trump Administration from the inside. Within days of the election, some Obama appointees who remained on the NSC apparently joined with some career intelligence and foreign policy bureaucrats across government to create the hashtag #Resistance movement. They selectively leaked highly classified information to their media favorites in order to make the new officials look inept and befuddled. Purported transcripts of Trump's phone calls with foreign leaders, notes taken during Situation Room meetings, and confidential conversations found their way into "breaking news" stories. These people, who hid behind the label of "anonymous sources," decided that they would take things into their own hands and stymie the Trump Administration. I'm sure they see themselves as patriots serving the higher good. But to me they are Washington insiders subverting the will of the American people who had, by electing Trump, just voted to reject them and their policies. They weren't preserving democracy by obstructing a duly elected President; they were vandalizing it.

Despite the small number of positions available to hire new staff members, the myth of the National Security Advisor's hiring power persists, and hundreds of foreign policy experts from outside government use every possible connection to get their resumes before an incoming NSA. Flynn was no exception and had a hard time saying no. He gave interviews and took calls from scores of his former colleagues, even those we were unlikely to ever hire. Consequently, a good deal of our time during the Transition was spent on personnel and staff organization issues, rather than developing policy.

Since most of Flynn's army career had been in military intelligence, he naturally gravitated toward those people for staffing the NSC. He didn't know many people in the wider foreign policy community and, given his background, didn't trust a lot of those he did. So we developed an unofficial division of labor: I recommended government alumni and people from thinktanks, the business world, and academia. Flynn focused on people from the military and military intelligence. I focused on China, Asia, and Europe. Flynn focused on terrorism, the Iraq and Afghan wars, the Middle East, and Russia. In addition to Flaherty and Badasch, the new people I insisted on hiring were China expert Matthew Pottinger to run the Asia shop, Putin expert Dr. Fiona Hill to head up Europe and

Russia, Ted Cruz's foreign policy advisor Victoria Coates, now in charge of Middle East policy, Joshua Steinman to head up the cybersecurity office, and Kenneth Juster for the international economics job, a jointly held appointment between the NSC and National Economic Council (NEC). (Juster is now US Ambassador to India). Rounding it out was one of the leading conservative intellectuals of his generation, Michael Anton, to run strategic communications.

These talented people ended up being some of the most effective national security officials in the Trump Administration. Not only were they able to navigate their way through several different National Security Advisors, they were effective advocates with President Trump. Since so much of Trump's policy emanates directly from him, his White House foreign policy experts play a more oversized role than is often the case with other presidents. Even though I left government in May 2017, these people stayed on and are responsible for many of the Trump Administration's foreign policy successes.

I knew from working in other Administrations that the Transition is usually devoted to turning the president-elect's campaign promises into policy proposals. For example, Kissinger and Nixon spent hours during their Transition period discussing the changes they wanted to make in the Johnson Administration's policies toward the Soviet Union and China and their approach to ending the Vietnam War. The Trump Transition was completely different, focusing more on procedure, process, and personnel. Even if we had written lengthy policy papers and prepared detailed briefing books, there was no one on the Transition team who would have had the time to read them. I figured we would get to policy-making once in office. My first priority was to survive the period without any major mishaps. We got through Thanksgiving and Christmas without any crises, so Flynn and his wife took a few well-deserved days off to vacation in the Dominican Republic between Christmas and New Year's, leaving me as the duty officer with Trump at Mar-a-Lago. Since Trump would be with his friends and family, and wouldn't be having regular meetings, my husband joined me, and we made a mini-holiday out of it.

Mar-a-Lago is Trump's Palm Beach resort. It is on the most desirable piece of real estate in one of the most exclusive and expensive resort towns in the country. It sits on a narrow barrier beach between Worth Lake on one side and the Atlantic Ocean on the other. Indeed, the name "Mar-a-Lago" means between sea and lake in Spanish. It is a vast 110,000-square-foot mansion, built in the 1920s for General Foods heiress Marjorie Merriweather Post, one of the wealthiest and most glamorous women of her time. It's filled with wall-to-wall gold leaf, Spanish tiles, and Italian marble, and radiates the excessive luxury of a bygone era. For nearly fifty years, Mrs. Post presided over elaborate house parties with the most famous people of her era—film stars, presidents, potentates, and celebrities. In her declining years, Mrs. Post thought of bequeathing Mar-a-Lago to the nation, to serve as a winter White House. Today it is just that, but not in the way she expected. While it is the president's Winter White House, it is privately owned by President Trump himself.

Mar-a-Lago is not like a typical resort. Even though it is a members only private club, it operates more like a personal home of a billionaire who has friends in for an extended house party. Trump doesn't keep a business office at Mar-a-Lago—he takes meetings on the oversized, down-filled silk brocade sofas in the lounge. Guests and members roam freely throughout the clubhouse and grounds, and Trump takes the part of the convivial host of a large, elaborate mansion from a gilded age.

My husband and I had dinner the first night in the formal dining room, where the walls were covered with hand-painted bucolic scenes of the European countryside. The ceiling was adorned with wall-to-wall cherubs and clouds. Gold leaf was on every remaining surface. The light was low, from crystal chandeliers overhead and flickering candles at the tables. As the maître d' wheeled the after-dinner cheese and port trolley to our table, I said to my husband, "This has got to be the most bizarre presidential Transition in American history." Mar-a-Lago is like a 15th century Florentine de' Medici palace, with Trump as the Renaissance prince.

During the day, my assistant, Lieutenant Commander Flaherty, and I set up our laptop computers at a table in the Mar-a-Lago breakfast room. I spent my days reading through emails, catching up on my foreign policy-related reading, studying NSC organization proposals, and flipping through the endless stacks of resumes. I also touched base with the fledgling Transition staff that was starting to assemble at the D.C. headquarters.

The only things on my schedule were one short meeting I had asked for with the president-elect, and to join him for the morning intelligence briefing. Flynn and I tried to check in once a day, but it was catch-as-catch-can since he had limited access to communications from the Dominican Republic.

Late in the day on December 28th, the media began reporting that President Obama was going to impose sanctions on the Russians in response to their election interference. Flynn and I were able to talk that evening, and I told him about these reports, although there was still no word on exactly what the Obama sanctions package would include or what evidence they had that drove their decision and its timing. I briefed Flynn on the decades-long history of back and forth sanctions and diplomatic expulsions between the US and the Soviet Union. I explained that throughout the Cold War we had episodes like this every few years, some more serious than others. For example, in the Reagan Administration we expelled a large number of their diplomats at the UN and at their embassy in Washington for spying. They retaliated by ordering hundreds of Soviets employed at our embassy in Moscow to stop working.

In the past, these episodes usually followed a fairly standard pattern: One country objected to some action they accused the other of doing, and imposed sanctions on individuals or institutions or expelled diplomats they deemed to be responsible. Usually the other country matched it with an equivalent, tit-for-tat retaliation, and that was the end of it. Sometimes, although less often, the other country made a lot of noise, but only retaliated with a pro-forma response and less than equivalent retaliation, thus de-escalating the situation. Very occasionally, the other country took things a step further with an escalatory response, which in turn risked provoking another round of retaliation and turning a fairly standard event into a crisis.

I offered my opinion that the way the Russians responded to President Obama's sanctions could be an indication of how they wanted their relationship with the new Trump Administration to proceed. My analysis wasn't terribly insightful, it was more or less what the pundits were saying on cable news.

I also started reaching out to several experts to get me up to speed. I called Dr. Fiona Hill, one of the savviest analysts of Putin in the country. She was the head of Russia and European department at the Brookings Institute, and I was hoping she would join the National Security Council in the same position. She chuckled that I was one of the few calls she would be willing to take while she was on vacation in California, at a shopping mall getting her daughter's ears pierced. She went into the mall's stairwell so she could hear me above the din. I asked her whether meddling in our elections is something Putin would have personally ordered? If so, why? What was he trying to accomplish? How was he likely to respond to Obama's imposition of sanctions? How would the sanctions impact Trump's goal of improving relations between the United States and Russia?

I also checked with cyber security expert and former White House Chief Information Officer Theresa Payton and asked her to explain to me in layman's terms how the Russians might have hacked into these systems. What were they technically capable of doing? Were they trying to cover their tracks, but we managed to discover them? Could they have deliberately left evidence so we would know they had done it? Payton explained the difficulties of attribution in a forensics case. We discussed whether the hacking could have been a false flag operation from the start, done by an independent group that planted digital artifacts to make it look like the Russians did it?

In addition, I called Robert O'Brien, an international lawyer from Los Angeles, who I was advocating for a post in the Administration. I asked O'Brien to remind me of how sanctions and expulsions had been done in the past. Could a president impose sanctions unilaterally, or did he need to go through a certification procedure which involved others, either in Congress or the intelligence agencies? (O'Brien became the chief negotiator on hostage affairs in 2018, where he earned the trust and confidence of President Trump, who appointed him National Security Advisor a year later, replacing John Bolton.)

I also had several conversations in person and by phone with Transition team members at Mar-a-Lago and in the Washington office. We hoped Russia would not escalate the situation with their response. Clearly, no one on our team wanted this to develop into a full-blown United States-Russia crisis on the eve of Trump's Inauguration.

Flynn and I talked again the next day, after the Obama Administration issued their formal announcement, and I read him the specifics of what the sanctions package consisted of—expulsion of diplomats, economic sanctions, and closing down Russian facilities. We discussed their potential impact on the incoming Trump Administration's foreign policy goals, and Flynn said he would be talking to the Russian Ambassador that evening.

I also pointed out that two things concerned me. First, the Obama Administration must have known about the hacking for weeks, if not for months, probably even well before the election. So why did they wait until now, just three weeks before Inauguration, to take action? Second, why did they say the intelligence report which led to Obama's decision to impose sanctions wouldn't be available for another week or two? Why the two-week gap between their decision to impose sanctions and releasing their supporting evidence? Normally, the decision and evidence would be presented together.

I was suspicious the outgoing Obama Administration might be trying to bait Trump into tweeting a criticism of their decision to punish Russia, and then a week or two later release definitive proof that Russia was guilty. After all, Trump had made no secret of his skepticism regarding charges of Russian hacking. During the first presidential debate he said, "It could be Russia, but it could also be China. It could also be lots of other people.... It also could be somebody sitting on their bed that weighs 400 pounds." Were Obama officials hoping to make Trump look foolish, or gullible, or soft on Putin just a few days before he was sworn in? That, too, would make it more complicated for Trump to improve relations with Russia once in office.

After the call with Flynn, I headed to the Mar-a-Lago ballroom for a meeting with Trump that I had scheduled several days before. My original goal had been to use this briefing time as a dry run to get a sense of the best way to brief Trump once he was in the White House. Most experts prepare lengthy briefing papers or detailed PowerPoint presentations for their bosses. I realized from the two debate prep sessions I had had with Trump before the election that the traditional briefing format wouldn't be effective with him. In this case, my cable news training was uniquely useful.

In television you have only a few sentences to make your point; most interviews are less than four minutes long. During my years as FOX News's National Security Analyst, I had learned to take complicated issues and condense them, in order to emphasize the key aspects of any situation. It's much more difficult than it seems. Anyone can speak for thirty minutes to make a point; it's far more difficult to make the same points in three minutes. It proved the best technique for briefing a president who had little patience for people who insisted on droning on.

I also wanted to use this briefing to get a sense of how deep Trump's background was on key national security issues, and to establish a baseline as we went forward. To that end, I had already prepared several short, unclassified, generic papers on China, the nuclear triad, missile defense, and the Iranian nuclear agreement. At the last minute I also added a short paper on Russian hacking, and attached to it a lengthy *New York Times* article by David Sanger on the Obama sanctions.

The ballroom, where we were scheduled to meet, isn't part of the original mansion. Trump added it when he renovated Mar-a-Lago after he bought it in 1985, but its design is in keeping with the rest of the mansion. It is another vast space, with white walls, elaborate Corinthian columns and gold leaf everywhere—on the walls, on top of the columns, on the moldings and on the ceiling. During the day the ballroom is suffused with bright Florida sunlight streaming through the floor-to-ceiling windows. At night the glow from the gigantic crystal chandeliers reflects on the white ceiling and walls. It's typical Trump glitz and glamour.

Trump was there, along with his senior team—Bannon, Priebus, Spicer, and one or two others—sitting informally around a table. I started by thanking him for the meeting, and said I wanted to take twenty minutes of his time to brief him on some key national security issues. It was at the end of a long day, and he said, "Make it ten." I began with missile defense, and everyone immediately jumped in with their own comments. I was somewhat surprised at this since missile defense is a complex issue, and one with which I had been involved since the 1980s when I wrote the first draft of Reagan's "Star Wars" speech. I had even taught a class on nuclear weapons at MIT when I was a PhD candidate in the 1980s. Nevertheless, the other aides all had something to say. I soon learned that this was how Trump liked to be briefed—everyone, informed or not, had an opinion and was eager to share it!

Knowing I had just a few minutes left, I switched to the Obama sanctions, briefly described what we knew, and gave them the same tit-for-tat assessment I had given to Flynn and to other staff members throughout the day. I used hand motions to demonstrate how, in past decades, the Russians had almost always responded in one of three ways—usually with an equivalent tit-for-tat (flat hand), occasionally with a de-escalation (fingers pointing downward), and very occasionally with an escalation (fingers point up). Their reaction to the Obama sanctions might give us a sense of how Putin wanted the United States relationship to proceed under President Trump. I also offered a note of caution that we should be careful about commenting on Obama's decision until Trump was back in New York and had his briefing from the intelligence community, which would take place in the next week or so.

Trump interrupted me and asked, "Do you think the Russians did it? (Meaning, hacked into the Democrats' computers and interfered in the election.) "Yes," I answered. Trump said he wasn't so sure and repeated the same doubts he had expressed in public several times before. He asked the others sitting around the table for their opinions. After a few minutes of a group conversation, Trump thanked me, got up from the table and headed for the door. As he was leaving, one of us mentioned that Flynn would be talking to the Russian Ambassador that evening, but I'm not sure Trump heard it.

I went back to the main building and that evening took a second call from Flynn. Flynn said he'd just spoken to the Russian Ambassador, and that their call had gone well. Flynn thought we were "going to be okay." He asked me how the briefing with Trump had gone, and I shared my frustration that everyone jumped into the conversation. Flynn chuckled and said, "Yeah, that's typical." I also told him that Trump made an interesting point—that Obama may have actually "done him a favor" by imposing sanctions, because it gave him some new leverage to use in negotiating with Putin. I signed off by saying that my husband and I would leave Mar-a-Lago in the morning, and then take a few days of vacation ourselves.

Although these events later became central issues in the Mueller investigation, at the time there was so much going on that they weren't my central focus. When Flynn said, "I think we're going to be okay," he gave me the impression that the Russian response to the sanctions was not going to be escalatory and that things were back on track. President Obama's imposition of sanctions would not prevent the incoming Trump Administration from exploring an improvement in United States-Russian relations. Frankly, I wasn't as concerned about precisely what Flynn and the Russian Ambassador were saying to each other, as I was about what the president-elect was saying to the world. If my suspicions were correct, and the Obama Administration's decision to announce sanctions the way they did was in part to lure Trump into saying something critical of their decision, it could turn out to be a major embarrassment just as he took office. Even if the Russians didn't turn this into a crisis, Trump's political enemies might use it to sabotage one of his main campaign promises. I was relieved when Trump issued a brief statement that evening saying it was time for "our country to move on to bigger and better things."

As expected, the next day the Russian Foreign Ministry announced that, "We will definitely respond to these actions. Reciprocity is a basic tenet of international diplomacy and international relations."[1]

The announcement went on to say they had submitted a proposal to President Putin for Russia to have an equivalent response to President Obama. But several hours later Russian Foreign Minister Sergei Lavrov was overruled by Putin himself. The Russian president said, "While we reserve the right to take reciprocal measures, we're not going to downgrade ourselves to the level of irresponsible 'kitchen' diplomacy." Putin said they would wait until Trump became president and then "proceed from the policy pursued by the Administration" of Donald J. Trump.[2]

Trump's Twitter response was immediate, and classic Trump: "Great move on delay (by V. Putin)–I always knew he was very smart!" Later that morning my husband and I left Mar-a-Lago to fly home to Long Island, and I put it all out of my mind. Flynn was back from his vacation and in charge again. I turned my attention to preparing for our annual Hogmanay New Year's party and packing up to move to Washington the next week.

After some back and forth with the Obama Administration, a week later Trump got the promised briefing on Russian interference in the election. On January 6th Director of National Intelligence (DNI) General James Clapper, Central Intelligence Agency (CIA) Director John Brennan, Federal Bureau of Investigation (FBI) Director James Comey, and National Security Agency (NSA) Director Admiral Michael Rogers traveled to Trump Tower to brief Trump, Pence, and the incoming senior staff. I jokingly referred to it as the "Four Amigos Briefing."

---

[1] "Comment by Foreign Minister Sergey Lavrov on recent US sanctions and the expulsion of Russian diplomats, Moscow." The Ministry of Foreign Affairs of the Russian Federation. December 30, 2016. http://www.mid.ru/en/foreign_policy/news/-/asset_publisher/cKNonkJE02Bw/content/id/2583996.

[2] MacFarquhar, Neil. "Vladimir Putin Won't Expel U.S. Diplomats as Russian Foreign Minister Urged." The New York Times. December 30, 2016. https://www.nytimes.com/2016/12/30/world/europe/russia-diplomats-us-hacking.html.

Flaherty called in the Secret Service and White House Situation Room to help set up a SCIF (Secure Compartmented Information Facility). The briefing was set for the small glass conference room on the 14th floor, right across the hall from our NSC office. Heavy blue floor-to-ceiling draperies were hung along the glass wall that faced the hallway in order to enclose the space. A large, mahogany oval conference table took up nearly the entire room, with President-elect Trump and Vice President-elect Pence sitting at either end. Flaherty found American and Armed Forces standing flags from somewhere and put them behind Trump and Pence. There were placards showing seats for Pompeo, Flynn, and Priebus on one side, and Clapper, Brennan, Comey, and Rogers, facing them along the other side. My chair was against the wall behind Flynn, alongside Spicer, Homeland Security Advisor-designate Thomas Bossert, and Vice President Pence's Chief of Staff Josh Pitcock. Trump's personal intelligence briefer sat behind the intelligence chiefs.

Since none of the other senior staff had yet to arrive, I welcomed the Four Amigos—Clapper, Brennan, Comey, and Rogers—when they arrived at the 14th floor lobby, and we waited for Trump, Pence, and the others. I chatted briefly with Admiral Rogers, who asked after my Navy daughter. But small talk with the other three was impossible. The Amigos, especially Brennan, Comey, and Clapper, were anything but friendly. They stood there silently and awkwardly, briefcases in hand. I shook everyone's hands and, as the only one who knew both sets of people, introduced them all around when my colleagues arrived. No introductions were necessary, of course; everyone knew who the others where, but at least it generated a few handshakes. But the air was decidedly frigid nonetheless.

The intelligence chiefs did most of the talking during the briefing. No one was allowed to take notes; cell phones and electronic devices had been surrendered before entering the conference room. Trump sat forward in his chair, forearms on the table, hands folded, erect throughout. He didn't interrupt their presentations, but he did ask a few questions afterward, mostly about sources and methods of intelligence gathering. Pence asked a few follow-up questions as well. When they were finished Trump looked to his staff and asked if anyone else had questions. One or two did ask them to clarify some of the things that they mentioned, but there was little discussion. Everyone was respectful. It was a standard intelligence briefing, where the experts did almost all of the talking—not at all like a Trump-style briefing where everyone jumped in to offer their own opinions.

Afterward, we all walked out of the conference room together, and Trump stood in the lobby for a few seconds to thank everyone for coming. As he turned to leave, Comey motioned him aside and I overheard him say to Trump he wanted to discuss "that other matter." Trump stood there waiting for Comey to continue, but Comey said they should talk in private. Trump waved Comey to follow him back into the conference room. According to press reports, that is when Comey told Trump about the infamous Steele dossier, which had lurid descriptions of weird sexual encounters in Moscow. Since then the Steele dossier has been thoroughly discredited as a politically-motivated hit job, with no grounding in reality, designed by charlatans and paid for by the Clinton campaign. Unfortunately, it also allegedly provided the basis for the intelligence community's launch of the Trump-Russia probe.

A few days later, the incoming NSC senior staff attended the Passing the Baton conference, hosted by the U.S. Institute of Peace. It's a two-day conference designed to share foreign policy insights between officials of the outgoing and incoming Administrations, and symbolizes the bipartisan nature of American foreign policy - that "politics stops at the water's edge"- to quote post-war Senator Arthur Vandenberg. But, of course, it doesn't and hasn't for years, especially when a new Administration sees itself as having a mandate to change the direction of America diplomacy.

Washington's foreign policy community was there in force—legislators, former government officials, journalists, and thinktank scholars. Outgoing National Security Advisor Susan Rice gave the first keynote address, recounting the Obama Administration's accomplishments and commenting on the state of world events. Flynn gave the second keynote address, offering a broad overview of the incoming Trump Administration's foreign policy goals. The two-day conference consisted of panel discussions, speeches, presentations, and what were supposed to be convivial conversations and meals, but it was decidedly uncomfortable for everyone. Most of the Obama Administration officials were arrogant and condescending. I didn't expect it would be otherwise, given that most were still reeling from Trump's upset victory. They no doubt viewed the people who would soon take over their jobs—jobs they had come to see as theirs by right—as interlopers and even as barbarians who were totally unqualified and unworthy of succeeding them.

After the formal presentations, the hundred or so people in attendance broke into smaller groups for an elaborate dinner and off-the-record conversations about the country's major national security issues. At the end of dinner, one of the journalists at my table, whom I had known from my previous stints in Washington, offered to share a taxi and drop me off at my new apartment a few blocks away.

During our ride, he expressed his dismay with Trump's choice of Flynn. I don't remember his exact words, but they were along the lines of saying Flynn shouldn't be the National Security Advisor–he didn't have the experience, qualifications, or intellectual firepower. It was an attitude shared by much of the Washington Establishment—the liberal media, the permanent bureaucracy, career politicians, and special interest groups.

Although I didn't recognize it as such at the time, two days later the *Washington Post* began a series of articles that would impact the first two years of the Trump Presidency. On January 12, *Washington Post* columnist David Ignatius wrote an opinion piece that set off a chain of events that helped lead to the Russia probe.[3] He posed a series of questions raised in part by the since-discredited Steele dossier, although Ignatius didn't refer to it by name. He said that an intelligence community investigation into possible Trump-Russian contacts "remains open." He wrote that "according to a Senior U.S. Government Official, Flynn phoned Russian Ambassador Kislyak" the day President Obama's sanctions against Russia were announced. "What did Flynn say, and did it undercut the U.S. sanctions? The Logan Act (although never enforced) bars U.S. citizens from correspondence intending to influence a foreign government about 'disputes' with the United States." Since Ignatius is known for his deep and long-standing connections to intelligence community sources, especially senior officials in the Obama Administration, the Washington media paid attention.

When I got to the Washington Transition headquarters that morning, Flynn was already there and furious that our press office hadn't shot down the story when the columnist asked for comment the night before. (NSC

---

[3] Ignatius, David. "Why Did Obama Dawdle on Russian Hacking?" *The Washington Post.* January 12, 2017. https://www.washingtonpost.com/opinions/why-did-obama-dawdle-on-russias-hacking/2017/01/12/75f878a0-d90c-11e6-9a36-1d296534b31e_story.html.

Communications Director-designate Monica Crowley was preoccupied with issues of her own over accusations of plagiarism and would herself be forced to resign within a few days. Two years later, however, she was appointed to the crucial position of Spokesman and Assistant Treasury Secretary for Public Affairs.)

The Ignatius article set off a flurry of new accusations against Flynn, damaging his credibility and effectiveness before the Administration even took office. The daily beating Flynn took in the press, plus his own unfamiliarity with his new role as National Security Advisor, meant he was easy pickings for the permanent bureaucracy, outgoing Obama officials, and incoming Trump aides hoping to encroach on his territory.

There is some evidence that Flynn was targeted from the beginning by some highly placed intelligence community and Justice Department officials, as a way to get to Trump. I didn't know it when Trump offered me the job of Deputy National Security Advisor two weeks after the election, but apparently Flynn had secretly been on the FBI's radar screen for months, going back to even before the election.

The media attacks against Flynn that had begun in November increased in frequency and intensity as we moved closer to Inauguration day. Many of the articles were by a number of well-placed reporters and seemed to come, at least in part, from the intelligence community. Not surprisingly, Flynn's outspoken criticisms over the years had made him lots of enemies within the Obama Administration and in Clinton circles, the permanent bureaucracy, the intelligence community, and the left-leaning thinktank world. Within days of his appointment, the media had cast Flynn as their favorite villain, second only to Trump himself.

The stories all followed a standard pattern and read something like this: "According to anonymous sources who are not authorized to speak on the record, General Flynn...(fill in the blank)." The articles would continue with several quotes from unnamed "Senior Government Officials," along with on-the-record quotes from former Obama Administration officials sprinkled in. Every article was labeled "breaking news", and repeated by radio, cable news, online, and print media. Almost all were one-sided and slanted, accusing Flynn of some wrongdoing or incompetence, but with nothing in Flynn's defense to balance them out. When one story line had run its course, it was followed by another detrimental story, or new spin on an old story. These attacks seemed coordinated and planned, with one story regularly following on the heels of the last one. There was rarely a day when Flynn was out of the news, and he was always portrayed in a negative light.

It was painful to watch. In just a few weeks, Flynn went from being a valuable asset to Trump during the campaign, to now being a major and constant liability. Flynn was my boss, and after I joined the Transition, he also had become a friend. I wanted him to succeed. I would wake up in the middle of the night, stomach clenched with anxiety, to check my iPhone for the next salvo of damning stories about him. There were so many, coming from so many news outlets, that it soon became impossible even to keep up with them all.

CHAPTER 15

Flynn Death Watch

When Trump finally arrived in Washington a few days before the Inauguration, he stayed at Trump International, his own marble and gold five-star luxury hotel two blocks from the White House. On January 20th, after taking the oath of office on the steps of the Capitol building, President and Mrs. Trump walked along Independence Avenue to the reviewing stand set up in front of the White House. After the bands and troops paraded by, the new President Trump walked across the North Lawn and into the West Wing of the White House. Flynn and I followed close behind. It had been a magical week of celebration. We were filled with enthusiasm and eager to pursue the new direction mandated by the American voters.

Despite my previous fears, the NSC staff was up and functioning on day one. The outgoing and incoming staff members who worked on the handover had done their jobs well, or as well as could be expected for such an earthquake of change from one president to the next. But then reality hit. The first crisis didn't come from abroad as I feared, but from within Washington, actually from within a handful of offices in the West Wing.

The barrage of negative press stories and swirling rumors about General Flynn were taking their toll. The anti-Flynn media frenzy actually escalated, now fed in part by leaks apparently coming from within the White House itself. During Oval Office meetings President Trump's attitude to Flynn showed none of the bonhomie of the Transition. He often blamed Flynn for the bad press, interrupting Oval Office briefings saying, "Mike, you've got to stop this." But there was nothing Flynn could do. Other than shouldering some of the workload, there was nothing I could do, either.

I felt a personal responsibility to help buck him up. But I felt an institutional responsibility as well. In those early days, the NSC was the only functioning part of Trump's new foreign policy team. Many Cabinet nominees were still being grilled by Senate committees, with their confirmation by no means guaranteed. Senior positions had been vacated by departing Obama officials, and Trump hadn't nominated his own people to take their places. It would take a number of days before Rex Tillerson was confirmed as Secretary of State. It fell to Flynn and me, as his deputy, to cover for everyone in the interim.

Adding to the confusion was the fact that every foreign government immediately wanted to forge a relationship with the new Administration. Not only was Trump himself an outsider and an unknown quantity, but so were the people around him, since he had refused to appoint establishment Republican insiders to his Administration. Understandably, foreign officials were flummoxed. They suddenly had to deal with people they didn't know, in hopes of learning about policies that were still in formation, led by a new president who seemed to relish his own unpredictability. They were in a scramble to connect to Trump and his senior staff. Because there was no clear chain of command in the West Wing, they sought entre wherever they could, all at once, with anyone and everyone.

The National Security Council needed take the lead in those first few weeks, but the National Security Advisor himself was wobbly. Flynn seemed unsure of himself from the very beginning. He was awkward in dealing with the media, Members of Congress, foreign leaders, and with the several hundred-person NSC staff we had inherited from the Obama Administration. Perhaps he already sensed he was on shaky ground with Trump, and worried that he might not last long in the job. Whether Flynn saw it coming or not, he was soon in well over his head.

The National Security Advisor is one of the most important people in any Administration. He is supposed to have the president's ear. He is supposed to bring the foreign policy, defense, and intelligence communities together and run the powerful interagency national security process for the president. He is supposed to be the president's intermediary with Members of Congress. He is supposed to be the president's personal conduit with foreign governments. He's supposed to give background briefings to the press to add depth and context to the president's policies. Although immensely powerful, he's also supposed to operate mostly behind the scenes. The one thing the National Security Advisor is *not* supposed to be is a magnet for damaging press stories and a political liability for the president.

There have been several reasons given for Flynn's firing, and they all have the ring of truth. But the one reason rarely mentioned was the constant drumbeat of attention-grabbing headlines criticizing Flynn. They were crowding out any good news about the new Administration.

Media coverage is very important for President Trump. He is a voracious consumer of it and clearly aware of just who on his staff is getting good press and who is getting bad. Too much good coverage and it looks like the aide is stealing Trump's thunder. Too much bad press and the aide is a drag on the Administration. Flynn was a public relations problem from the beginning. Further exacerbating the situation was the fact that his son, also named Michael Flynn, was a frequent, outspoken, and opinionated tweeter. Many assumed that his Alt-Right sympathies and conspiracy theories were shared by his father, and perhaps even President Trump himself. The foreign policy establishment, including those Republicans resentful at being passed over for plumb positions they had assumed would be theirs, were eager to criticize Flynn at every turn. They were the sources for many of the anonymous quotes and negative stories that recited Flynn's unsuitability for a job that usually went to a seasoned diplomat or foreign affairs scholar. President Obama's outgoing NSC staff members joined in the whispering campaign of leaks, designed to discredit Flynn with a drip, drip, drip of nasty stories. These were all damaging Flynn's effectiveness, his morale, and President Trump's confidence in him. Despite how much Trump may have personally liked Flynn, and felt a certain loyalty to him, things simply couldn't continue like this.

The Flynn death watch began two weeks into the Trump Administration. I really hadn't spent all that much time with Flynn after the Inauguration, other than joining him for President Trump's daily intelligence briefings. Our positions entailed different responsibilities. My focus was on taking stock of President Obama's existing foreign, defense, and intelligence policies, and coming up with plans to reorient them. I spent long hours each day in the Situation Room, chairing meetings with representatives from the national security community, reviewing their suggestions, and sending them back to the drawing board when they fell short.

Much of Flynn's day was spent at Trump's side, in briefings, at meetings, and during calls with heads of state. When Flynn was in his NSC office, it was to catch up on paperwork and hold staff conferences, or to host his own meetings with foreign dignitaries. Since the office serves as both a personal and ceremonial office, previous National Security Advisors had filled their bookshelves with memorabilia and personal photos with famous people, and covered their walls with historic paintings. Flynn hadn't brought anything from home until his second week, when he arrived with several cardboard boxes. They were unpacked and displayed, briefly, but packed up a few days later when Flynn was forced to resign in the third week.

Thursday morning, February 9th, just two weeks after the Inauguration, NSC Legal Counsel John Eisenberg came into my office, along with NSC Strategic Communications Director Michael Anton and shut the door. Anton said that in an interview with *Washington Post* reporters the day before, Flynn had categorically denied that he had discussed sanctions with the Russian Ambassador when the two spoke on December 29th, the day President Obama imposed sanctions on Russia and Flynn was on vacation in the Dominican Republic. According to Eisenberg and Anton, the *Washington Post* now had an actual transcript, or had been read a transcript, of at least one of Flynn's phone calls with the Russian Ambassador. They said the transcript showed that, contrary to what Flynn had just told the *Washington Post* reporters, the vice president, and others, Flynn *had* talked to the Russian Ambassador about sanctions, in very specific terms, and that Flynn himself had first introduced the topic.

Eisenberg, Anton, and I, along with one or two other aides, immediately walked through Flynn's open door and into his office. His head was bent down over his desk, pen in hand, and he was going through stacks of paperwork. He seemed oblivious to anything unusual, and barely looked up when we walked in. Anton is tall and thin, with a full head of salt and pepper, wavy hair, meticulously groomed and highly charged. In an agitated voice, with hands punctuating his points, Anton told Flynn that the *Washington Post* had a transcript of his call with the Russian Ambassador. Eisenberg is Anton's polar opposite in both looks and demeanor. He stood next to Anton—silently, briefing books under his arm—wearing a poker face along with a wrinkled suit. His choice of words was more measured and circumspect than Anton's, but he was clearly just as concerned.

Since the transcript contradicted Flynn's interview from the day before, the *Washington Post* was seeking clarification. Flynn didn't say anything, continuing to look down at the papers on his desk. He finally looked up and said, "You know, I've gone over it again and again in my mind and I honestly can't recall" whether we discussed sanctions.

We asked whether he had actually discussed "sanctions." Diplomats often speak in a kind of code, implying, inferring, and signaling a position, talking around a subject but not actually stating it directly. That way they would not be bound by it later if circumstances changed. When I talked to Flynn after he had spoken to the Russian Ambassador six weeks before, I had assumed that's what they had done. I did get the impression from Flynn that their phone call included discussion of President Obama's sanctions, but that they had probably talked around the subject, each conveying their continued desire to improve relations once Trump was in office, and implying that Obama's sanctions wouldn't derail that goal. That was how I could parse Flynn's continued insistence that he hadn't discussed sanctions with the Russian Ambassador. From what he told me at the time I thought that, "things are going to be okay," implied that their discussion covered sanctions, even if not directly or in so many words.

We pressed him. "Did you say the word *sanctions*?" Perhaps the situation might still be salvaged if Flynn had talked around the topic and not, as the *Washington Post* claimed, discussed "sanctions" with great specificity. After another long pause Flynn said, "I can't say that it didn't come up." He didn't strike me as dissembling, but as genuinely scared and confused—like a man who has just realized he is drowning, but who is powerless to save himself. I told Flynn he couldn't keep denying they discussed sanctions or say he couldn't remember if they actually had. I left Flynn's office, while Anton and the others stayed behind to craft a response to the *Post's* allegations.

I went back in my office and shut the door. I tried to collect my thoughts. My first reaction was wondering why the intelligence community was listening in on phone calls of the president's National Security Advisor. Did they have permission to do this and from whom? Could the intelligence community do something like this on their own authority? Even so, it could only have been ordered by people at the highest levels of the intelligence community, if not even higher, perhaps even from the Obama White House.

The transcript from Flynn's call with the Russian Ambassador happened during the Transition, in the closing days of the Obama Administration. If they were brazen enough to tap the phone of one of Trump's most senior advisors, who held the highest of security clearances, who else's phone calls had they listened in on? Trump's? His family's? Other Members of the senior staff? Were they still listening in on those calls even after Trump took office?

And how did these transcripts, which were so highly classified I wasn't even aware that they existed, much less cleared to read them, make their way into the hands of *Washington Post* reporters? Only a very few people would have had access to something as sensitive as these transcripts. Who had leaked them to reporters and why? Had senior Obama Administration officials authorized not just the wiretaps, but then approved turning the transcripts over to the press? How could any of this be legal? Had somebody gone rogue and done all of this without authorization? Something as significant as wiretapping the president-elect's National Security Advisor-designate would not have been done casually, or by accident, or by some mid-level bureaucrat. Authorized or unauthorized, sanctioned or rogue, it still could only be done by people so powerful that they didn't worry about getting found out. I felt like I had just been plunked down into the middle of a made-for-TV conspiracy drama.

The *Washington Post* ran their story on Thursday, February 9th, a month after their first story questioning whether Flynn had violated the spirit or the letter of the Logan Act.[4] It was followed by stories with additional detail from other publications.

---

[4] Miller, Greg, Adam Entous, and Ellen Nakashima. "National security advisor Flynn discussed sanctions with Russian ambassador, despite denials, officials say." *The Washington Post.* February 9, 2017. https://www.washingtonpost.com/world/national-security/national-security-adviser-flynn-discussed-sanctions-with-russian-ambassador-despite-denials-officials-say/2017/02/09/f85b29d6-eel1-11e6-b4ff-ac2cf509efe5_story.html?utm_term=.23ecce5469ec.

Thursday evening, President Trump had a scheduled phone call with Chinese President Xi. Given the time difference between Beijing and Washington, the call was arranged for late at night. President Trump took the call in the Treaty Room on the second floor of the White House Residence, in the first family's private quarters, rather than in the Oval Office. Even in the daytime the Treaty Room is rather dark, with heavy ornate drapes and swags, dark wallpaper and stiff furniture, in a style popular during the Civil War era. There is a large brass chandelier on the ceiling, but most of the light comes from a few table lamps scattered around the room, and from the brass bankers lamp on the large, heavily carved, wooden desk which dominates the room. Since it was very late at night, the room was even darker. I remember thinking how funereal it all seemed.[5]

Secretary Tillerson, Priebus, NSC China expert Matt Pottinger, and several other senior officials attended, including Flynn. We were all sitting around the room, when President Trump walked in and sat behind the large desk, directly under the painting which shows Lincoln and his Cabinet sitting at that same desk. It was Flynn's job to prep the President for the call, to give him a short briefing paper, and explain what topics were likely to come up. It was obvious that President Trump could hardly bear to have Flynn in the room. When Flynn walked over to the desk, and leaned over to show him the briefing papers, Trump just glared at him. Flynn walked back to his chair and slumped down with a hangdog look on his face.

The West Wing is a small place; inhabitants walk past each other dozens of times a day going to and from meetings. People's body language toward Flynn had suddenly grown markedly unfriendly. The next morning, Friday, February 10th, I walked with Flynn to the Oval Office for President Trump's intelligence briefing, which the vice president also attended. I suggested Flynn take the opportunity and apologize to Pence. We were already waiting in the anteroom when the vice president and his National Security Advisor arrived. Flynn asked Pence if he could have a word, and the two of them walked into the adjoining Cabinet Room and shut the door. After about five minutes they both came out, but neither

---

[5] "Readout of the President's Call with President Xi Jinping of China." The White House. February 9, 2017. https://www.whitehouse.gov/briefings-statements/readout-presidents-call-president-xi-jinping-china/.

was smiling. Whatever was said, it didn't seem to have fixed things. On my way out of the intelligence briefing I stopped at Hope Hicks's desk. "How bad is it?" I asked. She replied, "Bad. Really bad."[6]

Later that day Japanese Prime Minister Abe met with President Trump at the White House, and afterward the two held a joint press conference in the East Room. Chairs in the two front rows were reserved for White House officials, and Flynn was the first one to take his seat. He was all alone in the front row and glanced around to see where everyone else was. One by one the other officials arrived, but each avoided sitting next to him. The shunning had begun.

Later that day, Flynn accompanied President Trump and his entourage to Florida where he and the First Lady hosted Prime Minister Abe and Mrs. Abe at Mar-a-Lago for the weekend, for two days of meetings and Trump-Abe golf matches in between. It was the first major diplomatic event of Trump's presidency; it was also Flynn's first…and his last.

Adding to the drama of the summit meeting was the thing we had been worried about from the beginning: North Korea conducted a missile test just as President Trump and the Japanese Prime Minister sat down to dinner. Rather than a carefully scripted transpacific phone call between the two leaders, Trump was able to lean over during their first course of an iceberg lettuce salad to discuss it directly with Prime Minister Abe. Clearly, things were not going to be business as usual in the Trump White House.[7]

When President Trump and the White House staff returned to Washington on Monday, February 13th, it was obvious at the president's morning intelligence briefing that things had gotten even worse. Trump treated Flynn with disdain and refused to look at him or acknowledge him when he spoke. When the meeting ended, Flynn walked back to his office by himself and closed the door, which was unusual for him. Flynn always prided himself on being accessible and keeping an open door.

Flynn ventured out of his office several times throughout the day, always alone, and walked to the other end of the hall to the suite of offices

[6] Shuham, Matt. "Reports: Flynn Apologized To Pence Amid Reports He Talked Sanctions With Russia." Talking Points Memo. https://talkingpointsmemo.com/livewire/reports-flynn-apologized -to-mike-pence.

[7] Borger, Julian. "Missile crisis by candlelight: Donald Trump's use of Mar-a-Lago raises security questions." *The Guardian.* February 14, 2017. https://www.theguardian.com/us-news/2017/feb/13/ mar-a-lago-north-korea-missile-crisis-trump-national-security.

Priebus and Bannon shared. When Flynn returned, he went directly back into his office without saying a word, and again closed his door. At various points during the day, Priebus, Bannon, McGahn, Kushner, and others walked in and out of Flynn's office, always closing the door behind them. There was none of the usual bonhomie and greetings. It had been replaced by grim faces and silence. The rest of us in the suite were in the dark about what was going on with Flynn, but whatever it was seemed to have reached the crisis point.

At some point that afternoon, Kellogg and I, and several others on his immediate staff, knocked on Flynn's door, and went in. Flynn was looking down at his desk, going through the paperwork in his inbox. We asked what was going on. Was everything okay? Flynn kept his head down, focused on the papers he was reading. He brushed us off with, "No, no, it's okay. We're good." He continued looking at the papers on his desk, and we all trooped out.

We still didn't know what was going on when, at about 6:00 p.m. that evening, Kellogg and I walked down the hall to the Oval Office to witness Steven Mnuchin be sworn in as Secretary of the Treasury. Kellogg and I stood with our backs to the glass doors nearest the Rose Garden. Flynn was already there, standing on the other side of the room, near the door to the small dining room that adjoins the Oval Office. Usually these events are happy affairs, a brief break in an otherwise hectic day, and the senior staff are all invited to attend. Flynn was standing alone, looking forlorn, and the other senior staff members in the room avoided him. Everyone's discomfort was obvious. Kellogg turned to me and said, "It sure doesn't look like 'everything's okay.'"

After the Mnuchin swearing-in ceremony, we all went back to our respective offices, with Flynn again staying behind closed doors. An hour or so later, two of Flynn's aides came into my office, along with Kellogg, and shut my door. They said Flynn had been fired, effective immediately. Kellogg, who, along with Flynn, had been with Trump on the campaign trail, would be the interim National Security Advisor. Kellogg and I, along with the other aides, filed silently into Flynn's office. He was looking down at his desk, still working his way through the routine memoranda from his inbox. He looked up at all of us, with the saddest, most soulful eyes I think I've ever seen, and said, quietly, "I've really screwed up, haven't I?" It wasn't a question, and he didn't expect any of us to answer.

I asked if there was anything we could do to help him. Help with his resignation letter? Talk to his wife or anyone else and let them know? Was anyone coming to meet him at the White House? He said no, he still had some paperwork to get through. We all trooped out and closed the door behind us. I was struck that Flynn was still reflexively doing routine paperwork, reading intelligence reports, and signing off on memoranda, even as he was heading out the door for the last time. I don't think it had sunk in yet that when he left later that evening, he wouldn't be coming back. It was over. One of the last things Flynn said to us that day was, "You know, I joined the military to fight the Russians."

I left Flynn's office and walked the short distance down the hall to the Chief of Staff's suite. Priebus and Bannon were both sitting in the office when I arrived, and Priebus told me to close the door and sit down. They confirmed that Flynn had been fired, and that Kellogg had been named the interim National Security Advisor. I asked if they wanted me to resign too. They looked at each other, puzzled. They clearly hadn't given this any thought. They both looked back at me and Bannon said, "Geeze, you can't leave. Somebody's got to run the place!" Priebus added his agreement.

I left them and walked down the narrow staircase to Kellogg's West Basement office, near the Situation Room. We were both pretty stunned and shell-shocked, but agreed there was nothing more to be done that night. Kellogg packed up and headed home. I went back upstairs to the NSC suite. Flynn's door was still closed. Word of Flynn's firing had spread to the NSC staff across the street in the Executive Office Building, and several of them had gathered outside my office. Everyone wanted to know what would happen next, would they still have their jobs in the morning? Several of them had uprooted their lives, quit their old jobs, sold their houses and moved to Washington less than a month before; they were justifiably concerned.

I told them Priebus and Bannon had asked me to stay on, and I would try to talk with the president in the morning. But whatever happened in the days ahead, I said I would do whatever I could to make sure everyone's job was secure, either on the NSC or elsewhere in the Administration. I told them to go home. We would meet first thing in the morning for a senior staff meeting. The next few days would be difficult, so I packed up and headed home myself, telling Flynn's aide that I was available at any time, no matter how late, if Flynn wanted to talk.

The next morning, I remained behind in the Oval Office after the intelligence briefing, and asked President Trump if I could stay on as Deputy National Security Advisor. He said yes, definitely. He called Sean Spicer and Hope Hicks into his office and told them to "get it out there" that I was staying. Later that week, President Trump motioned for me to stay behind after the intelligence briefing. He said, "You know I had to fire Flynn. I didn't have a choice." I responded that it probably was inevitable. I said Flynn was a good man, but he was in over his head, and couldn't have lasted long in the job. Trump nodded slowly, in somber agreement.

Why had Flynn become the media's whipping boy? I think it was for a combination of reasons. One, the large number of Trump's critics who permeated the Washington Establishment—Democrats, the liberal media, embittered Clintonistas, and Never-Trump Republicans—all wanted Trump stopped dead in his tracks. They hoped to find ways to remove him from office and, failing that, to sabotage and disrupt his presidency. Perhaps they saw Flynn as Trump's weakest link, a way to harm the president by picking off one of his top advisors.

Perhaps people in Washington's foreign policy community resented Flynn for getting a job they thought should go to one of their own. After all, most National Security Advisors are drawn from the ranks of the left- or right-leaning thinktanks, depending on whether the new president is a Democrat or Republican. Flynn wasn't a member of any of these establishment "clubs." Perhaps they considered him unworthy to sit in the seat once occupied by Henry Kissinger, Zbigniew Brzezinski, Colin Powell, and Condoleezza Rice.

Perhaps it was a pre-emptive strike by some in the intelligence community who feared Flynn was planning a wholesale reorganization of their agencies, as the press was reporting.[8]

Perhaps it was an insatiable media looking for sensational stories to maintain public interest and keep their ratings up after a tumultuous, exciting, and highly profitable campaign season.

Perhaps Flynn had just made too many enemies along the way. There were a lot of people gunning for him from the beginning. But to be fair, he also gave them lots of ammunition—his over-the-top chants at the

---

[8] Paletta, Damian and Julian E. Barnes. "Donald Trump Plans Revamp of Top U.S. Spy Agency." *Wall Street Journal*. January 4, 2019. https://www.wsj.com/articles/lawmakers-officials-frown-on-donald-trumps-dismissal-of-u-s-intelligence-1483554450.

Republican Convention and on the campaign trail to "lock her up;" his son's constant tweeting and loud support of Alt-Right groups, which Flynn had done nothing to temper. It's one thing to criticize policies; it's another thing to bray for blood. Blood begets blood.

Perhaps it was his business ties and financial irregularities which had come as a surprise to many, myself included. Perhaps it was Flynn's connections to the Russians and other unsavory regimes, including Turkey. On election day, Flynn had an opinion piece in *TheHill.com* lauding Turkish Prime Minister Erdogan. It didn't sound to me like Flynn had written it; it wasn't his voice. It seemed to me more like Flynn had put his byline on an article authored by someone else.[9]

When I ran into Flynn in the lobby of the FOX News building a few hours after the article came out, I asked him, "What was that all about?" I had been critical of Prime Minster Erdogan for years—he had turned Turkey from a tolerant secular democracy into an Islamist autocracy. I assumed Flynn shared my assessment. He shrugged and mumbled something about having to get along with Turkey. I didn't think much more about it at the time, but his undisclosed consulting relationship with Turkey later became yet another red flag. Although Flynn never discussed his consulting firm with me, he had on several occasions expressed concern over his personal finances as well as those of his family members. Stories about Flynn's failure to reveal details of his business connections and past travel made their way into the media. Drip by painful drip, they helped guarantee a steady stream of disparaging news.

But once Vice President Pence determined that Flynn had lied to him, Flynn's fate was sealed. Pence is one of the most decent, unassuming, understanding, and forgiving people I have ever met. He doesn't let his ego get in the way of his judgment, or his principles. If he determined Flynn had deliberately misled him, Flynn would have to go—there could be no appeal.

I once had great respect for Flynn's professionalism as an intelligence officer and for his abilities as a national security analyst. But in the end, I realized that the Mike Flynn I thought I knew was only part of who he was. There was another part of him that had exhibited very poor judgment

---

[9] Flynn, Lt. Gen. Michael T. "Our ally Turkey is in crisis and needs our support." *The Hill.* November 8, 2016. https://thehill.com/blogs/pundits-blog/foreign-policy/305021-our-ally-turkey-is-in-crisis-and-needs-our-support.

and had needlessly cut corners in his personal and business affairs. It was almost like finding out the neighbor you've known and liked for years turns out to have a second family in another city.

There are probably as many theories of what really happened in the 2016 election as there are reporters covering the story. It's fertile territory for conspiracy theorists as well—everything from "Putin got Trump elected because he's a Russian agent" to "the FBI and Justice Department are part of a Deep State conspiracy that tried to keep Trump from winning, and when that failed, tried to destroy his presidency." In the end we may never know the truth, only that just about everyone behaved badly. There are no heroes in this story, and probably no happy ending.

The part that continues to baffle me is why Flynn did do some of the things that he has been accused of doing throughout the period from the campaign to the Transition to his brief tenure as National Security Advisor. I worked right alongside Flynn for several hectic months, and still haven't figured it all out.

The tragic irony not just for Flynn, but for the president and the country, is that the entire Russia investigation, the national hysteria, the collusion claims, and the obstruction of justice accusations all seemed to hinge on a supposed crime that had never been committed in the first place. As Trump said after Flynn was fired, while he didn't direct him to call the Russian Ambassador, he would have because it was Flynn's job to be in touch with foreign leaders during the Transition. As Trump said a few days after firing Flynn, "When I looked at the information, I said, 'I don't think he did anything wrong. If anything, he did something right… He was just doing his job.'"[10] Indeed, one of the goals of any presidential advisor is to prevent crises, not to exacerbate them. Given the hysteria over what later happened during the Russian collusion narrative, it is almost as if Trump's critics would have preferred the Russian-American relationship had descended into a full-blown calamity.

Ten months after leaving the White House as National Security Advisor, Flynn pled guilty to lying to the FBI when they interviewed him at his office a few days after the Inauguration. This is despite press reports that the FBI agents who interviewed Flynn said that they didn't think he was

---

[10] "Full Transcript and Video: Trump News Conference." *The New York Times*. February 16, 2017. https://www.nytimes.com/2017/02/16/us/politics/donald-trump-press-conference-transcript.html.

lying, just that he was confused.[11] Some have speculated that Flynn plead guilty to a crime he didn't commit in order to end his cripplingly expensive legal fees. According to press reports Flynn had already depleted his savings and been forced to sell his house, and could have faced millions more in legal expenses if he went to court. Flynn was living on his Army pension, had been unemployed since he left government, and was not a wealthy man to begin with. During the Transition he had often joked that the people in Trump's orbit could "pay off my mortgage with their petty cash."

There was also speculation in the media that he traded a guilty plea for "lying" in exchange for the Special Prosecutor not pursuing charges against his son, or to avoid more serious accounting and tax related charges against his consulting firm.[12]

Perhaps Flynn was hoping to make his mark in foreign policy. Every National Security Advisor since Kissinger has sought to achieve an historic breakthrough like he had with China in the 1970s. Maybe Flynn hoped to lay the groundwork for détente with Russia, in hopes of making diplomatic progress through his own special relationships and efforts. Not only could he then deliver a great achievement to Trump and win his appreciation, it would guarantee both of them a place in history.

Perhaps the Russians had played Flynn right from the start. Perhaps Putin never had any intention of getting into a crisis with the United States over the Obama-imposed sanctions and expulsions, coming as they did just three weeks before Trump was to take office. Putin had more to lose by continuing the antagonistic relationship between our two countries than we did. Plus, Trump had made it clear on the campaign trail that he would seek to improve relations with Russia once he took office. Why would Putin want to risk jeopardizing that just to get back at an outgoing Obama Administration?

If so, perhaps Putin wasn't going "to let a good crisis go to waste" as Obama's Chief of Staff Rahm Emanuel once said, and stage-managed the

---

[11] Leonnig, Carol D., John Wagner, and Ellen Nakashima. "Trump lawyer says president knew Flynn had given FBI the same account he gave to vice president." *The Washington Post*. December 3, 2017. https://www.washingtonpost.com/politics/trump-lawyer-says-president-knew-flynn-had-given-fbi-the-same-account-he-gave-to-vice-president/2017/12/03/5c59a620-d849-11e7-a841-2066faf731ef_story.html.

[12] "The Mystery of Michael Flynn's Guilty Plea." *Wall Street Journal*. May 6, 2018. https://www.wsj.com/articles/the-mystery-of-michael-flynns-guilty-plea-1525640861.

entire Russian response. By swooping in to dramatically overrule his Foreign Minister just a few hours after he promised Russian retaliation, Putin cast himself in the role of responsible senior statesman. Putin could take up the issue with the new president, and at the same time take credit for averting a crisis.

But perhaps, in the end, there is a simple but tragic explanation for Flynn's actions. Maybe his denials to the FBI were the result of faulty memory, poor judgment, and sloppy answers. I know Flynn was definitely preoccupied at the time trying to figure out his responsibilities for a job he was ill prepared to undertake. Perhaps he didn't appreciate the danger of taking a hastily arranged and seemingly inconsequential meeting with FBI agents in his first few days in office. Perhaps he was spooked by press reports that he had violated the Logan Act, which I doubt he or anyone else in the Trump orbit had ever heard of before Ignatius first brought it up in his *Washington Post* column in January. But once Flynn had gone down the track of insisting to the vice president and others that he hadn't talked to the Russian Ambassador about sanctions, he couldn't get off it.

Or maybe there is something to the conspiracy theories. Perhaps senior officials in the intelligence community did seek to sabotage the Trump presidency and Flynn gave them the opening they needed. Maybe the convenient leaks to *Washington Post* journalists about Flynn's contacts with the Russians were the work-around the intelligence community arranged to justify their investigations into the Trump campaign and Transition. That seems to fit a pattern they have used in the past when officials wanted to do something that otherwise might have been unacceptable. They would first leak information to the press, putting their own spin on the story. They could then point to the press story as evidence they needed to investigate the issue further. The Clinton-sponsored, FBI-promoted Steele dossier was certainly handled in a similar fashion. Once it was leaked, the press, predictably, went wild with speculation. The intelligence community could then point to these very same press stories (which their leaks made possible) as reasons for launching the Russia investigation.

This is all speculation on my part. I haven't seen Flynn since he walked out of his West Wing office on the night he was fired. We may never know what Flynn was trying to do. The transcripts of his calls with the Russian Ambassador have not been released. The irony is the only people outside of the intelligence services who do seem to know what Flynn and the Russian Ambassador actually said to each other in December 2016 are a select number of journalists from the *Washington Post* and other news organizations.

CHAPTER 16

White House Months

President Trump moved quickly to fill Flynn's vacancy. He briefly considered three Army generals: Kellogg, West Point Superintendent General Robert Caslen, and General H.R. McMaster. A week after Flynn was fired, Trump named McMaster as his new National Security Advisor. Like Flynn, McMaster was a career Army officer; like Flynn, he had never worked in the Executive Branch. But, unlike Flynn, McMaster had no previous relationship with Trump. The first time they met was at McMaster's job interview in Mar-a-Lago a few days before being appointed.

McMaster is a soldier-scholar and had been highly decorated for his involvement in both Iraq and Afghanistan. His book, *Dereliction of Duty*, is a classic and required reading for young officers. It is a well-researched, scathing criticism of the military and political leaders who led us into, and kept us fighting, a losing war in Vietnam. The media heralded his appointment, as did the Washington Establishment and foreign policy community. When McMaster arrived at the West Wing on Tuesday, February 21st, he was immediately swept into a day of meetings and administrative details.

I wanted to confirm with him that I would remain as his Deputy. Flynn and I didn't formally divide areas of responsibility; it had happened naturally. Like Flynn, McMaster's prior experience had been in the Middle East, the Afghan and Iraq wars. My area of expertise was Asia and China, plus, I knew the president, his thinking, and his style. I had been part of Trump's staff from the beginning of the Transition and had known several members of his Cabinet for decades. As a result, I thought McMaster and I made for a good fit. I get along pretty well with most people, so assumed McMaster and I would work together, with some obvious adjustments, as he put his own stamp on the NSC.

When I finally had a chance to meet alone with McMaster the next morning, Wednesday, February 22nd, I told him that the President had asked me to stay on, at least through a transition period, if not longer. He listened politely and said something non-committal.

Later that day, Priebus and Bannon called me into the Chief of Staff's office. Priebus told me to shut the door and take a seat. "Look," he said, "I just want to let you know upfront that this meeting isn't going to end well." He proceeded to tell me that McMaster wanted his own NSC staff, so I would have to resign, along with the other Flynn people.

I took a deep breath and said, "Wait a minute, guys. Just three days ago the president said he wanted me to stay. He said it to me several times and at different meetings in the days after Flynn left. He even called you and Spicer into the Oval Office and told you to get it out to the media. Are you now telling me that Trump has changed his mind in the last two days?"

Bannon shrugged and said it was one of McMaster's conditions for taking the job. He wanted me gone so he could have his own deputy. Reince cut in, "You must admit, it's only fair that McMaster be allowed to hire his own people. After all, Flynn hired you."

I replied, "No, actually General Flynn did not hire me; the president did, in part on the recommendation of Henry Kissinger. Trump himself called me on Thanksgiving Day to offer me the job. And, as you'll recall, Reince, because you were there, Flynn wasn't even present during my job interview with the president-elect at Trump Tower."

I went on to say, "Furthermore, I helped set up the NSC system and hired most of the new staff members when Flynn was still just feeling his way. I kept the NSC together during Flynn's tumultuous three weeks on the job. I held his hand during the resignation process and kept the system running during the interregnum. And just a few days ago you were begging me to stay."

I finished by acknowledging that, although Washington is a place where no good deed goes unpunished, this was a new low, even for Washington. I didn't think the president would want to reward my loyalty and steadfastness by firing me.

It was useless for me to carry on—they had already made their decision. So, I didn't say aloud what I was really thinking, that these rookies were pushing out the door the one person who knew how the West Wing and White House worked, who had decades of foreign policy experience, who had supported Trump long before they did, who understood and continued to support his agenda, and who was one of the few people who had a good relationship with him. Plus, they had just fired one of the only senior women on the White House staff, and probably the only senior citizen, other than the president himself. Brilliant, guys. Really brilliant.

Priebus rushed to assure me that my contributions were noted and appreciated, and that I was still a "part of the team." He said the president still thought well of me, but he shrugged and said their hands were tied. Later in the day, when I had some time alone with McMaster, I asked him if he indeed wanted me to leave. He vigorously denied it, and swore vehemently he wanted me to stay on, but said that Priebus and Bannon insisted I had to go. So, McMaster blamed Priebus and Bannon; Priebus and Bannon blamed McMaster—typical Washington profiles in courage—always blame the guy who's not in the room. To this day, I don't know who insisted I be fired: McMaster, Bannon, Priebus, or even President Trump. I don't really care; I just wish that one of them had been man enough to be honest with me and say it to my face. Ironically, Priebus and Bannon would themselves be fired within six months, and McMaster within a year—all in a decidedly humiliating fashion.

Bannon asked if there was another position I wanted at the White House or in the Administration. I answered that the National Security Council was the only job in Washington I ever wanted; there was no point in me staying there for anything else.

Bannon then asked if I wanted to be an Ambassador, and we discussed several countries—India, Australia, some European nations, and Singapore. Bannon made the case for Singapore—it was a crucial and increasingly important strategic ally for the United States. Plus, I had a background in Asia, and Singapore itself was the jewel of Asia. My Chinese was rusty, but I could always get a tutor. Since I didn't want to go away empty-handed, and certainly didn't want to live with the ignominy of being fired, I asked if I could let them know within the hour. I stepped out their office suite and into the hallway and called my husband. "Honey, I've been fired. I know we just moved to Washington three weeks ago, but would you be willing to get uprooted again and move to Singapore?"

After a long pause, my beloved husband of thirty-three years, my wise counselor, my closest confidante, and my biggest booster asked only one question, "When?"

The next day, Thursday, February 23rd, Priebus called me back to his office to say that President Trump would like me to send Priebus an email for the record confirming two things: First, that Trump had never called Flynn in the middle of the night to ask him whether a low dollar or high dollar was better for America. Second, that Trump did not direct Flynn to call the Russian Ambassador to discuss sanctions.

I responded to the first request by saying Flynn had told me several times that, despite press reports, Trump had never asked him about a high or low dollar, in the middle of the night or at any other time. Flynn added that the entire thing was crazy. "Why would a billionaire business-man ask me about that kind of stuff?"

I told Priebus that on the second point, I could not say one way or the other whether Trump did or did not direct Flynn to call the Russian Ambassador because I didn't know. I was at Mar-a-Lago the week between Christmas and New Year's while Flynn was on vacation in the Caribbean, and I was not aware of any Trump-Flynn phone calls, nor any Trump-Russia phone calls.

Priebus then asked if I could say something nice about Trump in my resignation letter. I said as for that, I would have no problem because I believed in Trump and was committed to his populist revolution from the beginning and remained so. "Look," Priebus said, "Trump just wants to make sure you say nice things about him when you go back on FOX."

"No problem there," I said. I left the other requests unanswered.

I walked back down the hall to my office, phoned NSC Legal Advisor John Eisenberg and asked if he could come to see me right away about something important. Eisenberg holds a joint position as the NSC's senior counsel, as well as being one of the top lawyers in the White House Counsel's office. He was one of my closest colleagues on the NSC and I trusted his judgment and wisdom in dealing with even the most difficult and sensitive issues. He is one of the great unsung heroes of the Trump Administration. A few minutes later Eisenberg walked into my office and closed the door. I told him I been fired the day before by Priebus and Bannon, and that my consolation prize was the Ambassadorship to Singapore, which I had accepted. I related that Priebus had just called me back to his office to pass along several requests from the president, which I repeated for Eisenberg. I told him the whole thing made me very uncomfortable, and asked for his advice.

Eisenberg reminded me that he wasn't my personal lawyer, which was how he often began before then going on to offer advice. He suggested that I not write the email. It would be bad for both sides. First, it would be awkward—why would I be emailing Priebus to make a statement for the record? Second, it was also a bad idea for the president because it looked as if my ambassadorial appointment to Singapore was in some way a *quid pro quo*. This is more or less what I expected Eisenberg to say, and one of the reasons I asked to meet with him in the first place. I didn't mention it to Eisenberg at the time, but I assumed he would immediately realize the request was inappropriate. I also assumed he would quietly get in touch with his other boss, White House Counsel Don McGahn, who might pass the word to Priebus that he should withdraw the request, thus solving the problem.

I took Eisenberg's advice and tried to see Priebus to say that, upon reflection, I didn't think it was a good idea for me to write the email, but I would be happy to say favorable things about Trump in my resignation letter and in any future media appearances, not because they asked me to, but because that was what I believed. I stuck my head in Priebus's office several times as the day went on, but he was either out of the office or in meetings. I figured if I didn't hear back from him, I would let the whole matter drop and not mention it again myself.

That evening, as I was packing up to go home, Priebus walked into my office and shut the door behind him. Priebus said, "Look, you don't have to write the email or the letter. Just forget I said anything about it. Forget we even had the conversation." I said I was still going to write a letter of resignation saying I believed in the president and in his mission. Priebus repeated, rather nervously, "You don't have to do that either. Just forget I ever mentioned it."

The next morning, President Trump motioned me to stay after our morning intelligence briefing to congratulate me and to tell me what a great place Singapore is. He said, "Singapore, how cool is that!" as if nothing had happened.

I never took the request as anything more than a rookie mistake. In the world of business, it wouldn't have been unusual to ask for a favor when granting a favor. But in Washington it could be interpreted differently. Not only could it be seen as unethical, it could even be considered illegal. I knew the Singapore job was not conditional on my writing the email regarding Flynn; it was my consolation prize for getting fired without cause from the NSC. But the whole thing had been very badly handled.

First, President Trump tells me I can stay at the NSC, and Bannon and Priebus insist I had to stay to run things. A few days later Bannon and Priebus fire me, saying it was at McMaster's insistence. At the same time, McMaster swears that firing me wasn't his idea, that he's not the kind of person who would do that, but it was what Bannon and Priebus wanted. Bannon and Priebus offer me the Singapore post, then Priebus asks for the email for the record regarding Flynn. Meanwhile, the president himself congratulates me saying Singapore is a terrific place, one of the best cities in the world and I would have a great time there. He said, "You know, a lot of people wanted that job!" I got the impression that the president thought it was *my* idea to leave the White House for Singapore. He saw it as a promotion.

I was distinctly uncomfortable with the entire episode. Given the level of chaos and duplicity all around me, I was concerned that any one of them could twist it, or leak it, or use it to his advantage at some point in the future. My husband suggested I write a memorandum for the record, outlining everything and including a timeline of events. It was the first time in my career that I considered such a step prudent or necessary. I wrote the memorandum and forgot all about it—until the Mueller investigation.

As I was mulling all of this over, I recalled a conversation I'd had with one of the stalwarts of the Washington Establishment two weeks before the Inauguration. He observed there seemed to be no clear division of responsibilities among the senior staff, and predicted we would have even more than the usual set of difficulties. He said in previous Administrations virtually everyone reported to the president through the Chief of

Staff. But with the Trump team, there appeared to be three people in that position—Chief of Staff Reince Priebus, Senior Counselor Steve Bannon, and Senior Advisor Jared Kushner. They seemed to have overlapping portfolios, and it wasn't clear who had the final word with the president, or who determined what did or didn't make it into the Oval Office. He said this would lead to confusion and undue complications in those critical first few months.

His prediction turned out to be prophetic. There were endless stories of chaos in the White House, dysfunction at the National Security Council, and a nest of vipers in the West Wing. Not only was there constant jockeying for power among the inner circle for face time, attention, and pride of place, there were repeated arguments between the globalists and nationalists, between the interventionists and the isolationists, between the free traders and the protectionists. It wasn't clear who actually spoke for Trump on any of these issues, even though all claimed to do so.

Added to this was Trump's propensity for handing out assignments based on whoever was in the room at the time, and on who was currently in or out of his favor. He bounced ideas around with the people around him and asked for their opinions. It made for constant competition among even the closest of his aides. But in the final analysis, Donald J. Trump was the only one who made decisions, and he had no problem overruling others, including sometimes even himself. It did little to build the we're-all-in-this-together approach they would need to weather the inevitable criticisms every Administration quickly faces. And they were going to need it more than other Administrations because Trump had been elected to shake up the Washington Establishment. Little wonder that they viewed him as a usurper, and threat to their power. They were unwilling to give Trump or his people the benefit of the doubt. That meant everyone outside of the White House was gunning for everyone inside, and the people inside were gunning for each other too.

It took me some time to figure it out, but much of the constantly negative media coverage was being fed by the people closest to Trump. They were some of the "anonymous sources" quoted in the established and respected publications, which now churned out story after story about the chaos in Trump land. They gave reporters an unending supply of the one topic that so captivates Washington—West Wing palace intrigue. Aides took to supplying the media with unattributed leaks, badmouthing their colleagues, and puffing themselves up. But the real audience they were aiming at was an audience of one—the media-savvy man who sat in the Oval Office.

There have been lots of theories about why President Trump's first few months in office were so tumultuous. But the problem wasn't just an organization chart oversight, as my friend implied. The management system didn't happen by accident. It was the way Trump wanted things to be. This was the how he had operated his business empires for years, and with great success. He forced aides to compete with each other for his attention and to advance their own policies. By dividing power without clear divisions of responsibility, he ensured no one of them was powerful enough to overrule the others or make decisions in his name.

Trump bristles at being managed by anybody. He has said often enough that he is his own Chief of Staff. There is something to that claim. He sets things up so that he makes all the important decisions himself. He often keeps the reasons for his decisions close to his vest and announces them when he thinks the timing is right. Make a mistake, take credit for something that Trump believes belongs to him, or try to push him to do something he doesn't want to do, and you could be fired at any time, and without warning. Trump is the only one in charge and he wants you to know it. Everyone else is expendable.

Adding to the sense of chaos and uncertainty was President Trump's habit of constantly polling the people around him on what they thought about each other, and who would make good replacements for them. He openly discussed all of this not just with his staff, but with his friends. Not surprisingly, almost everything found its way to the press—and never in a nice way. It led to a steady stream of stories quoting "anonymous sources" about whose head was on the chopping block. Everything was breathlessly reported as "breaking news." This kept the D.C. rumor mill churning with stories about pandemonium in the West Wing at a fevered pitch. It was great for the media's bottom line, and for Trump's unrelenting daily domination of the news cycle.

President Trump takes great pride in being unpredictable and is very effective at keeping his adversaries off balance. But when that unpredictability extended to his staff, it made the Trump White House a difficult place to work, especially in the early months when people were still feeling their way. You never knew from week to week whether you'd be working there the week after that. You could be fired or forced to resign. Or someone else could be fired, and you could be promoted to replace him. You never knew when you looked at your Twitter feed whether you'd be praised or humiliated. The constant feeling of uncertainty took its toll. No one had job security. One week you'd be in favor, the next week you'd be on the outs. You didn't know who you could trust; and confiding in anyone was risky. There was no sense of the camaraderie that I had experienced in other Administrations, even during the darkest days of the Watergate crisis.

All this kept the senior staff on edge, and eager to be at the president's side at all times to protect their interests. The only thing more important than face time with Trump was air time. Trump is a prodigious consumer of news—newspapers, news magazines, radio, and especially cable news and Sunday morning talk shows. If an aide could get booked on a news show, it gave him the excuse to personally check in with Trump beforehand for guidance. If the interview went well, Trump would often phone afterwards with congratulations, and then later mention the aide's good performance to others. If someone wanted to push a certain policy with him, it was more effective to do it on television than during an in-person briefing where Trump might interrupt with an unrelated comment, and cause the interview to veer off course.

Critics laugh at President Trump's obsession with the news, implying that he's watching cable news instead of working. But I think his news watching habit is one of the secrets to his success. Most presidents get captured by a Washington media that just loves to obsess over every jot and tittle that happens or might happen in politics and government, especially when it involves gossip and scandal. They dissect the latest opinion polls, looking for trends. They spend hours raking over who's up and who's down. They join countless panel discussions that dwell on the most insignificant aspects of policy and personnel. They're so focused on the minutiae of what is going on in Washington that it's easy for them to lose track of what really matters to the rest of the country.

President Trump's TV watching habits let him stay in tune with the average American. He watches what they watch. He knows what matters to them. He knows the things that seem like earthquakes in Washington barely get a second glance in the rest of the country. News isn't just what happens inside the Washington Beltway. It's what happens around the country, at kitchen tables, at sports events, in the workplace, and at the malls. He connects with issues average people care about, that Washington overlooks. Sure, Trump may get riled up about the negative stories carried by the liberal anti-Trump press, and he can't resist letting off steam by tweeting up a storm about it. But he also knows that most Americans aren't paying that much attention to Washington's 24/7 news cycle. They may read his tweets, glance over a few headlines, listen to the evening news or radio talk shows, but they're not spending several hours a day poring over opinion pieces in the "failing" *New York Times,* or glued to the Twitter feed of snarky liberal reporters. If he could only trust his own common sense and stop rising to the bait of the anti-Trump media, he'd probably be more popular. At times, his tweeting is self-defeating, as it only serves to call attention to things the rest of the country doesn't notice or care about.

CHAPTER 17

Turning Campaign Promises Into Policy

Even though McMaster, Bannon, and Priebus wanted me gone, they couldn't run the interagency Deputies Committee policymaking process without a Deputy National Security Advisor. The Deputies are the number two officials of most departments and agencies. They are, in effect, the chief operating officers of their organizations, the ones responsible for day-to-day management. They are also the backup for the number one officials, the Cabinet secretary or agency head, who are often on the road. Finally, they are also members of a powerful interagency group, chaired by the Deputy National Security Advisor, who assesses the departments and agencies positions on key national security issues and makes recommendations to the Principals Committee (a subset of the Cabinet) and the president.

It took McMaster several months to find my replacement, so I stayed on at the NSC during the interim. I kept my head down, while the chaos was swirling around, and used the extra time to continue the interagency reviews of the Obama Administration's policies and come up with recommendations for changing them. I chaired several of these Deputies Committees each week as we worked our way through the range of foreign policy, defense, and intelligence issues, and reoriented them to the Trump agenda. We began with the most immediate and longstanding problem, North Korea.

President Obama told President-elect Trump in their Oval Office meeting right after the election that the first national security crisis Trump could face was over North Korea's nuclear weapons program. Trump had pledged on the campaign trail that he wouldn't let North Korea get nuclear weapons capable of reaching the United States.

Prior to becoming Deputy National Security Advisor, I had been an outspoken critic of both Republican and Democrat Administrations' North Korea policies, which ping-ponged back and forth with carrots and sticks, between diplomacy and sanctions. Previous presidents had imposed sanctions in order to get the North Koreans to the negotiating table, then rewarded them for showing up by dropping sanctions and offering them inducements to slow their nuclear program. Once we gave the North Koreans what they wanted, they would inevitably break the agreement and restart their nuclear and missile programs, picking up where they had left off. The cycle would then begin again, with the North Koreans another step closer to developing nuclear weapons and long-range missiles. Every president since Jimmy Carter had tried and failed to stop North Korea's nuclear weapons program. After a few years of effort but no success, President Obama adopted the policy of "strategic patience," which really meant he couldn't figure out what to do, so was kicking the can down the road to the next Administration.

Trump wanted all options with North Korea on the table for his consideration, including even establishing a direct, regularized relationship with them. In the late days of the Transition, John Thornton, the former President of Goldman Sachs and an old graduate school friend of mine, said he was hosting a lunch for the outgoing and incoming North Korean Ambassadors to the United Nations and would introduce me to them if I wanted.

Thornton and I arranged to be at the same restaurant that day so I could "accidently" bump into them and be introduced to the North Koreans. I asked Danielle Hagen, one of the best people in the Transition communications office, to come with me to lunch. We arrived a bit after Thornton and the North Koreans and sat at a table across from theirs. I walked over to the table, said hello to Thornton, and he introduced me to the North Korean diplomats, pointing out that I was President-elect Trump's Deputy National Security Advisor. I said hello to the two thoroughly surprised Ambassadors and remarked that we looked forward to working with them. Then I beat a hasty retreat back to my table. After sharing a plate of french fries, Hagen and I left. I never heard from the North Koreans, who were no doubt confused about the "coincidence" of meeting me, nor did I expect to. But it fit in with Trump's own preference to always do the unexpected.

As we got closer to Inauguration day, one of the things I worried about most was the very real possibility that North Korean President Kim Jong-un would test a nuclear weapon or long-range missile before we were up and running or even had a North Korea policy. We made it through January 20th without incident, thankfully, but knew it was only a matter of time.

I called for a Deputies Committee meeting on North Korea our first week in office. I sat in the chairman's seat, with representatives from State, Defense, Treasury, the Joint Chiefs, the CIA, and other departments and agencies around the long table in the Situation Room. The suite had undergone extensive renovation since I had first worked there over forty-five years before. But it was still a windowless room with a low ceiling and wood paneled walls, a mahogany table, and high-backed leather chairs. And, yes, it looks just like the Situation Room you see in movies.

After brief introductions, I went around the table and asked one after another for their observations and recommendations. It seemed like they had dusted off the Obama briefing papers and stamped a new date on the top. To be fair, since they had received no new instructions from the Trump Administration, they were still operating under guidelines from the outgoing Administration. In fact, since no new Trump Administration officials had been appointed or confirmed, most of those attending were Obama holdovers—sitting in the same chairs with the same briefing papers as they had for the last few years. I was the only new person in the room.

I said, "None of these plans have worked in the past. What makes you think they'll work this time around? Go back to your agencies and come back in a week with some *new* ideas. Don't just bring back the same old stuff. It's probably been at least a year since your last North Korea review. Have circumstances and capabilities changed since then? If so, does that make for new opportunities or vulnerabilities for either side?"

One of the strengths of President Trump is that he's not bound to "this is the way we've always done things in the past" thinking. So I told them to "think outside the box, *way* outside the box. Open the aperture. Don't dismiss anything out of hand." I threw my arms out wide and wiggled my left hand, "everything from regime change," and wiggled my right hand, "to accepting North Korea as a nuclear weapons state". I threw my arms up and down and wiggled my hands again. "Everything from covert and cyber to military action to diplomacy."[1]

The head of the NSC's Asia office, Matt Pottinger, and his very talented colleague Allison Hooker, who had spent decades studying North Korea, became the point people with the agencies and departments. The Pottinger/Hooker team is brilliant, and Pottinger, our original "China" guy, has been one of the most effective, successful, and enduring members of the National Security Council staff. He's had the guts to occasionally disagree with Trump, but never without good reason and sound arguments, and sometimes is even able to bring Trump around to his way of seeing things. But I will leave those stories for him to tell.

Over the next two weeks, I spent hours with experts across government looking for pressure points. I met with former U.S. diplomats, foreign leaders, Asia experts, and international businessmen and bankers. One of the most senior and well-respected North Korea experts in the intelligence community came to my office to deliver a briefing. As it was wrapping up, he thanked me enthusiastically. He said, "I've been waiting years for someone to ask me what I really think and have the guts to finally bring Kim to task." The problem was after twenty years of trying and failing to stop North Korea's nuclear program, there were *no* good options left. Nothing was without risk, and no one of them had a high likelihood of success. Those had all been tried in the past and failed.

But there were some partial options, in each of the economic, diplomatic, and military categories. It was possible to pick out a few threads in each category and pull them together to create a plan to exert simultaneous pressure on all fronts. Instead of alternating between diplomacy and sanctions, as previous Administrations had done, we recommended doing all of them at once, then slowly turning up the dial on North Korea.

---

[1] Sanger, David E. and William J. Broad. "Trump Inherits a Secret Cyberwar Against North Korean Missiles." *The New York Times.* March 4, 2017. https://www.nytimes.com/2017/03/04/world/asia/north-korea-missile-program-sabotage.html.

This became the foundation for Trump's maximum pressure campaign, as noted in President Trump's National Security Strategy, published in December 2017. At the same time, Trump offered an alternative future to Kim, even suggesting he would welcome Kim to the Oval Office "if conditions are right."[2,3,4]

The question was how to convince Kim that his nuclear weapons were no longer an asset but were increasingly becoming a liability. Over the last several years, Kim has begun to stress the need for economic development, occasionally even making it more of a priority than military power. Was there a way to nudge that thinking along? The goal was to demonstrate to Kim that clinging to his nuclear weapons would do more harm than good when it came to ensuring his regime's survival—that creating a world class modern economy that delivered prosperity to their people was more important than their nuclear weapons for keeping him in power.[5]

I cannot speak for the Trump Administration today. I left the White House over two years ago and much has transpired since in American-North Korean relations, including Trump's summit meetings with Kim, and their direct personal correspondence. But watching from the sidelines, it seems that Trump is continuing the strategy we developed in the early days of his presidency. He continues to dial up the pressure while at the same time offering a tangible demonstration of an alternate future. The points of leverage remain applying simultaneously both maximum carrots and sticks. To date it has had middling success.

Trump himself seems to have intuitively arrived at a third point of leverage with Kim–his ego.

---

[2] Rogin, Josh. "Trump's North Korea policy is 'maximum pressure' but not 'regime change.'" *The Washington Post*. April 14, 2017. https://www.washingtonpost.com/news/josh-rogin/wp/2017/04/14/trumps-north-korea-policy-is-massive-pressure-but-not-regime-change/.

[3] Lubold, Gordon, Nancy A. Youssef, and Dustin Volz. "Trump Administration Resumes Pressure Campaign on North Korea." *Wall Street Journal*. May 25, 2018. https://www.wsj.com/articles/trump-administration-resumes-pressure-campaign-on-north-korea-1527240600.

[4] U.S. Department of Defense. "Department of Defense Press Briefing by Pentagon Chief Spokesperson Dana W. White and Joint Staff Director Lt. Gen. Kenneth F. McKenzie Jr. in the Pentagon Briefing Room." *Paper*. May 24, 2018. https://www.defense.gov/Newsroom/Transcripts/Transcript/Article/1532246/department-of-defense-press-briefing-by-pentagon-chief-spokesperson-dana-w-whit/.

[5] Yong, Kim Hwan. "Kim Jong Un Seeks Economic Development Amid Sanctions." Voice of America. January 4, 2016. https://www.voanews.com/east-asia/kim-jong-un-seeks-economic-development-amid-sanctions.

Any negotiation or relationship with Kim Jong-un will always be personal. He doesn't care about the welfare of his people, unless it figures in keeping his regime in power. He is a brutal dictator—the majority of his people live in poverty, the equivalent of forced labor on farms and in factories. Kim holds absolute power over what his people see, read, and hear. They are brainwashed into believing Kim and his family are their saviors. Any dissent, especially coming from his closest advisors, is dealt with by barbaric punishment and execution. That's one of the reasons previous Administrations' attempts to urge Kim to improve the lives of his people have fallen on deaf ears. He simply doesn't care.

Trump's approach plays to Kim's ego. Sometimes he flatters Kim, strokes his ambitions to be a great world leader, and dismisses suggestions of regime change. Other times he trash talks Kim, and threatens him with war. He's luring Kim into getting accustomed to being at the table with world leaders. You can see by Kim's body language that he loves what only Trump can give him—a place on the world stage. But what Trump gives with one hand he can pull away with the other. He has already cancelled one summit meeting, and presumably would have no problem walking away from Kim if he doesn't deliver. Trump could tweet that the failure is all Kim's fault, and then move on.

It wouldn't be so easy for Kim. Without Trump's support, Kim will no longer be traveling around the globe and hobnobbing with world leaders. He will be back in the Hermit Kingdom going to military parades with his sycophantic generals. It would be a blow to Kim's ego, and he would also lose face at home. He would risk the enmity of the United States and our allies, seen as responsible for keeping North Korea in isolation and poverty, and revert back to being the world's pariah nation. Kim has just as much if not more riding on a successful U.S.-North Korean relationship than Trump does.

I think that is why Trump chose to meet Kim first in Singapore in 2018, and then in Vietnam in 2019. Singapore is one of the wealthiest, most modern, and high-tech cities in the world—and it has been built in less than fifty years. Vietnam, the country America fought with for nearly a decade a generation ago, is now a modern, thriving, and relatively prosperous nation, albeit one still ruled by the Communist Party. Holding their summit meetings in these two Asian nations couldn't help but drive home the point to Kim and his senior leaders that this could be North

Korea's future, too. The movie trailer Trump prepared for Kim before the Singapore summit might have been corny, but it was aimed to appeal to Kim's ego, to show he can make North Korea a modern wealthy society, and himself be hailed as a man who changed world history...or not.

Critics have complained that Trump's meetings with Kim grant him the legitimacy on the world stage that he craves. I agree. I think that's the whole point; he craves it. Might he be willing to give up something in order to keep it? But there is another audience looking at all those pictures of Kim and Trump hobnobbing together—the North Koreans. Pictures of the two men shaking hands, walking together through two modern Asian cities is a significant symbol to the North Koreans. Those pictures give the implicit promise, especially to the leadership cadre around Kim, that they too will soon reap the economic benefits of cooperation with the United States.

Years ago, a Chinese official told me that when he was growing up in the 1960s, it was hammered into their heads that America was evil, corrupt, and China's mortal enemy. Suddenly, in February 1972, there were images everywhere - on the sides of buses, on billboards, and on newspaper banners - of Mao and Nixon smiling and shaking hands at a summit meeting in Beijing. The message was unmistakable—overnight, America had become China's friend. Mao was personally invested in its success. The official said that if the U.S.- Chinese relationship failed, if China did not receive the anticipated economic and political benefits their new friendship promised, Mao himself would lose face. It seems to me Kim has made a bet similar to Mao's of fifty years before. Kim needs the relationship with the United States to succeed.

The more Trump lures Kim and his entourage to interact with the world, the less likely it will be for Kim to continue to keep his people, especially his mid- and senior-level people, in the dark about the rest of the world. I have no illusions that the North Korean people would ever rise up in rebellion; they've been brainwashed and terrified for too long to question their Supreme Leader. Kim remains in power because the people around him are too afraid and invested in his regime to challenge him. Could that change now that they have had a taste of the outside world? Might they finally decide they've had enough of Kim's reign of terror? Maybe, maybe not. But Trump's approach has given us another angle of leverage over Kim. So, as Trump is fond of saying, "We'll see."

Allison Hooker had worked on the NSC for several years but had never been inside the Oval Office. One of the things I did from the beginning was break with tradition and bring NSC staff members into the Oval Office to personally brief President Trump. These are the professionals who give their all, day in and day out, but rarely get the recognition they deserve. They were excited about the prospect of meeting the president, but it was always a challenge to warn them beforehand that briefing Trump was a unique experience. He is not a passive recipient of information. There is constant give and take, and everyone in the room is allowed an opinion, expert or not. He constantly interrupts, peppers you with questions - seemingly out of nowhere - and argues if he disagrees with your analysis. In the end, if you hold your ground, and make your case, you might walk out of the briefing exhausted, but with the realization that you have given the president of the United States what he needs to do his job.

We walked into the Oval Office and I said, "Mr. President, let me introduce you to Allison Hooker. She's your Korea expert here on the NSC, and has been working on the North Korean problem for decades." Allison is a striking woman—thin, elegantly dressed in silk dresses and chiffon scarves, with long silver hair, which she sometimes wears up and other times leaves loose down her back. Trump turned his attention from me to Allison. He was clearly impressed that he had a North Korea expert, especially one who didn't look like what he figured a North Korea expert would look like. He was very gracious, asked a few questions, and then looked her right in the eye and asked, "Would you want to live in North Korea?"

Allison paused for a second before answering; after all, it was an unexpected question. She came prepared to talk about Kim Jong-un, his nuclear program, his missile program, his relationship with China, his economy, and his military. But she hadn't thought about *that* question in advance.

But she looked him right back in the eye and said, "No, Mr. President, I would never want to live in North Korea, not under any circumstances."

It seemed like an odd question, but it actually made sense. Trump wanted to know how bad the living conditions were, perhaps gauging whether this would be a point of weakness for Kim that he could exploit down the road.

As I continued working in the West Wing, it became apparent that McMaster and Trump weren't a good fit. McMaster had been an Army man since his early teens, first at a military high school, and then at West Point. He was used to being briefed, and briefing others, in a certain way, with lengthy PowerPoint presentations using military jargon. Trump's style is completely different. He immediately takes charge of a briefing and turns it into a multi-party discussion, where he gets to offer opinions and ask questions, whether on topic or not. Lord help anyone who expects to stick to an agenda. President Trump takes the conversation where he wants to go. He tends to get diverted if something you're discussing triggers something else on his mind and he can veer off on tangents. The style is disconcerting to just about everyone, but it works for him. It's hard to fault it when Trump's approach has built a multi-billion-dollar business empire. It helped him win the presidency against all odds, and create more economic growth than we have seen in decades, more jobs for many Americans, and the lowest unemployment rates in our entire history.

Trump has a limited attention span for information he's already digested. "Yeah, yeah, I got it. What's next?" means he doesn't want to waste time on something he already knows, and you should move on to the next item. Finally, when a meeting or briefing goes on too long, Trump will fidget, look down at the papers on his desk, fiddle with the phone, or interrupt you and change the topic entirely. That is his signal that the meeting is over. To keep talking is pointless; Trump is no longer in the receive mode. You should thank him for the meeting and depart. You can always catch up at the next briefing. To keep talking when he's clearly finished, and his mind has moved elsewhere, risks alienating him altogether. To Trump, personal chemistry is very important, and it is always up to you to make it work, not him. This is something that McMaster never seemed to figure out. They did have genuine policy differences across the board, but what really damaged their relationship was their personal incompatibility and McMaster's disinclination to adjust his approach.

Secretary of State Rex Tillerson and Trump were more in sync on policy, with the exception of their differences on how to deal with Iran. But they also had significant differences in style. Tillerson was a CEO used to delegating to subordinates, Trump is a CEO who wants to make the decisions himself. Tillerson spent his meetings with Trump giving him a status report. "Mr. President, here is what I've done with Prime

Minister X, this is the approach I'm taking with President Y." Tillerson briefed Trump on the actions and decisions *he* had made, how *he* was negotiating, and which policies *he* was pursuing—all the while thinking he was doing what Trump wanted. But Trump wants to be the one in charge, especially when it involves negotiating strategy, or the timing and tactics of dealing with foreign leaders. Trump takes great pride in his deal-making abilities. He wants to decide these things for himself, not be told by an aide what he's done on Trump's behalf and in Trump's name, even if that aide is the Secretary of State, and the respected former CEO of one of the largest and most successful corporations in the world.

Perhaps Tillerson would have had a more effective relationship with the president if he had used a different approach and asked for Trump's guidance beforehand instead of briefing him on what he had already done. If Tillerson had said, "Mr. President, I'm considering using this approach with Prime Minister X. What do you think?" Or, "I'm having a hard time with President Y. He keeps making outrageous demands. How should I handle it?" Trump would probably have agreed with him nine times out of ten, and it would have made Tillerson a more effective Secretary of State because he would be speaking for the president. Furthermore, Trump could have also provided Tillerson some useful insights and advice.

Trump bristles at "being managed." He doesn't want the staff, especially an ever-changing staff, to make decisions for him, or take it upon themselves to eliminate options before he's even had a chance to weigh in. That's one of the reasons he announces major policy changes on Twitter, sometimes surprising even his closet advisors. That's also why he likes tweeting out his firing and hiring announcements, occasionally without a heads up to the person being fired or hired. It allows Trump to keep the whip hand and to remain totally in charge of his own agenda. Unfortunately, it also creates unnecessary resentment with people he fires. Instead of giving them a dignified send off, he sometimes delights in skewering and humiliating them in public. Some get their revenge by providing the media with a steady stream of criticism of Trump from "anonymous sources".

In many ways both McMaster and Tillerson had the same problem with the president. They never figured out how to work with Trump—who, granted, has a unique style, which is often difficult to adapt to. The trouble for them is once you're a CEO, or have all those general's stars on your shoulders, you've probably forgotten what it's like to have an actual day-to-day boss, or the importance of figuring out how to read that boss. Put simply, they each failed to rework their approach to fit Trump's way of doing things. They didn't click with him. McMaster and Tillerson were professionals, and to them it was all business. It didn't matter if you liked someone or not. But with Trump, personal chemistry is critical. For senior members of his Administration, diplomacy begins at home.

Most of the presidents I've known, or worked for, or studied, eventually came to enjoy the foreign policymaking part of the job. Even those who come into office more focused on economic or domestic matters ended up relishing their role as Commander in Chief, and leader of the free world. When they were dealing with foreign leaders they could operate with a freer hand and have more leverage than when dealing with dozens of argumentative, oppositional, and obstructive Members of Congress. Trump is no exception.

Finding someone to take my job as Deputy National Security Advisor proved more difficult than anyone anticipated. From time to time in meetings, Trump would make a crack that there were lots of people who wanted the Singapore job I'd been offered, a whole lot more than wanted the NSC job. He occasionally needled McMaster when we were together for Oval Office meetings. "You know she's really good. You're nuts to get rid of her." McMaster would smile self-consciously, but never said anything in response. While personally flattering, President Trump's compliments didn't change things; he would simply shrug and move on to something else. Over time, McMaster and I grew to have a good relationship. I came to respect his abilities as a manager and his success in putting a chaotic NSC on firmer footing.

One of McMaster's lasting achievements was producing the Trump Administration's official National Security Strategy white paper, which laid out a different strategic vision, and charted a new course from recent Administrations. Capturing Trump's "America First" agenda, it argues that the US needs to compete more effectively to retain and regain its economic, political, and military advantages. The lion's share of the credit goes to Nadia Schadlow, who began by laying out the main principles, patiently working them through the interagency process, and then producing a clear and forceful document. Then she did what few people in

Washington ever do -she let others get the credit for a final product that was well received by Trump's critics as well as his supporters.

Two of the most talented people I worked with in the Trump Administration are Ivanka Trump and her husband, Jared Kushner. Unfortunately, they will never get an ounce of credit for their contributions, especially from a Washington Establishment which doesn't like New Yorkers as a general rule, and resents the couple's wealth, business success, and unique relationship with the president. In the early days of the Administration, the anti-Trump media was particularly vicious in criticizing them. But both Jared and Ivanka, in their own different ways, have had great impact, especially behind the scenes. Because neither are typical Washington insiders, they are able to bring a fresh perspective to problems which have plagued us for years.

The first thing you notice about Ivanka is how attractive she is—tall, thin, and elegantly dressed. The second thing is that she is unfailingly polite and poised. She doesn't talk at people; she listens to them. She solicits their opinions and values their advice. In a business where the favorite topic of most people is themselves, it's very effective. If you want to get the spotlight on a project, get Ivanka on board and she'll let you take the credit. If you're trying to get a recalcitrant politician to cooperate, ask Ivanka to make the call. She has gained enormous influence in the Trump Administration and uses it wisely to advance causes she believes in. Ivanka is a stalwart champion for women's empowerment, in an Administration which is often criticized, unfairly, for being anti-woman. Whether it is the Working Family Agenda, Child Tax Credit, or workforce and job retraining and development, Ivanka has been the guiding hand.

Trump put Jared Kushner in a difficult position in the first few months in office. Trump was used to operating as a sole proprietor, involved with all major initiatives, and making the big decisions himself. It's difficult enough if you're running a business empire, but nearly impossible if you're running the country. Trump set the White House up so he would be in charge, with a weak Chief of Staff, and an unclear chain of command. And, as in business, he relied on his immediate family, whom he had confidence in and knew he could trust. The result was Trump delegated almost everything that mattered to his son-in-law, whom he had confidence in and knew he could trust. Things eventually sorted themselves out, with others taking up some of Kushner's responsibilities, which left him free to focus on criminal justice reform, and Israeli-Palestinian peace.

Kushner, a businessman himself, understands that the key to making any progress in the Middle East isn't by starting with the politicians who have a vested interest in keeping the enmity going. It's by getting investors and businessmen, who see the practical advantage of working across sectarian lines, to lead the way.

His approach resonates with something I learned a decade ago when I was in Israel. I was taping two segments for my FOXnews.com show, *DEFCON3*. The first was a panel discussion with Israeli and Palestinian politicians, the second with Israeli and Palestinian businessmen. While I was in the studio interviewing the politicians—who each recited their standard litany of grievances against the other—guests for the second panel were sitting in the green room. My husband was there too, and said it was a far more interesting conversation than the one I was having with the politicians. The Israeli and Palestinian businessmen, who all knew of each other, had never actually met. After introducing themselves, they started talking about business possibilities. They discussed that if their two countries were allowed to trade, the Palestinian companies could be the portal for Israeli goods to be exported throughout the Arab world. The Palestinian agri-businessman asked the Israelis about growing heirloom tomatoes and other produce in the West Bank for export to high end Tel Aviv and European restaurants. The Israeli businessman discussed supplying materials to the Palestinian real estate developer. While the politicians were dug into their same old ruts, the entrepreneurial businessmen were trying to figure out how to make money with each other.

Kushner's proposal is a two-part plan of economic investment and political agreements. He has worked out of the spotlight to line up a large investment fund devoted to developing the economies in Palestinian and neighboring states. It is an ambitious undertaking, and details are still being worked out, but hopefully this different approach can gain traction where previous efforts have failed.

Staying on at the NSC for those extra months meant that, in addition to supervising the reorientation of national security policies, I could continue doing something near and dear to my heart: mentoring the young, and even not so young men and women on the NSC staff. Those first few months of the Trump Administration were a rough environment, especially for a staff of professionals who were tossed into the political maelstrom of one, two, three and now four NSC Advisors, each of whom wanted to purge the staff of his predecessors.

I particularly enjoyed working with the women, not just on the NSC but throughout my life. I was a female trailblazer of sorts in the foreign affairs arena, although I never had a grand design for my career. For me things unfolded more or less by accident, by taking one step at a time. As opportunities started opening up for women of my generation, I was able to take advantage of them. But I was also able to find happiness and contentment in my personal life—with my husband of thirty-five years, our five children and stepchildren, and now grandchildren.

For the generation of women who have come after me, the multitude of options open to them can be overwhelming at times, and trying to take advantage of them all simultaneously can be exhausting. My motto is a woman fortunate enough to live in today's America can have it all, but it's hard to have it all at the same time. For me, life has been lived in chapters. Each chapter is unique onto itself—some emphasize career, others education, marriage, and family. Even the chapters in my working life have been varied. My career hasn't been in just one area. I've spent time in government, in the media, politics, and government again. My chapters aren't balanced within themselves, but taken all together, have allowed me to live a multi-faceted life of great personal and professional fulfillment.

I was happy to have the time I had on the National Security Council, but in many ways wish it had lasted longer and been done under different circumstances. But the dye was already cast when McMaster arrived at the White House. There was no looking back for either of us. The one thing I did succeed in getting was a promise from McMaster to keep several of the most talented of the original NSC staff members—Flaherty, Pottinger, Eisenberg, Anton, Badash, and Coates—who were soon able to prove their own worth. Ironically, after I left Washington, McMaster and I bucked each other up when Trump continuously humiliated him in public, and I was caught up in the partisan politics of the Senate confirmation process.

In any event, I handed things over to my replacement, Army Major General Ricky Waddell on May 19, 2017 and then I walked out of the West Wing for the final time, forty-seven years after I first walked in. My plan was to ride off into the Washington sunset, await Senate confirmation to be the U.S. Ambassador to Singapore, move halfway around the world, stay there for several years, and then retire. That's not how things turned out. As they say, if you want to hear God laugh, tell him your plans.

CHAPTER 18

The FBI Comes Calling

I take no pleasure in telling the tale of my experiences with the FBI, with the Office of Special Counsel, or with Congressional investigations. It was a painful period of my life and one I would sooner forget. Most people who go through it are so relieved to have it over that they want to put it behind them and get on with their lives. As a result, the rest of the good and decent people in the country have no idea what goes on behind the curtain. It's not a pretty sight.

But I believe it is a tale worth telling because it illustrates how dangerously perverted the system has become. It is also a cautionary note to the American people that these politically-motivated investigations have unintended consequences. They shove our very real problems to the sidelines while those inside the Beltway remain obsessed with scandals that the rest of the country doesn't really care about. But they also cast doubt and suspicion on our governmental institutions when some powerful people in the Washington Establishment attempt what amounts to reversing election outcomes if they don't like the results. Investigation after investigation, impeachment effort after impeachment effort serve to paralyze our elected officials. They also gnaw away at our people's faith in the democratic system itself. Furthermore, they put our national security at risk, as our adversaries exploit the madness of our internal divisions and political paralysis to their own advantage.

For me, it all started on the morning of August 29, 2017, three months after I had left the White House. I was at home in Southampton, Long Island and went for my regular hour at the gym. I returned home and, just as I was heading for the shower, my cell phone rang with a number I didn't recognize. It was a poor connection, but the caller identified himself as a Special Agent of the FBI. He asked if we could set up a meeting, but the rest was garbled. I said I couldn't hear him very well. He said, no worries, he and his partner had driven up from Washington and were right outside my house. Could they come in? My initial reaction was this was probably another routine interview for a friend who was being considered for a federal appointment, or a colleague whose security clearance was up for renewal, just like the dozens I had participated in before. Figuring it wouldn't take long, I said yes and within a minute there were two FBI agents at my door, flashing their credentials.

They said they were from the Office of Special Counsel Robert Mueller and wanted to ask me a few routine questions. I must have looked shocked because one of them said, "You can't be surprised that we want to talk to you." Actually, I was surprised. As I understood it, the Office of the Special Counsel, or "OSC" to the Beltway crowd, was supposed to determine whether the Russians had interfered with the 2016 elections and, if so, how, and what steps could be taken to prevent the Russians or anyone else from doing so again.

I didn't see how those topics involved me. I wasn't a part of the Trump campaign, other than participating in two, one-hour debate prep sessions with Donald Trump, along with some two dozen other experts. I wasn't appointed Deputy National Security Advisor until two weeks after the election, when the Transition had already begun. Throughout my seven weeks on the Transition team and four months in the West Wing of the White House, I had no contact with any Russians, let alone the Russian Ambassador, other than a quick handshake in a long receiving line the day before Inauguration.

When they arrived, I was at home alone since my husband had left to run some errands right after I walked in the door. (It was only later that I realized the FBI agents had probably already been waiting outside our house, parked out of sight, and only phoned once they saw me drive in and my husband drive out.)

I asked the agents if I needed to have a lawyer present, or have someone with me to take notes. They said while they couldn't tell me *not* to have a lawyer present, the only thing they wanted from me was to get a sense of what happened during the Transition and at Trump Tower. I naïvely took them at their word.

Nevertheless, I called my husband and asked that he come home. He is a retired investment banker but had some legal training. He had gone to law school and briefly practiced law in the 1960s. I didn't have a lawyer lined up for this sort of thing, and wasn't sure I needed one. I hadn't done anything wrong, or broken any laws, and assumed if I answered their questions as best as I could remember, everything would be fine. Plus, I wanted more than anyone to figure out how the Russians interfered with the 2016 election, and was glad to help with that effort.

While the agents and I waited uncomfortably for my husband to return, I asked them whether I was under some sort of investigation. They emphatically and unequivocally said no. I was not under investigation, I wasn't a person of interest, I wasn't a target of any investigation. I was just a "fact witness," someone they hoped could give them background information, and put events of the period into context.

I asked how long this would take. They had "a few" questions to ask and said they wouldn't take too much of my time, maybe two or so hours. I warned them that anything I could give them was obviously from memory, off the top of my head, and about events that had occurred some nine months before and that I had not thought much about since. They assured me they weren't out to catch me with "gotcha" questions. I believed them and agreed to go ahead.

My husband arrived about twenty minutes later, arms full of groceries, mail, and dry cleaning, and joined us. He listened to the agents' questions and to my answers. He left a few times to answer the phone but sat in for most of the interview. The agents gave no indication that this was anything other than the way they characterized it—a fact-finding mission.

We sat at my dining room table, the agents in their white shirts, dark suits, and ties, me in my gym clothes and sneakers. The senior FBI agent, who was part of the Washington office and had been assigned to the Mueller team, took the lead and asked most of the questions. The junior agent, from the Philadelphia field office, took notes, occasionally speaking up to add points of clarification. The senior agent opened a folder with newspaper clippings, and showed them to me one at a time, putting each one back into the folder before he brought the next one out. Keying off the newspaper articles, he fired off a series of questions:

How did I come to work on the Transition team? Had I been part of the campaign? Did I know Trump or any of the campaign officials, and for how long? What was our relationship? How did I know General Flynn? Were Flynn and I personal friends? When did I first meet him? How did I get the job? Who interviewed me? How did I interact with Flynn, Trump, and others on the Transition? What was the relationship between the Transition offices in Washington and the Trump Tower operation? What was the layout at Trump Tower like? Who was there? Where did people sit?

How did I spend my time? Where did I spend my time? What were my responsibilities? How was the National Security Council structured? Did I write position papers or brief the president-elect or others? Was working with Flynn during the Transition period any different after the Inauguration? What meetings did I attend with foreign officials? Did Flynn meet with foreign officials? When did I meet with the president-elect during the Transition and once we were in the White House?

I prefaced just about every answer with the caveat that if I got something wrong, or didn't remember something with complete accuracy or certainty, it wasn't intentional. I was just human, and my memory wasn't perfect. Generally speaking, I'm not very good at remembering specific dates, times, or numbers. My memory has always tended more toward recalling my impressions, people's emotions, their reactions, and attitudes. I can recall some events rather clearly but not others, or snippets of conversations, but not everything that everyone said. I also remember things more as snapshots in time than with full and total recall. I must have sounded like a broken record, because they reassured me several times that they knew it was a busy time and didn't expect me to remember everything. They told me not to worry, and repeated that these were not trick or "gotcha" questions; they just wanted to get a sense of how things operated.

They switched back and forth from questions about the Transition period to after the Inauguration. They asked the same questions again and again, but each time in slightly different language, and then moved ahead with another issue. They then circled back to topics they had discussed an hour before. After two or so hours I asked them if they wanted to take a break and have some coffee or something to eat. They declined, so we pressed on.

They asked about the pre-Christmas United Nations Security Council vote to condemn Israeli settlements on the West Bank. They showed me newspaper articles which discussed the UN vote to help refresh my memory. They asked about the president-elect and about Flynn, Kushner, and others. Had any Transition officials called or met with foreign leaders regarding the United Nations Security Council vote? Which Transition officials called which foreign officials and what did they say? Did they ask for their positions, or try to change their votes? Did I talk to any foreign officials about the UN vote? Did Flynn or others have previous relationships with these foreign leaders? Who took the lead on this?

The agents then moved on to whether Trump or any senior staff members had contact with the Russians during the Transition. Did I meet privately with any Russians? Did Flynn? Did others? Did I or anyone else join Flynn in these meetings? What was the nature of Flynn's relationship with the Russians? Did I know about meetings with Russians during the Republican Convention or after the election?

They spent several hours asking about what had happened at Mar-a-Lago during the last week of December 2016, when Flynn was on a four-day vacation to the Dominican Republic and I had joined the president-elect and senior staff at Mar-a-Lago. Since my interim security clearances had come through just a few days before, it was the first time I was eligible to be the NSC duty officer, attend the president-elect's daily intelligence briefings, and read the daily classified cables. The Mar-a-Lago trip was my solo debut as the senior NSC official with Trump.

The lead agent read a series of prepared questions off his notes: Who did I meet with at Mar-a-Lago and how often? Did I meet with Trump? Did I attend his daily intelligence briefings? How did I first learn President Obama would impose sanctions? Was I aware Flynn and the Russian Ambassador talked during the period when Obama had imposed sanctions on Russia? Did I listen in to Flynn's calls with the Russian Ambassador? How often did Flynn talk to or meet with the Russians? Who initiated the calls? Why was I at Mar-a-Lago between Christmas and New Year's? Did I remember which days I talked to Flynn from Mar-a-Lago and how many calls we had? What was discussed? Did Flynn and I discuss Obama's sanctions and the possible Russian response? Who else did I talk to during this period? Who did I meet with? What did we discuss? Was I surprised that the Russians did not retaliate when Obama imposed sanctions?

They zeroed in on Flynn. Was I aware Flynn met with the FBI a few days after the Inauguration? Did I know Flynn briefed Vice President-elect Pence prior to his January 15, 2017 interview on *Meet the Press*? What was the relationship between Pence and Flynn? Did I know Flynn lied to Pence? To others? When was I first aware he would be fired? Did I talk to him after he left the White House? Who on the Transition staff reported to whom? Who were the decision makers? What was the process? Did I think Trump put pressure on Comey to drop the Flynn investigation?

Throughout the interview, I pointed out that I was working entirely from memory about events that happened months before, when a lot of other things were going on in my life. My recollections were not precise or clear, especially about timing of calls and emails and the topics covered in them. I prefaced most of my responses with those same caveats.

As the interview finally wound down, in the late afternoon, I asked again about my status. They repeated what they had said at the beginning of the interview - that I wasn't a target or subject of any investigation, that I was a fact witness who could give them context. The senior agent thanked me for talking to them about events which I probably hadn't thought of since I left the White House.

I asked them what happens next? They said in all likelihood, nothing; I probably wouldn't hear from them again. *But* they might want to check a few things with me later. I left the house with them, and as I walked them to their car the senior agent thanked me for being so generous with my time. He said I had been very forthcoming and cooperative, and it was helpful to their investigation. He said it was "good for them, and good for me". At the time, I thought it was an odd thing to say, but didn't give it a second thought.

After the FBI interview, I got in touch with former Attorney General Michael Mukasey. He was a Yale Law School classmate of my husband's and their friendship has continued for the last fifty-five years in New York. He was surprised the agents just showed up at my house without warning, but said that from their questions and the way they handled things, I was just a witness, and it sounded like I would be fine.

We also talked to another close friend, the prom   t litigator Robert Giuffra (who would later represent me). He agreed with the former Attorney General, it sounded like I was just a fact witness.

Given the press frenzy surrounding the Mueller investigation, we worried that if I did "lawyer up," most of the press would probably point to that as evidence that I knew I was guilty of some serious crime. In retrospect, this hesitancy was a big mistake. It caused me a lot of pain, anguish, and expense, and put me in potential legal jeopardy.

I heard nothing for two weeks and hoped that was the end of the matter, but it turned out to be just the beginning. In September 2017, I got a call from the junior of the two FBI agents asking for a second interview. They wanted to follow up on a few questions. I asked if my status had changed, and he confirmed on the phone that I was just a fact witness, not a target, or someone they were investigating, or a person of interest to them. I asked again if I needed a lawyer and got the same answer as before. They couldn't advise me *not* to get a lawyer, but this second interview would be similar to the first one, only shorter. They just wanted to go back over a few things, and maybe show me a few documents to refresh my memory. Once again, I believed them.

I got in touch with Mukasey again, explained the FBI wanted a second interview, and asked if we could use his law firm's conference room in Manhattan rather than meet them at our Long Island home. Mukasey wasn't my lawyer; I didn't think I needed a lawyer, and neither did he.

On September 14th, 2017 my husband and I met Mukasey at his law office in midtown Manhattan. When the two FBI agents arrived, we introduced them to Mukasey. He is a highly respected former Attorney General, and long-time Federal District Court Judge known for his intelligence, wisdom, and integrity. It was all very friendly. The agents seemed honored to meet him, and Mukasey asked them to pass along his personal regards to Robert Mueller. They had worked closely together when Mueller was FBI Director and Mukasey the Attorney General.

Mukasey left and gave us use of the conference room. I asked the agents again to confirm that I was not being investigated, that I was not the target of their investigation, and that I was not a person of interest. They again assured me that I was just a fact witness, who could give them a sense of how things had worked, the timeline of events, and provide context. Once again, I believed them.

Most of their questions focused on the same topics we discussed in the first interview. In addition to press stories, this time the senior agent showed me parts of emails, email chains, and selected sentences and paragraphs taken from emails that I had received, written, or was copied on. Some of the email chains that he showed me weren't complete; some emails were missing from the sequence, some emails had the sender and recipient blocks removed, some were only fragments of longer emails, and some were out of chronological order—all of which made it difficult for me to recall their context. The senior agent brought each document out of his folder, one at a time, showed it to me, and then replaced it in his folder before bringing out the next one. I asked if I could see all the emails at once to give me a sense of the flow, but the Senior Agent refused. He claimed showing them to me one at a time would be better to refresh my memory. It didn't of course, but that was his argument nonetheless.

I hadn't seen these emails for nearly a year, and had forgotten about a lot of them. I pointed out that I had, as legally required, turned over all my Transition and White House calendars, schedules, and phone logs, as well as emails, computers, and cell phones to the Government Services Administration (GSA) at the end of the Transition, and to the NSC and White House when I left government—and no longer had access to any of them. I hadn't kept personal copies of anything. (According to later press accounts, the Office of Special Counsel had obtained these records from the GSA, and controlled access to them.) I asked the senior agent if I could keep the emails or make copies of them. He responded, "That's not how this works."

They asked about several people and events, and then turned to the United Nation's Christmas Eve vote to censure Israel. They went over the same ground that we covered in the first interview. The agents then asked whether I knew about the Logan Act. I was surprised by their question, and asked how they knew about it, since it is an obscure law passed over two hundred years ago which had never been enforced nor its constitutionality tested in the courts. The only public reference to it in years was in Ignatius's *Washington Post* column in January 2017. The FBI agents chuckled and admitted they had never heard of it either, but had looked it up when prepping for our interview.

The Logan Act was enacted in 1799 and bars a private citizen from interfering with U.S. foreign policy by trying to influence a foreign country. The Act is generally not known outside of the foreign policy community and even then, only by old-timers like me. I hadn't thought about it for years. The only reason I was familiar with it at all was because in 1968, the outgoing Johnson Administration had accused the incoming Nixon Administration of violating the Logan Act. They claimed Nixon and Kissinger had sabotaged Johnson's Vietnam peace negotiations during the Transition period in order to steal the credit for themselves, even though it was unlikely there was anything on the negotiating table to sabotage. In fact, the Vietnam War plagued the Nixon Administration for another four years. The peace negotiations dragged on throughout his first term and the Paris Peace Accords were not signed until 1973, after Nixon's re-election.

Frankly, I always thought those accusations of Logan Act violations were sour grapes on the part of outgoing Administrations; their excuse for leaving office with unfinished foreign policy business, or their attempts to avoid blame for their foreign policy failures. President Jimmy Carter had failed to get American hostages out of Tehran after 444 days of negotiations and a botched rescue mission, which had contributed to his re-election defeat. When Iran released the hostages on the day Reagan was sworn in, the Carter Administration was quick to accuse Reagan of violating the Logan Act and having sabotaged their negotiations with Iran.

Every time an outgoing Administration cried Logan Act violations, the incoming Administration's lawyers inevitably jumped in to dismiss the claims, arguing that it was probably unconstitutional anyway. A president-elect is hardly a private citizen and in two hundred years no one has ever been successfully prosecuted for violating the Act. In foreign policy circles, it has never been given much weight. Former and even future government officials, former presidents and presidential hopefuls, and even private citizens meet with foreign leaders all the time. I doubt if all they talk about is the weather or their grandchildren. It always seemed to me that accusing someone of a Logan Act violation, especially just weeks before they assume office, is like arresting a political opponent for driving fifty-six miles an hour in a fifty-five-mile an hour speed zone. Yes, it might technically be a violation of the law, but it's a petty accusation and has never been enforced—and for good reason.

Regardless, the FBI agent's questions bore down on the Logan Act. Did alarm bells go off in my head that what Flynn and others were doing was a possible violation of the Logan Act? Did I warn them about it? Why not? Were Trump Transition officials trying to undermine Obama's foreign policy? Were they aware they were violating the Logan Act?

After the agents finished this line of questioning, they moved on to Flynn's contact with the Russian Ambassador in late December, when President Obama imposed sanctions on Russia and I was in Mar-a-Lago with Trump. They had covered it in detail in the first interview, but this time they focused on it with even greater specificity. The senior agent showed me more redacted emails, again only one at a time. For the most part, they covered the same topics they had during the first interview. As they had then, they asked the same questions several times, each time with a slightly different wording. They also jumped around from one topic to another and switched back and forth between the Transition period and after the Inauguration. They seemed most interested in possible Logan Act violations by Trump and Flynn. In addition, I got the impression from the way the agents framed the questions that they were suspicious of Flynn's relationship with the Russians, and that they were trying to find evidence of wrongdoing between Flynn and the Russians that they could tie to Trump.

This second interview lasted about five hours. As we finished, I asked what would happen next, and they said they might need to get in touch again to clarify some things, and perhaps ask me to testify before a grand jury. I asked them again whether my status had changed, and they assured me that I was not a subject or target of an investigation, nor a "person of interest." Once again, I believed them.

After the agents left, Alan and I told Mukasey about their focus on the Logan Act. It was so obscure that even the former Attorney General had to look it up. Mukasey pulled the volume on Title 18 of the U.S. Code off his shelf, which contains all of the federal criminal statutes. He looked up the Logan Act and read it out loud. He was stunned that the Special Counsel appeared to be considering charging Trump or his officials with violations of this particular act.

The junior FBI agent called a month later to arrange a third interview in October and again to ask some additional follow-up questions. As before, we met in Mukasey's law offices, and again Mukasey greeted the agents at the door. They had already run into each other at Reagan Washington airport earlier that day as all three of them boarded the same flight to New York. This time they passed on Robert Mueller's personal greetings to Mukasey. Once again, everything was friendly and the agents were cordial. I assumed that if I was in trouble or needed a lawyer, the agents would have told me. Mueller and the agents knew that Mukasey was helping me, if only to loan us the use of his conference room. If there was a problem, I thought that the agents would have said something to him. There were smiles all around, and Mukasey left. He saw no need to stay for the interview, so only my husband remained.

Again, I asked if my status had changed in any way, and they confirmed that I was still a fact witness. Once again, I believed them. This time the agents asked about the Comey firing. They focused on events that happened during the weekend before his dismissal, when I was the NSC duty officer at Trump's golf resort in Bedminster, New Jersey. Had I met with Trump on Air Force One or at Bedminster? Who else was with us? What did we discuss? Where did we meet? Did I know Trump was planning to fire Comey? Did I discuss Comey with Trump or anyone else? Did I know why Comey was fired? What was Trump's mood that weekend? On Air Force One? Did he seem agitated?

They zeroed in on Trump's son-in-law, Jared Kushner, who was at the Bedminster resort that weekend as well, staying at his own villa with his wife and children. Had Kushner met with Trump that weekend? Had I met with Kushner? Was Kushner on Air Force One when we returned to Washington Sunday night? Was his family with him? Was he with Trump in the president's quarters on the plane? What about his wife, Ivanka, and their children? Where were they? Did I meet with Trump on the plane? Who was with us? What did Trump say to me; what did I say to Trump?

The agents then returned to much of the same territory they had already covered in the two previous interviews. They showed me partial excerpts from a few more emails and some numbers from phone logs. Again, they zeroed in on the time I was in Mar-a-Lago in December 2016, when President Obama had issued the sanctions. Who did I talk to about Obama's sanctions, in meetings or on the phone? Who did I talk to during the day at Mar-a-Lago? At dinner? What had I done during this particular hour? Who did that phone number belong to? Why did I talk to this person? What did I talk about on this particular call or on that one?

Their main focus was on Trump and Flynn and on connecting the two of them during this period. Did I meet with Trump? When? Where? Who else was present? What did Trump say about the sanctions? Did he ask questions? What did others say? When did Flynn talk to the Russian Ambassador? When did I talk to Flynn? What did we discuss? Did I pass along orders from Trump to Flynn? From others to Flynn? Did I tell Trump that Flynn was going to talk to the Russian Ambassador? Did I tell others about his call? Why did I send this particular email? Why was I copied on that email? What did I think about the Russian sanctions? Russian election interference? Russian hacking?

They moved on to the events surrounding Flynn's firing, and brought out some more press stories and documents. What about this press report? Was it accurate? Did I know in advance Flynn was going to be fired? Did anyone discuss Flynn's firing with me? We had gone over all these things in the previous two meetings, and I thought my answers were consistent. I reminded them again that without access to my phone logs, emails, and text messages from the official government devices, I couldn't be 100 percent sure that my recollections were accurate or complete. As they had in the two earlier interviews, the FBI agents jumped around from topic to topic, and then back again asking the same question using slightly different words.

My impression from their questions was that they believed Flynn and others, but especially Trump, had committed some sort of crime, and they were searching for evidence. It was less clear to me what they thought that crime might be—a Logan Act violation, lying about knowledge of Flynn's contacts with the Russian Ambassador, colluding with the Russians, or interfering with their investigations. They didn't say it in so many words, but I got the clear sense that they suspected that I might have been the missing link connecting Flynn and the Russians to Trump.

As this third interview was winding down and we were getting ready to leave, the senior FBI agent pulled one more document from his briefcase. It was a subpoena, bearing that day's date of October 19th, 2017, ordering that I turn over to the Office of Special Counsel all documents, text messages, and emails that were on my personal phone and computers for a twenty-two-month period. Later, I received a second subpoena on November 21st, 2017, ordering me to appear before the grand jury in person on December 1st to give testimony. If I had a lawyer, he would not be allowed to participate or be in the jury room while I testified. I was stunned, especially given his repeated insistence that I wasn't a target, just a fact witness. On receiving the first subpoena, I asked if this was an indication that my status had now changed? Had I suddenly gone from just a fact witness to someone under suspicion? The senior agent again assured me that my status had not changed, that I was still just a fact witness, and not under investigation myself.

Yet, something clearly had changed. If I was just a fact witness, voluntarily cooperating with them throughout our three interviews, why would they now issue me a subpoena? Why had they been so friendly with the Attorney General Mukasey before the last two interviews? If I had known at the beginning of their final interview that they intended to hand me a document subpoena at the end of it, I would immediately have postponed the interview and gotten legal counsel, or at least have asked the former Attorney General to remain in the conference room while they questioned me.

A few days before the scheduled grand jury testimony, a close family friend, Murdo MacLeod, died suddenly at his home in Argyll, in western Scotland. My husband and I made hasty plans to fly out December 2nd to participate in his funeral and burial, and be with the grieving family. I called the junior FBI agent to ask that my grand jury testimony be delayed until after we returned from the funeral. It was at the same time the Flynn guilty plea was announced, along with his Statement of Offense, which referenced Flynn's calls with a "Senior Official of the Presidential Transition Team ('PTT official')" which the press soon reported was me. The junior agent agreed to put off my testimony and said they would be in touch.

One of the OSC's lead prosecutors, Brandon van Grack, called my husband just after we arrived in Scotland for the funeral. Van Grack confirmed that my status had changed and recommended that I get legal counsel. I had suddenly and inexplicably gone from being a fact witness to something worse. This was despite their continued assurances that they were not playing "gotcha" with the questions; that I did not have access to my government records other than the excerpts of text messages and redacted emails that they showed me out of order and out of context during our three interviews; that I didn't work on the campaign; and that I never met with Russians during the Transition or in the Administration.

CHAPTER 19

Investigated by Mueller, Harassed by Congress

After a long drive from Glasgow through the Scottish Highlands, where we had no cell phone coverage, we arrived at the MacLeods. While I was putting the finishing touches on my eulogy, my husband was able to reach Robert Giuffra by phone in New York and asked for his advice. In addition to being one of my husband's closest friends, Giuffra is a senior partner in litigation at the Sullivan & Cromwell law firm. He is considered one of the best lawyers in the country. Today, Giuffra's practice mostly focuses on big cases for corporate giants like Volkswagen and Goldman Sachs. Giuffra is a New York lawyer, but he knows his way around Washington, too. After working in the Reagan White House and clerking for Chief Justice William Rehnquist, he was Chief Counsel to the Senate Whitewater Committee. Giuffra successfully represented lawyer E. Robert Wallach, a close friend of Reagan's Attorney General Edwin Meese, and former New York Senator Alfonse M. D'Amato's brother, Armand.

When my husband described the turn events seemed to have taken with the Mueller investigation, Giuffra realized at once the extent of the legal jeopardy I was now facing. Not because I had done anything wrong during the Transition or while I worked in the White House, but because I was now vulnerable to being charged with lying to the FBI.

A "perjury trap" is what is called a "process crime," where the prosecutors can claim someone's faulty memory isn't faulty at all, but a deliberate effort to evade or lie. They can threaten to charge someone with lying and committing perjury merely on their say so, without letting the person know how they had arrived at that conclusion, what evidence they had, or what documents had led them to believe it so.

In my case, the FBI agents had their notes from my three long interviews (for which I had no legal counsel present). It wasn't an official verbatim transcript, only what they had written, which I was not allowed to review for accuracy, or see what they had recorded as their questions or my answers. I had spoken to the FBI agents without any access to my Transition or Administration records, and had only been shown excerpts of emails that I sent or received, without knowing the context of what came before or after. I was flying blind against the risk of a perjury prosecution.

Giuffra immediately got in touch with Mueller's office to get a sense of what was going on. He knew Mueller from the Volkswagen emissions case that they had both worked on. They confirmed that it was as bad as Giuffra thought it might be. Mueller's lawyers told him that some of my answers to the FBI agents were inconsistent with the facts as they knew them. Fortunately, Giuffra was able to work with the White House and Trump Transition office and get them to provide some of my emails, text messages, and phone records from the Transition period. I hadn't remembered many of them, especially the routine ones dealing with scheduling and personnel, until I saw them again. I didn't find that surprising.

The Transition period was a fairly chaotic time. I received dozens of phone calls and over a hundred emails a day. I was in the process of moving from New York to Washington. I was heading to a new job in an organization I hadn't worked in for decades, and which I would be responsible for managing. To complicate things even more, almost no one on the Transition or senior staff had had any familiarity with the White House or Executive Branch, or even with the federal government. I devoted considerable time to helping them prepare for their new positions.

Once Giuffra was able to obtain the files, I finally had something tangible to work with.

I read through hundreds of documents, including emails, phone logs, and calendars. I was able to reconstruct a rough timeline around the key events the Mueller people were interested in, especially those several days at Mar-a-Lago when Obama imposed sanctions on the Russians. Giuffra and his Sullivan & Cromwell partner, Alex Willscher, a smart former federal prosecutor, grilled me eight to ten hours a day over the next several days. Giuffra and Willscher pressed me to remember in precise and minute detail what I did, who I met with and what we discussed, who I talked to on the phone and what topics we covered, who I exchanged emails and text messages with and why, and what news stories I read. They pressed me to explain what was going through my mind at the time, what issues I was concerned with.

Giuffra and Willscher were able to take all of this information and write a "proffer," a lengthy preview of the points I would make at a subsequent in-person interview. Giuffra phoned the Mueller prosecutors handling my case and went over it with them in detail. They had a favorable reaction to Giuffra's proffer. They trusted him, but the implication was clear—I was in legal jeopardy. I was told to report for an in-person interview with their key prosecutors on December 22nd, 2017 in Washington.

My husband and I flew to Washington the day before the Mueller interview, as did Giuffra and Willscher. We met at Sullivan & Cromwell's Washington office for several more hours, doing one last review of the questions the Mueller team might ask. I couldn't take any notes into my interview with the Special Counsel prosecutors, so I made sure to have the precise sequence and substance of the dozens of meetings, and phone calls and what was discussed in each, as well as the emails and text messages, firmly in my head, so I wouldn't get tripped up.

The next morning, December 22nd, Giuffra, Willscher, and I were picked up by a young female FBI agent in a van with darkened windows at the Sullivan & Cromwell offices at 9 o'clock and driven to the Special Counsel Mueller's offices in Southwest Washington. We approached a non-descript office building and pulled into the loading dock entrance. A guard checked our identification, and a large, gray, metal garage door rose, closing immediately behind us. We parked, got out of the van, and walked single file through a narrow, basement corridor. We arrived at a solid gray steel door, and were buzzed into a small ten-by-ten cinder block room, where we locked our cell phones and any electronic devices in gray metal lockers.

The FBI agent escorted the three of us into a windowless room with a low ceiling and several long gray metal conference tables and gray metal folding chairs. The OSC prosecutors and FBI agents were already in the room when we arrived, and we were introduced all around. Mueller and Giuffra exchanged friendly pleasantries. Mueller then turned to me. When he shook my hand, I was surprised to see he held my gaze a little longer than I expected. He seemed a kindly man, and I was taken a bit back. I expected someone sterner looking, even gruff. It was an odd juxtaposition to what I knew would come next—a long and grueling interrogation by his team of prosecutors and investigators.

Mueller then left the room, and we all took our seats at the table. I was on one side, flanked by my two lawyers, Giuffra and Willscher, and the lawyers and FBI Special Agents who would conduct the interview on the other. All five of them simultaneously opened their five-inch wide, three-ring binders and notebooks sitting on the table in front of them. My two lawyers pulled out their yellow legal pads, hunched over them with pens poised, ready to take copious notes. I sat there with my hands in my lap. It suddenly popped into my head that this was like a meeting I attended decades ago, in Panmunjom, on the Demilitarized Zone between North and South Korea, although, in that case, the low-ceilinged room had windows.

The senior-most official was James Quarles, who looks like a stern, Old Testament prophet—tall with a full head of white hair, prominent penetrating eyes behind thick glasses, and a long, white, handlebar moustache. Quarles is a veteran Washington lawyer. At the beginning of his career he was a young prosecutor in the Watergate investigation, which forced Richard Nixon's resignation. Now, forty-five years later, Quarles was investigating yet another President.

The lawyer in charge was Andrew Goldstein, a former prosecutor from the U.S. Attorney's Office for the Southern District of New York. Goldstein looks more like a college professor than a killer prosecutor. Goldstein struck me as tough but fair, genuinely wanting to understand what had happened during the Trump Tower Transition and early days of the Trump Administration. His questions and demeanor throughout the interrogation suggested that he was interested in getting facts, no matter where they led, rather than someone who had already made up his mind on what the verdict should be and was looking for a crime to justify it.

The other interrogator was Justice Department prosecutor Brandon Van Grack, who looked like a shorter, younger version of James Comey— dark hair, pale white skin, handsome but with an expressionless poker face. He wore a dark suit, solid dark tie, crisp white shirt, had perfect posture, and sat stiffly erect in his chair. Rounding out their team were the two FBI Special Agents–the lead investigator for my three lengthy interviews and the female FBI agent who drove us to and from the interview.

There were no real surprises in their questioning. Giuffra and Willscher had anticipated the likely topics and prepared me well. But it was relentless, tense, and exhausting. As with the three previous FBI interviews, I found the challenge was in following their format. They would ask rapid fire questions, switching back and forth from one topic to another, and one time period to another, and then circle back to the same questions again, but worded slightly differently. I forced myself to remain on high alert for hours on end, knowing that one slip up might prove fatal.

They had large binders in front of them, with pages of questions they planned to ask me, as well as my emails, text messages, phone logs, and schedule (including some I still did not have access to) and presumably everyone else's as well. I had been shown some of them before in previous interviews with the FBI agents. Van Grack also presented several additional documents, which I hadn't seen nor recalled.

They asked about my opinions on Russia policy. Did I have conversations with anyone on the campaign regarding Russia? During the Transition? Did I talk to Flynn, Bannon, Richard Gates or Stephen Miller? Did I have any conversations with Trump after the election? What was my background with General Flynn before being appointed Deputy National Security Advisor? Prior to the week in Mar-a-Lago in December did I sit down with Flynn or Trump to discuss policy? Did I discuss post-Crimea sanctions? Why did I go with President-elect Trump to Mar-a-Lago? When did I meet with Trump there? On December 28th, after I learned from the press that Obama was going to impose sanctions on Russia, who did I talk to at Mar-a-Lago? Did I reach out to experts? Who? How did I know them? Did I speak to Trump or anyone before he spoke to the press or tweeted about Russia? Why did Trump say what he did about Putin?

When did I talk to Flynn? How often? What did I discuss? Did I direct Flynn to call the Russian Ambassador or did he volunteer to make the call? What did Flynn and I discuss regarding sanctions? What was discussed during President-elect Trump's intelligence briefing at Mar-a-Lago or when I met on December 29th with Trump and other senior officials? Did I discuss Russian hacking with them? Sanctions? Other subjects?

After these general topics they zeroed in on what I had done hour by hour, sometimes minute by minute, during four specific days—the day before Obama imposed sanctions, the day the White House officially sanctioned Russia, the day Putin announced the Russian response, and the day afterward when Flynn called me after I returned home to Long Island to say the Russian Ambassador told him their call had made a difference in Russia's response. Who did I talk to at Mar-a-Lago? On the Transition team? On the outside? What did we discuss? Why did I call them?

They showed me emails that I had not seen before: Why did this person send me that email? Why did I write this memo? Who else worked on it? Did I tell others at Mar-a-Lago that Flynn was scheduled to talk to the Russian Ambassador? Did I report back to them after Flynn told me the results of his call? What was my reaction to the sanctions? How did others react? What about this email? What did I say during this phone call? Why did I send that text message? Why did I forward that email? Why did I talk to this person a second time? What was going through my head at this time? What did Flynn tell me to say to the president-elect or others at Mar-a-Lago? What did Trump or others tell me to say to Flynn? Did I discuss sanctions with Trump or others? What did he say? What did they say? Did I discuss what the Russians might do in response? Where was I sitting during this call? Where did I have dinner? Who was with me? Did I see Trump during dinner? Others from the Transition? Who did I pass in the hallway?

They didn't say it outright, but I got the impression from their questions that they believed there must have been some sort of a quid pro quo between Flynn and the Russians, or Trump and the Russians, over sanctions, and that was why Putin suddenly overruled his Foreign Minister and did not retaliate. Several of their questions seemed to suggest they thought I was lying for someone or covering up something. They zeroed back in on Trump, implying that I must have been the conduit between Trump, or other senior staff members, and Flynn, passing along their orders to him and reporting back to them on his results. Did Trump himself, or any of the senior staff, instruct me to direct Flynn to call and make promises to the Russians? Did Trump know that Flynn was talking to the Russian Ambassador? Did Trump or any other senior officials on the Transition have any conversations directly with Flynn?

Van Grack pointed to a sixty-minute gap on December 29th when I didn't text, email, or use my phone. He said I had been active both before and after that period, but during that hour I went silent. Was that when I met with Trump? Or with senior staff members? The implication was that this sixty-minute gap must have been when I got my marching orders from Trump to pass along to Flynn. I pointed out it that the sixty-minute gap was during lunchtime. I had left the Mar-a-Lago clubhouse for an hour to take a slow stroll along the beach with my husband.

The interview went on for nearly eight hours. I had a few energy bars my husband had slipped into my purse that morning. I could ask for short bathroom breaks, but otherwise we went straight through, adjourning for a lunch break when my lawyers and I gobbled down some sandwiches. We resumed thirty minutes later and went through to the end of the day.

I was grilled by five skilled and aggressive lawyers and FBI Special Agents, who had taken a series of Trump tweets, public statements, news reports, phone calls, text messages, emails, and meetings by Trump, his inner circle, and even some peripheral advisors, and hypothesized their own theory of what happened. Simple rookie mistakes on the part of people unfamiliar with the ways of Washington, the inability of many to remember things accurately without access to their records, the chaos of the Trump Transition, and Trump's absolutely unconventional way of doing things could be made to seem like a carefully organized conspiracy of silence, collusion, obstruction of justice, and intentional wrongdoing.

Several days later, I was still pretty rattled. I told my older daughter about the interrogation, especially their questions and implications about Flynn and Trump. She laughed and said, "Well, Mom, since no one told you what to say to Flynn, what they're implying is that after you and Dad walked along the beach, you, on your own initiative, told Flynn what to say to the Russian Ambassador. The Russian Ambassador then passed it on to Moscow, and Putin immediately folded. He reversed Russia's previous position and didn't dare retaliate to Obama's sanctions. It wasn't just

Flynn who was following your orders—it was Putin too! So, Mom, you were running Putin's foreign policy! Who knew you were that powerful! We never thought so when we were growing up!"

A month or so later the Mueller team wanted me to come down to Washington for another interview. At this point, I had already spent more than twenty hours over the course of three FBI interviews. I had been through several intense all-day sessions with my lawyers to prepare lengthy "proffers" of detailed testimony on everything I could recall. I had spent eight grueling hours with the Mueller prosecutors. I couldn't imagine what more they wanted from me. It had already gone on for nearly six months, and I felt like there was no way out of this nightmare. At that point I was so worn down and disillusioned that I turned to my lawyers and pleaded, "Just tell me what they want me to say, and I'll say it."

After a lot of soul searching on my part, and relentless encouragement from my husband, I decided that if the Special Counsel decided to charge me with lying to the FBI, I would not plead guilty to a crime I did not believe I had committed. I would stand trial, with the full understanding of what that would entail—hundreds of thousands, if not millions of dollars in legal expenses, years of litigation, and the certain end to my career. What I could not do, even though I was sorely tempted, was admit to some type of lying I did not feel I had done, or to lie about the actions of others. I knew I couldn't live with myself if I took that path, even if the consequences of not doing so were personally catastrophic.

In the end, the Mueller team did not demand I come to Washington for another interview. Nor did they charge me with any crime. Since I couldn't provide them with any more information than I already had, I wasn't all that useful to them. I couldn't link Trump or others to Flynn's phone calls with the Russian Ambassador or link Trump to Russia. I would probably have been a good scalp to pin to their wall with a perjury trap, but I had one of the best lawyers in the country on my side, so getting my scalp would not have been easy. According to press reports, their investigation soon moved on from Flynn and the Logan Act to other topics, including claiming porn star hush money payments as campaign expenses, and Trump's business interests.

The Mueller report came out over a year later. After their exhaustive investigation, they found no evidence that Trump or Flynn or anyone on the campaign had colluded with the Russians to influence the election. I was mentioned throughout their final report, with no indication of any wrongdoing on my part, despite the perjury traps that were laid. Even so, for months I still woke up in a cold sweat from nightmares of people knocking on my door in the middle of the night, charging me with non-existent crimes, putting me in handcuffs, and hauling me off to jail.

I had worked in Washington before. I had seen up close what happened during the Watergate and Iran Contra investigations. I was not inexperienced, nor was I naïve, nor was I oblivious to the dangers. Even so, I learned several hard lessons during this ordeal. First, I should never have met with the FBI agents without a lawyer present. I should have immediately retained the best counsel I could find, regardless of expense.

Second, I took the FBI agents at their word, that I was only a fact witness helping with their inquiry. Even though my first three FBI interviews seemed friendly, they were not. Just "telling the truth" as you remember it isn't as simple as it sounds. There is a large gray area in people's memories, or at least mine, in recalling past events with 100 percent accuracy. Therein lies the danger. If you are asked the same question, but in different words, in one interview or in different interviews over time, your answer cannot deviate, even slightly. There is similar jeopardy if you think you remember something that later turns out with some other discovered evidence or testimony to be incorrect, or only partially correct, or if you do not remember something when others do, or recall it differently. It is difficult to prove to interrogators that any of these are unintentional human errors, and not deliberate lies, especially if they are determined to find a crime.

Finally, I should have devoted the same amount of extensive and expensive preparation with lawyers for my first three FBI interviews as I did in preparing the proffers and being interrogated by the Mueller prosecutors. In these special investigations the government has all the power, all the resources, and all the rights. The prosecutors decide what documents and evidence to share with you. They decide whether you are telling the truth or not, without telling you the basis for their decision. They can charge you with some sort of crime if they choose to, knowing you face the choice of pleading guilty without a trial; or making special arrangements with them to implicate others; or spending years in court, fighting the entire power and might of the U.S. government. If so, you are likely condemning your family to ruinous legal expenses, and yourself to shame and unemployability. To me, the experience seemed to turn our justice system on its head. It was not innocent until proven guilty. If they decide you have committed some crime, you have to bear the burden of proving yourself innocent, without necessarily having access to all the documents and information they do.

All that being said, I don't believe the Mueller prosecutors singled me out or treated me any differently than they did others. They were professionals, dogged and thorough, and most of them the kind of people you want protecting the nation's security against terrorists or hardcore criminals. It wasn't them as much as it was the process, and the viciously partisan environment in which we now live. The role of a special counsel is to be relentless and ruthless in uncovering any wrongdoing within the scope of his mandate. They run down every rabbit hole, chase every conspiracy theory, assume people are lying and covering up instead of just people with imperfect memories. It is one of the most powerful investigatory tools at the government and intelligence community's disposal. That is why the process should not be initiated unless there are serious and verified grounds for doing so. What should never happen is for the process to be used as a weapon against political enemies. Given the tribal toxicity of today's Washington, it is even more important, and more difficult.

The late Justice Antonin Scalia, one of the most brilliant minds in the history of the Supreme Court, sent a cautionary note to the nation in 1988 when he wrote,

> *"nothing is so politically effective as the ability to charge that one's opponent and his associates are not merely wrongheaded, naïve, ineffective, but, in all probability, 'crooks.' And nothing so effectively gives an appearance of validity to such charges as a Justice Department investigation and, even better, prosecution."*[1]

The Office of Special Counsel spent two years, $35 million, interviewed 500 witnesses, and issued 3,500 subpoenas. They had dozens of crack lawyers and FBI agents on their team. It was the most thorough investigation in United States history. If there was any wrongdoing, they would have found it. Mueller's final report found no conspiracy between

---

[1] Pierce, Jr., Richard J. "Morrison v. Olson, Separation of Powers, and the Structure of Government." *The University of Chicago Press Journals, The Supreme Court Review* 1988 (1988). https://www.journals.uchicago.edu/doi/abs/10.1086/scr.1988.3109619?journalCode=scr.

the Trump campaign and the Russians. As Senate Judiciary Committee Chairman Senator Lindsey Graham said, "It's finished."

Unfortunately, however, my experience with the Mueller team wasn't the end of the matter for me or for the country. The Democrats in Congress are determined to drag the country through endless anti-Trump interrogations, hearings, inflammatory accusations, and public horse whippings, covered in rapturous detail by the Trump-hating liberal media. It is difficult to comprehend how legislators and their staff think they are going to uncover illegalities that the Office of Special Counsel could not discover when looking through the microscope at everyone and everything. But perhaps that's not the point.

The Congressional committees want in on the action, too. They have all but declared they are no longer in the business of writing, evaluating and passing legislation, confirming nominees, or ratifying treaties. They're now in the business of investigating President Trump and everyone around him. It's much better for raising their profiles, getting on cable news, fundraising, running for reelection, and even campaigning for president. Merely being legislators is rather hum drum by comparison.

My first experience was with the Senate Foreign Relations Committee in the summer of 2017, and confirmation hearings to be the U.S. Ambassador to Singapore. After a much delayed but rather routine round of meetings with staff I was given a formal confirmation hearing with senators and, after an additional delay, was voted out of Committee.

Instead of proceeding to vote on my nomination, however, Democrat staffers brought me back for several additional rounds of meetings and questions. At one point a Democrat staffer said I would not be confirmed unless I turned over to them my Transition files and records. They wanted to know what foreign officials I met with during the Transition, who else was present at the meetings, and what was discussed. Unless I was prepared to give them "names, dates, and topics," they would put a hold on my nomination and not allow it to go forward for a vote by the full Senate. When I said I no longer possessed those records because, as required, I had turned them over to the GSA at the end of the Transition, nor did I have access to them, the lead staffer said, "That's your problem, not mine."

I was caught in the middle, which was probably what the Democrats intended. To give them what they demanded, I would have had to violate the president's right to assert Executive Privilege. The White House was taking the position that communications among the then-president-elect and his advisors about foreign policy during the Transition was covered by Executive Privilege. The Democrats on the Hill didn't agree. If I didn't give the Democrat staffers what they demanded they would hold up my nomination indefinitely.

While I was still dangling in limbo, on December 1st, 2017 Flynn pleaded guilty to lying to the FBI. Democrat Senator and now presidential candidate Cory Booker immediately accused me of lying to the Senate Foreign Relations Committee in one of the written questions for the record I had submitted five months before. In Flynn's Statement for the Offense, he said he spoke to a "Senior Transition Official" (which the press identified as me) both before and after his call with the Russian Ambassador on December 29th to discuss what, if anything, to communicate about sanctions, and afterward to report on the substance of his call with the Russian Ambassador, including their discussion of sanctions.

Booker pointed to the written question for the record he had sent to me several days after my hearing, which began with a three-paragraph-long series of accusations about Flynn and mentioned other matters that I was not involved with. Booker's final sentence, the one with a question mark at the end, switched topics and asked, "Did you ever discuss any of General Flynn's contacts with Russian Ambassador Sergey Kislyak directly with General Flynn?" I answered in writing that "I am not aware of any of the issues or events as described" in his opening paragraphs, in essence responding to the lengthy lead-in to his question, not the single final sentence. I did not, in effect, answer the precise question about Flynn's conversation with the Russian Ambassador on December 29th, 2016 in that answer.

However, Booker asked the same thing two questions later, which I did answer. Booker's written question asked, "Were you aware of General Flynn's conversation with Russian Ambassador Sergey Kislyak on December 29, 2016 at any point before Vice President Pence's interview with CBS's 'Face the Nation' on January 15, 2017? If you were aware of Flynn's conversation with the Russian Ambassador prior to Pence's interview, did you discuss Flynn's contact with Kislyak with Pence or any other Senior Transition Officials?"

I responded that, "Any conversations I may or may not have had with General Flynn would have been confidential. As such, it would be inappropriate for me to comment on them," which is the response I was directed to make by the White House Counsel's Office. Neither they nor I were attempting to cover anything up, or lie to the Senate.

In normal times this sort of thing could have been explained as just a difference in interpretation of the question and not intended to be disrespectful or disingenuous. But these are not normal times, and Senator Booker was preparing to run for president. Washington is consumed by outrage fever and gotcha partisan warfare, and no one is willing to give any quarter.

As I was preparing to explain all this to Booker's staffer and the rest of their committee, I got word that I shouldn't bother. I had heard from several sources, and later read in an article in *The Atlantic* that Ranking Member Senator Ben Cardin told his staff to "Please make this go away."[2] I was told that several Democrat staff members bragged, "We're never going to let her be confirmed!" When I heard from a reporter that yet another Democrat staffer joked, "The only way that KT McFarland is getting to Singapore is if she swims," I decided I had finally had enough.

I was tired of being a plaything for Democrat senators and their staffers. Rather than remain in limbo indefinitely, I asked President Trump to withdraw my nomination in early 2018.

Dear President Trump,

I am asking that you withdraw my nomination to be the U.S. Ambassador to Singapore. My prolonged confirmation by the Senate in an election year will not help advance our critical relationships in South East Asia, and is precluding me from serving this country in other meaningful ways.

I have come to this decision reluctantly, because I believe in your mission. You have unleashed the country's great engine of economic growth. You have brought millions of once disengaged Americans into the political debate. You have laid the foundations for a new foreign policy that puts America's interests ahead of, but not at the expense of, our obligations to others.

You have honored me not once, but twice-over, by appointing me Deputy National Security Adviser in the early months of your Administration, and

---

[2] Entous, Adam. "The Agonizingly Slow Downfall of K. T. McFarland." *The New Yorker*. January 29, 2018. https://www.newyorker.com/news/news-desk/the-agonizingly-slow-downfall-of-k-t-mcfarland.

nominating me as Ambassador to Singapore. For those opportunities I will be forever grateful.

I have served in four Administrations, beginning in 1970 as a young college student working part-time on Henry Kissinger's National Security Council Staff. I returned to that same office more than forty-five years later, as your Deputy National Security Adviser, at a desk just a few feet away from where I began. But our great nation has moved mightily in those decades. I have been blessed to be part of that first generation of women who could choose to have a full professional life, but also a full family life. When I began my career I never dreamed a woman could serve at such levels of government. I am proud that it is now a matter of course for my children's and grandchildren's generations.

While I am withdrawing from this nomination, I have no intention of withdrawing from the national debate. My life has been guided by the principle that when the good Lord closes a door, He always opens a window. I have spent over four decades seeking to advance our nation's security, and will continue to do so in the years ahead.

With great respect and admiration,

KT McFarland
February 2, 2018

President Trump accepted my request reluctantly, chastising Democrats for choosing "to play politics rather than move forward with a qualified nominee for a critically important post." He urged me to use my "considerable wisdom and skill as a commentator to explain to the American people how to make American foreign policy great again."

I was one of the most qualified ambassadorial nominees put forth by President Trump. From Singapore I could have been the president's personal eyes and ears for the entire Indo-Pacific region. Because of my background, I could have helped develop our policies and conduct diplomacy in an area crucial to America's long-term economic and security interests. I could have played an important role in America's efforts to push for North Korean de-nuclearization. But because some career politicians would rather put their own ambitions ahead of the country's, I became another casualty in Washington's unending political wars. Afterward, out of respect for the ongoing Mueller investigation, President Trump, and the process, I stayed out of sight and didn't immediately resume my career on cable news, radio, and the lecture circuit.

After I left the White House and withdrew my ambassadorial nomination, I received repeated demands from several House and Senate Committees and their staffs similar to the ones I received from the Senate Foreign Relations Committee. They wanted me to turn over my Transition files—emails, text messages, phone logs, and schedules—the majority of which I did not have access to, and to appear voluntarily to be grilled before their committee staffs in the hopes they could catch me in perjury traps of their own making.

The Senate Select Committee on Intelligence took their requests for my voluntary cooperation a step further. They subpoenaed me to appear before their staffers in February 2019, the week my husband was scheduled for surgery for aggressive prostate cancer in New York. Only after my lawyers provided them with signed letters from doctors and surgeons did they agree to a three-week delay. When my husband's post-surgical recovery developed complications, Giuffra asked if we could delay the interview again. They refused. Giuffra asked if we could conduct the interview in New York, which they had originally offered to do. They refused. We offered to have the interview conducted via video conference, or with written questions—all under oath—so I could remain in New York with my husband during this period. They again refused.

So, after another several days of extensive preparation with Giuffra, Willsher, and their talented young associate, Amanda Shami, we flew to Washington in early March for a hearing with about a dozen Senate Intelligence Committee staffers. Their interview was to cover events during the Transition. They covered much of the ground that had already been covered in great detail by Mueller's staff, although their questioning was far less precise or professional. At least six staffers, in addition to their staff attorney, jumped in with questions, some contradictory, and some vague. Giuffra, concerned that my answers to their sprawling questions could be taken out of context, or misinterpreted at some later date, cleared up any misunderstanding by himself asking me a series of precise questions to which I offered precise answers.

The hearing went on for most of the day, and a number of times the staffers asked questions that could implicate the president's Executive Privilege, including insisting that I tell them what Trump said in his daily intelligence briefing and other similar meetings. Giuffra was back and forth on the phone with President Trump's White House lawyer, Emmet Flood, throughout.

As we were nearing the end of their interview, and they continued asking questions that they knew I was not allowed to answer, the lead interrogator said, "we have a plan" on how to deal with the Executive Privilege issue. Their plan was to hold me personally in contempt of Congress for refusing to answer questions we understood involved the president's Executive Privilege. Their position was that a president-elect is not entitled to any Executive Privilege during the Transition. Giuffra forcefully objected to their tactics, and we all got up and left the room. The interview was over. Giuffra sent a strong letter to the Senate Intelligence Committee several days later, citing their incorrect interpretation of the law, and their insistence on bullying a private citizen, rather than resolving their dispute with the White House over the scope of my testimony.

I have received similar subpoenas from the House Intelligence and House Judiciary Committees. They want to investigate the same things the Office of Special Counsel did, and promise to hold me and others hostage to their efforts. Do they really think they will find anything the FBI and Justice Department professionals did not? Or is their goal to harass Trump and everyone who has served in his Administration? Is their goal to punish Trump aides and supporters by forcing them to incur ruinous legal expenses? Every subpoena they issue, no matter how frivolous or redundant, costs the witness tens of thousands of dollars in legal expenses to gather documents, prepare for interviews, and anticipate "gotcha" questions. None of these expenses are reimbursed—by insurance, by your government employer, by the Congressional committee. Committee members and their staffers realize that, which is perhaps one of the reasons they do it. They also know these investigations and hearings guarantee fawning applause from the anti-Trump media, which serves to raise a legislator's profile, political support, and even campaign contributions.

We would all like to believe that our justice system is based on the premise that people are presumed innocent until proven guilty. It is not the individual who must prove his innocence. It is the government which must prove his guilt. Most of us don't think about it much at all.

We assume our legal system is just and it punishes the wrongdoers and exonerates the innocent.

Until I was myself drawn into the Mueller investigation, I had always assumed that people accused by the Justice Department or Special Prosecutors were guilty. I never had much sympathy for them because I thought they would not have been charged with a crime unless there was an unequivocal, airtight case against them. I didn't know until I went through it myself that the accused, whether innocent or guilty, has to spend thousands, tens of thousands of dollars to defend himself against a government with unlimited resources and budget.

For example, perjury is supposed to be intentionally lying, either on a document, government form or in person, to an official of the FBI, Justice Department, Congress, or other government agency. Yet, in today's highly charged political environment, human errors such as misremembering phone calls, emails, or text messages from years before, or unintentionally omitting items on government documents, can be painted as deliberate lies and charged as crimes.

In the Age of Trump the stakes have become so high, the consequences so great, and the temptation so alluring, that justice can take the backseat to opportunism, ambition, and greed.

Washington is so obsessed with partisanship, and that means investigations into presidential candidates and senior officials have become weaponized tools that one party uses against its political opponents. Ambitious prosecutors and investigators can abuse the system for their own ends, and deny due process or selectively enforce laws. Yet there is rarely a penalty for their actions.

These politically motivated investigations do lifelong damage to people's lives and their families, even to those who are innocent. I was in the White House during the Watergate scandal and knew many who got swept into the maelstrom for no reason other than that they worked for Richard Nixon. They had nothing to do with the original Watergate break-in or the cover-up that followed. They were people who in normal times would have left their White House jobs and gone on to success in the private sector. But because they worked in the Nixon Administration they were deemed radioactive. Doors that should have been open to them were slammed shut for years because potential employers didn't want the hassle of any connection to a national scandal.

I was in the Reagan Administration during the Iran-Contra affair. Many people pulled into that investigation bore a heavy financial burden from legal expenses; it didn't matter whether they were guilty or innocent. The air of suspicion for even being called to testify hung over them for the rest of their lives. One close friend even attempted suicide. What about the dozens, even hundreds of others, who have had to go through this process, not only in the Trump Administration but in previous and probably future Administrations?

It is not just the damage these politically motivated investigations do to individuals by savaging their reputations and marking them for life. They can destabilize the presidency itself, set off constitutional crises, and sow doubt into the legitimacy of our most important institutions. These endless investigations, launched against every president since Nixon, cause us to lose confidence not just in some of our leaders, but in the effectiveness of democracy itself.

Throughout our history, once elections were over, the winners went on to govern for their full terms of office. The losers accepted defeat. They went home to lick their wounds and try again at the next election. But now, losers immediately cry foul. They challenge the validity of our electoral system and demand investigations and interrogations, sometimes before the winners have even taken office.

Most of those called to public service are good and decent people who want to make their country a better place. But not everyone. In today's toxic environment, some have decided that Trump is so evil, his threat to the nation so extraordinary, that they are no longer bound by tradition, norms, or even laws. They believe they're justified in bringing down presidents; in effect nullifying election results. The liberal mainstream media and Democrat presidential hopefuls scream that the president and his family, advisors, and former business associates must to be "brought to justice."

As I write this in the fall of 2019, there is some evidence that highly placed Hillary Clinton supporters in the intelligence community had an anti-Trump "insurance plan" in place before the election. If Hillary won, no one would be any the wiser. But if the unthinkable happened and Trump won, they could activate the plan and claim he won unfairly with the help of America's arch enemy. As Attorney General William Barr said, they saw themselves as above the law, as guardians of the republic.

They seemed to think they were justified in doing whatever necessary to stop Trump from governing, including overruling the will of the people. Unless these people are themselves brought to justice, and their hidden abuses of power brought out into the sunlight, the witch hunts they launched against Donald Trump are likely to be visited on the next president and beyond.

Some in Congress, especially the House, have decided they will not accept the conclusions of the Mueller report, and are conducting their own investigations. Others are expanding scope into new areas, including Trump's past business projects, his personal life, and his children. They are determined to put everything under a microscope until they find a crime, any crime, that can be pointed to as justification for launching the greatest reality show in the history of television—"The Impeachment of Donald Trump."

CHAPTER 20

Impeachment

I have seen firsthand what happens during an impeachment process. It has ramifications far greater than whether a president is guilty or innocent of any crime. It brings the entire nation to a halt, and leaves us weakened and vulnerable to foreign adversaries.

I was a young aide on Kissinger's staff in the West Wing in the early 1970s, when Richard Nixon became embroiled in the Watergate scandal. He had just been re-elected by a landslide in 1972, despite being hated by the liberal intelligentsia and Washington insiders.

The *Washington Post* reported a break-in in the Democratic National Committee headquarters in the Watergate office building a few months before the election, but no one gave it a second glance. The burglars were eventually traced back to several people on the Nixon re-election committee. Higher-ups in the Nixon Administration went into damage control mode to cover up the connection. But the story didn't stay buried. The Senate formed a Watergate Committee to investigate wrongdoing and demanded the creation of a Special Prosecutor with subpoena powers operating independently of the Justice Department.

What had been dismissed as a "third-rate burglary" by the White House Press Secretary in late 1972 had become a full-scale White House crisis by spring 1973, especially after the resignation of White House Chief of Staff Bob Haldeman and Domestic Affairs Advisor John Ehrlichman, who were later charged with being co-conspirators in the Watergate cover-up scandal.

One by one my colleagues in the West Wing were brought in to testify publicly before the Senate and summoned to meet behind closed doors with the Watergate Special Prosecution Force. We also learned that there was a previously unknown Oval Office taping system that recorded President Nixon's meetings.

Every week investigative reporters Bob Woodward and Carl Bernstein had a new story on the front page of the *Washington Post*, with details of the investigation, and who was involved in the cover-up. It later developed that Woodward and Bernstein had a secret source within the Administration, an anonymous FBI official nicknamed "Deep Throat," who supplied them with a constant stream of revelations.

The offices I passed regularly on my way to Kissinger's suite began emptying out as staff members who were forced to resign were not replaced. The West Wing began to resemble a ghost town. Meanwhile, those of us on the NSC were working overtime while we followed through on foreign policy success after success—the Paris Peace Accords which ended the Vietnam War, the opening to China, arms control agreements, and détente with the Soviet Union. The Richard Nixon the world was reading about daily in the pages of the *Washington Post* and the *New York Times* was portrayed as an evil and conniving criminal. The Nixon we saw was a president who, working with Kissinger, presided over a golden age of American diplomacy.

The Watergate scandal dragged on and on for nearly two years. The Senate and the Special Prosecutor demanded Nixon turn over tapes of his meetings in the Oval Office. Nixon refused. Nixon's Republican allies in Congress became increasingly skeptical and guarded as the scandal grew. Meetings the new Chief of Staff, General Alexander Haig, had with the Congressional leadership became more frequent, and more pessimistic. Vice President Jerry Ford stopped meeting with Nixon to avoid the appearance of impropriety. In late July 1974, the Supreme Court denied Nixon's claim of Executive Privilege and ruled that he must turn over his Oval Office tapes to the Special Prosecutor. Three days later, the House Judiciary Committee adopted the first of three articles of impeachment. The death watch had begun.

Deputy National Security Advisor General Brent Scowcroft (who held the post I would come to occupy in the Trump Administration) asked our West Wing Staff to pull together briefing books in the likelihood that we would soon have a new president. I stood at the Xerox machine for hours copying everything from the NATO Treaty to transcripts of President Nixon's most confidential communications with foreign leaders. No one knew whether Nixon would resign, stay in office and be impeached by the full House and stand trial in the Senate or, in desperation, possibly even end his own life.

Nixon spoke to the American people for the last time from the Oval Office on August 8th, announcing that he would officially resign the presidency the next day, August 9th, 1974. I worked in the Situation Room late into the night, and came back early the next morning. We were still pulling together briefing papers and three-ring binder notebooks when my office mate and immediate boss, Peter Rodman, said we were all invited to the East Room to hear President Nixon bid farewell to the staff. We left and joined the stream of staff members coming over from the Old Executive Office Building, and together walked across the West Basement hallway, up the stairs and past the Press Office, through the Colonnade and into the White House Residence.

The Cabinet officers and White House senior staff and their spouses all had seats up front. I arrived a bit behind the crowd, and all the chairs were taken. I stood along the south wall, at the back of the East Room near the large windows, leaning against the long yellow brocade drapes. President Nixon and Mrs. Nixon, their two daughters and sons-in-laws, Julie and David Eisenhower and Tricia and Ed Cox, walked through the audience to the raised podium on the eastern wall, between the historic paintings of George and Martha Washington.

I was amazed by their composure, and moved by Nixon's words. No teleprompter, no papers, he just spoke from the heart. The press, of course, criticized him for being maudlin, but I thought he seemed touchingly vulnerable. To this day, I don't know where Nixon summoned up the courage to say farewell to his staff. He was such a private man, and now to see him stripped of dignity, to have fallen so far, so fast, with no one to blame but himself, was painful to watch. The most powerful man in the world, who had been reelected less than two years before in the greatest landslide in United States history, had been forced to resign the presidency or face impeachment, trial, and removal from office for "high crimes and misdemeanors." It was one of the most stunning political reversals in modern times.

After he finished speaking, President Nixon and his family walked across the East Room and past row upon row of their most loyal supporters and staff. Those seated stood up and joined those of us standing along the walls in applauding the departing president. Most of the women were crying and everyone looked woefully sad.

The Nixons walked right past me into the Green Room, and on to the Portico and down the stairs to the South Lawn. When President Nixon had entered the East Room, just a few moments before, he had the vast machinery of the entire U.S. government at his disposal, and the mightiest military at his command. But when he left that room, he was about to become the *former* President Nixon, broken and humiliated with his grief laid bare for all the world to see. He had failed at the one thing that he had spent his entire life seeking—the presidency. He had done great things during his years in office, but that would all be forgotten. The name Nixon would forever be linked to the Watergate scandal and the shame of being the only president in American history to resign from office.

Some of the Cabinet and senior staff walked slowly behind the Nixons like a funeral cortege, and those of us standing along the wall brought up the rear. We all walked down the staircase and stood on the South Lawn. We hung behind while the Nixons, who were joined by Vice President— soon to be President—Ford and Mrs. Ford. They walked to Marine One, the presidential helicopter that was to take the Nixons to Andrews Air Force Base for their final trip to San Clemente, California. As the Nixons walked up the helicopter steps and ducked into the doorway, we all stood on the lawn, behind the Fords, and waved goodbye.

No one said a word as we walked back to the Situation Room and resumed working on the briefings books for the new president. Two hours later, the same group of us walked back to the East Room, me again standing along the southern wall, and watched as Vice President Gerald Ford was sworn in as the 38th President of the United States.

Despite the high emotion of the times, Nixon was never charged with a crime. A month later, President Ford pardoned him to end our "long national nightmare." Nixon's guilt was never proven, and recently released evidence indicates that the rush to indict Nixon was probably more about politics and personal unpopularity than any personal criminal conduct. Even so, some of the senior members of the Washington elite hated Nixon with such intensity that they were furious he had escaped trial, conviction, and prison.

Today, history seems to be repeating itself. A president despised by the liberal elites. A Washington press corps committed to covering him as a craven criminal, even before uncovering scandal. A Special Prosecutor conducting a lengthy and wide-ranging investigation into the president, his campaign and his advisors. Senior people at the FBI seemingly set on destroying his presidency. Ambitious politicians from the opposition party feeding the media's frenzy, launching investigations and endeavoring to remove him from office, with some even hoping to run and take his place in the White House. An entire Washington Establishment committed to his destruction.

No American is above the law, including the president. That is why the Founding Fathers included in the Constitution a mechanism which gives us the ability to remove a sitting president from office. But they also set the bar for impeachment very high, requiring both the House of Representatives and Senate, as well as the Supreme Court to be involved. They guaranteed that impeaching a president wouldn't be done lightly, or get caught up with the hot political tempers of the day. It could only happen with the overwhelming support of the American people, working through their elected representatives in Congress.

No matter what the final outcome, a vote in the House to impeach a president, and conduct a subsequent trial in the Senate, comes at great cost to the nation. It dominates our national attention span for months, crowding out other issues of importance. There is only so much oxygen in the Oval Office, and if a president is forced to expend much of it on legal proceedings, the day to day business of government crawls to a halt. Legislators on both sides of the political aisle hold their breath, waiting to see which way the wind blows before deciding whether to take a stand on important domestic and international issues. The president loses the clout to pull together the coalitions necessary to get legislation passed. Cabinet officers and other senior officials are unsure how to act in the midst of such controversy when there is little direction from the top. A vice president, who might otherwise share more of the burden of governing during these periods, is advised to stay neutral and on the sidelines, lest he be tainted should he have to replace the president. Our adversaries and enemies, and even some of our friendly competitors, sense weakness and division at our seat of government and move out smartly to take advantage of the situation.

When I was in the West Wing during Watergate, and Nixon was preoccupied with the Special Prosecutor's investigation and Congressional hearings, those of us inside "the bunker" joked that General Haig, Nixon's Chief of Staff, was running the country while Secretary of State Kissinger was running the world. It was gallows humor, but it spoke to the underlying truth—that while a president is under investigation, a lot of the routine business of government simply doesn't get done. Things fall into a state of suspended animation.

However disruptive these crises may have been in the past, they pale in comparison to anything in the Age of Trump. His critics are more obsessed with the constant stream of stories featuring new bombshell revelations, breaking news scandals, and non-stop investigations. When the Mueller report was finally finished, it was clear that many of the press stories during the course of those two years were little more than speculative gossip, some were simply made up by ambitious politicians and journalists. Michael Wolff, author of the controversial bestseller on the early days of the Trump presidency, was at least up front about it. After admitting that many of the accounts he got from Trump insiders were "baldly untrue." Their "looseness with the truth, if not with reality itself, are an elemental thread" of his book. The "version of events" he offers isn't necessarily true–only that in his opinion they could have been true, even if he made it up.[1]

The anti-Trump frenzy is likely to get even more intense in the months leading up to the 2020 election. There will be a crescendo of calls for the biggest reality television extravaganza of all time: "The Congressional Investigation, Impeachment and Trial of Donald Trump." Previous presidential scandals dominated our national attention; this one will entirely overwhelm us.

These constant scandals, investigations, and prosecutions cannot help but have a corrosive effect over time. The wounds don't heal quickly. This swirl of intense emotions, once released, are not so easily put back inside

---

[1] Wolff, Michael. *Fire and Fury*. New York: Henry Holt and Company, 2018.

the box. After the crisis subsides, the losing side wants to "get even" the next time around.

For the first 200 years of our history, we had impeachment proceedings for only one president, in 1866, when Vice President Andrew Johnson succeeded to the presidency of a divided nation after Lincoln's assassination at the end of the Civil War. Those two centuries were filled with the normal nastiness of American politics, no different from today. Political battles were fought every four years as one party sought to replace the other in the White House. Throughout almost all of our history, though, the victor would become president and take charge of the Executive Branch. The defeated candidate would fade into history, and the losing party set about finding new candidates with new ideas who could win the next election. But in modern times, the effort has been to try to hobble or actually remove a president *during* his term of office.

In the nearly fifty years since the Nixon presidency, every single president has faced some kind of impeachment effort or investigation. Some were more serious than others, but they all sought to wound or delegitimize a sitting president. After the Watergate scandal, Nixon's forced resignation and President Ford's pardon, Republicans investigated President Carter for incompetence in the Tehran hostage crisis. Democrats investigated the Reagan Administration for illegal arms sales and secret negotiations in the Iran-Contra Affair.

House Republicans voted to impeach President Bill Clinton for perjury and obstruction stemming from a sexual harassment lawsuit. He was impeached by the House, and tried before the Senate with Supreme Court Chief Justice William Rehnquist presiding. Clinton was acquitted when the Senate failed to get the two thirds majority necessary to remove him from office. Democrats investigated George W. Bush and his Administration for making fraudulent intelligence claims to justify the Iraq War and for the Valerie Plame affair. Republican "birthers" claimed Obama was not born in the United States, and therefore constitutionally ineligible to be president. Congressional Republicans held several investigations focused on former Secretary of State Hillary Clinton's role in the Benghazi attacks. Democrats and senior officials of the intelligence community launched the Russia probe into the Trump campaign, seemingly to de-legitimize him even before he took the oath of office.

While the impeachment process and the upcoming presidential election are proceeding down two separate tracks, they are inextricably bound together, with each affecting the other.

For the most part, impeachment is an Inside-the-Beltway affair. Voters do not get a say in the matter, other than indirectly through their already-elected representatives in the House and Senate. The presidential election, on the other hand, plays out all across the land: beginning with the nominating process of caucuses, and primaries, and conventions. It will all come to a climax on the first Tuesday in November 2020. Yet because of the Electoral College, our national presidential election is in reality fifty separate elections, all held on the same day.

It is worth noting that the two most serious presidential impeachment efforts in modern times—against Nixon and Clinton—both occurred during their second terms, after each President had won a landslide re-election victory. As a result, neither Nixon nor Clinton had an opportunity to take their case to the voters. They had already been reelected before Congress launched impeachment proceedings, and by the time they were finished neither Nixon nor Clinton would face the voters again. Nixon had already resigned the presidency and Clinton was term-limited out. The impeachment procedures against them were entirely run by the Washington Establishments of their day, not the voters who had just reelected both presidents.

The "Impeachment of Donald Trump" will be different. It will play out in the months before the presidential election, and be fresh in voters' minds when they go to the polls in November. Trump will face the voters again. And, as with any previous election where the president is running for a second term, the vote becomes a referendum on the incumbent. They will decide to keep him in office for a second term.

But the 2020 election will also be an after-the-fact referendum on the Democrats and impeachment. Will Congressional Democrats and their presidential standard bearer be seen as justified in trying to remove Trump from office before the election? Or will they be seen as spoilers who wasted the country's time and abused their legislative power by harassing and hounding a duly elected president for their selfish political gains? If so, Trump will be reelected, probably by a landslide. As I write this in the fall of 2019, it is simply impossible to predict how this ends, for either side.

What we do know is that presidents, congressmen and senators are increasingly turning to scandal driven investigations—and even impeachment efforts—as political weapons wielded by one party against the other. A president investigates the campaign of the opposing party's candidate. A House or Senate chamber controlled by one party investigates a sitting or former president of the other party. This is all done under the guise of national security or oversight responsibility, but it is the politics of personal destruction and a perversion of government's legitimate responsibilities. Legislators weaponize their oversight function and investigate the political opposition. Presidents weaponize their law enforcement functions and investigate their opponents. The number, and level of intensity, of these investigations is accelerating with each Administration.

The Founding Fathers did not intend for elected officials of one party to conduct non-stop investigations and prosecutions of the other party whether in or out of office. That is why they made it complicated and difficult to remove a president from office. But that's where we are today. Republicans investigate the Clintons, both Bill and Hillary. Democrats get their revenge and investigate Trump, his family, his business, and his aides. They comb through decades of someone's life, looking for any crime, even something insignificant that gives them an excuse to launch formal investigations in hopes of finding a way to remove Trump from office.

Now that the Mueller investigation has found no evidence that crimes were committed, attention has begun to focus on why senior officials from the Obama Administration launched these investigations into a presidential candidate of the opposing party on such obviously flimsy evidence in the first place. The tables are turned, and the investigators themselves are now being investigated. Whatever the outcome of these efforts, the next president and his Administration will likely face even more pressure for investigations and calls for special counsels than Trump. More gridlock, more scandal, more non-stop hysteria. We seem doomed to repeat this cycle of retribution—an eye for an eye—until we are all blind.

We will never know the harm these investigations do to the ability of our officials to do their jobs, except with hindsight. But it is safe to assume that no presidential Transition going forward will be allowed a guarantee of confidentiality. Every conversation, every email, every phone call will be assumed to be publicly available. To be safe, every official may have to consider insisting that his personal lawyer be present in every meeting.

To ensure one's words are not taken out of context or deliberately twisted, perhaps it will be necessary to have verbatim notes or tape recordings of meetings, phone calls, and conversations, even when staff members are speaking among themselves. Everyone should consider keeping personal copies of these records, lest they be denied access to them in the future. Perhaps these steps sound extreme, but I certainly wish I had taken some of them when I worked on the Trump Transition.

While America seems focused on whether Donald Trump paid hush money to porn stars and claimed it as a campaign expense, or said something he shouldn't on a phone call with a foreign leader, China is moving rapidly into the 21st century, poised to dominate technologies of the future. They have already moved hundreds of millions of people out of poverty in a generation. In another decade or so they could overtake the United States as the world's largest economy. They are building the infrastructure to create Eurasian land and sea-based trade routes.

Two decades ago, it looked like the world was embracing the American example of democracy and free market capitalism, and modeling their own countries along the lines of ours. But after two failed wars, the Great Recession, and our current political turmoil and dysfunction, the rest of the world looks at us with dismay and disgust.

I had to bite my tongue during my confirmation hearing to be the U.S. Ambassador to Singapore. Several senators kept hammering away that I should tell the Singapore government to be more like ours. They took it for granted that everyone the world over wants what we have, wants to live like we do, and wants to be just like us. The irony is while we have been stuck in gridlock and mired in scandal for years, and the majority of Americans think we're headed in the wrong direction, opinion polls show Singaporeans are among the happiest people in the world, both with their government and lot in life. We think of ourselves as the highly evolved pinnacle of civilization. Others, not so much.

Those who doggedly pursue inquiries into every aspect of Trump, his presidency, his family, and his business in hopes of uncovering some crime or at a minimum preventing him from doing his job may believe they're advancing the nation's interests. They brag about having the moral courage to "stand up to the president" while they quietly fill their campaign coffers with cash, loudly announce their presidential campaigns, and sign lucrative book and television news contracts. I have never thought it took much strength of character to pat yourself on the back for having the guts to join a groupthink gabfest.

But it is not just their hypocrisy that offends me, or their self-righteous assumption that they know better than the voters who elected Trump. It is what they are doing to the long-term interests of our country. They are demonstrating to the world that America's government has become hopelessly dysfunctional. We are a once great nation that used to win wars, push out the frontiers of science and technology, inspire imagination, and send men to the moon. Today, we can't even get a majority of Congress to vote to secure our own borders in what leaders of both parties admit is a crisis.

The face we now show to the world is one of an American democracy so consumed by political infighting that we are no longer capable of solving even the routine problems of modern society. We have become a nation no longer able to summon the will to fix our education system, repair our crumbling infrastructure, or ensure prosperity for all our people. Our adversaries are moving out smartly to take advantage of our temporary insanity. They are telling the world that the American model of democracy and free market capitalism, once so admired and emulated, no longer works. They are offering the world a different governance model, and a different political and economic system. They tell the world, "Look at what we have achieved in just a few decades. Follow our example. Let us lead you. Authoritarian government and state capitalism are the wave of the future. Democracy is dead."

But perhaps the greatest tragedy of all is the damage this does to our national security. Our adversaries, enemies, competitors, and even some friends, sensing our political divisions, realize this is an ideal time to exploit our weaknesses. We are so preoccupied with headline grabbing investigations, special prosecutors, trials, and media frenzy that we are not paying attention to how others can take advantage of us.

For the first three years of his presidency, Trump has had to operate under the constant cloud of suspicion. Our adversaries pay close attention to the American media. What they see is hour after hour of pundits, politicians, and pontificators all predicting that Trump will be impeached…he won't finish his term…he certainly won't be reelected. Many of them have concluded that they can just wait him out, especially when his foreign policy has been aimed at pressuring them to give America better trade and security terms. Once Trump is gone, they can go back to enjoying the good old days when America did their bidding. You can hardly blame them. Why should our adversaries fear Trump's threats? Why should our competitors renegotiate trade deals? Why should our allies believe Trump can make good on his promises? Why should any of them give up the American trade and security subsidies they've enjoyed for years?

Who knows whether the North Koreans would have been more amenable to giving up their nuclear weapons in exchange for economic success? Who knows whether the Chinese would have been less aggressive in the South China Sea or more willing to agree to fairer terms of trade and investment? Who knows if NATO's allies would have been more likely to increase their defense budgets? We may never have the answers to those questions, but it is a cardinal rule of diplomacy that a leader who is weakened at home is even more weakened abroad.

I won't judge the intentions of others, but the consequence of the constant drumbeat of the Trump-hating media fanning the flames of scandal, outrage, and division is the fact that our competitors, adversaries, and even our enemies don't have to do a thing. They can sit back and watch America tear itself apart. Throughout history, many great nations haven't been destroyed by war or invasion; they have destroyed themselves from within, by civil war and internal dysfunction.

CHAPTER 21

The Administrative State

Trump's victory was so unlikely and so unexpected that to this day Hillary Clinton, the Democrats, and liberal media have simply refused to accept it. Most candidates have a hard time acknowledging defeat, but for the Clintons and their supporters it was all but impossible. Hillary Clinton began her campaign with an overwhelming lead, she had the entire Clinton machine behind her, she raised and spent hundreds of millions of dollars more than Trump, and had the press, entertainment industry, and the punditry on her side. She even had the support of the Never-Trump Republicans. Throughout the campaign, every poll had her ahead by double digits, even on the morning of the election. Her supporters just couldn't wrap their heads around the idea that Hillary Clinton had lost, especially to a supposed buffoon like Donald Trump.

The only way they could rationalize the 2016 election result was to insist that it must have been stolen, most likely with help from the Russians. First, the Russians nurtured a grudge against Bill Clinton for bringing former Soviet-dominated countries into NATO. Second, Putin himself loathed Hillary Clinton, dating from her failed attempt to reset United States-Russian relations, as well as to her support for Ukrainian nationalists during her years as Obama's Secretary of State. Finally, while

Hillary kept to her anti-Putin theme during the campaign, Trump said he wanted to improve United States-Russian relations.

Team Hillary convinced themselves that the only way Trump could have won was with the help of Vladimir Putin, who was desperate to keep her out of the White House. From there it wasn't much of a leap for the Trump-hating Washington Establishment to conclude that the Russians colluded directly with his campaign, and probably with him personally. Ipso facto, Trump was an illegitimate president, and any lengths were justified to stop him from governing. This explanation was more palatable to the Washington Establishment and liberal media than having to admit that their confident predictions that Hillary would win were wrong, and that the country had in effect just overwhelmingly rejected continued rule by the Washington elites.

Many career bureaucrats took Clinton's defeat especially hard, because they would have to hold their noses if they were to stay in their jobs and report to Trump and his people come Inauguration day. When Trump had the audacity to keep his campaign promises and set about reorienting foreign and economic policy, cutting government regulations and refusing to fill his Administration with Washington insiders, the entire governing class rose up against him. The fact that he was blunt, disrespectful, and occasionally vulgar enraged them even further.

When those of us on Trump's team arrived in the nation's capital a few days before the Inauguration, the Washington Establishment treated us as alien invaders. Outgoing Obama officials and some members of the permanent bureaucracy, including the intelligence and foreign policy community, found ready opportunities to whisper in the ears of journalists about the egregious failings of the Trump team. Stories of "chaos in the West Wing" led every front page. Trump was routinely compared to Hitler and Stalin. Some career government officials, especially in the intelligence and foreign policy communities, no longer saw it as their duty to be non-partisan civil servants. They believed Trump was so evil and the threats he posed to the nation so atrocious that traditional norms of behavior no longer applied. According to press reports, there was even an attempt by the senior-most bureaucrats at the Justice Department and FBI to remove him from office under the 25th Amendment, with what they hoped would be the concurrence of Vice President Pence and the majority of his Cabinet.

If they couldn't remove Trump from office, they could at least throw sand in the gears and make it difficult for his people to carry out his agenda, especially when it came to cutting their budgets and reducing their power. Bureaucrats who resisted Trump from within, and their allies in the media, saw themselves as modern day freedom fighters, battling behind enemy lines to sabotage the occupying forces. They began an unofficial hashtag #Resistance movement. They would try to delay, dilute, or undo the results of what they believed was a flawed election. People who voted for Trump had made a mistake; they had been duped by a reality TV star and conman. They saw themselves as the guardians of the republic and it was up to them to make things right by doing whatever they could to foil Trump and his misguided policies.

The permanent bureaucracy knew how to do it, and they had all the weapons at their disposal—anonymous leaks, "lost" emails, text messages and paperwork, bureaucratic delays, slow-walking implementation, tangles and layers of rules and regulations, and procedures and protocols. The incoming Trump Administration had no idea they were walking into a silent buzzsaw. Fired FBI director James Comey summed up an attitude shared by the Trump-haters when he talked about sending FBI agents to the West Wing to interview National Security Advisor Mike Flynn on his third day in office. "I probably wouldn't have… gotten away with [it] in a more … organized Administration,"[1] implying that he knew it was wrong but did it anyway because he didn't think he'd get caught.

Trump had never before run for office. He assumed that if you win an election, you're automatically and indisputably in charge of the government, and the vast Executive Branch does your bidding. After all, that's how it is in business. You buy a company and after the contract is signed, it's yours to run. You can bring in your own team and fire people who are underperforming or working against you. You have a bottom line of profit and loss, of input and output, and constant employee evaluations. If you conclude they're redundant, too expensive or not up to the job, they're gone. In government, it's just the opposite. If a president and his officials don't like someone in the permanent bureaucracy, too bad. They are civil servants and can't be fired. They belong to their own powerful

---

[1] Ruhle, Stephanie. "Why James Comey says President Trump should not be impeached." *MSNBC.* December 10, 2018. https://www.msnbc.com/stephanie-ruhle/watch/why-james-comey-says-president-trump-should-not-be-impeached-1393767491877.

labor unions, have connections all across the Washington Establishment, and have what amounts to lifetime job tenure and automatic pay raises.

On the other hand, the president and his team are only in office temporarily. If government employees don't like a president or his appointees, they can sit back and wait them out. Presidents come and presidents go, but the permanent bureaucracy stays on forever.

Some of my fellow conservatives believe there is a Deep State, a conspiracy within government that continues to rule, regardless of who's elected to office. Whether or not there is a Deep State plot against Trump, there is a permanent Administrative State which leans heavily Democrat in vote and view. It is an enormous bureaucracy that has institutional interests of its own and, like all bureaucracies, seeks constantly to expand not just in size, but in power, scope, and privilege.

Not surprisingly, the majority of career bureaucrats subscribe to the liberal Democrat's tax and spend/big government agenda. They share the belief that our modern economy and society have become so complicated that a large, permanent Administrative State is necessary to manage them. Therefore, the American bureaucracy grows ever larger, exercising ever more control over more aspects of our lives. Since there are no bottom-line budget restraints—our federal government runs an annual deficit of about a trillion dollars and can always borrow more—the unaccountable Administrative State grows ever more expensive and powerful.

Over the years attempts to reform the Administrative State, cut its budget, shrink it, even efforts to slow its rate of growth have been opposed and met with foot-dragging, resistance, and occasionally even outright obstruction. Not even the immensely popular Ronald Reagan, who pushed through tax cuts and regulatory reform *and* was the most successful and popular president of the era, was able to cut the size of government. The most he could do was reduce the rate at which government grew.

Trump had run on a vigorous anti-Washington platform, vowing to cut both the size of government and its regulations. He set out immediately to reform and reduce the regulatory bloat and got tax cuts passed. One way to cut government, short of a major overhaul of the bureaucracy, was to leave many senior government posts empty. Not surprisingly, it made him about as popular in Washington as a skunk at a family picnic. It should come as no surprise that Trump only garnered 4 percent of Washington, D.C. voters.

That said, no one, even I, anticipated the degree of resistance that the Washington Establishment elite and permanent bureaucracy would mount against his presidency. President Trump and his most senior advisors were unfamiliar with how Washington worked. They were unaware of the myriad ways Washington has to thwart a president and his people. Early in my White House tenure, I arranged for Flynn to meet with Henry Kissinger. Most of the meeting was spent discussing foreign policy, especially China. As we finished the meeting, Kissinger wanted to give Flynn a piece of advice about how difficult it would be to run the National Security Council interagency system. In typical Kissingerian style, he used humor to make the point: "In my experience, when a president asks the Pentagon to do something, there is a 75 percent chance they will carry out to the best of their ability what they believe are his orders. If the president asks the State Department to do something, there is an 80 percent chance they will take it into consideration when carrying out what they believe to be their responsibilities!"

In other words, winning the election isn't the last step before assuming the mantle of governing, it's only the first step. The next step, which is often even harder than winning an election, is bending a resistant, behemoth bureaucracy to carry out the new president's agenda.

CHAPTER 22

Weaponized Media

Washington is called a company town, where government is the "company," and everything and everyone revolves around it and the political infighting that never ceases.

I've always thought Washington is more like a high school microcosm, only on a larger scale and with much bigger stakes. In high school everything that could potentially happen while you're there is of all-consuming importance, crowding out what is going on outside of school and the rest of the world. Your entire universe is the students and teachers inside the bubble of the school and the sports fields.

Yet to outsiders it often seems like a lot of fuss about nothing. And, as is often the case with adolescents, everything is blown way out of proportion. There is lots of drama and anxiety. There are cliques and constantly shifting friendships, rumors, and romance. There are the rich kids, the poor kids, the jocks, the nerds, and, of course, the phonies. The Friday night football game—who gets to play and who you party with afterward—takes on life-altering importance. Who gets to sit at the cool kids' table at lunch is watched and gossiped about by everyone in the school cafeteria. Who is hooking up with whom is a breaking news scandal, only to be replaced a day or two later by another fresh breaking news scandal. And in today's world, everything that happens to the students is chronicled 24/7 by social media. But social media is more than just a bulletin board for the latest news. It has become the weapon students use against one another.

The same thing has happened to the news business—it has been weaponized and sent into battle. For decades, we adhered to the same way of doings things, with media mandarins in Washington and New York who deciphered politics, politicians, and policies for the nation. The evening news, the daily paper, the morning and afternoon drive-time radio shows all featured the professionals who studied the stories of the day, and explained them to the rest of us in terms we could understand. They were the gatekeepers, the interpreters, and the middlemen between the people and their leaders.

This gave our media stars enormous power. We trusted them, even more than we trusted the politicians they reported on. But back then they didn't abuse that power. For decades, they brought us non-partisan, unbiased reporting. You could watch the greatest news anchors of the day—David Brinkley, Walter Cronkite, and Harry Reasoner—deliver the nightly news for years and still have no idea who they had voted for. Opinion pieces and editorials were properly confined to the editorial pages. There was a clear division between the opinion and straight news sections of papers. But over the years, the line between news and opinion became blurred. News stories took on a partisan twinge reflecting the conservative or liberal biases of their news organizations. Editorials and opinion pieces rarely strayed from the party line. The writers who wrote contrarian stories were phased out. Journalists came to see themselves as people who weighed in on and influenced the news rather than just reported it.

Over 90 percent of the media consider themselves liberals, Democrats, progressives, or socialists. Even when they do keep Republicans in their lineup, they're most likely Never-Trumpers. As former CNN contributor Stephen Moore pointed out, the only Republican commentators on his former network are the ones who hate Trump.[2]

Most in the liberal media are so similar in outlook and background that a sort of groupthink prevails. All their friends are liberal Democrats, all the people they work with, all the people they meet through their kids,

---

[2] Heath, Wade. "Exclusive: Former CNN Pro-Trump Contributors Allege Network 'Openly Despises Conservatives.'" *Mediaite*. May 24, 2019. https://www.mediaite.com/tv/cnn-claims-balanced-coverage-but-former-pro-trump-contributors-disagree-were-squeezed-out-involuntarily/.

think identically about politics. They relate to the people who live on the East and West Coasts, who attended the same elite universities, live in wealthy sections of large cities, read the same books, like the same movies, do the same sports, and share a similar outlook on life. It's not that they intentionally discriminate against people who don't think the way they do; they just see them as being wrong, or stupid, or uninformed, or bigoted, or…well, take your pick. Because they rarely encounter people who do see things differently, they attribute all sorts of negative characteristics to them. It's easy to belittle and stigmatize people you don't know. The small enclaves of conservatives who live in the coastal cities, especially Washington, New York, Boston, Los Angeles, and San Francisco, tend to hunker down, stick together, and stay out of sight.

The pro-Trump conservatives tend to follow FOX News, Fox Business News, the *Wall Street Journal*, the *New York Post*, some online publications, and most of talk radio. They, too, associate mostly with likeminded folks. They're often the people who live in what liberals derisively call the "flyover states" in the heartland, the South, and the Midwest.

When I moved from New York to Washington in January 2017, just before the Trump Inauguration, I needed to find a new dry cleaner, grocery store, dentist, doctor, and beauty salon—all the mundane things people do when they move. I had been going to the same Long Island hairdresser for thirty years, so I asked around if any of my friends or friends' friends knew a good beauty salon in Washington. One friend called me back and passed along a point of clarification from her Washington connection: Was I looking for a Republican or Democrat beauty salon? I was stunned and asked my friend to check back for an explanation why that mattered. She said, "Well, think of how few secrets there are at beauty salons." Apparently, in Washington, even hairdressers are divided along partisan lines!

I guess I shouldn't have been surprised. I know from personal experience how exhausting it is to have every conversation turn into a cross-examination of your personal beliefs, and defense of your integrity and intelligence. The result is we find it easier to divide up and live in our own parallel, self-reinforcing universes. Both sides whip up their followers—the liberal media chant "Trump is a Nazi and racist who must be stopped at all costs;" the conservative media chant Trump is "Making America Great Again." Their TV screens scream: Stay tuned for the latest "breaking news!" Their newspapers have bold-faced headlines reporting on the latest end-of-the-world scandal. Cable news and online publications update their stories every few hours with "the latest," so you tune in or click on, only to find a repetition of the story *du jour*, perhaps with an additional quote from a new anonymous source. We've become addicted to rumor, scandal, and gossip, and the news media is our daily supplier.

Three years into Trump's presidency, his opponents have become even more apoplectic. They point to his divisiveness, coarse rhetoric, chaotic management style, and constant tweetstorms as evidence that they were right about him all along. They're convinced Trump is a uniquely terrifying phenomenon, and that he's taking a wrecking ball to the Constitution, toying with enemies and allies alike and literally destroying the country. They've turned up the volume on criticisms, committed to thwarting his policy initiatives and getting him impeached and removed from office. Even after the Mueller investigation found there was no collusion between Trump (or any other Americans) and the Russians, many still fantasize about the FBI knocking on Trump's door, slapping him in handcuffs, and escorting him from the White House to the jailhouse.

Not surprisingly, Trump has responded by counterpunching with rhetoric of his own—the liberal mainstream media are the "enemy of the people." "Fake news" charges appear almost daily on his Twitter account, and he regularly rails against the "failing" *New York Times*, the "ratings losing" CNN, and offers blunt criticisms of just about every reporter and executive at MSNBC, CNN, the *New York Times*, and the *Washington Post*.

Despite this continuing 24/7 barrage of negative press coverage from an antagonistic and highly partisan media, Trump's supporters are still with him. By every conceivable measure the economy is achieving historic highs, with more people of every ethnic group and class having jobs than ever before. Tax rates are down, business investment is strong, tax revenues are going up, and the stock market is soaring. Trump has renegotiated major trade agreements in America's favor, gotten our security allies to cough up more for our common defense, and even brought North Korea to the bargaining table. His approval ratings remain steady, and if the presidential election were held tomorrow, there is a good chance he would win again. And he would do so without the support of the coastal elites, especially the voters in Washington D.C., California, and New York.

The news business has changed in the decades since Walter Cronkite, slowly becoming more partisan. But it has changed at warp speech in the last few years. The weaponization of media has been led by several things: the transformative power of social media; the vast expansion of reliance on "anonymous sources;" and President Trump himself. They feed on each other, amplify each other, and provide people inside the Beltway with a constant stream of gossip about palace intrigue swirling around for front page reporters and cable news's talking heads to thrive on.

The early years of the Trump Administration were filled with many ambitious, backbiting, and self-promoting people. That's more or less par for the course in the upper reaches of politics. Some of them saw their job as letting Trump be Trump. Others saw their job as saving the country by preventing Trump from being Trump. It makes for a volatile mix, but it's further exacerbated by Trump's own governing style. He tends to play staff members off each other so that no one has any real sense of job security. Nobody fully trusts anybody, and with good reason. Trump's White House is a constantly swirling whirlwind. There is always another crisis, another scandal quoting "anonymous sources," another firing, hiring, or rumored fall from grace. There is never such a thing as a normal day, so you never have a chance to catch your breath. It's emotionally exhausting, because everyone is on 24/7 high alert. There is no way to predict who the next "breaking news" story will be about. You? Your boss? Your colleague? Every morning you walk into the White House wondering if it might be your turn, perhaps even your last day. Things have settled down a bit since I left the White House, but I gather from my former colleagues that much of the anxiety remains. There is a cost to Trump's unique management style.

In the Age of Trump, where nearly every lead news story is Trump-related, there is pressure on reporters to get the "inside scoop" about anything that's happening or might be happening in the West Wing, even if it's just gossip from "anonymous sources" that's been dressed up as breaking news. In the first year just about everything leaked in one fashion or another. It didn't matter whether it was a top-secret White House Situation Room meeting, or people joking around over lunch in the White House Mess. It could be a small meeting in the Oval Office, or a large meeting in the Executive Office Building Auditorium. The leaks were not only betrayals of trust and security, they were usually an incomplete or highly slanted version of events, or sometimes just downright wrong. The reason Trump's calls of "fake news" find resonance is because some news is fake. Even so, these stories are effective in reinforcing the media's narrative of chaos and confusion in Trump land. But the consequences don't stop there. They also have the potential to do damage far more significant than just the trashing of their political opponents.

Their actions play right into the hands of our foreign adversaries who are always looking for ways to exploit our domestic disagreements and set us against each other. Other nations, especially authoritarian dictatorships, realize that American democracy needs compromise and trust to succeed. The Kremlin has sought to exploit our political differences for over sixty years, going back to the Cuban Missile Crisis and Vietnam War. They've always sought to fan the flames of division with their disinformation and information warfare campaigns. Now, with the United States gripped by hyper-partisanship, which is amplified by social media, our adversaries can fan those flames into a wildfire. Trump's opponents are so fixated on destroying him at home, they rarely focus on the geostrategic consequences of American political dysfunction.

In my experience, the press portrayal of a meeting or conversation usually has some element of truth to it, that is then elaborated on and spun in a direction often contrary to what had actually occurred. A casual aside, when taken out of context, and selectively edited, and recounted by one or more "anonymous sources" sounded nothing like it did when I was in the room and said it or heard it firsthand. Deceptively characterized, even the most innocuous comments can be made to appear sinister and conspiratorial.

After Mike Flynn was fired, I gave Trump my elevator pitch to keep me on. He waved his hand dismissively. "Yeah. It's already been decided. You're going to stay. Why?"

Relieved, I answered, "Well, the *New York Times* is reporting that I'm being fired along with Flynn."

Trump exploded. "Who said that? Where's that coming from?" he asked me. I answered, "They're quoting anonymous sources."

There is nothing that sets off a Trump tirade more than quotes about him from anonymous sources.

He shouted out the door, "Hope? Hope! Get Spicer in here. Now!" Trump fumed. "Anonymous sources! Who are these 'anonymous sources'?

They're just making it up, and claiming they've got fifteen anonymous sources. There aren't fifteen people in the entire White House who know about this stuff. It's more fake news from the failing *New York Times*."

As he was talking, the rest of the staff filed into the Oval Office for the morning intelligence briefing, and took their usual seats around Trump's desk, but realized something was up…again. Spicer appeared at the door, out of breath, and clutching his notebook. Priebus was right behind him.

Before they could say anything, Trump said, "Get it out there. Tell them she's staying. Their so-called anonymous sources are fake news! It's more fake news!" I had to wonder, though, whether the "anonymous sources" were the people I worked alongside every day.

As Deputy National Security Advisor, it wasn't my job to speak directly to the media. In fact, it was frowned on. That's why there is a White House Press Office and communications directors on all the major staffs and departments. They're the ones who are supposed to work with the media on a daily basis, push back on stories that are wrong, and give context and background to decisions. The rest of us are supposed to keep our heads down and carry on with the day to day work of government. But that's not how it always happened.

In the early days of the Administration, after Flynn's firing, I received a flurry of emails, texts, and phone messages from reporters, never on my work phone or government email, always on my personal cell phone—the one I use to talk to my husband and kids—and my personal email. They would all say more or less the same thing.

"Hi, it's *XXX* from *YYY*. I'm working on a story in which you figure prominently. Give me a call as soon as you get this. I want to give you a chance to comment."

Or, "I'm working on a story about your colleague, *XXX*, and wanted to run a few things by you. I'm working on deadline so call me back right away."

They all, without exception, offered to talk to me on whatever terms I wanted—off the record, on background, anonymously. According to press accounts, some reporters even offered to throw their readers off the scent by saying the official had declined to comment. In return, that same official would give them gossip and juicy quotes the reporter attributed to "anonymous sources."

Maybe it's a legitimate media query, an honorable reporter giving you an opportunity to refute the charges against you; but it's still a thinly veiled blackmail threat. "We'll trade trash on you for trash you give us on some-one else." Or it's a plea bargain: "You give us good quotes on something and we'll drop the most egregious of the accusations against you." Or it's the beginning of a mutually advantageous relationship. "We'll let you off the hook this time, but you have to keep feeding us inside information (in other words, gossip) about your colleagues. In return we'll make sure you get good press." It's no surprise that oftentimes officials who got treated well by the press are most likely the ones doing the anonymous leaking and the spinning.

At this point you've got several options.

You can pass the query along to the press office, which is what you are supposed to do. But it's not what the reporter wants, since he approached you outside of channels. If you refuse to play ball, the reporter can punish you for it, by printing gossip and dirt about you, as I found out to my detriment. I wouldn't leak and paid for it with consistently negative press.

You can call the reporter back and find out what he knows. He could say he's come across some allegations against you, or conversations that cast you in a negative light. What is your response? Now you're faced with a moral dilemma and are tempted to engage in something right out of Kevin Spacey and *House of Cards*—you trade information. You go "off the record" and give him something about somebody else in the White House, which may be true or not, and he agrees to rewrite his story to cast you in a better light, or to take you out of the story entirely. If you've dodged the bullet this time, it means that you're now one of his "sources." And you can be sure that he'll keep coming back for more.

If you don't give the reporter something he can use, or don't call the reporter back, or if the email goes unnoticed in your spam folder, you are cannon fodder. You wake up in the middle of the night, and frantically check your inbox, or your Google alert. Is the story online yet? You're dying a thousand deaths while you wait…a day…two days…maybe for-ever. This could mean the end of your entire career. No matter what, you never rest easy again.

In today's world of anonymous sources, a reporter isn't expected to reveal his sources to his editors, or even to stand by their veracity. He can give equal weight to someone who was there in the room when the decision was made, or someone who has information secondhand or thirdhand, or someone who just made it all up. It's what Trump calls fake news, and it's true! There are unscrupulous reporters who claim a dozen anonymous sources for a story about a meeting where there were only three other people in the room. There is no penalty for getting something wrong—either for the reporter or the news organization. Just the opposite. There is a significant personal benefit to getting a story out first, or even better, having an exclusive, even if it's just speculation.

Most of the time these sorts of stories are about personalities and palace intrigue rather than policy. They are the stories that get top billing and get the reporter on a cable news panel that night or the next morning. Gossip always wins. If you are not part of this insider's game, or hold opinions that differ from the groupthink of the mainstream media, or follow the rules and don't leak, you risk becoming everyone's piñata.

Next time you hear a story about chaos in the West Wing, count how many quotes are from "anonymous sources." Eliminate those since they're coming from people who have a vested interest and aren't willing to attach their names to it. They're often nothing more than unsubstantiated rumors. See what you're left with. It's often just implications and innuendo, but it's what passes for news these days.

I'm not saying all reporters are like this, or even the majority. The veterans, the real professionals, work through channels and query public affairs officers with legitimate questions. They double- and triple-check their sources. They verify facts and quotes. They adhere to the rules "off the record" or "on background," even when it's to their disadvantage. Those with integrity are unwilling to divulge their sources, even if it means running afoul of the law and risking jail time. They write stories you may not like, but they're more or less fair, and give all points of view a hearing. They focus on policy and substance, facts, and figures. They don't offer their opinions on the news pages, nor let their biases show through. But they're increasingly seen as the dinosaurs: large, slow, consuming extensive resources, and slowly dying off.

There are a growing number of reporters who deal in gossip, insinuations, and character assassination. And they're the ones who tend to make the headlines, who get the talk show gigs. They're the ones who light the bonfire and then offer to sell tickets to watch it. In the 24/7 era of constant news coverage, they're often the ones who set the pace.

Gresham's law says that "bad money drives out good" and so it is with today's media. For the person consuming the news—increasingly online—the trusted reporter writing from behind the paywall of a prestigious international journal is being displaced by some internet blogger who may, or may not, follow the same rules, or any rules at all. One result is that today, even some of the most hallowed news outlets have now tossed journalistic standards aside to provide clickbait headlines. If a story isn't remotely accurate, it's really no problem, it can always be edited online later. Now everything is instant access, via social media or internet publications. News is accessible online throughout the day, and the latest breaking news stories are constantly changing. The goal is to be first and sensational, not necessarily accurate. There is a reason Trump's charge of "fake news" resonates so well with so many Americans. It's true and in some ways the media is running a protection racket.

I experienced this myself firsthand. In early December 2017, my husband and I were on a red-eye flight from New York to Scotland. By the time we landed in Glasgow, the *New York Times* had published a bombshell story claiming that not only had I admitted the Russians had interfered in the election, but that I had confessed that Trump had conspired with them to do so. The *New York Times* quoted from two emails I had written during the Transition as confirmation of the crimes. It was the *New York Times* scoop of the year—the supposed smoking gun that proved that Trump and the Russians had colluded to steal the election.

The problem was that their breaking news bombshell was fake news. Yes, I had written two emails, but the quotes from them were taken out of context, selectively edited, with large sections deleted, and conveyed the opposite meaning to what I wrote. It was no different from taking the sentence, "I do not think it's going to rain today" and deleting the words "do not."

In fact, when read in its entirety, my two emails to the senior staff discussed the odd timing of the Obama Administration's decision to impose sanctions on Russia just three weeks before Trump's Inauguration. I speculated on Obama's possible political motives, including my suspicion that they might be trying to sabotage any chance of improving relations with Russia once Trump was in office. I urged that we wait to make any comment until after we had all the facts from the intelligence community report. As for the Russians, I pointed out that they'd been meddling in American politics for decades, as we had in theirs.

Did the *New York Times* deliberately edit, twist, and spin my words just to get a sensational story? Or were they mere tools in the hands of Trump-haters who fed the fake news? In any event, the *New York Times* later had to edit the online version of their story four times, each time removing more of the juicy, breaking news scoops. But the damage was done. By the time our red-eye flight touched down in Scotland, six hours later, I was all but accused of treason.

There were no consequences to the *New York Times*. On the contrary, their sensational story probably got them a big spike in readership that day. The anti-Trump liberal media ignored the *New York Times*' rewrites and went with the far more titillating original story, repeating it endlessly, and for days.[3, 4]

Trump's Twitter feed has a daily dose of accusations about the "failing *New York Times* and *Washington Post*," "Fake News CNN" and criticisms of reporters, news anchors, and columnists. Some of his supporters cheer him on; others have heard them so often they're immune to them. His critics dismiss these as his childish temper tantrums, or evidence that he's unfit to be president. I cringe when I read them, as do many of my conservative friends. But he's got a point.

Once respected national media figures routinely call President Trump a Nazi, a liar, mentally unhinged, corrupt, a traitor, a Russian agent, a bully, a tyrant, and on and on. They pummeled him for two years with made up stories, gossip and speculation while Special Prosecutor Mueller and his team silently conducted a thorough and lengthy investigation into every aspect of the Trump campaign, and Russian interference in the 2016 election. When they found no evidence of collusion, the press, encouraged by the Democrats in Congress, moved on to look elsewhere in the hopes of finding some crime that could be linked to Trump—his businesses, his family, his taxes, and his non-traditional foreign policy. The media are now like a dog with a bone—they will never stop harassing Trump. Over 90 percent of all news coverage of Trump was and remains

---

[3] Adams, Becket. "That New York Times article on Trump transition official saying Russia had 'thrown the US election' isn't what you think it is." *Washington Examiner*. December 4, 2017. https://www.washingtonexaminer.com/that-new-york-times-article-on-trump-transition-official-saying-russia-had-thrown-the-us-election-isnt-what-you-think-it-is.

[4] Adams, Becket. "New York Times forced to heavily amend another supposed K.T. McFarland 'scoop.'" *Washington Examiner*. December 5, 2017. https://www.washingtonexaminer.com/new-york-times-forced-to-heavily-amend-another-supposed-kt-mcfarland-scoop.

viciously negative, even after (or in spite of) finding no connection between Trump and the Russians.

Yet the media have a little secret. News organizations—on both sides of the political divide—never want to discuss just how good Donald Trump has been for business. With the exception of Fox News, cable news networks had been in a ratings slump for years. Then along came Donald Trump. He has almost singlehandedly resurrected them. He has made media rock stars out of print reporters from the *New York Times* and *Washington Post*, as they add punditry to their journalist credentials. He has boosted hitherto unknown online publications to become successful must-reads. Trump has been crucially important for a business which is undergoing massive transformation, seemingly overnight. Cable networks began nearly four decades ago. They opened up opportunities not only for more channels, but for more news shows. Over two decades ago the internet opened up seemingly endless opportunities for online news outlets—from online publications, online podcasts, online radio, and even online television channels.

The way we access news, the way it's packaged, the platforms in which it is presented, and the ways in which it's paid for are changing rapidly and fundamentally. A generation ago the barrier to entry to create a newspaper, or magazine, or cable news channel was so high that only large, diversified, cash-rich corporations with a large infrastructure could contemplate it. It wasn't so long ago that our news came to us once a day, along with commercials and print ads by large companies, via a handful of distinguished journalists, writers, editors, and reporters working for media giants. But those days are gone.

Today, it's not that there is suddenly a lower barrier to entry—there is no barrier to entry—all you need is a computer and a blog. There is no large organization to support, no journalists to manage, no generous compensation, health care, or retirement packages. You don't even need a building. All you need is a website and a computer. Scratch that. You don't even need a computer—a smart phone will do. *The Drudge Report*, read by over 100 million people a day, started out 20 years ago on Matt Drudge's home computer. Today it is the one of the most powerful media publications in the world, and still only has a handful of employees. It's online and it's free.

Meanwhile, several older news organizations, with their high salaries and legacy costs, plus their dwindling advertising income, are struggling to make ends meet. Once powerful news magazines have gone bankrupt or sold for a fraction of what they were once worth. Others have been forced to cut staff, eliminate their print editions, and gone completely digital. They've erected paywalls, which means you can read them if you pay several hundred dollars a year for a digital subscription. Publications which have managed to survive have done so because they no longer appeal to a broad-based market or offer unbiased coverage. They've become full-time Trump bashers.

Media is a profit-driven business, which prospers under crisis and controversy. In this respect, Donald Trump has been a gift from the gods. As CNN President Jeff Zucker said, they've seen an unprecedented "bump" in television and digital audiences. "CNN's been around for thirty-seven years. This is the most-watched year in the history of CNN on television."[5]

Shortly after Trump secured the Republican nomination, I was in Washington with a group of well-known journalists. Trump had just had his first sit-down interview with a major newspaper. One of the reporters who interviewed Trump regaled everyone with stories of what an idiot he was. He said Trump kept bouncing from one thought to another, saying the first thing that came into his head. Another writer shook his head in wonderment and said, "How does he dare to think he can run for president?" A year or so later, both reporters were only too happy to get interviews with President Trump. They might despise him, ridicule him, look down their noses at him, but they know Donald Trump is terrific for their business. He is making them famous—and rich.

In the Age of Trump, much of the media, like much of the Washington Establishment, is no longer neutral nor non-partisan. They have lined up against Trump, both during the campaign, the Transition period, and now that he is in office. They have abused the trust of the American people, and are no longer honest brokers. But they have also abused their position in a second way. They have been so driven by their bloodlust and

---

[5] Anapol, Avery. "CNN chief: Trump has made American journalism great again." The Hill. November 30, 2017. https://thehill.com/homenews/media/362545-cnns-zucker-trump-has-made-american-journalism-great-again.

hatred for all things Trump that they uncritically fed the flames of the Russia probe, which now turns out to have been a hoax from the start.

For more than two years, they held the nation hostage to their anti-Trump Russia obsession. Special Prosecutor Mueller was disciplined and for the most part silent about his probe until his team was ready to file criminal complaints or issue their final report. No leaking, no speeches, no whispering in the ear of favorited reporters. So the media, Democrats, and Never-Trumpers filled the void with their own fantasies dressed up as facts: "Trump will be charged with conspiracy, collusion, obstruction of justice—any day now. Anonymous sources claim investigators have evidence that Trump worked with the Russians to steal the election. Trump is owned by Putin's oligarchs. Trump obstructed justice by firing Comey. Trump is going to fire Mueller and shut down his investigation." These and other seemingly authoritative speculations from the liberal anti-Trump media's talking heads were a constant feature of the 24/7 news cycle. Now it turns out all to have been "fake news" from the very outset. As former Attorney General Mukasey told CNN's Chris Cuomo: For three years, Washington journalists have been on TV news shows "inhaling their own exhaust fumes and getting high on them."

The media faces two real dangers as a result of the approach they've taken in the Age of Trump. First, they should be careful of what they wish for. Ever wonder why some journalists and pundits are so eagerly calling to impeach Donald Trump? Nothing will drive up ratings more than impeachment hearings. The Watergate hearings in the summer of 1973 were watched by 80 percent of the American people, and that was in the day before there was a TV in every room or live-streaming device in everyone's hand. Trump's impeachment hearings would be the ultimate reality TV show, with hundreds of millions of people watching, on their televisions, computers, laptops, smartphones or watches. What could be better for the media than getting to indulge in nonstop, breathless coverage of Trump's supposed crimes and criticisms, and getting paid handsomely to do so?

What they've not figured out is what will happen in the post-Trump era. Will readers and viewers still pay attention and pay for the privilege when he is gone from the scene? Or will their ratings disappear in a giant poof. Might they be clamoring to kill the goose that has been laying golden eggs for them?

Second, I'm reminded of the story about the weather forecaster. In one town all the weather forecasters on TV, radio, and in the paper predicted dark and stormy weather. So the people took their umbrellas to work, dressed their kids in raincoats for school, and cancelled plans for the family picnic. But the weather forecasters were wrong. The day turned out to be beautiful and sunny, without a cloud in the sky. The same thing happened the next day—the weather forecasters all predicted ferocious wind and rain. Once again it was bright and sunny. Same thing happened on the third day, and so forth. At a certain point, one person got fed up, stuck his head out the window and figured out the weather for himself. And soon everyone else did the same. The result? A lot of unemployed weather forecasters.

The media has led us on a merry chase for over three years with their dire predictions about the coming demise of Donald Trump. They've warned his economic plans of tax cuts, deregulation, and readjusted tariffs would lead to a stock market collapse and to massive unemployment. In fact, the opposite has happened. Trumponomics has launched one of the greatest periods of economic expansion in our history, with record low unemployment across every socio-economic group in society. They've warned us he was a Putin puppet, and would capitulate to Russia on every matter. In fact, Trump has been much tougher on Russia than our last two presidents. He has rebuilt the military, increased serious sanctions on Russia, and given lethal weapons to the people of Ukraine. The media made promise after promise that the Mueller report would prove that Trump had committed any number of traitorous crimes and was sure to be hounded out of office. In fact, the Mueller report came up empty, and Trump's popularity has risen accordingly. Like the weather forecaster whose predictions never come true, at a certain point, people will just tune them out.

CHAPTER 23

America's Political Civil War

On the day Donald Trump was inaugurated president, I walked into my new office in the West Wing of the White House. It was January 20, 2017, and I retraced the same steps I had first taken forty-seven years before, as a college freshman, when I arrived for my part-time job as a night shift secretary for Dr. Henry Kissinger, President Nixon's National Security Advisor. When I started at the White House in 1970, it was before the women's movement, before equal access to higher education, scholarships, position or pay, and a lifetime before the #MeToo movement. In those days the highest position in the West Wing most women could aspire to, no matter how qualified or experienced, was as a secretary or administrative assistant to a man. Now, nearly half a century later, my appointment as Deputy National Security Advisor was considered routine.

When I sat down at my new desk, just a few feet from my original desk, I was fulfilling the dream of a lifetime. It the only Washington job I had ever wanted, the opportunity to be one of the Senior Foreign Policy Makers in a government of the most powerful nation the world had ever known. Moreover, I would hold that position during a period of enormous challenges and possibilities, with a mandate from the American people to make sweeping changes. I couldn't wait to begin.

When I walked out of the White House for the last time, just four months into the new Trump Administration, I couldn't wait to leave. Despite being one of the most capable and experienced people on Trump's staff, I became collateral damage in the Michael Flynn affair, and was asked to resign with the arrival of a new National Security Advisor.

I soon found myself caught up in the Mueller investigation, even though I hadn't been part of the campaign, nor had any contact with any Russians during the Transition. As I was pulled deeper into the Russia probe, it seemed to me like I was being given a choice, a devil's choice: If I yielded to prosecutorial pressure and falsely accused others of wrongdoing, perhaps implicating even Trump himself, or ultimately confessed guilt to having committed a minor crime that I didn't believe I had I committed, I might be able to sidestep the worst of a political witch hunt.

By taking that path, I might be able to avoid escalating and ruinous legal expenses and be free to get on with the rest of my life. But doing so would mean betraying everything I believed in, and possibly doing great damage to the Trump presidency, to the populist cause, and to the nation. In the end, I decided to accept the battering of investigators and prosecutors rather than sacrifice my integrity and lose my soul. But I was under no illusions of just how traumatic and excruciatingly painful it could all become, not just for me but for my family.

For a year after my resignation, I was hounded by reporters peddling fake news stories leaked by people pursuing their own agendas. Legislators and Congressional committee staffers harassed me for months, hunting for anything they could claim was a crime, no matter how insignificant or obscure. Under the guise of "protecting democracy," investigators had become inquisitors and prosecutors had become persecutors. Their focus on me eased up by mid-2018, when they seemed to move past the Flynn part of the investigation and into areas which seemed far more fertile territory for the anti-Trump consortium.

* * *

I concluded that it was time for me to drop out, to disappear from view, and try to pick up the pieces of my shattered dreams. My husband and I left the country for an extended visit to Scotland—to the rural Western Highlands and Hebridean islands. Our close friends, the extended MacLeod clan, took us in. We spent weeks living in remote Scottish villages, without television, internet, emails, or cell phones. We had to shoo sheep, shaggy Highland cattle, and long-horned wild goats out of the way to drive on unpaved single-track roads to get to the local market. We went for days having little or no contact with anything other than four-legged farm animals. It turned out to have been the perfect way to leave the day to day gossip and machinations of Washington behind, and to try to get some perspective on my recent experiences.

I also wanted to check my homework, so to speak. Were my reasons for supporting Trump still valid? I re-examined whether it had been a mistake to reject the beliefs of a lifetime, and to break ranks with the Washington Establishment and the people I'd known and respected for decades. They believe that a global community managed through international organizations is better for preserving peace than independent nation states. They think the best way to run the country is for a large professional bureaucracy to oversee the complexities of modern society.

I had once believed in those things too. But after nearly two decades of foreign policy failures, I had come to the realization that those ideas weren't working, and that the people promoting them were too invested to switch gears. Instead, they doubled down on failure. "We just need to stay in Afghanistan a little longer, with some additional troops and resources. Victory is right around the corner." "Everything here at home will improve, if we only add more stimulus packages and give the economy a little more time to recover." The economic and foreign policies they continued to champion may have worked in the past, but they no longer protected America's interests at home or abroad. The Washington Establishment had grown just as stale as its ideas and agendas.

Their risky tax and banking agendas contributed to the financial crisis of 2008. Their response was government bailouts for everybody, except the American working and middle classes. For the people in Washington and on Wall Street, things went back to business as usual. Our political leaders didn't take the financial community or other special interest groups to task because their support was essential for their re-election campaigns. They didn't promote pro-growth policies for some of the same reasons, instead declaring that low growth rates and high unemployment were the new normal. Their solution was to increase taxes, grow the bureaucracy, increase regulation, and launch expensive new stimulus plans. The result wasn't the economic growth they promised, but a prolonged Great

Recession that was uniquely hard on farmers, domestic manufacturers, and blue-collar workers.

As a result, the American Dream fell out of reach for millions of Americans. The people in Washington who were making the rules—and their families and friends—were doing just fine, some even better. It is no surprise that the five richest counties in the country are in the suburbs surrounding Washington, D.C. But for the millions of Americans living in the heartlands of our country, there was no recovery in sight. Their small towns were dying. Their home values plummeted along with their savings. Their neighborhoods were no longer safe. They had to send their children to schools that were not just failing to prepare them for the working world, but were often beset by violence and drugs. Some were contending with a growing opioid crisis. Others racked up huge college loans for themselves or their children, with little prospect for repayment.

Our working and middle classes are the very backbone of the nation. They are the people who work hard, save, sacrifice for the future, and hope to give their children a better life with more opportunities than they had. Yet for the last twenty years more and more American families were falling out of the bottom rungs of the middle class, and many working-class families were unable to climb into it. Leaders told us they were starting to see the "green shoots" of economic growth. When that turned out to be a mirage, they said the economy actually was recovering, but it wasn't apparent because it was a jobless recovery. A jobless recovery for people without jobs isn't a solution to the problem. Meanwhile, the plight for many of our working and middle classes went from temporary to permanent hardship.

Instead of addressing these mounting concerns, our leaders were digging us deeper and deeper into debt, by voting for mountains of new programs and creating an ever-larger Administrative State, without the means to pay for any of it. When they did create jobs, they were usually government jobs which cost the government money, not private economy jobs which added to the government's coffers. To make ends meet in the near term, the United States had to borrow from our foreign adversaries and competitors. Our politicians literally went on a spending spree with our national credit cards, substantially increasingly our national debt in order to temporarily buy the good will of voters so they could get re-elected. When those bills finally come due, these politicians will be long gone.

In the foreign policy arena, things were just as bad. The irony is that some of the very countries our government borrows from are the same countries our government also provides very substantial trade and security subsidies to. At the end of World War II, the United States gave generously to the war-ravaged nations—friend and foe alike—to rebuild their infrastructure and industrial base. We extended favorable loans and trade agreements. A generation ago, we extended another round of subsidies and assistance to what were termed "developing nations" to kick-start their economies.

But after decades of favoring their industrial development, often at the expense of our own, those same nations are now fully recovered, and are now our peer competitors. They no longer need our assistance and we can no longer afford to provide it. Yet the Washington Establishment and the foreign policy community of both political parties want no recalibration of our trade or security agreements. They insist on calling these outdated agreements "free trade," implying that they are tariff-free and make for a level playing field. In reality, they are far from it, perpetuating as they do the trade subsidies to countries which no longer need our assistance but continue to want it anyway, and then use that very advantage to undercut American products.

Similarly, at the end of World War II, we entered into security agreements with our allies and even our former enemies. Because they were economically and militarily devastated, we agreed to provide a disproportionately higher share of the manpower and equipment toward our common defense. Doing so would allow our partners to focus their resources on rebuilding their infrastructure and industrial base and creating substantial welfare and social programs.

These nations have long since recovered from World War II and can afford to spend far more on their armed forces and increase their contributions to our defense alliances. In recognition of this change of circumstance, previous presidents, both Republican and Democrat, have urged our allies to do just that for decades, but to little effect. For the most part, our security partners have made excuses and stalled, deferred, and delayed paying for their own defense, and American officials have failed to hold them to account. As a result, we've continued our security subsidies, even as the threats against us and our allies have grown substantially.

Perhaps the biggest failing of all is that for years most of Washington's foreign policy experts, both liberal and conservative, were so consumed with the Middle East and fighting the terrorism that originated there, that they were blind to everything else. We have spent American blood and treasure fighting in foreign wars with little chance of success, all too often propping up dictators who don't like us, in countries that don't matter. The foreign policy establishment has wasted trillions in these wars of intervention, while failing to prepare us for future challenges from far more substantial national security threats.

The foreign policy establishment refused to see the strategic threat posed by a rising, expansionist, and unsparingly mercantilist China. They were willfully blind to the gathering storm, assuring everyone that the Chinese leaders had no designs on seizing the commanding heights of technology. They assured us that the Chinese would soon open up their economy and society as they joined the community of nations and became more developed. They insisted that China would become a responsible stakeholder in the American-led liberal world order as it grew in economic and political stature. They believed in Chinese benevolence and their assurances not to become a military threat in the South China Sea or the Pacific. But now, as is becoming increasingly apparent, our experts have been wrong all across the board.

For years the Chinese have exploited our generosity and been relentless in pursuit of their development at our expense. Two decades ago they kept their ambitious goals quiet. But they have become more openly aggressive in the last few years. They now make no secret of their plan to replace us as the world's dominant nation, both economically and militarily. Within a few decades, China will be in the position to impose a new international order which favors their interests, and those of other authoritarian nations, at our expense. They call it a new global order with "Chinese Characteristics."

After putting some time and distance between myself and Washington, and giving these questions quiet and considerable thought, I concluded I had been right to break ranks with the Washington Establishment and foreign policy community during the 2016 election. Their programs, policies, and ideas simply were not getting the job done. They were stuck in

Groundhog Day, the same people repeating the same mistakes they had made for years, reluctant to change with the times, especially because it often meant challenging the domestic and foreign s, il interest groups they had been answering to for decades.

That's why I turned to Trump. I knew he was divisive and unconventional. But that's what the country needed: someone determined enough to break through the false promises of conventional wisdom, someone tough enough to stand up to the well-entrenched Washington Establishment, and someone persistent enough to do whatever it took to move the country in a different direction. We needed someone who would do in 2016 what Ronald Reagan had done in 1980: fix the economy by restoring economic growth and creating jobs; rebuild the military; tame the welfare state; get out of hopeless, fruitless, costly, and unnecessary wars that went on forever; stand up to our allies and together recalibrate our outdated security agreements; confront our trade partners and insist on fair and reciprocal agreements; staunch the theft of our intellectual property; and ensure that America continues to remain the land of opportunity. Finally, and most importantly to the future of the nation, someone who put the American Dream back within reach of all of our people, especially the working and middle classes who had been ignored and left behind for the past two decades.

That is why I supported Donald Trump and was honored to be part of his Administration. I knew Donald Trump wasn't like normal politicians. But normal was no longer working. All the other candidates were too invested in maintaining the status quo and in protecting their positions and privileges to even try to bring about major change. They were so entrenched that only a political revolution could shake their grip on power. We were well past the point where merely alternating the presidency between traditional candidates of two parties held out any possibility of fixing things. We needed changes even more pronounced than those of the Reagan Revolution of nearly forty years before. We needed another political revolution.

The Trump presidency has been more chaotic and divisive than any in my lifetime; his combative personality exacerbates the already eroding civility of Washington. I know he can be petty, uncouth, and unpredictable. I know he can be a mean, stubborn S.O.B. I worked for him and experienced it all firsthand on a daily basis sitting across from him in the Oval Office. I paid a heavy personal and professional price to be part of his Administration. But even knowing how it would turn out for me personally, I would do it all over again. That's because Donald Trump, for all his faults and shortcomings, has turned out to be the only person willing to take on the governing elite and disrupt their status quo. Trump is stubborn enough to keep fighting, despite the forces arrayed against him. He will never back down or cave in to their demands. Trump has the self-confidence, guts, and perseverance to keep going until he's won.

In spite of operating under the cloud of multiple investigations over allegations he knew to be groundless from their very outset, in spite of having to endure the relentless and personal scorn of a savage and hostile media, and in spite of being in an anti-Trump city where prominent members of his Administration are harassed in public, he has managed to do what most professional politicians never do—he has actually tried to keep his campaign promises. He has had unprecedented and historic success in growing the economy, creating jobs, and repairing the damage done to our working and middle classes. He began reorienting our status quo foreign policy from his first day in office. He has put America's interests first and recalibrated our trade and security relationships. The fact that he has done so by ignoring members of the Washington insider's club, has enraged them even further.

If anything, I am now more convinced than ever that what we are experiencing now is not just a group of Democrats, Never-Trumpers, and the liberal media who have made common cause in their efforts to get rid of Trump. It is an entrenched self-perpetuating Washington Establishment locked into a battle with the American people over who is sovereign. Is it the American electorate who voted for populism and nationalism with Donald Trump as their flagbearer? Or does the ultimate power rest in the hands of the entrenched Administrative State and the governing class who are using the system to get rid of Trump and everything he stands for?

In some ways, I wish I had come to a different conclusion. It would be far easier for me to write a book saying that, upon reflection, I had been mistaken. If I recanted and said I should never have rejected the conventional wisdom of the Washington Establishment, I would be embraced and welcomed back into the establishment's fold. If I confessed that I was wrong to put my faith in Trump, and now believed that he deserved to be turned out of office, I would no doubt be applauded by the coastal elites and invited to appear on endless broadcasts, all for supposedly recognizing the error of my ways.

But I have reached an age and stage of life where those things matter less to me than being true to my core beliefs and conscience. Even if I stand largely alone, even if I'm belittled and condemned by the Washington Establishment, I will remain committed to populism and nationalism and, yes, very much to Donald Trump, warts and all. While there is breath left in me, I will fight for the average, common man, and to ensure that the American Dream is open to all our countrymen. I will not turn my back on the principles that have made America great for nearly all of our 250 years.

PART THREE

WE THE PEOPLE

CHAPTER 24

We've Always Had Revolutions

Most of us have a sense that something isn't right in America these days, and hasn't been right for some time, even if we don't all agree on the causes or solutions. We may accept that division is normal in a democracy and that hundreds of millions of people living across thousands of miles can't be expected to all agree on everything. We understand that a democratic government requires compromise and cooperation to function effectively. Yet, something still seems very much off-kilter. Our divisions are more widespread, more corrosive, and more insurmountable than even a few years ago. In today's Washington compromise and cooperation are seen as vices to be avoided rather than virtues to be embraced. To consult with the other side is to be accused of political treason and to invite a primary challenge from the extremist wings of one's own party.

It's almost as if Washington has become like that post-apocalyptic horror movie of a decade or so ago, when a bicycle messenger has an accident, and is rushed to the hospital in a coma. He is put into isolation. When he regains consciousness a month later, nearly everyone is dead. He pieces it together to realize an experimental rage virus had escaped from a lab and swept the land. Once infected, people became so uncontrollably hateful that they attacked and killed each other.

Euphemistically, this seems to be what's happening in America today. This sense of unease prevails among us despite a most welcome turnaround in our economy, which has gone from sluggish to booming in just three years' time. We seem more consumed by tribal warfare than ever before, even though more people are employed than in any time in in our history—regardless of gender, race, or ethnicity—and the standard of living is rising all across the board.

For the first time in nearly two decades, we are not involved in large scale foreign wars. We are living in undeniably good times, especially when compared to just a few years ago; yet the sense of negativity seems to be growing. Washington and the media seem angrier, louder, and less willing to ever listen to people who don't agree with them. Groupthink prevails. The vitriol seems to coalesce in the seat of government, leading to the natural question of whether Washington is the cause or the effect of it. Some point to Trump, and insist he is personally and solely responsible for our divisiveness. Others point to Congress, the Democrats, the Administrative State, and the liberal media.

When I began my search for answers, I didn't just focus on my own recent experience. I wanted to look at things through a broader lens, and put events into a bigger perspective. Admittedly, Washington has spent the last few decades going from one scandal and investigation after another, targeting both Republicans and Democrats. But in the Age of Trump, these investigations have gone into overdrive and become inquisitions, and the nation's normal business has been pushed aside.

Trump's enemies have long since decided to remove him from office. They just had to find a crime–any crime will do. For two years our national attention span was consumed by the Russia scandal, and all its spin-off investigations. But when the Mueller probe came up empty, they immediately set about looking for new crimes. His offensive personality and questionable character…his dealings with Ukraine…his tax returns. Now we are absorbed by the impeachment melodrama which has taken on a life of its own. Should that fail, they're convinced they will have done so much damage to him, that reelection will be impossible. The question is why is it happening now?

Part of it is self-interest. Bitter Clintonistas and Never-Trump Republications could point to the Russian collusion narrative as vindication that Trump should never have been elected, and the follow-on investigations

304

and spin-off scandals proof that he shouldn't remain in office. Ambitious legislators see this as a unique opportunity to advance their own careers, especially those seeking to run for president, and to fill their campaign coffers. It is a race to the bottom to see who can make headlines by leveling the most egregious allegations against the duly elected president. A weaponized, Trump-hating press corps have discovered they can take the moral high ground by attacking him, while at the same time reaping the benefits of fortune and fame. Trump was ratings gold, and Russia-mania a boon for all their businesses.

The efforts of the anti-Trumpers aren't necessarily coordinated or organized. They don't need to be. They are like a school of fish in the ocean, or a flow of birds in the sky: coordination is instinctive and automatic. Their focus is driven by people from the various Washington power circles who have vested interests in taking down any outsider, especially one as unacceptable to them as Donald Trump. The entire Trump presidency consisted of the Washington Establishment fighting back against Trump and his populist movement.

This has an added benefit of sending an unmistakable message to anyone outside Washington's approved set of candidates who might be contemplating a run for president: "Don't even think about it. If we can do this to the rich and powerful Donald Trump, we can do it to anyone."

Trump's supporters, in contrast, weren't necessarily Republicans or conservatives or blue-collar Democrats. The thing that united them all is that they are anti-Washington.

The battle lines are drawn. You're either anti-Trump or pro-Trump. The anti-Trumpers point to his shortcoming of character, outlandish behavior and propensity to fight with everybody all the time. They focus on how he acts and what he says. The pro-Trumpers ignore his over the top claims, cringe-inducing comments and angry tweetstorms and focus on what he does. Trump has created a record number of jobs, and lifted the standard of living working and middle-class Americans. He has put America's interests first, rebuilt the military, stopped the forever wars, and stood up to China.

This is the debate that dominates our national conversation. The forces arrayed against Trump would have us believe it is all about him. Remove him from office one way or another, everything can go back to pre-Trump normal, and the country will be just fine. Trump would have us think it's all about him. He is Donald J. Trump, after all, and this is the Age of Trump. As a result, it is difficult to step back and see things from a broader perspective. But I believe there is something far greater happening to the country than a fight over Donald Trump. I believe we are in a pitched battle over where power ultimately resides in the America of today and tomorrow. Is it with the elites or the common man? Who is in charge? Who has the final word?

Will America be governed by the privileged and the powerful who set the rules that the rest of us live by? Are we to be governed by an entrenched governing class made up of the Washington Establishment, the permanent bureaucracy, the Administrative State, career politicians of both parties, and the special interests which support them, the liberal media, academia, the entertainment industry, Wall Street, social media, and tech giants?

Or should power remain in the hands of the common man, the average American voter, the little guy who by himself has neither privilege nor power, only the rights guaranteed to him in the Constitution, especially the right to make his own decisions. That right to choose doesn't mean he always chooses wisely. He is sometimes ill-informed, he doesn't always bother to vote. When he does, he will make mistakes, have false starts, and change his mind. If so, he will have to live with the consequences of his decisions. But they are his to make.

To try to make sense of this conundrum and put my own experiences in some sort of perspective, I turned to American history. Have we been through anything like this before? I started at the beginning, with the Revolutionary War and the birth of our nation. I looked through the last 240 years, right up to today.

What I found surprised me. Despite what we may think, American has been through viciously divisive periods before, some far worse than the one we're living through today. With the hindsight of history, we can see them as inflection points, the transitional periods between an old system that had broken down, and a new one still largely in formation. Sometimes these transitions took years, even a decade, to reach completion. But we have always gotten through them, and emerged as a nation transformed, as if we had been born anew. And every single time we have built a new society that was stronger, more prosperous, and more united, with ever expanding freedoms and opportunities for more and more of our people. This recurring theme of having returned to and rediscovered the interests of the common people is what gives me faith that our country will survive this current period of division.

* * *

Our Founding Fathers had the foresight to create a democratic system of self-government, where all power is ultimately vested in the hands of the people. The Declaration of Independence gave the American people—former colonists under England's boot—the right to overthrow a monarch judged wanting. The Preamble to the Constitution begins with three words: "We the People." Common, average Americans have the right to rise up and replace the governing class whenever they become too entrenched, too self-serving, and too ineffective to serve a dynamic American society. We can vote people into leadership positions, but we can also vote them out.

Our Founding Fathers understood that by vesting power in the hands of average Americans there would inevitably be tensions. It is only natural that people in positions of power and privilege want to keep them and will go to great lengths to do so. The most far-sighted of our Founders also recognized that, in part because of immigration and changes in how people earn a living, America would be a constantly evolving nation—socially, economically, technologically, politically, geographically, ethnically, and demographically.

Yet it is the very nature of governments to become complacent over time and settle into a status quo way of doing things. So, while the people and policies in government stay the same, our dynamic society changes. We revolt against the governing class out of right, as well as necessity.

That is just what we have done time and again throughout our history, beginning with the American War for Independence. We did it in the 1830s with Jacksonian democracy. We did it again in the 1860s with the Civil War, and again in 1900, to constrain the power of monopolies created in the Industrial Revolution. We went through the Great Depression and World War II in the 1930s and 40s. We had the Reagan Revolution in the 1980s, and now, today, we are in the midst of another grassroots populist revolution. The Trump Revolution will likely be followed by another tug of war looming on the horizon, between the people and all-powerful tech giants of the digital age. Each time our political revolutions have been different, with their own unique causes and circumstances. But the result every time has been a national movement that elects new leaders who advocate different policies and take the country in a different trajectory than the one it was on.

Let's examine a couple of these periods in a little more detail.

In the mid-1770s America consisted of thirteen individual colonies, each with their own governors appointed by King George III, and each ruled separately. Some of the colonies chafed under English rule, especially over added taxes and an unresponsive monarch. The thirteen colonies soon banded together and to declare their independence, raise a citizen army, and fight for freedom from English rule. They rejected the governing class of their day, the English overlords who ruled the colonies on behalf of a distant and detached King.

In the beginning, the rebels seemed sure to lose. They were a citizen militia of farmers, laborers and merchants pitted against the most powerful, well-trained army in the world. The Americans slogged through privation and defeat after defeat, until they were able to turn things around and fight and win on their own terms. The newly liberated colonies then came together to write and ratify a Constitution. They created a government of, by, and for the common man. It was the only democracy in over 2000 years, and the world's first constitutional democracy. The new Americans replaced the governors of the British Crown by electing their own representatives. "They" became "We the People."

For the next forty years, the United States was governed by the revolutionary generation and their heirs—the landed aristocracy of Virginia and the wealthy merchant class of New England. But over the years the country changed. New waves of immigrants arrived from the British Isles and from northern Europe. Pioneers moved westward and settled new communities. New states joined the Union. Our people became small farmers, city merchants, and laborers. The population moved and changed—geographically, economically, demographically, and ethnically. The governing class bequeathed by the Founding Fathers grew apart from and no longer represented the people it governed.

With time the American revolutionaries and their successors became the new establishment, and eventually an entrenched governing class. They reinforced the status quo of the post-revolutionary period and failed to keep up with the rapidly changing American society. They, too, lost touch with the people they governed, and dissatisfaction grew. People demanded more rights, not the least of which was the right for the people who didn't own property to vote.

Shortly after the War of 1812 a populist movement developed, arguing that the ruling class had become too entitled, and too unresponsive. Americans were ready for a new kind of leader—a frontiersman, a man of the people who would speak for them and stand up to what had over the years become an entrenched Washington Establishment. The people turned to General Andrew Jackson, who reflected the national mood when he wrote in July 1832 that, "The rich and powerful too often bend the acts of government to their selfish purposes." The Jacksonian Democracy movement of the 1830s expanded suffrage and ushered in a new era in which common folk from all across the our newly growing country became the guiding force in American politics.

This new group of Jacksonian Democrats replaced the old guard. But over the years they, too, settled into power, and themselves became the new Washington Establishment, determined to protect the status quo. Meanwhile, America continued to change. Over the next forty years new waves of European immigrants came to America, settling in the ever-expanding cities and farms across the North American continent. Fissures grew between the agricultural South, which depended on the plantation system and slave labor, and the urban manufacturing North, which advocated emancipation, and the West, which was being settled by single-family homesteaders. The Washington Establishment of both parties was no longer up to the job of bridging the gap. In 1860 another unlikely leader emerged—a former one-term Congressman from Illinois, Abraham Lincoln.

Lincoln became president almost by accident. The frontrunners, each of whom represented a different faction of the newly formed anti-slavery Republican party, canceled each other out. Lincoln was the first Republican candidate to be elected president, thus triggering the seven slave-holding southern states to secede from the Union and to form the Confederate States of America. Their secession set off the bloodiest war in American history—the Civil War between the industrialized, abolitionist North and the agrarian, slave-owning South. After four years of brutal conflict that pitted cousin against cousin, the South was devastated. They had no choice but to offer unconditional surrender. The North emerged victorious and relatively undamaged. Slavery was abolished, and the tug of war between states' rights and the federal government was decided in favor of preserving the Union.

While the Civil War may not have started as a grassroots national movement to replace the political establishment, by the end of the war it had the same effect. The ruling elites in the South—and the North—were replaced by a new group of leaders. The Industrial Revolution expanded rapidly in the years after the Civil War and launched a great boom in manufacturing. The American citizenry was expanded to include the freed slaves and waves of new immigrants who settled in the growing cities and worked in the new factories. Once again, the country changed.

While it took the agricultural South decades to recover from the Civil War, the North embarked on a fast-paced industrial revolution that spread from the East Coast and Midwest to the Southwest and beyond the Rockies to the West Coast. Over the next forty years or so a new breed of industrialists rose up. They built railroads, steamboats, and roads to carry agricultural products from the West and Midwest to cities in the East, and goods manufactured in eastern cities to the rest of the country. American coal fueled the factories, ships, and trains, and American steel built those industries at a dizzying pace.

By the turn of the 19th century our fast-paced industrial progress gave rise to great Trusts, which were the oligopolies in the manufacturing, transportation, and energy sectors. These corporate giants used their wealth and power to exploit factory workers and rural farmers. The "robber barons" were not the political leaders of the day, but they controlled them through donations to political machines. Once again, a national grassroots movement grew up, which demanded workers' rights and insisted that government clip the wings of the industrial and financial titans.

In 1901 Vice President Theodore (Teddy) Roosevelt was sworn in as president following the assassination of President William McKinley. Although born to wealth and privilege, Roosevelt became a champion of the country's emerging working class, who were being exploited by the banking and manufacturing monopolies that had grown up with the Industrial Revolution.

He embraced the progressive reform movement and immediately took on both the Washington Establishment and Wall Street corporate oligarchies that controlled the new American manufacturing, transportation, and financial services industries. He believed they had become so power-ful that they crushed competition and trampled the rights of the workers. As president, Teddy Roosevelt was the "Trust Buster." He restored the balance between the competing interests of the American people and the industrial giants that employed them and moved the center of politi-cal power from the Legislative to the Executive Branch. His progressive movement introduced a series of laws to grant workers' rights, ban child labor, and regulate commerce, food, and drugs. Roosevelt also expanded America's global presence by creating a blue-water navy that would go anywhere in the world. This gave Roosevelt and the United States the abil-ity to play a role on the diplomatic stage. Eventually, women even won the right to vote!

But by the 1930s, that enormous creative energy of the Industrial Rev-olution had run out of steam and financial speculation was rampant on Wall Street. The stock market crashed in 1929, and the nation was soon plunged into a massive Great Depression, with widespread unemploy-ment among factory workers. At the same time, midwestern farmlands and western prairies were hit with several years of drought and dust storms. They suffered massive crop failures and owners of these small farm holdings were pushed off the land.

The political leaders of the day, especially President Herbert Hoover, were judged incapable of leading the country out of crisis. In 1932 Amer-ican voters chose another radical reformer, Franklin Delano Roosevelt (FDR). Like his distant cousin, Teddy Roosevelt, FDR had also been gov-ernor of New York, and championed the cause of the common man. FDR promised a "New Deal" for the American people and put many of them back to work with government-related jobs designed to help build our nation's infrastructure. During his unprecedented four terms in office, FDR rapidly expanded the power and reach of the central government to deal with the twin scourges of the Great Depression and, after the Japa-nese attacked Pearl Harbor, with World War II. But what started out as temporary emergency measures became permanent. Big Government had arrived and now was here to stay. It continued to expand in size, cost, scope, and complexity throughout the next four decades.

The postwar period was a heady time for America. We emerged from World War II virtually unscathed: self-confident, victorious, and united. Despite the attack on Pearl Harbor, the American mainland was untouched, so our great industrial war machine remained intact. Our political system evolved to deal with the postwar challenges at home and abroad, and our economy grew rapidly. Our society had finally assimilated the millions of immigrant families that had flocked to America during the first half of the 20th century. Returning veterans went to college in large numbers, thanks to the GI bill. They moved their families to the suburbs and the great American Middle Class was born.

The optimism of the 1950s and 1960s was soon followed by political assassinations and social unrest of both the civil rights and anti-Vietnam war movements of the 1960s and 1970s. That is the period when I came of age and arrived in our nation's capital to attend George Washington University. My entrance coincided with the low point of another forty-year cycle, the end of the post-World War II era.

As a member of President Nixon's and then President Ford's White House staff, I watched as the old political establishment began to crumble. Inflation rates skyrocketed. Energy prices went up and gasoline supplies went down, creating long waiting lines at filing stations across the country. The Soviet Union built up its nuclear forces, tightened their hold on the Communist Eastern Europe, and expanded their influence around the globe. By the late 1970s more and more of our countrymen, now referred to as "the Silent Majority," had concluded the leadership of both the Republican and Democrat parties had run out of ideas and energy. Republicans rejected their traditional candidates in favor of the one candidate who wasn't part of the Washington Establishment—conservative California Governor and former movie actor Ronald Reagan. He won over working class voters from the Democrats, and was elected in 1980.

Reagan promised to take the country in a very different direction, and he succeeded beyond anyone's expectation. The Reagan Revolution cut red tape and curtailed the massive, job-crushing government regulatory system. He cut personal and corporate taxes significantly all across the board. He rebuilt the military, and restored their pride. He repaired the damage done to the armed forces and the spirit of our men and women in uniform during the Vietnam War and its aftermath. Within three years, the economy had gone from "stagflation"—the combination of high inflation and high unemployment—to one of stability, economic growth, and new job creation that reached dizzying proportions.

At the same time, Reagan stood up to the Soviet Union, targeted their economic weaknesses, and won the Cold War without firing a shot. Millions of new jobs were created, while "Reaganomics" and his Peace through Strength national security program ushered the country into one of the longest periods of peace and prosperity in our history.

But, as seems to be our wont, over the years the Reagan gains were chipped away at by more and higher taxes (which slowed the economy), and with massive and expensive new government programs as a result of the September 11th attacks and the Great Recession. Instead of being temporary fixes, they became permanent after the initial crises were over. Two decades of fighting unsuccessful wars in distant and unimportant places took their toll on the United States armed forces, and also on the federal deficit.

By 2016, fed-up Americans once again turned to an outsider, Donald Trump, for many of the same reasons they turned to Reagan thirty-six years before—because the Washington Establishment was seen as no longer being capable of solving our problems. Or, as Reagan himself said during his first inaugural address: "Government is not the solution to our problem. Government is the problem."

These political revolutions seem to happen in America fairly regularly every forty years or so, even though their causes have all been different, and they were not triggered by any one thing. Sometimes they were a reaction against too much government and regulation, which threatened individual freedoms, and hampered economic growth. Other times they were in response to too little, when the government of the day had insufficient authority to meet the new demands of an emerging era. Sometimes our rebellions have been over economic failures; sometimes, over injustices. Sometimes they have been a tug of war between the states and the federal government. Three of them—the Revolutionary War, Civil War, and World War II—were borne in violence. Others—the Jacksonian Revolution, the Industrial Revolution, and the Reagan Revolution—were more about achieving economic, social, and political reforms.

Different as they have been, these revolutions seem to share some common traits:

- They happen when the establishment leaders of both parties become disconnected from the people they govern. They're seen as being more concerned with keeping themselves in power and perpetuating the status quo than in adapting to new conditions. As a result, they alienate many of the people they had always counted on as their base. For example, because Lincoln was elected by the abolitionist Republicans, after the Civil War the defeated southern states became a solid wall of Democrat voters for decades.

- They begin when weak political parties and their lackluster leaders are no longer able to hold coalitions of people together. Parties break apart and then reform into new coalitions with different political goals, often led by outsiders. For example, Trump has reformed the Republican Party into one that now caters to the middle and working classes, instead of the Bush Republican Party which gave preference to corporate America, Wall Street, and the neocon war hawks.

- They coincide with major changes in how people earn a living. They also happen when the country experiences rapid demographic and geographic changes in our population. For example, the Industrial Revolution created a new class of super-wealthy oligarchs and a new urban working class. With time the workers demanded the breakup of monopolies and better working conditions.

- Many occur during periods of fundamental change in how we communicate with each other—the telegraph during the Civil War, radio during the Great Depression and World War II, film and television during the Reagan era, and the world wide web and social media with Trump.

These revolutions happen because we are a dynamic people and thrive on change. Every aspect of our society and culture is constantly adapting, evolving, and advancing. New immigrants continue to arrive from all parts of the world; we advance methods of agriculture; we engineer new ways to recover the resources lying right under our feet; we invent technologies which then launch entirely new industries; we have groundbreaking advances in science and medicine. Our free markets, forward-leaning and entrepreneurial, offer constant opportunities for rich and poor alike. These are the things that are built into our national DNA.

But a nation that is constantly reinventing itself is also a difficult nation to govern. Government in our modern, complex society is, by its very nature, large, structured, and bureaucratic. It just isn't nimble enough to keep up with the needs of the people it is supposed to govern. Added to this is the fact that people drawn to government and bureaucracies tend to be more risk averse and unwilling to make the leaps to keep up with rapid change. It is even more so because entrenched governing classes are usually reluctant to adapt, especially if it means giving up their privileges and perquisites of office, or rejecting the powerful special interest groups that support them and the status quo. American society and business are constantly pushing toward tomorrow, while government and the Washington Establishment remains stuck in yesterday. The result is we have an entrepreneurial society but not an entrepreneurial government. And over time, tensions are bound to occur.

Our Founding Fathers had no illusions about human nature. Along with patriots and honest citizens, they understood that the vain and venal will always be drawn to power and money, like moths to a flame. They realized that even people who begin as selfless public servants could become so enchanted with power that they would seek to keep it at any cost. Even in a democracy, our leaders can, over time, come to forget they work for us instead of the other way around. As the nineteenth-century British philosopher Lord Acton so famously observed, "Power tends to corrupt and absolute power corrupts absolutely."

The men who wrote our Constitution had firsthand experience with the temptations and dangers of concentrating power in just a few hands. That is why they created a system of checks and balances, with the power of government spread across Legislative, Executive, and Judicial branches. They were three co-equal branches and no one of them had absolute power over any aspect of our governance. The Legislative Branch, made up of an elected House of Representatives and Senate, could write and debate bills, and vote for them, but they had to be signed by the president to become law. These laws, if challenged, could be sent to the Supreme Court to decide whether they should to be upheld or struck down as unconstitutional. The Executive Branch, led by the president, was responsible for enforcing the laws, but Congress has oversight of their actions. Supreme Court Justices and Federal Judges hold their seats for life, but they must be appointed by the president, and confirmed by the Senate. Everyone in government—congressmen, senators, presidents, vice presidents, and judges—would be elected directly or indirectly by the voters. As one of the authors of the Constitution, James Madison, said to the Virginia Constitutional Convention, "The essence of Government is power; and power, lodged as it must be in human hands, will ever be liable to abuse."

Our Founding Fathers also understood a universal truth that governments, if left unchecked, will always expand—in size, scope, cost, control, and arrogance. They understood human nature and realized people with power and privilege would not willingly give them up without some nudging. Even as they wrote the Constitution and elected the first leaders of our country, they recognized that, with the passage of time, even this new governing elite was likely to become entrenched and less responsive to the needs of the people. Eventually, it, too, would need replacing.

The Framers of our Constitution gave us the right to do just that, with regular elections, and charged us with the responsibility to do so when the majority of voters deemed it necessary. After fighting for our freedom on the battlefield, they made it possible for future generations to fight for it at the ballot box. Our Founding Fathers expected us to have these peaceful political revolutions periodically. They are not to be feared, but expected. They are the normal ebb and flow of American governance.

For people who like their governments neat and tidy, these regular populist upheavals are a bit unnerving, especially to outsiders. Other countries look on with wonderment and even with a bit of dismay. But that is who we are. It has been part of our national DNA from the outset. There is nothing unprecedented about the grassroots political revolution we are currently in the midst of. The tug-of-war between centralized control and individual freedom—between the power of big government and the rights of the common man—has been with us from the very first breath of our Republic.

Many Americans think that what we are experiencing today, especially in Washington, is uniquely terrible—that things have never been this bad, that we have never been this divided. Others accuse Trump of being a dictator who is trying to overthrow the Constitution. Others point to a coup attempt by people high up in the intelligence community and permanent bureaucracy to override election results and destroy Trump.

But a stroll through history shows that we have gone through periods just as divisive, bitter, and vitriolic as the one we are going through today. In fact, as crises go, the one we are in now isn't even one of our most difficult. It's just that history is always prettier in hindsight. It seems more united, purposeful, with the rough edges all smoothed out. The reality is a little different. We lurch through these periods, stumble, lose our way and fall, only to regroup and rise to fight again. Different groups emerge, political parties break up into factions, and the deck gets reshuffled. But eventually, it is these political revolutions that bring genuine change.

That is what we are living through now, and it will likely go on for several more years. Many find it disheartening, and are sickened by what they see in Washington, as the old guard fights off the new, and different groups challenge each other. We ask ourselves whether this is finally the end, whether this great experiment we call America will survive. But that's exactly what people thought during the Jacksonian Revolution, during the Civil War, during the Industrial Revolution, and during the Great Depression.

If history is any guide, we will eventually pass through this political revolution too. The extremists will once again be marginalized, normal people will become fed up with the nastiness, the old establishment will increasingly become irrelevant, and - after fits and starts of trying this and that—we will find our way back together again.

I have confidence that the American people will ultimately prevail. One of the things that will help us through these years of turmoil is to remember what unites us instead of what divides us, to remember why what we have is worth preserving and fighting for, and to remember what Makes America Great.

CHAPTER 25

Remembering American Greatness

During one of the Republican debates in a presidential election cycle a few years ago, the moderator asked the candidates to raise their hands if they believed in American exceptionalism. Hands shot up. The moderator, a liberal from an even more liberal news channel, smiled smugly, as if he had scored a major "gotcha" point. But it was a dumb question and a waste of time. Did the moderator really think any candidate for the Republican nomination would keep his hand down, saying, in effect, that he did *not* believe in American exceptionalism? Even worse, the moderator missed the opportunity to ask an obvious follow-up question that actually would have been interesting: *Why* do you believe in American exceptionalism? What evidence is there to support your assumption that America is different from any other great nation today or in history?

My generation, the Baby Boomers, are the children of the Greatest Generation. Our parents survived the Great Depression and won World War II. Many of our grandparents were immigrants who assimilated into an evolving American society. Our forebearers lived the American Dream and were unabashed nationalists. We Baby Boomers took American exceptionalism as our birthright. We recited the Pledge of Allegiance every morning in grade school. We memorized Lincoln's Gettysburg

Address in middle school. We read the Declaration of Independence and studied the Constitution in high school. We were at the forefront of the civil rights and women's rights movements in our college years. We were members of the most admired, most generous, most powerful, and richest country in the world. Everything about American was exceptional.

But that idea of American Exceptionalism has faded over the years, giving way to identity politics, political correctness, multiculturalism, and moral relativism. Our schools no longer study the Founding Fathers or examine the concepts in the Declaration of Independence or Constitution. They no longer read the stirring speeches of Jefferson, Lincoln, FDR, or Reagan. Today's students are taught that no one culture or government or value system is better than any other. College campuses across the country are destroying the symbols of our past and the heroes of our history because in their eyes our forebearers don't measure up to today's societal norms. Our most celebrated educators insist that America's story is one of oppression, exploitation, and discrimination. They're convinced our country's flirtation with American greatness has done more harm than good.

It's almost as if people are ashamed of the very idea of American Exceptionalism. Yet, it is when we insist on forgetting our history that we lose track of the values and the qualities that formed us. And that's when confusion creeps in, even into the minds of those who aren't part of the liberal elites. We start to wonder whether America really is special? Were we ever? The doubt becomes contagious—more and more people have come to regard American Exceptionalism, if it ever even existed, as something in our past, not in the present, and certainly not in our future.

The fashion today, especially among the liberal, democratic coastal elites, is to walk away from the concept that America is special. When he was first running for president, then-Senator Barack Obama met with a group of donors in ultra-liberal San Francisco and took the opportunity to deride those who believe in American exceptionalism as nativists and jingoists—those people who "get bitter…[and] cling to guns or religion or antipathy to people who aren't like them or anti-immigrant sentiment or anti-trade sentiment as a way to explain their frustrations." Obama's attitude was echoed eight years later when Hillary Clinton told a group of her donors that half of Trump's supporters could be put in a "basket of deplorables…[who are] racist, sexist, homophobic, xenophobic,

Islamophobic." In other words, patriotism and nationalism are not just out of style, they're dangerous. They are to be despised, not celebrated.

As arrogant as they may have sounded, Clinton and Obama were just giving voice to a worldview now commonly accepted by the elites that dominate the Democrat Party, academia, the mainstream media, the entertainment industry, thinktanks, and the liberal intelligentsia—and are even shared by some in the Republican establishment. They used to say those things in whispered voices, behind closed doors. Now they're so captured by their self-reinforcing echo chamber that they say these things out in the open

Today, if the only thing you knew about America was learned by watching the Democrat presidential candidates' debates, you would conclude that America had a dark and dirty history, that American society had few redeeming qualities. You would believe that the country had very few virtuous leaders—past or present—other than the ones celebrating themselves on the debate stage.

Liberal elitists believe there's nothing so great about a system of government that puts power into the hands of all people equally. On the contrary, it can be dangerous to rely on people they believe are undereducated, ill-informed, and narrow-minded to make the right decisions. They believe the country needs people like them to govern, to tell people just how they should act, what they should want, and how they should think. They believe in big government and in the nanny state, but only if they're in charge.

On the campaign trail they talk about people's rights, the needs of the underprivileged, the discriminated against, the unemployed, and the unassimilated. They present themselves as the saviors who will look out for these people in exchange for their votes. But take that concept a step further and it seems that they are asking voters to make a trade—we will give you everything you want, if you give us the power to make all your decisions for you. We will decide what is best for everyone—we will give deserving people what we think they need, and we will take things from the people we think don't deserve what they have. No free market capitalism, no leaving things up to the voters to decide, no live and let live, only an all-powerful government, concentrated in their hands.

These elites also believe the best future for everyone is a world governed by international organizations and global institutions, which they, of course, also expect to be in charge of. They believe that the greatest threats to the homeland aren't from unemployment, the $20 trillion-plus national debt, our crumbling infrastructure, the lost American Dream, a rising China, or terrorists, but from racism, discrimination, police officers, the Second Amendment, hate speech, deregulation, and those who have the audacity to believe American leaders should put America's interests first.

In his final years in office, President Obama increasingly talked about the "rules-based international order," "the global community," and our "commonly shared values." He embodied the liberal elite's worldview that the notion of American exceptionalism was a dangerous relic from the bygone days of the twentieth century. He spoke for the people who are convinced that in the twenty-first century, nationalism is passé, and patriotism is only for losers. National borders no longer matter, and any responsibilities of citizenship are optional. Their disdain for national pride, as well as all things Trump, was on full display when the liberal elites, goaded on by the Washington press corps, uniformly opposed a display of American innovation and salute to our Armed Forces on July 4, 2019. Trump was accused "of exploiting the nation's birthday party for his own political ends…[that] bolstered the President's narrative that he is a strong commander in chief and a decisive leader….at the start of his reelection race."[1]

I think they're nuts. I believe we are a great nation, and that American Exceptionalism is real, tangible, and bears constant recounting. But this doesn't happen naturally; it isn't automatically inhaled just by being in America, or passed down through our national DNA. It has to be explained, nurtured, and encouraged.

The Greatest Generation is now passing from the scene. They survived a Great Depression in the 1930s, defeated Fascism and Nazism in World War II, created the post-war liberal world order, and restored the American Dream. Then, in their final years, they triumphed over communism and won the Cold War without firing a shot. National pride was something they felt in their bones, and American Exceptionalism was something they earned for all of us with their own blood, sweat, and tears.

---

[1] Collinson, Stephen. "Trump calls bluff of critics in July 4th speech." CNN. July 5, 2019. https://www.cnn.com/2019/07/05/politics/trump-july-4th-speech/index.html.

Today people don't appreciate what the Greatest Generation or previous generations did to win and maintain our freedoms, create the American Dream, and build the world's longest lasting and greatest self-governing nation. It's not because they are ungrateful, but because most of them remain uninformed about our history, our unique form of government, and the long record of our achievements. We no longer routinely teach our young people civics, ethics, or American history. On the contrary, the emphasis today is on what's wrong with America.

People can't appreciate something they've never been taught and don't understand. It's hard for them to value as special the privileges that they have always enjoyed. They take them for granted and, to the extent they think about them at all, assume they are our birthright and they'll never have to do anything to maintain them. If you have never learned what it is about America that makes it exceptional, you're unlikely to be willing to sacrifice for it, or even to recognize when it starts slipping away. Trump, for all of his unorthodox tendencies, does understand this American quality—and is rightfully proud of it.

It would take a far longer book than this to list all the attributes that make America a great nation. So, forgive me if I recount just a few that I think are the most consequential.

First, our national identity is a melting pot society that is uniquely our own. No other nation has the same mix of people, drawn from all corners of the earth, and blended together over the decades to create a unique American culture. We are the amalgamation of all the people who have come here over the centuries, each adding something to the melting pot that is American society, each helping to create something that can be found in no other country. You don't have to belong to a certain race, practice a certain religion, or come from a certain place to be an American. That privilege is open to anyone, as long as they play by the rules and enter the United States legally.

This ideal is so ingrained in our national identity that we often fail to appreciate how rare it is. From the beginning of recorded history, peoples have fought along ethno-sectarian battle lines—whether it's the Sunnis warring against the Shiites today, or the Persians battling the Greeks in ancient times. Some have been so preoccupied fighting each other—sometimes for millennia—that they have failed to develop modern societies.

Sure, we've had our bumps along the road—the "Irish need not apply" signs in Boston and Philadelphia shop windows in the 19th century, Japanese internment camps in World War II, and the "Whites Only" bathrooms in the South in the 20th century. But for the most part, our history has been one of assimilation and inclusion. Today's immigrants do struggle at first, but within a few years their children are hanging out at the mall with Mayflower descendants. A black man won the presidency—twice—elected by the descendants not just of slaves, but of slave owners. We may be a nation of immigrants from every corner of the earth, but by and large over the years we have found a way to live together in relative harmony. Instead of fighting over the American Dream, our immigrants assimilated and quickly set about achieving it. We have welcomed all, and then absorbed them to create a new and unique American culture, where the whole is greater than the sum of the parts.

That's why I love watching old movies about World War II. They always begin with a polyglot group of soldiers—the long, lean Texas cowboy, inevitably called "Tex;" the wisecracking Italian kid from Brooklyn; the tall, blond Scandinavian from Minnesota; the Appalachian hillbilly; the southern gentleman; the Boston Brahmin. At the beginning, they spend as much time brawling with each other as they do fighting the Nazis. But by the end of the movie, they have become a band of brothers, each of them willing to put his life on the line for the others. They may have gone to war as strangers, but they finished the war as Americans.

When I was a little girl, I spent my Saturday mornings at Catholic catechism class in the Italian neighborhood of Madison, Wisconsin. I sat in the same chairs and was taught by the same nuns who some three decades before had taught my Sicilian-American father. After the nuns taught us the seven deadly sins, they ordered us out of those chairs and onto our knees to recite the rosary and pray that Senator John F. Kennedy would be elected president. I doubt if they even knew he was a Democrat. As far as they were concerned, he was a Catholic, and that was all that mattered. The nuns said it would take a miracle for a Catholic to be elected—and we were praying for that miracle.

Sure enough, Kennedy narrowly beat the sitting vice president, the Protestant Richard Nixon, in part because the large block of Irish and Italian Catholics came out en masse to vote for him. Yet, thirty years before, when my parents were children, New York Governor Al Smith had lost the 1928 presidential election in part because he *was* a Catholic. From rejection to acceptance in a generation—and by the third generation, being Catholic was regarded with political indifference. My children could care less about a presidential candidate's religion. Moral values, yes; religion, no. America does not only assimilate; we evolve.

Or at least we used to. My Sicilian grandmother was somewhat of a celebrity in her neighborhood—unlike everyone else, she was actually born in America, a year after her parents "got off the boat." I never knew my father's father, an immigrant from Sicily who died young from lung disease. By all accounts, he didn't speak much English, despite having been a soldier in the U.S. Army and surviving a gas attack in World War I. Nonetheless, when my father was growing up, my grandparents always told him, "Speak English! Be an American!" And his friends, all the children of immigrants, were told the same thing—whether it was at home, at school, or at baseball practice. The only place they were free to speak Italian was at the neighborhood Italian Workmen's Club.

This pattern was repeated in every home in immigrant families for generations. Be an American! Get an education! Work hard! Get a good job! This is the land of opportunity! This is America—so go live the American Dream! And they did. They built a great nation with people who had come here from every corner of the earth, speaking every language, practicing every religion. As each new generation arrived, they, too, were added to the great melting pot. What keeps pouring out is a new, constantly changing American culture not to be found anywhere else in the world.

Compare this to the massive and enduring problems multiculturalism has caused in Europe. Those cultures have never been particularly welcoming to immigrants. But in recent decades they've opened their doors, in part as a humanitarian gesture and in part to guarantee a work force to support their aging populations. These immigrants speak different languages, have different cultural and religious traditions than their host countries, and possess meager employable skills. That wouldn't have been a problem in America—the immigrants who have always come to our country had challenges similar to those who are now coming to Europe. But we welcomed and assimilated them, and Europe has not.

Instead, some countries in Europe promote what amounts to an anti-assimilation policy, where immigrants live in unofficial states within the state. Their invitation was the opposite of ours: Come to Europe. You can live in your own communities with your fellow immigrants, keep your own customs and continue to speak your native tongue. We will provide you with state-sponsored schools where your children can study your ethnic traditions in your original language, with teachers from your own culture. You can take your grievances to your own courts with judges who mete out decisions based on your own traditions. You can live alongside us in parallel societies, as though you never left home—but never as equals.

Europe's arrangement hasn't worked. A great many of their immigrants, even onto successive generations, are unable to find rewarding jobs or to move out of their segregated communities. With the very best of intentions, these European nations have condemned their immigrants and their children to being permanent aliens in their new lands. It has fostered unemployment, poverty, and resentment. Even German Chancellor Angela Merkel, herself one of the leaders of open-door immigration, admitted several years ago that their form of multiculturalism has been a failure. The legacy of that failure is in part what drives the political divisions all across Europe today.

Why has a combination of cultures worked in America but not in other parts of the world? Because while we acknowledge the diversity of Americans, we also ask them to join us in creating a new and ever-evolving American society and culture. We expect our immigrants to pour their customs and culture into the great melting pot to which previous generations of immigrants have already contributed. We expect our immigrants to embrace our culture, the same way we expect our society to evolve by embracing them. It is this cultural dynamism that makes America different from any place else in the world. Assimilation is one of our greatest strengths.

Despite all of this, many Americans remain enamored of European multiculturalism. For the past decade or so we have walked away from the very thing that unites us—our American culture—in favor of a society divided along social, economic, ethnic, ideological, and regional lines. It's discriminatory and judgmental, we're now told, to expect someone to assimilate, study our history, or even to learn to speak English. My father's immigrant generation worked hard to be called Americans. But that has gone out of fashion. We no longer refer to ourselves simply as

Americans—we're hypothecated Americans: Italian-Americans, Vietnamese-Americans, Hispanic-Americans. And which nationality is supposed to come first? The foreign one! The American label is tacked on second, almost like an afterthought.

We have become so afraid of giving offense to one or another group or individual, or being accused of intolerance and prejudice, that many of us walk around in a state of constant self-censorship, lest we say something politically incorrect. Identity politics has supplanted the sense of common purpose our forefathers had. The notion that we are part of something bigger than ourselves, united by shared values, is seen as either hopelessly quaint or aggressively selfish. For lots of reasons, some well-intentioned, others not, we are urged to divide into groups and set against each other—old against young, white against black and Hispanic, coastal elites against heartland commoners. As a result, we're in danger of losing our American-ness, that very thing that made us great. We have always been a wonder in the world, precisely because we have found a way to transcend race, ethnicity, religion, and class and grant equal rights to all. It is a pity to sacrifice all of that, as many would have us do, on the altar of multiculturalism and identity politics—and become like every other society which by history, tradition, or circumstance, continues to pit one group against another.

The problem with identity politics is how it slices and dices our society up into pieces, and encourages each of them to claim an injustice. I would be charitable in saying that the leaders of the grievance groups feel compelled to right what they see as a wrong done in years past. A less charitable explanation is to point out that they tend to do very well for themselves by exploiting division to raise their profiles, fundraise, and keep themselves in positions of power and influence. If they were ever to actually solve the problems of the grievance groups they champion, they might find themselves out of a job.

In the current mud wrestling fight over immigration, both sides have lost track of two important elements. First and foremost is the fact that we are a nation of immigrants. It is one of our greatest strengths. But, secondly, unless new citizens are willing to assimilate and join American society, and longtime citizens willing to welcome them into the fold, immigration can become disruptive and turn into one of our greatest weaknesses.

Trump has proposed a solution to our immigration problem: a wall with a big door, and regularizing our immigration process and enforcing the laws. This door amounts to a welcome wagon for every new legal immigrant, where they must master English, learn and obey American laws, and become productive members of their community in order to reap the rewards of citizenship. Sadly, many in our governing class have no interest in this solution. Why? Because like many things in Washington these days, each side uses the issue as a wedge issue to whip up their base, and as a club to beat over the other side's head. Neither side is willing to compromise in order to give the other side a "win." These people seek to score political points by being the self-appointed leaders of identity groups, and championing multiculturalism at the expense of Americanism. Meanwhile, the rest of the country, citizens, legal immigrants, and even undocumented illegal immigrants, all suffer for their selfishness.

By failing to address critical elements of the immigration crisis, we are also turning away some of the most talented students who come to our universities from abroad. America has the best higher education system in the world. Our colleges and universities, particularly our graduate schools, are ranked in the top tiers and attract talented, highly motivated students from all over the world. We educate them here, oftentimes at our own expense, with scholarships and grants. When they graduate, many want to remain and make their lives here, contributing to America's continued success and helping us maintain our technological prowess. Some of our most successful high-tech companies have been created or led by immigrants, who remained after graduating from American universities. Instead of sending them back to their home countries to compete against us, we should staple a green card application and work visa to their college diplomas, and create jobs right in America.

Reagan's final speech was an ode to immigrants, a love letter really. He quoted from a letter a man wrote to him, "You can go to live in France, but you cannot become a Frenchman. You can go to live in Germany or Turkey or Japan, but you cannot become a German, a Turk, or a Japanese. But anyone, from any corner of the Earth, can come to live in America and become an American."[2]

---

[2] "Remarks at the Presentation Ceremony for the Presidential Medal of Freedom." Ronald Reagan Presidential Library. January 19, 1989. https://www.reaganlibrary.gov/research/speeches/011989b.

Reagan said this constant stream of immigrants throughout our history was "the great life force of each generation of new Americans that guarantees that America's triumph shall continue unsurpassed into the next century and beyond." Reagan was right—our melting pot society is essential to our greatness. It is part of why we are able to reinvent ourselves as individuals and as a nation, and why we remain a dynamic people. "Thanks to each wave of new arrivals to this land of opportunity, we're a nation forever young, forever bursting with energy and new ideas, and always on the cutting edge, always leading the world to the next frontier."

Second, America is the land of opportunity. We hold out the promise to all of our people—immigrant and longtime citizen alike—that in America anything is possible. Or, as Walt Disney once said, "It you can dream it, you can do it." If you work hard, plan, save for the future, and live in peace and harmony with your neighbors, you can pass on to your children a better life than you have had, with a higher standard of living and greater access to education and opportunities. We usually associate this with prosperity and financial achievement. But the American Dream is more than that.

During my first year at Oxford University, I was invited to join the Amazons, as the only American member of a decidedly English woman's club. Today, Oxford has many American students; forty years ago, not so many. One of our major events was the annual dinner—our college version of a grand Downton Abbey affair. Each of the twenty Amazons was expected to invite two male guests—not necessarily boyfriends, just classmates and friends. The Amazons all wore long dresses and the men tuxedos. We had arranged for a very elaborate dinner, beginning with sherry in the college library and finishing with port and cheese in the lounge, with a different wine pairing for each of the several dinner courses.

I was new to Oxford life, so chose my two escorts with great care. One was a young economics don, a brilliant junior professor with a sardonic wit. The other was an urbane undergraduate in his final year, whom I had met in my political theory tutorial. I didn't think they knew each other but was sure they would prove entertaining dinner partners for me and the other Amazons. Both were bright, witty, and open-minded enough to be friends with an American. Both loved politics and debate.

I was already in the college library, sipping my dry sherry, chatting with the Amazons, when my two gentlemen walked through the door, both looking dapper in black-tie and dinner jackets. I made the introductions, but instead of making small talk, the two men glowered at each other. I tried everything to warm them up, nattering away about the university gardens, the latest rock bands, and British and American politics. Nothing. The two men would talk to me, but they refused to talk directly to each other. I had no idea what was wrong, but clearly I had made some major mistake. The evening was a complete disaster, and my two handsome escorts made their excuses and both left well before dessert. I was an abandoned Amazon sitting alone in the lounge, with my glass of port and wedge of cheese.

The next day, one of my sister Amazons pulled me aside to explain what had happened. The young economics don was a grammar school boy who had gone through Oxford on a scholarship, waiting tables to make ends meet. His mother was a charwoman, which I later found out meant cleaning lady. His tuxedo was from the second-hand bin of Oxfams, the British equivalent of the Salvation Army. The politics student, on the other hand, had an "Honourable" in front of his name, which meant his father was of a peer of the realm. Someday he would inherit his father's title and become a duke himself. From age eight on he had gone to boarding school at Eton and was now a student at the snootiest of Oxford Colleges, Christ Church. His tuxedo was custom made by a tailor on London's famed Saville Row. My sister Amazon reassured me that because I was an American there was no way I would have known about the unbridgeable social gap between them, but it was clear to everyone else at the dinner. When I asked her why the son of a charwoman and the son of a duke both accepted me as equals, she laughed and said, "Because you're an American, of course!"

I had made the ultimate faux pas. These two men were wonderful and talented individuals, but according to the British customs of the times, they were unlikely to be friends, or even polite acquaintances—ever. All because they were born into different and adversarial social classes. No matter what successes or failures their own lives would hold, they would always see themselves—and each other—as being irreconcilably different. Britain may have given both men an Oxford education and, when they graduated, supposedly presented them with equal opportunities in the job market. But they could not do the one thing that we Americans do so well—allow them to be accepted and judged by their own merits.

Many European countries still have aristocracies and royal families who inherit their place in society. We Americans might find the British class system fascinating, but not necessarily admirable. Instead, we respect people who "make something of themselves." We cheer for the self-made man who pulls himself up by his bootstraps, or the woman who cracks the glass ceiling. We love an underdog. Our heroic tales are of young people who overcome adversity, go up against great odds, persevere in the face of failure, and ultimately triumph.

We have a classless society, which makes social mobility an American right. Your place in America doesn't depend on who your parents are, but on what you make of yourself. Being born poor doesn't mean you have to die poor or be looked down on or disrespected. Being born to wealth is no guarantee you will keep it. Reinvention is part of our American birthright.

When I was in the Ford Administration, young West Wing staff members like me would occasionally be invited to come to the East Room for the after-dinner entertainment following very elegant, formal state dinners. One of the grandest of all was the State Dinner that President and Mrs. Ford held for Queen Elizabeth and the Duke of Edinburgh. We got dressed up in evening gowns and tuxedos and waited in the expansive downstairs hallway of the White House, while the dinner guests ate upstairs in the State Dining Room. Just before the final dinner toasts, we were ushered up the broad marble staircase into the East Room and slipped into seats in the back rows. Once the State Dinner finished, the official guests would walk from the State Dining Room to the East Room for the concert and take their front row seats. I don't remember who the musicians were, but I do remember catching a glimpse of the Queen.

A few days later I went to the White House photographers' office in the West Basement, which was then located right across from the Situation Room. I pored over White House photographer David Kennerly's thumbnail slides. Bingo! David had captured the perfect moment when Cary Grant was introduced to Queen Elizabeth.

Hollywood heartthrob Cary Grant, some twenty years the Queen's senior, as ever debonair in his tuxedo, offered just the slightest bow of his head as he shook the Monarch's extended hand. The Queen, resplendent in a yellow gown and jewel encrusted crown, was beaming up at him like a schoolgirl. It was hard to tell who was the more starstruck, but if I had to guess, I think it was the Queen.

For decades Cary Grant epitomized the suave, sophisticated gentleman. But he started life as Archie Leach, a working-class boy from Bristol, England, the son of a tailor's presser. He came to America, changed the way he walked, talked, and dressed, and was reborn as Cary Grant. What if he had stayed in Bristol? He might have become an actor, but would never have become the very image of an upper-class English gentleman. Coming to America changed everything. Archie Leach left England and became Cary Grant, who decades later dazzled even the Queen.

What is it about America that makes this possible? Aren't we and the Brits, for example, a lot alike? Yes and no. We have a special relationship with the British—a common language, shared values, and we fought two World Wars as the closest of allies. But scratch that surface and we're different. The British have a class system that values pedigree, often more than achievement. For us, it's the opposite. Where we start out in life is not necessarily where we end up. We celebrate people who rise on their own achievements.

Reinvention requires not just hard work and a few lucky breaks, but opportunities—a good education, jobs, equal treatment, and equal rights. It may have taken us a while, but we have constantly marched toward providing equal opportunities to all of our people, regardless of race, color, creed, gender, or sexual orientation. Not only is it the right thing to do, but it is the smart thing to do. It is difficult for a democracy to hold itself together over time unless all of our people feel they have a fair shot at achieving the American Dream.

Third, we are a nation that has always looked to the future, rather than one that dwells on the past. One of the things I find fascinating about Facebook is how people fill out the line for "Hometown." Most people write in where they live now, not where they were born or where they grew up. It says a lot about Americans. The past isn't as important to us as the present—and the future. Trying new things, going new places, working at new jobs, carving out the wilderness, and venturing into space are all things to be encouraged, not frowned upon.

It has meant that we have been at the forefront of innovation and technology at least since the Industrial Revolution. We built a transcontinental railroad, steel factories, and oil refineries as part of our post-Civil

War industrial and manufacturing revolution. We mastered the steam engine and built trains, cars, and planes. Our inventors discovered electricity, invented phonographs, telephones, and televisions. We were the first to harness the power of the atom.

Young American inventors built the first computers and microprocessors; our entrepreneurs created the information age by connecting computers to pass information across telephone lines; and then launched the digital age by connecting the world through the internet. American scientists, inventors, and entrepreneurs have been at the cutting edge of every aspect of our modern lives from cameras to iPhones to microchips to wearable medical devices. Our scientific know-how, our innovative society, and our free market system have made it possible for America to become, and then remain, the world's high-tech superpower.

That is why we must do everything in our power to retain our technological leadership. As I mentioned earlier, President Xi has committed his country to *Made in China 2025*. They seek to use whatever means necessary—legal, illegal, overt, and covert—to develop, invent, buy, persuade, demand, cajole, bully, and steal what's needed to become the dominant manufacturers of the ten critical technologies of the future. Xi realizes that the country that dominates the technologies of the future will dominate the future of the world. He intends for that country to be China, and China alone.

America, on the other hand, has become complacent over the last two decades. We have been the world's tech superpower for so long that we assume it will always be the case. But technological innovation doesn't happen by accident. It needs constant reinvestment and replenishment. Our development model has been for government to invest heavily in basic research, designed to innovate and introduce new products and services. The private sector then turns these inventions and discoveries into commercial products and makes further innovations of its own.

According to David Goldman, columnist for the *Asia Times*, "Without exception, every key component of the digital economy was invented in a U.S. corporate or government laboratory with funding from the Defense Department or NASA."[3] America led the digital revolution in large part because of the Reagan defense buildup of the 1980s. But for the last thirty

---

[3] Goldman, David P. "How Not To Restore American Industry." *Townhall.* August 9, 2019. https://finance.townhall.com/columnists/davidpgoldman/2019/08/09/how-not-to-restore-american-industry-n2551451.

years or so we haven't kept pace with federal funding for basic R&D. In the 1980s we spent 1.3 percent of our GDP on basic R&D; today we spend only 0.7 percent.

The Asian model of industrial development is different. In Japan, South Korea, Singapore, and now China, the government subsidizes capital-intensive investment—factories, equipment, and infrastructure. They're good at mass producing things that we invent. They're so good at it that many of the essentials of the digital age—electronic devices like computers, memory devices, mobile phones, cameras, and flat screen televisions—which were designed in the United States are now made in Asia.

The commercial consequences of this have an impact on American jobs, which is bad enough. But the national security implications are profound, even dangerous. Our advanced weapons systems are dependent on electronic components that may have been invented in the United States but are increasingly manufactured overseas, where costs are cheaper. One example is microchip manufacturing. Micro-processing was invented in the United States, but the manufacture of these components has largely moved overseas, to countries which are not just economic competitors, but could someday be military adversaries. They control the supply chain. What happens if they decide to stop selling us components which are essential for our advanced weapons systems? In a must-read *Wall Street Journal* article, Goldman and technologist Henry Kressel[4] make the case that "If the U.S. loses all of its most advanced chip-fabrication capacity, it will be like a country without a steel industry in the age of artillery—at the mercy of its enemies."

If we are to maintain our technological edge, we should focus on what we're good at—thinking and experimenting and coming up with creative ideas which can create entire new industries. We must continue to do everything we can as a society—encourage private industry, champion inventors, incentivize manufacturers, provide basic government-funded research and development, and improve our primary and secondary education systems to stress the study of science, technology, engineering,

---

[4] Kressel, Henry and David P. Goldman. "Silicon, Not Steel, Will Win the Next War." *Wall Street Journal*. December 23, 2018. https://www.wsj.com/articles/silicon-not-steel-will-win-the-next-war-11545598669.

and mathematics—if we hope to continue to retain our technological dominance.

America can and should remain the innovation engine of the world. The Trump Administration is absolutely right to restrict Chinese access to U.S. technology, by adopting more stringent measures on what they are given access to, allowed to buy, or manage to steal. But that alone is not enough.

Trump's first term has been focused on pro-growth policies, which has resulted in sudden and extraordinary economic success. He should now build on that by focusing on pro-innovation policies which encourage new private and public sector research and development. Technology will advance, with or without us leading the way. Washington is going to have to encourage innovation across the science, technology, engineering, and mathematics spectrum for us to stay competitive in the decades ahead. In the past, American scientists, technologists, engineers, and mathematicians have always led us and the world into the future. It's what we're good at; it's part of who we are. We must continue to do whatever is necessary to keep it that way.

Many of the qualities that make America a great nation rest on the foundation of free public education for our children, and even for our adults. A good education opens the door to the land of opportunity for all our people. It provides many of the tools we need to take advantage of those opportunities. It teaches us about American history and government, so that we can value our democracy, and understand why it is worth keeping. It helps our immigrants assimilate into our society. It gives us the skills we need to discover, create, invent, and build our future. It is essential for a self-governing society. Thomas Jefferson, author of the Declaration of Independence, and the third President of the United States, wrote that, "An educated citizenry is a vital requisite for our survival as a free people."

Finally, America is a generous nation. We have built the richest and most powerful country in the history of the world and then, instead of using it to exploit the weak, conquer lands, or build empires, we have used it to do good for others. We came to Europe's aid not once, but twice, to win World Wars and to save their beleaguered nations from defeat. When these wars were won, we did not demand reparations from the defeated, even though they were the aggressors. Rather, we did what no other conquering nation in the history of the world had ever done before. We turned around and helped rebuild the defeated, not just our allies, but our enemies as well. We could have demanded lands or riches as the spoils of war. As Secretary of State Colin Powell once said, "Did we ask for any land? No. The only land we ever asked for was enough land to bury our dead, and that is the kind of nation we are."[5]

In the end, the reason America is great is because of a combination of all these things—we're the land of opportunity, a melting pot society, at the forefront of technology and innovation, and ever generous and forgiving. I could also add a dozen other characteristics of America that add to our greatness.

But in the end, American greatness comes from also knowing our purpose in the world, that intangible, but very real, sense that we Americans are part of something bigger than ourselves. It is our confidence that America isn't just another great power, in the world's long history of great powers, but holds a unique place in the hearts and minds of people throughout the world.

---

[5] "Be Heard: An MTV Global Discussion With Colin Powell." U.S. Department of State Archive. Accessed September 24, 2019. https://2001-2009.state.gov/secretary/former/powell/remarks/2002/8038.htm.

CHAPTER 26

Why America Is—
and Remains—Exceptional

Over the years, while in and out of government, I've given a great deal of thought to the follow-up question that liberal moderator should have asked the candidates at that Republican presidential debate. What exactly is it that makes America exceptional? Most of the candidates on that stage would have answered by ticking off a number of characteristics: Our melting pot society; our creativity and inventiveness; our free market system and the economic opportunity it provides to all; our dynamism; our history; our success and prosperity, our hard work ethic; our democratic system of government; our economic power and military might; our generosity; our pioneer spirit; and our willingness to explore the unknown.

But many nations today, and throughout history, have possessed some of these qualities. While they may be great nations, I wouldn't necessarily consider them exceptional. What separates America from the pack, what makes us *exceptional* is what we then do with all these qualities. We use them to do what no other nation does—we periodically reinvent ourselves as a nation, not just as individuals.

America was founded on the principle of reinvention. When our Founding Fathers wrote the Declaration of Independence, they reinterpreted the rights of man. When they wrote the U.S. Constitution, they reinvented government.

The American Dream offers each of us the opportunity to write our own destiny. Archie Leech came to America and became Cary Grant. Abraham Lincoln was born in a log cabin, taught himself how to read, and became one of our greatest, most eloquent presidents. The coddled New York blue blood Teddy Roosevelt overcame his childhood infirmities to become so rugged that he stared down a grizzly bear while exploring the Wild West.

America is an exceptional nation because it makes this personal reinvention possible. But even more profound is that we also have the power to reinvent the nation. Our Constitution vests all power in the hands of the common man and then gives us the right, indeed tasks us with the responsibility, to create and recreate our society so that it continues to answer to our needs. America is constantly changing and evolving, and because our society is dynamic, we need leaders who can keep up with us. Our Founding Fathers understood this, and made it possible for us to have periodic, peaceful political revolutions. Our greatest leaders have recognized the need for change and have led the way.

For hundreds of years, waves of immigrants have come to our shores from all corners of the earth. Pioneers spread out across the continent settling the wilderness. Inventors and entrepreneurs created the Industrial Revolution. College dropouts invented the first Apple computer in their parents' garage and launched the information and digital age. These people not only reinvented their own lives, they recreated American society, time and again. When government was reluctant and slow to change, the American people demanded them to do so.

My husband, Alan, was involved in the founding of the National Constitution Center in Philadelphia. As the building was going up, and the exhibits being laid out, he tried to describe how the Constitution Center would be different from other museums. I had never understood what Alan meant until we went to the grand opening on July 4th, 2003. When the doors opened, we filed into an upside-down auditorium. The stage was an empty circle in the round, on the ground floor. The seats started at the stage and moved up and up, row by row. The theater was covered by a dome, with bare walls. When the doors closed, the lights dimmed, and an actor stepped into the spotlight, standing alone in the well of the theater.

He narrated the story of the founding of America, with patriotic music in the background and a light show playing across the dome, showing how America had come to be.

As he led us through the events and phases of America's development, the images across the dome changed, as did the sounds. The narrator described how we began as a nation of immigrants, how we tamed the wilderness, how we formed a rag tag militia to fight and defeat the greatest army in the world to win our independence. The narrator went on to explain how our Founding Fathers wrote a Constitution that created a new form of government. He pointed out that our new citizens say the Oath of Allegiance, and our leaders and military all take their oath of office, not to a king, or general, or dictator, or cleric, but to *an idea*. We swear to protect and defend the Constitution of the United States, the document that sets out the principles by which we are governed—the rights as well as the responsibilities. He talked of how our forefathers fought a great and bloody Civil War that freed the slaves and kept the nation united. He described the women's suffrage movement and the Civil Rights era. The narrator ended his presentation with a description of how we continued to defend our freedom from fascists and communists and terrorists in the 20th century. It left me with the unmistakable and unshakeable belief in the dynamism, optimism, and basic goodness of Americans.

This live one-man performance, called *Freedom Rising*, left the audience silent—enraptured by what was unfolding before us. When the lights came back on there were even a few of us discreetly wiping tears from our eyes. It turns out a lot of us do want to believe in the beauty of the American Constitution again, but we've been talked out of it by leaders who would have us focus on what divides us, instead of what unites us; what's wrong with America instead of what's right.

If you were to draw a diagram of the flow of power before the American Revolution, it would have God on top, with an arrow pointing directly down to the king, and little arrows going out from him to parliament, the aristocracy, the military, the church, and then to the common people. On July 4th, 1776 representatives of the thirteen American colonies signed a Declaration of Independence, laying out the case for why we had to take up arms against Britain. In so doing, we turned that flow chart on its head. Instead of being subjects of a king who got his power from God, we declared that the Creator gave the rights to "life, liberty, and the pursuit of happiness" directly to the common man, without any intermediaries.

Our Declaration of Independence claims it as a universal principle that all men are created equal. It is the people alone who have the right to choose our leaders, and to replace them. It is more than just a right, however; it is also our responsibility to do so if we determine those leaders fail to protect our interests. The Declaration of Independence states "it is their right, it is their duty, to throw off such Government, and to provide new Guards for their future security."

Our War of Independence went on for seven years. When British General Cornwallis surrendered to General George Washington at Yorktown, legend has it that the British Army band played an old English ballad, "The World Turned Upside Down." The most powerful and professional army in the world had just been defeated by a Colonial Army and militia of farmers, shopkeepers, and laborers. The world was turned upside down in another way as well. Common citizens would now, for the first time in millennia, have the right and responsibility to govern themselves.

After some fits and starts, seven years after Yorktown, the thirteen colonies ratified the Constitution of the United States of America. The framers of the Constitution, the men who created it, were concerned that just throwing off the king and putting power in the hands of the people wasn't alone a sufficient guarantee that freedom would survive. They knew all too well the corrupting influence of power, how it was the very nature of government to expand and add to its power by chipping away at the rights of the people.

So they did something both brilliant and enduring: they gave us a Constitution of divided government, replete with a system of checks and balances, designed to put constraints on government power. They put all power in the hands of the voters, with no one having special status. Those who hung around their local taverns tippling from their tankards and complaining about the British were to have the same rights as those who fought alongside George Washington and suffered through that winter at Valley Forge. If our government overstepped its bounds or failed to do the people's bidding, we would have a built-in right to another revolution, albeit peaceful this time, at the ballot box. In this new United States of America, commoners have the right to choose their own leaders, and through them to write their own laws, administer government, and create a military. That is why The Preamble to the Constitution begins with these three words: We the People...

These periodic political revolutions that make our reinvention possible have always been populist revolutions, from the bottom up, not from the top down. But they have all been led by extraordinary people, and outstanding presidents—the Founding Fathers, George Washington, Andrew Jackson, Abraham Lincoln, Teddy Roosevelt, Franklin Delano Roosevelt, Ronald Reagan. They all battled against the governing class of their day. Having disrupted the status quo, many of them also led us in a new direction, and helped reunite a divided nation. They did so by bringing the people along with them every step of the way. They all knew for change to become permanent, it had to be embraced by the people, not just imposed on them from above.

President Trump has shown that he is willing to stand up to the Washington Establishment. He has been a great disrupter of status quo policies that may have worked years ago but have not changed with the times. The sentiments that drove this grassroots populist revolution were already stirring, but it was Trump who gave them voice and purpose. It was Trump who started us down a very different path, one that would answer to the needs of all our people, not just the coastal elites, or Wall Street, or the grievance groups.

The question is whether Trump will also be the president who finishes the job he started. Can he pivot from being a counter-puncher always ready to take the next swing, and instead be a leader who brings us back together as a society? Will he become the leader who patiently explains to the American people why he has taken the path he has, and how it will lead to a better, stronger, greater nation? Can he become the leader who rises above the fray, and unites the people including even those who once opposed him? Or will that task fall to the leaders who come after Trump?

President Trump alone knows the answer. He is already a president of consequence. But if he can move from being a divider to a uniter, he will go down in history as of one of our great presidents.

I've always thought there were three types of presidents. The first group are those who slavishly follow popular opinion. They live by focus groups and polls, choosing their words and adjusting their policies accordingly. They do what their pollsters say appeals to voters at that particular moment in time. These presidents tend not to be great leaders because they followed the political fashions of the day, rather than lead us to someplace better. Bill Clinton was like that. They're the sugar-high presidents. We like them while they're in office but, ultimately, their ideas and leadership leave us unsatisfied. History tends to forget these presidents within a generation or so.

The second kind of president pays no heed to polls or to popular opinion. He's convinced that he is right, his motives pure, and his principles universal. Even if the American people don't agree with him at the time, he contents himself with the thought that in the end time will prove him right. George W. Bush and Barack Obama were of this sort. These presidents may have the best of intentions, and on a personal level can be charming, likable, and popular. But there is an arrogance about them. They assumed history would validate them, so they didn't bother to take the time or make the effort to bring the people along with them. They never paid us the compliment of thinking they had to convince us of the merit of their arguments. They just plowed ahead. History does remember these presidents, but not always for the reasons they assume. Sometimes—surprise! surprise!—history proves them wrong, and occasionally, catastrophically wrong.

There is a third, much rarer, type of president. He takes polls into account, but they don't define him. He doesn't need focus groups to tell him if he's at odds with what's popular at the time. But rather than abandoning his convictions like the first type of president, or ignoring the people's wishes like the second type, this third type of president goes to enormous lengths to bring his case directly to the people. He makes a great effort to explain to us why he believes as he does, and then works patiently to bring us around to his way of seeing things, even if we are initially skeptical. He doesn't pander to us; he doesn't ignore us; instead, he works hard to lead us to a new place.

This third sort of president doesn't tell us what to think; he explains to us why he believes a particular course should be taken and then lets us decide for ourselves. He doesn't try to fool us with false promises. He doesn't tell us what we want to hear in order to get elected and then do whatever he wants once in office. He doesn't say one thing to one group and something different to another group. He carefully lays out his arguments, in language we can all understand. Sometimes he asks for us to go in a completely new direction, at odds with our current thinking.

Sometimes he has to persuade us to delay our desire for immediate gratification, to sacrifice now so that later we, or our children, will have a better life.

Unfortunately, this type of president is quite rare. That's because it's so much more difficult to get things done if you have to take the time and make the effort to convince the American people to follow your new direction. It is far easier for a president simply to rule by imperial command, and sign Executive Orders which don't require congressional approval. But, their dictates only last for that president's time in office, then cease with the next president. Those changes don't endure to become part of the fabric of our society. It is only this third type of president—the one who presents the case to us and then lets us decide—who changes history.

These are the presidents we put in the history books, the ones we make monuments to. It's Lincoln at Gettysburg, FDR in his fireside chats, Reagan on the cliffs of Normandy. These are the leaders who give voice to what we're thinking, take time to connect with us, mourn with us, challenge us to do great and difficult things, and cheer us on when we do them. And when victory comes, these presidents step back and give the credit to the American people.

They led political revolutions which were disruptive, often acrimonious, and sometimes even violent. The greatest of these presidents have not just stood up to Washington and disrupted the status quo, they've gone on to heal our divisions, to unite us once again. First, they make war against the Washington Establishment, then they make peace with it.

The last time we went through one of these political revolutions was in the 1980s. Ronald Reagan defied conventional wisdom and led the nation to new economic and foreign policies—which brought us one of the greatest periods of peace and prosperity in American history. Yet our political revolutions inevitably awaken the forces of division that rent our national fabric. The cycle is not complete until the people are brought back together again. There is always the all too human temptation once these revolutions have run their course to assign blame and settle scores. Our greatest leaders, including even those who launched and fought those revolutions, knew that unless the wounds of division were healed, the country couldn't move forward. We needed to move past the anger and discord to find our way home again—if we were to once again realize our common purpose and shared destiny.

I saw this firsthand at the 1984 Memorial Day ceremony at the Tomb of the Unknown Soldier in Arlington National Cemetery. Despite being the most famous symbol of America's sacrifices in combat, it bore no acknowledgment of the Vietnam War, even a decade after that war had ended. No unknown soldier from that war had yet been interred to join the remains of other unknowns from World Wars I and II, and the Korean War. This is because, until Reagan, our leaders had taken the approach that the less said about Vietnam the better.

Reagan righted that wrong. On May 28th, 1984, an army caisson carried the remains of an unidentified Vietnam War soldier from the U.S. Capitol, where he had lain in state, to Arlington National Cemetery for burial at the tomb. Men and women of our armed forces formed a cordon all along the route through the streets of Washington, across the Memorial Bridge, and into the cemetery. It marked the final step in a weeklong series of ceremonies honoring our Vietnam veterans.

Arlington National Cemetery is one of the most serene and peaceful places in Washington, despite being filled with row upon row of white crosses marking the graves of America's fallen heroes. But as I stood in the audience on that bright and sunny day, I'm ashamed to admit that I was more concerned with whether Reagan would utter some of the phrases I had submitted to the White House speechwriters than with the gravity of the ceremony.

As I looked around the crowd, though, I suddenly realized that it wasn't all about me. It was about the veterans in the audience—especially those who had fought in Vietnam. Some were in wheelchairs; some had long hair in ponytails and scraggly beards. Some wore bandanas around their heads, and some had medals pinned to their faded camouflage uniforms. Most of them looked like they had lived lives that were very much the worse for wear. They remained silent, many with tears running down their cheeks.

When these soldiers returned from Vietnam—a war in which they had been drafted to fight—they hadn't been met by their fellow citizens waving flags and patting them on the back for defending our freedom half a world away. They were scorned and spat upon. They were called baby killers. When they tried to slide back into their old lives, many had trouble, and the military didn't provide them with the counseling and care they needed. We left them to suffer in the shadows and in silence.

For more than a decade we had pretended our Vietnam veterans didn't exist, because to recognize them and care for them as we should have, we would have had to acknowledge America's failure in a tragic chapter of our history. But Reagan knew that until we acknowledged the Vietnam War, and separated out the brave men and women who fought in that war from the war itself, we would never be made whole. He didn't spend his time assigning blame for past mistakes. Instead he celebrated our veterans, acknowledging their service, and finally laid to rest the ghosts of Vietnam. He knew even better than his countrymen that it wasn't just about righting a wrong done to our veterans; it was about bringing us together and healing the soul of our nation. It was a moment that stays with me to this day.

A year or so ago, I was sharing this story with my fellow Reagan alumnus Ed Rollins. Rollins was in charge of the landslide victory in Reagan's 1984 reelection campaign, and he is one of the giants of American politics. We often trade Reagan stories, like old soldiers laughing at the good and bad times we shared. I was talking about that day at Arlington when Ed asked if I knew what had happened after that. I didn't, so he filled me in on what transpired two days later, when President Reagan flew to Colorado Springs to give the commencement address to the some one thousand graduating seniors at the Air Force Academy. Rollins was part of the president's entourage when they arrived at Falcon Stadium for the ceremony. There were thirty thousand people in attendance: the graduates in dress uniform sitting in white folding chairs on the field, and their families and friends in the stands.

Everyone was excited. This was the first time in many years that the Commander in Chief had given the commencement address, and the cadets, their families, and the entire Air Force Academy took it seriously. The stadium is built on a breathtaking site. There are no tall trees or buildings on the horizon, just clear blue sky. When you're in that stadium, it seems like you're on the top of the highest point in the world. As Rollins recalled it, the day was gloriously sunny—but hot.

Tradition calls for the keynote speaker to give the entire graduating class the oath of office, and then remain on the stage while the top one hundred graduates file up one by one to receive their diplomas. The speaker gives each newly minted officer his all-important "first salute" and then shakes his hand. Then, out of respect for the speaker's time, he gets escorted off the stage while the remaining nine hundred of the graduates get their diplomas, first salutes, and handshakes from other VIPs in the official party.

But on that day, as the ceremony was about to begin, Rollins said Reagan looked at the program, then leaned over to the Air Force Academy Superintendent and asked a question. Would it be all right if they broke with tradition that year and let Reagan give the first salute to each of the one thousand graduates? The Superintendent said, "Mr. President, you're their Commander in Chief, and you can do whatever you would like. But I've got to warn you, sir, it's a hot day, and saluting an additional nine hundred first lieutenants is going to add at least another hour, if not more, to your day." Reagan said that would be just fine, leaving Ed Rollins and the aides in a scramble to readjust the rest of the schedule.

One by one, the rest of the brand-new officers stepped up to the stage to receive their first salutes from their Commander in Chief. Rollins said the excitement was palpable. It was one of the first classes to graduate women, and some were so excited that they jumped up and hugged the president instead of shaking hands. Even Reagan's aides stopped worrying about sticking to the almighty schedule and were swept away by the patriotism of the moment. Most of them had been with Reagan two days before at the Memorial Day ceremony at the Tomb of the Unknown Soldier, surrounded by the graves of the men and women who had made the ultimate sacrifice to keep us free. Now they shared the joyous excitement of the Air Force's newest officers, their lives stretched out in front of them, and listened as Reagan told them, "America's future will be determined by your dreams and visions." The Air Force Thunderbirds flew overhead, leaving their white contrails. In keeping with tradition, the new graduates tossed their old cadet caps in the air.

Afterward, Rollins joined the president in the limousine as they drove back to the airport and Air Force One. Rollins leaned over and told President Reagan, "Sir, you did a great thing for those young men and women. They'll remember that for the rest of their lives, getting their first salute from their Commander in Chief."

Reagan replied, "Oh, Ed, I didn't do it for them. I did it for me. If I have to send any one of them into harm's way—and believe me, I won't hesitate to do it if I must—I want to do so having looked into their eyes, seeing them as young men and women, not numbers on a page." Reagan had spent Memorial Day looking into the tear-filled eyes of some of our long-forgotten veterans. Two days later he looked into the smiling eyes of the next generation of America's warriors.

America is a great nation for many reasons. But we are an exceptional nation for only one—that we have within our hands the power of regeneration. We can reinvent ourselves as a nation, just as we can reinvent ourselves as individuals. It doesn't happen as automatically or as a matter of right. Once we come to realize our leaders are out of step with the people, we can't just stumble along and keep doing what we've always done because it's familiar and comfortable. We have to earn it, to go through our catharsis, to adapt and change.

I believe that is what we have done during these periods of creative destruction throughout our history, beginning the first time we shook off the governing class with the Declaration of Independence and Revolutionary War. We did it again during the Jacksonian Revolution, during the Civil War, the Progressive movement, the New Deal, and the Reagan Revolution. That is what we are in the midst of doing now, with the Trump Revolution.

We enter each one of these periods with a growing dissatisfaction with Washington and the powers that be. The dissatisfaction grows, and forms a national grassroots movement of the people against the status quo governing class. We battle it out—in town halls across the country, in the halls of Congress, and finally in our presidential elections. Sometimes we have even fought it out on the battlefield. These periods are not harbingers of our doom or signs of the end of American greatness, even though the establishments of the day may have called them that. Indeed, they are to be welcomed as the very essence of what is unique about America. They are how we renew and regenerate, how we disrupt the stale governing elites, sweep them out of office, and make a fresh start.

What emerges at the other end of them is a nation reborn, one that keeps some of the old, and adds some of the new. We evolve, and we reinvent America. The Constitution gives us the right to do it, and provides the means by which to do it. Our dynamic American society demands it. Our technological, entrepreneurial, and innovative nature gives us what we need to make it possible. Our tendency to find great leaders just when we need them most is what carries us through these periods of transformation. It is our shared belief that all men are created equal, and have the right and the ability to govern ourselves, that motivates us to persevere through tumultuous times.

These periods of creative destruction are our lifeblood and our legacy. They are what have always propelled us into the future. It is through these peaceful political revolutions, that are uniquely American, that we come to regenerate and reinvent ourselves, not just as individuals but also as a nation. They are, in fact, what *does* set us apart from other nations. They are the way we avoid following the path taken by other great empires throughout history—to rise, shine, and eventually decline. These periods of challenge and change may be miserable to live through, as we know only too well today, but they are in fact what make America an exceptional nation. We start along the same path as other great nations of the past. But then we part ways. While other nations inevitably and permanently decline, we do not. We may decline, for just a little while, but then we do what we have always done throughout our history. We reinvent ourselves and rise again. Perhaps Lincoln said it best, in the darkest days of the Civil War, that our country has "a new birth of freedom".

Look around you. The future is in all our hands. It is not up to a group of elites, or a permanent governing class, or a bunch of power-grabbing ideologues, or some self-appointed saviors to reinvent America for the 21st century. It is up to average, common, regular American citizens. We are the people whose task it is to bring about America's next revolution. That is why our Declaration of Independence, signed on July 4th, 1776—the document which launched the greatest experiment in the history of all mankind—is founded on the belief that all men are created equal. Then, a decade later, having won our independence, our Founding Fathers drafted a six-page Constitution, which continues to guide us on a path of constant renewal. It begins with these three simple, yet earthshaking words: *We the People…*

Acknowledgments

Today, most books of this type are written by a ghostwriter who takes an author's stories, or ideas, and turns them into a polished memoir, or a policy platform.

REVOLUTION is different. It is the story of my own experiences, written in my own words, by my own hand. It does not presume to be a scholarly history of the period, or a comprehensive political manifesto. The theories, observations, and analysis are mine alone. They are based on the lessons I have learned over nearly five decades in public affairs, culminating in my rough and tumble times with the Trump presidency.

REVOLUTION retraces the beliefs of a lifetime spent in the foreign policy establishment, then rejecting them to become part of the Trump Revolution. I believe it is these populist revolutions that lie at the heart of democracy in America—the perennial struggle between the governing class and the governed, between Washington and the rest of the country. This book is ultimately a journey of discovery, as I came to realize that these periods of creative destruction, and the ability to reinvent ourselves, not just as individuals but as a society, are an essential part of what makes America an exceptional nation.

But no journey is without mentors to point the way, colleagues to offer constructive criticism and encouragement, and friends to help pick you up and dust you off when you falter. Those people have been many, far too many to mention here. But there are some whose efforts are truly special. To them I owe a special debt of gratitude.

First, to my legal advisor, Robert Giuffra, and his colleagues at Sullivan and Cromwell: Alexander Willsher and Amanda Shami. Because of his friendship with my husband, Giuffra was willing to take a detour in his legal mega-practice in order to represent me during the Mueller investigation and Congressional enquiries. Without his brilliant and tenacious legal counsel, my life might well have taken a tragic turn, and been caught up by and destroyed in the crossfire of the Russia probe.

My husband's law school classmate and friend of fifty years' standing, former Attorney General Michael Mukasey, was a pillar of strength and wisdom throughout. He characterized the FBI and Office of Special Counsel's investigation as "boiling the ocean" to see if anything floated to the top. It helped me put things in perspective.

My government career spanned four Administrations—beginning as night shift secretary in Dr. Henry Kissinger's West Wing office in the 1970s up to the Deputy National Security Advisor to President Trump in 2017. I encountered people in the Nixon, Ford, and Reagan Administrations who had a formative effect on my own thinking. I also had mentors and role models—especially Henry Kissinger, who remains a friend to this day. It was through Kissinger that I learned the value of seeing things through the eyes of others. It was through Ronald Reagan that I learned power of challenging the conventional wisdom when you believe it's wrong. It was through Donald Trump that I learned the importance of tenacity, of getting back up every time you're knocked down, to keep fighting for what you believe in. All three of these men had the courage of their convictions, and because of it they were able to change history.

I owe special thanks to my former colleagues in the Trump Administration and the National Security Council, who I won't mention individually here, because they all appear in the pages of this book. There is one person that stands out above all others, however, and deserves my special appreciation: Navy Commander Sarah Flaherty. She was at my side throughout my time in the Trump Administration, and stayed on after I left. She represents the very finest example of talent, integrity, and service to the nation.

To the late Terry Martin, a former CBS producer, who helped launch me on this course, years before Trump came on the scene, by reminding me of the significance of the Reagan Revolution. To Geoffrey Shepard, the youngest lawyer in the Nixon White House, now president of the Nixon Legacy Forums, who over the years has become a good friend, confidante, and editor.

To American Conservative Union Chairman Matt Schlapp and President Daniel Schneider, who together resurrected that great organization. They have made it into a powerful force not just in our own country, but throughout the world. As Margaret Thatcher once said, first you win the argument, then you win the election. I am honored by my continued association with them.

To Michael Carlisle, founder and president of Inkwell Management. Although Carlisle and I sit in opposite sides of the political aisle, both of us believe what unites us as Americans is more important than what divides us. Carlisle has guided this book all along the way, encouraging me to toss aside the trivial in favor of the lasting message. To Carlisle's deputy, Michael Mungiello—a genuine wunderkind—who helped with organization and editing.

To Anthony Ziccardi, publisher of Post Hill Press, and managing editor Madeline Sturgeon. Post Hill Press is at the vanguard of the new wave in publishing—an independent house providing a bare bones charter operation. It gets a book into print quickly, while leaving editorial control to the author.

To my friends and former colleagues at FOX News, starting with the late Roger Ailes and his wife Beth. Roger was willing to take a bet that hiring a woman over the age of 50, and a brunette at that, to talk about issues in the traditionally all-male domain of national security would be successful. In doing so he broke all the rules. Sure enough, his bet paid off for us all, and launched my media career.

I owe special thanks to my former colleagues at FOX, who have become friends along the way. To Lou Dobbs, who was the first person to recognize that working and middle-class Americans had been left behind by globalism. To Bill Hemmer, who works harder than anyone to get the story right, but who makes it seem effortless when he's on the air. To Martha MacCallum, who is living proof that good guys (gals) deserve to and can finish first. To Lynne Jordal Martin, who taught me how to be a better columnist, and who has single handedly propelled the Opinions page of FOXNews.com into the top tier. To all the other talented people on air and off at FOX News and Fox Business News. Thanks also to Suzanne Scott and Tom Bowman who first welcomed me to FOX over a decade ago, and now have welcomed me back.

Our family has been privileged to have life-long, multi-generational friendships with the Clan MacLeod, beginning decades ago with the twin MacLeod brothers, Kenny and the late Murdo MacLeod. When the Mueller investigators were finally finished with me, in February 2018, my husband and I headed to Scotland and were taken in by the MacLeods. We went off the grid for weeks, staying in remote guest houses in the Hebrides and Western Highlands. Kenny MacLeod encouraged me to write about my experiences, and lent me his ancient stone boathouse on the shores of Loch Fyne where I wrote the first draft of this book. Eighteen months later I returned there and put on the finishing touches.

To my children and their spouses—Andrew and Gretchen McFarland and their children Arabel, Alasdair, and Lachlan; Gavin McFarland and his daughters Louisa and Georgina; Fiona McFarland and her husband Matt Melton and their baby-to-be; Luke and Baylie McFarland; and Camilla McFarland. Being the Matriarch of Clan McFarland is the most rewarding job I will ever have, or could hope to have.

I acknowledge that I was lucky enough to be born in an age when the doors of opportunity were beginning to open for women, even if I had to kick a few open myself. One of the great joys of my life has been to see the generations of women after me, and help mentor a few of them along the way, especially my daughters, Fiona and Camilla. They are both the embodiment of my hopes, and the fulfilment of my dreams.

It was my daughter Fiona who, more than anyone, urged me to write a book I thought mattered, not the trashy tell-all others were pushing me to do. While she was still a teenager, Fiona thought I should get off the Mommy track and back into politics after September 11th. Fifteen years later she held my hand through the trying times of the Trump White House and Mueller investigation and, after everything was said and done, surprised everyone by entering politics herself.

But most of all to my beloved husband, Alan Roberts McFarland. He has encouraged me when I needed it, admonished me when I deserved it, and always taught me how to distinguish between what was passing and what endures. My greatest blessing has been to walk through life with him at my side.

President Nixon's National Security Advisor Henry Kissinger and Chinese Premier Zhou Enlai, Beijing, July 1971. I helped staff this first secret meeting between officials of the United States and People's Republic of China. The handshake has symbolic significance because two decades before, President Eisenhower's Secretary of State, John Foster Dulles, pointedly refused to shake Zhou's hand at an international meeting in Geneva.

Being presented to Pope Paul VI by Ambassador Henry Cabot Lodge and Kissinger at the Vatican, July 1974.

100 WAYS TO WIN EVERY DAY!

Triple Chance WINGO

NEW YORK POST

METRO
TODAY'S RACING

TODAY
sunny, 45-60

TONIGHT
mostly fair, 25-30

TOMORROW
partly cloudy, 45-60

Details, Page 2

TV listings: P. 95

THURSDAY, MARCH 24, 1983 **30** CENTS

5½ cents - beyond 50 mile state, except L. I. **AMERICA'S FASTEST-GROWING NEWSPAPER** © 1983 News Group Publications Inc. Vol. 182, No. 110

ABC AVERAGE
SALES EXCEED

960,000

Reagan unveils historic space-age counterpunch

STAR WARS PLAN TO ZAP RED NUKES

★ **PRESIDENT Reagan**, in an historic address to the nation, last night unveiled a dramatic new space age defense strategy aimed at destroying Soviet missiles in the event of a nuclear attack.

★ **The President** showed aerial photographs of Soviet installations in Cuba that, he said, posed the most critical threat to the United States since the Cuban missile crisis of President Kennedy's administration.

★ **Introducing** a new program to develop a galactic defense umbrella rather than first strike nuclear weaponry, Reagan asked: "Would it not be better to save lives than to avenge them?" Comprehensive coverage begins on Pages 4 and 5.

Teen dies in freak elevator horror
PAGE THREE

AX SIX AIDES IN PURGE AT SCANDAL-HIT STATE AGENCY
PAGE TWO

Front page of the *New York Post* the morning after President Ronald Reagan's historic "Star Wars" speech. I wrote the first draft of the speech, which was originally intended to make the case for Reagan's defense buildup and nuclear deterrence policy. Reagan himself added the key paragraphs announcing his plan to build a missile defense system. I was invited to the White House for the speech and the small reception Reagan hosted afterwards for American scientists and others who were involved in launching his Strategic Defense Initiative (SDI).

At the podium in the Pentagon Briefing Room in 1984 when I was Deputy Assistant Secretary for Public Affairs, and head of the speechwriter's office.

Official Defense Department photograph

Receiving the Distinguished Civilian Service Award from Reagan's Secretary of Defense Caspar Weinberger in January 1985. It is the Defense Department's highest civilian honor.

China's Great Hall of the People, Beijing. I joined other Nixon Administration Alumni Jack Brennan and Robert C. "Bud" McFarlane, as well as Christopher Nixon Cox, on a trip to Beijing, Hangzhou, and Shanghai to commemorate the 40th anniversary of Nixon's historic trip to China.

(Left) Mar-a-Lago is all gilt, glitz, and glamor. The clubhouse is like the personal palace of a Renaissance prince. This oil portrait of a young Donald Trump hangs in the small bar off the main lounge.

(Bottom) After getting sworn into office in the East Room, I brought my family to my tiny West Wing office, and then the Roosevelt Room for a picture. Surrounding me left to right are Camilla, Fiona, Alan, Gavin, and Georgina McFarland. Missing are the rest of the family—Louisa, Andrew, Gretchen, Arabel, Alasdair, Lachlan, Luke and Baylie McFarland, and son-in-law Matthew Melton.

In the first military action of his presidency, less than three months after taking the oath of office, Donald Trump ordered the destruction of Syrian airfields that had been used in President Assad's chemical weapons attack on his own people. It was a gutsy decision, in part because Trump and his senior advisors were in Mar-a-Lago in the middle of a summit meeting with Chinese President Xi Jinping. I remained in Washington with Vice President Pence and other officials to help coordinate events from the White House Situation Room. The U.S. Navy flawlessly executed their plan, news of the attack did not leak beforehand, and the entire operation was a complete success.

As I prepared to leave the White House for the last time, I escorted my first boss, Henry Kissinger, to a meeting in Oval Office with my final boss, Donald Trump. For me it was a life coming full circle. I began my career in 1971 as the night shift secretary on Dr. Kissinger's West Wing Staff. I ended it some forty-five years later, as Deputy National Security Advisor to President Trump, sitting at a desk just a few feet from my original one.

My farewell picture with President Trump in the Oval Office, May 2017.

After leaving the Trump Administration, I got caught up in the Mueller and Congressional investigations for months. When they were finally finished with me, my husband and I left the country for the most remote parts of the western highlands and islands of Scotland. I spent months reflecting on my own experiences in the Trump Administration and trying to make sense of what was happening to America. This book is the result.

Walking to the MacLeod boathouse in Lochgilphead, Scotland.